THE COLLECTED WORKS OF GONZALO DE BERCEO IN ENGLISH TRANSLATION

Translated by
JEANNIE K. BARTHA,
ANNETTE GRANT CASH,
and RICHARD TERRY MOUNT

Coordinating editor
ANNETTE GRANT CASH

ACMRS
(Arizona Center for Medieval and Renaissance Studies)
Tempe, Arizona
2008

*The publication of this volume has been greatly assisted by
a grant from the Program for Cultural Cooperation between
Spain's Ministry of Education, Culture and Sports
and United States Universities.*

Library of Congress Cataloging-in-Publication Data

Berceo, Gonzalo de, 13th cent.
  [Works. English. 2007]
  The collected works of Gonzalo de Berceo in the English translation /
translated by Jeannie K. Bartha, Annette Grant Cash and Richard Terry
Mount ; coordinating editor, Annette Grant Cash.
    p. cm. -- (Medieval and Renaissance Texts and Studies ; 327)
  Includes bibliographical references.
  ISBN-13: 978-0-86698-373-0 (alk. paper)
  1. Berceo, Gonzalo de, 13th cent.--Translations into English. I. Bartha,
Jeannie K. II. Cash, Annette Grant, 1943- III. Mount, Richard Terry, 1944-
IV. Title.
  PQ6397.A7E5 2007
  861'.1--dc22

                                                            2007013636

∞
This book is made to last.
It is set in Adobe Caslon Pro,
smyth-sewn and printed on acid-free paper
to library specifications.
Printed in the United States of America

We dedicate this text to John E. Keller,
without whom this work could not have been accomplished.
He encouraged and enlightened us, edited the text,
and has been our guide and devoted friend throughout the project.

TABLE OF CONTENTS

II. The Hagiographical Poems

III. The Doctrinal Poems

ACKNOWLEDGMENTS

We gratefully acknowledge the meticulous and scholarly copyediting of our manuscript by Dr. Leslie MacCoull. Her efforts on our behalf have improved our work. We also thank Roy Rukkila, Managing Editor of MRTS, and his staff for their kind attention and careful work on this project, and our respective universities for their support.

JKB, AGC, RTM

Introduction

A definite need for translations of all of Gonzalo de Berceo's works has inspired three scholars/translators to produce this collection. They realized that without specialized linguistic training many students, teachers, researchers, and general readers did not have access to Berceo's thirteenth-century Castilian language. The three translators—Jeannie K. Bartha, Annette Grant Cash, and Richard Terry Mount—had also become aware of a revival of public interest in miracles, angels, and the appearance of new or hitherto neglected shrines. What can be termed "everlasting shrines" venerated down through the ages—such as Santiago de Compostela (Spain), Canterbury (England), Lourdes (France), Fatima (Portugal), Guadalupe (Mexico), and most recently Medjugorje (Yugoslavia [Bosnia and Hercegovina])—consistently receive vast numbers of faithful pilgrims, many of them ailing, who pray for miracles. New reports of miracles wrought by the Blessed Virgin Mary are frequent. For example, a well with water which some regard as curative was visited by thousands on a farm near Conyers, Georgia. The owner avowed that she received messages from the Virgin. Many of Mary's images are said to weep human tears, and the Church has not proved all of these manifestations as frauds. Stigmata are occasionally confirmed by the Vatican, notably those of Padre Pio, a Franciscan Capuchin friar, canonized in 2002 by Pope John Paul II as St. Pio of Pietrelcina, Italy. This same year Pope John Paul II also conferred sainthoods on Juan Diego, the Nahua Indian of Mexico to whom the Virgin of Guadalupe appeared in 1531; on Pedro de San José Betancourt, a Spanish monk who lived and did charity and missionary work in Guatemala in the seventeenth century; and on Josemaría Escrivá de Balaguer, the Spanish priest who founded the religious organization Opus Dei. Many other examples could be adduced. These miraculous persons, places, and occurrences can be compared with those which Berceo's works extolled, of which his best-known and most studied is *Milagros de Nuestra Señora* (*Miracles of Our Lady*).

Histories and critical works on medieval Hispanic literature abound. Therefore, this general introduction and those provided for the individual poems will be brief, offering information useful to readers unfamiliar with Berceo and his copious outpouring of renditions from medieval Latin works into the Spanish of his times.

Gonzalo de Berceo was born toward the end of the twelfth century in the region known as La Rioja in the hamlet of Berceo, which exists today. He was still alive in the early years of the 1250s. He is the first Castilian writer whose name we know, proclaiming his identity at a time when authors preferred anonymity. Part of his education was received in the Benedictine monastery in San Millán de la Cogolla, which is still active and thriving. Berceo labored as a secular priest, not a monk. His work was for the most part administrative and legalistic. It is likely that he served the abbot as his notary.

Berceo's poetry can be classified according to form and content into four groups: 1) poems concerned with the Blessed Virgin Mary—the aforementioned *Milagros de Nuestra Señora*, the *Loores de Nuestra Señora*, and the *Duelo que fizo la Virgen*; 2) the lives of local saints—the *Vida de San Millán*, the *Vida de Santo Domingo de Silos*, the *Vida de Santa Oria*, and the *Martyrio de San Laurencio*, which was not finished; 3) two doctrinal poems—the *Sacrificio de la Misa* and *De los signos que aparescerán antes del Juicio*; 4) and three hymns—"Veni Creator Spiritus," "Ave Maria Estrella de la mar," and "Tu, Christe, que luz eres."

Berceo's poems are the first in Castilian written in a metrical form known as the *mester de clerecía*, which indicated that the meter was a learned and literate form used by monks in monasteries. It is also known as *cuaderna vía* ("fourfold way") because it consists of monorhymed quatrains of fourteen-syllable lines divided by a caesura or pause. Another term applied to this meter is "alexandrine," because it is employed in some medieval poems about Alexander the Great produced both within and outside of Spain. Some critics have labeled full rhyme as dull and monotonous. They are mistaken. This metrical form was easy to memorize. Full rhyme has other virtues, but first and foremost it possesses certain powers. It caught its audience in its net and carried it along with force. Once entrapped, once accustomed to its metrics and trained to the regular and unchanging cadence, readers or hearers surrendered to the *cuaderna vía*'s spell. Furthermore, within this structured and studied fabric, the effect of Berceo's language is colloquial and loquacious.

Berceo and his contemporaries adored the Blessed Virgin and knew of her miracles. They also knew of the existence of local saints and their lives and miracles. However, these accounts were written in medieval Latin prose, useless to the vast illiterate public. Berceo in his rhymed quatrains relayed stories/poems his contemporaries could understand. No saint himself, he had practical as well as pious motives. He wanted to attract pilgrims and contributors to the shrines and monasteries of these saints so that they could thrive and continue their doctrinal and charitable works. He strove tirelessly, and, we believe, successfully.

The title of this collection, *The Collected Works of Gonzalo de Berceo in English Translation*, is appropriate. Jeannie K. Bartha, Annette Cash and Richard Terry Mount wisely decided that true translation of meaning could not preserve rhyme, which is so embedded in the sounds and cadences of each language that it cannot be transferred to the other with any sense intact. Therefore, they gave us a reliable version in prose. An egregious example of rhymed "translation" of poetry can be found in the sprightly and sometimes indecorous rendition by Elisha Kent Kane of Juan Ruiz, Arcipreste de Hita's *Libro de buen amor*. Kane indeed transferred full (English, not Castilian) rhyme, and kept fairly close to the spirit of the original, but all too often he lost exact meaning, making his version more of a personal creation than a scholarly work.

Berceo was not strictly a translator. He molded his Latin sources to his own purposes, so that his poems are not exact translations of the originals, which are in some cases prose. They are, rather, renditions which frequently contain statements and passages not in his sources. This is not because of faulty understanding of Latin, which he read very knowledgeably. Berceo's narrative poems could be used in sermons, to instruct as well as to entertain (*enseñar y deleitar*), the two-fold aim of medieval moralistic literature. In addition to being read, they could well have been recited, sung, or chanted with musical accompaniment, perhaps with dramatic gestures on the part of the performers. David Flory theorizes that they were used to instruct young would-be clerics.[1] Richard Kinkade suggests a kind of theater-in-the round setting.[2] Berceo, we believe, had additional motives. Pulpit preachers had captive audiences, but there were clerics who preached in public squares and in the countryside. Moreover, another variety of spectacle rivaled all preachers. Minstrels traveled about singing and playing many kinds of instruments. Their performances narrated and dramatized stirring, heroic, and heart-rending deeds in an older metrical form, the "*mester de juglaría*" or the art of the minstrels, which was transmitted orally in a meter of loosely sixteen syllables (8/8) with assonant rather than full or consonant rhyme. This is the metrical form of the twelfth-century *Poema de Mío Cid*, for example, and is very natural to the Spanish language, characterizing much Hispanic poetry, both popular and learned, to this day.

Berceo's cultivated *cuaderna vía* lasted as a prevalent style throughout the thirteenth century and well into the fourteenth, where its aims and contents differed considerably. Only very rarely did it appear any later, until the nineteenth and twentieth centuries, when it was revived by the poets of Modernism and the Generation of '98, who employed many types of traditional forms in artistic and/ or artificial ways.

---

[1] David Flory, *Marian Representations in the Miracle Tales of Thirteenth-Century Spain and France* (Baltimore: Catholic University of America Press, 2000).

[2] Richard P. Kinkade, "Sermons in the Round: The *Mester de Clerecía* as Dramatic Art," in *Studies in Honor of Gustavo Correa*, ed. C. Faulhaber et al.(Potomac, MD: Scripta Humanistica, 1986), 127–36.

Berceo has been accused by critics of writing nothing original. It is true that his sources, all in Latin, are known. However, there is a special kind of originality in his works. He transposed the contents of his sources, the miracles of the Virgin and the lives of saints (whatever their time or place), into the homely context of his familiar existence. He forged his nascent Castilian vernacular into a literary instrument, using it to create new and unusual vocabulary filled with words found nowhere else, yet perfectly understandable by all, including earthy expressions which are quite surprising. For example, in number 8 of the *Milagros de Nuestra Señora*, a sinner deceived by the devil had castrated himself. The poem chattily points out that this unfortunate yet repentant chap thenceforth had to urinate in a special fashion, in case the audience was wondering about the practical details. Yes, this occurred in the Latin account, but more conservatively and with fewer details. Berceo's texts are salted with colorful idioms and proverbial expressions, a key to the colloquial vernacular of his times as well as to his own inventiveness. In the guise of his authorial persona, he insists throughout that he is only a simple man who cannot read Latin and is required to use the language of his rustic neighbors even for his biblical and historical characters. As he says in the "Encomienza" or introduction of the *Vida de Sancto Domingo de Silos*:

> Quiero fer una prosa en román paladino,
> En qual suele el pueblo fablar à su vecino, ...[3]

All these stratagems, which obeyed the dicta of various manuals of versification and advice to preachers of the times, served to put his audiences at ease and engaged their attention. Thus, while seeming to be one of the folk, he deliberately uses language to create and persuade.

The amount of Berceo's poetic output is phenomenal. The twelfth and thirteenth centuries were an amazingly fertile period of linguistic and cultural activity on the Iberian Peninsula (and elsewhere in Europe). Berceo can be compared with his contemporary, King Alfonso X, "El Sabio" ("The Learned" or "The Wise"), who also aimed to entertain and edify through his scientific and artistic projects. These two could have known each other or of each other's works, but there is no hard evidence that they did. Alfonso, like Berceo, was sincerely pious and a devotee of the Virgin Mary. He compiled, sponsored, and in part authored the *Cantigas de Santa Maria*, a collection of over four hundred hymns and miracle tales, a species of ex-voto to his divine patroness and protectress. The contents include widely known miracles from the European tradition, manifestations at

---

[3] Gonzalo de Berceo, *Vida de Sancto Domingo de Silos y Vida de Sancta Oria, Virgen*, 3ª ed. (Buenos Aires: Espasa-Calpe Argentina, S. A., 1953), 9.

local shrines, and personal experiences. Nineteen of the miracles of St. Mary in the *Cantigas* are also narrated by Berceo in *Milagros de Nuestra Señora*.[4] Like Berceo, Alfonso departed from Latin and couched his collection in a vernacular Romance tongue, in his case not Castilian (his preferred language for his other scholarly and literary projects), but Galician-Portuguese, the medium of the courtly tradition of that time (influenced by the Provençal troubadours, who wrote and performed artistic poetry in *langue d'oc*, or the Romance dialect used in Provence, France) and also the authentic folk speech of Galicia, the northwestern part of the Iberian Peninsula, site of the famous shrine of Santiago de Compostela. Both authors were literate and learned, and their intended audiences included both upper and lower classes. Both took a stance of quaint simplicity to reach all elements of the populace and spoke/wrote "román paladino" (in the case of Berceo, Castilian, and in the case of Alfonso, Galician-Portuguese). As king, Alfonso could exercise his royal patronage to produce true "luxury editions," in exquisite calligraphy with lavish illustrations and musical accompaniment. Three of the four extant manuscripts of the *Cantigas* are illustrated with beautiful miniatures in stunning color and gold adornment. Musical notation exists for all of the 420 songs (much enjoyed by musicologists and musicians of today, who perform and record the songs with twenty-first-century means). While perhaps in great part this abundance of King Alfonso's studios was aimed at the noble society of the court, the books and their pictures were large and could be seen by many assembled people, who could also hear the poems as they were read aloud or sung to the accompaniment of numerous kinds of instruments, as depicted in the miniatures. Enjoyment and understanding could take place on many levels. Anybody who could crowd into the hall or church could receive a threefold impact—verbal, visual, and musical. The meter *cuaderna vía* occurs among the many other verse forms in the *Cantigas*, where it is set to music. Although Berceo's poems were primarily intended to be read or recited, they might have sometimes been sung as well. At any rate, no music or illustrations are provided. However, the vividness of the language, which evokes images both visible and audible for the reader, supplies the lack.

Some historians of Old Spanish literature have suggested that Berceo received higher education at the University of Palencia, but this cannot be ascertained. Others will soon offer what many believe may be substantiated proof that Berceo rendered into his *cuaderna vía* the tremendously lengthy *Libro de Aleixandre*, which he would have based on an Old French manuscript the original of

---

[4] In the order of *Milagro* = *Cantiga*, the correspondences are: 1 = 2; 24 (or 25) = 3; 16 = 4; 21 = 7; 2 = 11; 18 = 12; 6 = 13; 7 = 14; 17 = 19; 3 = 24; 23 = 25; 8 = 26; 9 = 32; 22 = 33; 14 = 39; 20 = 47; 19 = 86; 13 = 87; 15 = 132.

which was the Latin *Historia rerum in partibus transmarinis gestarum* of William of Tyre in the late twelfth century. Berceo had sufficient education to translate or render into Castilian this very lengthy book. Whether he was the translator/renderer or not, we have decided that it cannot be included in this collection.

To translate Berceo's collected works into English has required extensive linguistic and cultural knowledge. These translators have risen to the task, and thereby have ensured that these delightful, moving, and classic works of a remarkable medieval author will live in the contemporary world.

John E. Keller
Kathleen Kulp-Hill

TRANSLATORS' NOTES

The Praises of Our Lady, The Lamentation of the Virgin,
The Life of Saint Dominic of Silos, The Martyrdom of
Saint Lawrence, The Sacrifice of the Mass, The Signs
Which Will Appear Before Judgment Day, and *The Hymns*

JEANNIE K. BARTHA

In translating Berceo's works, I have relied predominantly on Brian Dutton's critical editions. However, I have also worked very closely with other editions indicated in my Abbreviations and/or Bibliography under Primary Sources. Wherever I have preferred the reading of another edition, I have indicated this in a footnote.

I have respected the integrity of Berceo's style, maintaining his quatrain division. In almost every case, I have been able to preserve Berceo's line-by-line structure. Very rarely have I found it necessary, due to the exigencies of English syntax and for purposes of comprehension, to alter the order of his line structure. For stylistic reasons, however, I have often altered the order of Berceo's hemistichs within his lines. I have made no rhyming attempt whatsoever in my translation of these works.

For a thorough background in the sources used by Berceo, I refer the reader to the editions of Brian Dutton.

My objective has been to preserve the medieval flavor of Berceo's language but at the same time to modernize the text sufficiently so as to be able to make it appealing to the contemporary reader. Thus I have not used a completely prose style in rendering Berceo's works into English. Rather, I have attempted to give some rhythm and meter to the lines, which will be particularly evident if the lines are read aloud.

In dealing with the problem of how to translate into English the Spanish names found in these works, I have consistently translated into their English equivalents the names of persons historically known to have existed. For other persons, such as those named in the miracles performed by St. Dominic of Silos, I have generally rendered their names into modern Spanish wherever possible.

I have chosen to modernize certain Old Spanish spellings such as *nn* with *ñ* and *ſ* with *z*.

As to when and where to employ the English auxiliary forms of *shall* vs. *will* and *should* vs. *would*, I have for the most part followed the modern American English usage of *will* and *would*. However, I have sometimes allowed myself to be guided by style in choosing *shall* and *should* over *will* and *would*.

Translating Berceo has been arduous work, but also an inspiring and rewarding labor of love. I have found myself continuously challenged emotionally, spiritually, and intellectually as if on a personal mission — or better still, on a pilgrimage. It is my hope that these works will resonate in similar ways for the reader of the twenty-first century.

∼

The Miracles of Our Lady, The Life of Saint Aemelianus of La Cogolla, and *The Life of Saint Oria*

ANNETTE G. CASH
R. TERRY MOUNT

Our translations in the present volume have been guided by the same philosophy and methodology which carried us through the work on our original collaborative translation *Miracles of Our Lady* (Lexington: University Press of Kentucky, 1997). Our foremost consideration as we have revised the *Miracles* and independently translated the two saints lives has been to present in English readable translations which preserve the meaning and something of the flavor of the original works. We have made no attempt to adapt our translations to English rhyme and meter but have preferred to maintain, insofar as possible, the strophe divisions of the originals so that each strophe in English is a faithful and readable translation. Where English grammar and syntax allow, the sense of each line of verse and even of each hemistich has also been preserved. Occasionally, of course, the exigencies of English have required the rearrangement of some of the lines within a strophe. While we have not tried to cast Berceo's Spanish into the language of his English contemporaries, we have aimed to create through vocabulary, syntax and style the feeling in present-day readers that Berceo is speaking to them from a world in which saints and miracles were a vital presence in the lives of Christian believers.

Our translations are based on Brian Dutton's editions, but we have found invaluable the work of other editors and, in the case of *The Life of Saint Oria*, the translation done by Anthony Lappin (Oxford: Legenda, 2000). On the rare occasion that we depart from Dutton, we have acknowledged the fact in footnotes.

I: The Marian Poems:

The Miracles of Our Lady,
The Praises of Our Lady,
and *The Lamentation of The Virgin*

Introduction to *The Miracles of Our Lady*

TRANSLATED BY RICHARD TERRY MOUNT
AND ANNETTE GRANT CASH

The Miracles of Our Lady is a collection of twenty-five miracles of the Virgin Mary which are preceded by an allegorical introduction. The form of these miracle tales, though they vary in length, is simple, as is Berceo's style in general. There is a discernible, basic pattern in the presentation, which varies somewhat according to the particular situation. Keller describes it as follows:

> [T]he poet lays the scene, giving the name of the city and the name of the protagonist. He then describes the protagonist and acquaints us with his qualities.... Those of evil intent receive graphic treatment also.... If some evil antagonist is a character, he ... is presented early by the poet.... After such introductory scenes and characterizations, the miracle runs its course, ending almost invariably with one or more quatrains which relate the reward for piety and devotion or the punishment for sin and a reminder that the Virgin is a constant protectress. (*Gonzalo de Berceo*, 60–62)

Wilkins offers an outline that focuses on the "dramatic form" of Berceo's miracle-tale structure:

> The typical scenario of the *Milagros*, based on the original Latin, pits the Virgin Mary, the protagonist, against the opposing force, the devil and his cohorts. A secondary character involved in the conflict is usually a faithful Christian follower of the Virgin who has erred and yet, eventually and miraculously, is saved because of repentance, or, more often, some saving grace or redeeming feature which the sinner possesses. We can subdivide the plot of each miracle as follows: the beginning: point of attack, exposition; the middle: rising action, crisis, falling action; and the end: the resolution. Aside from some tragic situations in the rising action and those of a few secondary characters, the *Milagros* do not have catastrophes or tragic outcomes, and, for that reason, we can describe the end of the plot in terms of its successful resolution. The third-person narrative and direct discourse are so firmly blended in the *Milagros* that the resultant dramatic form is far removed from the Latin prose versions. ("Dramatic Design," 310)

This work is an example of the extensive literature of miracles of the Holy Mother which had great currency during the Middle Ages. Among these are the *Miracles de Notre-Dame de Roc-Amadour* (*Miracles of Our Lady of Rocamadour*, twelfth century) and the *Miracles de la Sainte Vierge* (*Miracles of the Holy Virgin*) of Gautier de Coincy (1177–1236) in France and the *Cantigas de Santa María* (*Canticles of Holy Mary*) of Alfonso X the Wise (1221–1284) in Spain. Other more general works in this category are the *Speculum Historiale* (*Mirror of History*) of Vincent de Beauvais and the *Legenda Aurea* (*Golden Legend*) of Jacobus de Voragine. Because of similarities in presentation of the *Miracles* of Gautier de Coincy and of Berceo's own *Miracles*, it was once thought that the latter poet might have based his work on that of the former.[1] However, Richard Becker in 1910 brought to light a Latin collection (MS.Thott 128) found in the Library of Copenhagen which most likely served at least indirectly as model for both Berceo and Gautier. This collection contains all of Berceo's miracles except "The Robbed Church"; moreover, the miracles in common appear in the same order in both collections.[2] "The Robbed Church" is perhaps taken from Spanish oral tradition since it deals with a Spanish subject. It should be noted that Kinkade in 1971 proposed another Latin manuscript (MS.110 of the Spanish National Library) as a more direct source for the *Miracles*.

The allegorical introduction is the most famous and most highly praised part of Berceo's creation. Its precise source remains a mystery.[3] The central metaphor, that the Virgin Mary is a perpetually green meadow where the pilgrim can rest and enjoy spiritual delights, is an elaboration of the often described *locus amoenus*, or "pleasant place," of the Middle Ages. Here the *locus amoenus* serves as an allegorical setting that frames and sets into perspective the twenty-five miracle tales of the Virgin's miraculous intercession. While in most of the tales she intervenes in some way on behalf of her devotees, she is also quick to punish the incorrigible or those who have offended her so severely that they are beyond redemption.

---

[1] See T. J. Boudet, *Les vieux auteurs castillans* (Paris: Didier, 1861–1862). For a description in English of some of the problems of the sources of the *Miracles*, see J. E. Keller, *Gonzalo de Berceo* (New York: Twayne, 1972), 44–50. See also B. Dutton, ed. *Obras Completas 2* (London: Támesis, 1971), 13–14, and the commentaries following each miracle tale.

[2] Dutton reverses the order of the last two miracle tales in his critical edition so that "The Robbed Church" is the twenty-fourth and "The Miracle of Theophilus" is the last. We have followed this as well as other such suggestions of his for reordering quatrains. For the rationale for retaining "The Miracle of Theophilus" as the twenty-fourth and "The Robbed Church" as the last of the twenty-five tales, see Fernando Baños, ed. *Milagros de Nuestra Señora* (Barcelona: Crítica, 1997), lxii–lxxii.

[3] For a thorough presentation on the sources of the introduction, see Dutton, *Obras* 2, 36–45.

Berceo's poetry in general reflects the importance of the widespread and ever-growing devotion to the Virgin Mary that reached its apogee in the thirteenth century. The *Miracles* is but one of his three major poems devoted to her (not counting the hymn "Ave Sancta María, estrella de la mar"), and she is of signal importance, though by no means the central figure, in *The Life of Saint Oria*. In two of these works, the *Praises* and the *Miracles* (specifically the introduction to the *Miracles*), Berceo devotes concentrated attention to the evocation of the Virgin's role in the fulfillment of the law and prophecy of the Old Testament. The poet's insistence on Old Testament events and figures reflects (with particular emphasis on the role of Christ's mother) the generally held view that the Old Testament was fulfilled by the coming of the New Testament messiah in what Warner has referred to as "one unbroken chain of prophecy" (*Alone of All Her Sex*, 62).

Obviously written within this tradition, the introduction to the *Miracles* represents a compact but evocative narration which is followed by a gloss containing many of the same images of prophetic and typological fulfillment found in the *Praises*. This allegorical introduction is the portion of Berceo's work richest in imagery and symbolism. Berceo opens the poem with a quatrain of exhortation to his audience. He names himself as a pilgrim in the second quatrain, and the allegorical narrative begins. The narrative proper ends with a comparison of the meadow to paradise in quatrains 14 and 15. This comparison is not casually made; the correspondence Virgin-meadow-paradise is the key to the allegory and to the meaning of the *Miracles* as a whole. The Virgin is linked symbolically to the Garden of Eden, the earthly paradise lost, and the fall of mankind. Her part in the salvation of mankind, as the Second Eve, is Berceo's central theme. Just as God in his infinite goodness created Eden, so has he created this second garden paradise, this Second Eve — Mary — who leads humankind to the third and heavenly paradise. Quatrain 15 continues with imagery of the Fall and evokes the whole history of humankind in the Christian framework, suggesting that the meadow (Mary) undoes the sin of Adam and Eve.

With quatrain 16, Berceo expresses metaphorically his desire to take the husk off the allegory in order to expose its underlying meaning. He begins the gloss, explaining the significance of the various aspects of the narrative and the attributes of the garden. For example, the birds of the meadow represent all those who sang the virtues of Our Lady — including the prophets (like Isaiah) and the patriarchs. Then, in quatrains 31–41, he arrives at an extensive series of allusions to the Virgin as fulfilment of prophecy. In quatrain 31, he explains the flowers of the meadow as representing the names or titles of the Blessed Virgin. And in quatrains 33–41, he lists these names giving varying degrees of explanation, but none so complete as those found in the first section of the *Praises*.

The following titles are bestowed upon the Blessed Virgin because they have been interpreted as prophetic of her or have been applied to her through typological exegesis: fleece of Gideon (34a); sling of David (34c); fountain (35a); closed gate (36a); Zion (37a); throne of Solomon (37c); vine; grape; almond; pomegranate (39a); olive; cedar; balsam; palm (39c); staff of Moses (40a); rod of Aaron (41ab).

The fleece of Gideon is considered a prefigurement of the virginity of the Blessed Mother and is one of the best known of such symbols (Raby, *Christian-Latin Poetry*, 371). The sling of David in the well-known David and Goliath story (1 Samuel 17) prefigures her in that she launched the stone, her son, into the world to strike down evil and bring salvation.

The fountain is most likely the sealed fountain of the Song of Solomon: "A garden enclosed is my sister, my spouse; a spring shut up, a fountain sealed" (Song of Solomon 4:12) which was considered a prefigurement of her virginal womb. This idea of her unblemished virginity is also behind the interpretation of the closed gate of Ezekiel (Ezekiel 44:1–3) that is seen in the *Praises*, and the image of the Closed Gate appears here again in Berceo's words: "she is called the Closed Gate; / for us she is open, to give us entrance" (*Miracles* 36a).

She is Zion (37c), or the virgin daughter of Zion, evoked in so many Old Testament passages such as "Sing and rejoice, O daughter of Zion: for, lo, I come, and I will dwell in the midst of thee, saith the Lord." As the Throne of Solomon (Mi 37c) described in 1 Kings 10:18–20, the Virgin is unique in beauty and virtue, for "there was not the like made in any kingdom." The gold of the throne symbolizes her charity, the ivory her chastity. The association with Solomon also associates her with wisdom and justice.

In quatrain 39, she is vine, grape, almond, pomegranate, olive, cedar, balsam, and palm. These images are consistent with the garden enclosed of the Song of Solomon (4:12) which holds among other things an orchard; however, they seem more specifically to relate to the twenty-fourth chapter of the *Book of Ecclesiasticus* in which the female figure Wisdom says:

> I grew tall like a cedar in Lebanon ...
> I grew tall like a palm tree in En-gedi ...
> like a beautiful olive tree in the field..
> like a vine I caused loveliness to bud,
> and my blossoms became glorious and abundant fruits.
>   (Ecclesiasticus 24:13–17)

Both of these passages were applied typologically to the Virgin Mary.

The last two names are staff of Moses and rod of Aaron. The staff of Moses, Berceo says, confounded the sorcerers of Pharaoh and opened the waters of the sea for the children of Israel but closed them on the pursuing Egyptians (Exodus

14:21–27). Because the staff was significant in the salvation of Israel and acted contrary to the laws of nature, particularly when it spontaneously turned into a serpent, it was seen as a prefigurement of the virginal conception of Christ in Mary (Warner, *Alone of All Her Sex*, 62). A similar interpretation was applied to the Rod of Aaron, the last of Mary's names mentioned by Berceo in the introduction and used also in the *Praises*. God caused Aaron's rod to bloom and produce almonds as a sign that Aaron was chosen and that the Israelites should not continue to resist his leadership (Numbers 17:1–8).

It is clear from the *Praises* and the introduction to the *Miracles* that the figures which Berceo gives as prophetic prefigurations of the role of the Virgin serve to elevate her to a level of importance in human salvation very near, if not equal, to that of Christ. While Mary's elevated position may not adhere to strict Catholic theology, neither is it a strange aberration that makes Berceo's perception of her role unique. Rather, his perception of her role is formed by a centuries-old tradition that found its fullest flowering in the writings of St. Bernard in the twelfth century. Furthermore, Berceo's insistence on prophetic fulfillment links his work to the long chain of previous writers in both West and East and serves artistically as one element of unity in the works. Prophecy is of particular significance as a unifying motif within Berceo's Marian works and sets them and their audience within the continuum that leads to salvation.

The *Miracles* within the Context of Pilgrimage

In the ninth century, the tomb of the Apostle St. James the Greater (Santiago to the Spanish) was found in Galicia in northwestern Spain, and the shrine there established became the goal of the famous pilgrimage to Santiago de Compostela.[4] The impact of the pilgrim route crossing northern Spain from the Pyrenees to Galicia was not only religious but also economic, cultural, and political. Pilgrimages to Santiago were particularly promoted during the eleventh century by King Sancho el Mayor of Navarre. The Cluniac order established itself along the route and provided lodging for the travelers. Since this was a French order, the trans-Pyrenees connections were an important force in bringing new ideas from the rest of Europe, especially France, into the Iberian Peninsula. The monasteries themselves vied for pilgrims and even those not on the direct pilgrim

---

[4] Still today thousands of pilgrims, whether by motor vehicle, bicycle, or on foot, follow the traditional route to visit the shrine of Spain's patron saint in Santiago de Compostela. Many, as in Berceo's day, take side trips to the monasteries of San Millán and Santo Domingo de Silos. For an account of the modern-day experience, see E. Stanton, *Road of Stars to Santiago* (Lexington: University Press of Kentucky, 1994).

route served as lesser destinations or side trips for pilgrims. Michael Gerli points out that in the eleventh century the Monastery of San Millán de la Cogolla (Berceo's monastery) had acquired the pilgrim hostel of Azofra near Nájera on the Santiago route. Pilgrims who stopped there were no doubt encouraged to make the excursion to San Millán to pray in the sanctuary of the Virgin Mary. Gerli believes that Berceo's *Miracles* were probably read or recited in Azofra in order to entertain pilgrims and, perhaps more importantly, to entice them to go to San Millán to pay homage to the Blessed Mother (Gerli, *Milagros*, 23). Be that as it may, San Millán was known to attract pilgrims in its own right as many came to pay homage to Saint Millán or to the Virgin, whose cult was firmly established there.

The reader of Berceo's *Miracles* will note not only the importance of the concept of pilgrimage in the work but also the orality of the text. The fact that the work was written to be read or recited and even acted out for an audience of religious pilgrims explains to a large degree both the motivation for the work's composition as well as the nature of its presentation. With his analysis of the "dramatic design" of the *Miracles*, Wilkins raises the possibility of the work as an antecedent of Spanish drama. Other scholars have gone a step further suggesting that works such as the *Miracles* actually were acted out through mime while a reader (possibly the poet himself) read or recited the narration. This view, by placing the *Miracles* and other *clerecía* works within the tradition of dramatic art, helps to fill in the three-century gap in the early development of Castilian "drama."[5]

---

[5] See especially M. Gerli, "Poet and Pilgrim: Discourse, Language, Imagery, and Audience in Berceo's *Milagros de Nuestra Señora*," in *Hispanic Medieval Studies in Honor of Samuel G. Armistead,* ed. idem and H. L. Sharrer (Madison: Hispanic Seminary of Medieval Studies, 1992), 140–51; and Richard P. Kinkade, "Sermon in the Round: The *Mester de Clerecía* as Dramatic Art," in *Studies in Honor of Gustavo Correa*, ed. C. B. Faulhaber, idem, and T. A. Perry (Potomac, MD: Scripta Humanística, 1986), 127–36. Kinkade offers his study as a plausible explanation for the apparent lacuna between the twelfth-century *Auto de los reyes magos* (*Play of the Three Wise Men*, the earliest extant religious play in any vernacular) and the fifteenth-century *Representación del nacimiento de Nuestro Señor* (*Representation of the Nativity of Our Lord*) by Gómez Manrique. Further discussion of manifestations of dramatic "staging" techniques in Spain in the thirteenth century, especially as related to the *Canticles of Holy Mary* of Alfonso the Wise, can be found in J. E. Keller and R. P. Kinkade, *Iconography in Medieval Spanish Literature* (Lexington: University Press of Kentucky, 1984), 16–17, and in J. E. Keller, "Drama, Ritual, and Incipient Opera in Alfonso"s *Cantigas*," in *Emperor of Culture: Alfonso X the Learned of Castile and his Thirteenth-Century Renaissance*, ed. R. I. Burns (Philadelphia: University of Pennsylvania Press, 1990), 72–89.

Gerli has shown that what he calls the inscribed audience of the *Miracles* is in fact an audience of pilgrims for whom the work's language, discourse, and imagery are specifically tailored. The central human figure in the allegorical introduction is the narrator who presents himself as a pilgrim, a stratagem by which the poet-narrator immediately identifies himself with his audience and gains their confidence as well as their interest. Moreover, two of the miracle tales have pilgrims as their human protagonists: "The Pilgrim Deceived by the Devil" and "The Shipwrecked Pilgrim Saved by the Virgin."

The Translation

Considering the importance accorded Berceo's *Miracles*, it is surprising that there was no complete English translation until 1997.[6] This can be explained in part by the fact that the work was not generally known in Spain until the eighteenth century when Tomás Antonio Sánchez rediscovered and published Berceo's works. While its importance as one of the monuments of medieval Spanish literature is firmly established, the difficulties of translating the *Miracles* with its stringent versification pattern and Latinized syntax may have daunted many who might have considered undertaking the project. This translation, based on Brian Dutton's critical edition of the *Miracles*, is a revised version of the 1997 Mount and Cash translation published by the University Press of Kentucky. The translators thank the Press for permission to include this amended introduction and translation of the *Miracles* in this volume and are grateful to colleagues and reviewers who have made numerous suggestions for its improvement. Presenting in English a readable translation that preserves the meaning and something of the flavor of the original remains our goal.

R. Terry Mount

---

[6] Mount and Cash translation: see bibliography.

Works Cited

Baños, Fernando, ed. *Milagros de Nuestra Señora*. Barcelona: Crítica, 1997.
Becker, Richard. *Gonzalo de Berceo. "Los Milagros" und ihre Grundlagen*. Strassburg: Universitäts-Buchdruckerei, 1910.
Beltrán, Vicente, ed. Gonzalo de Berceo, *Milagros de Nuestra Señora*. 3rd ed. Barcelona: Planeta, 1990.
Boudet, Théodore Joseph, comte de Puygmaigre. *Les vieux auteurs castillans*. Paris: Didier, 1861–1862.
Devoto, Daniel, ed. Gonzalo de Berceo, *Milagros de Nuestra Señora*. Odres Nuevos. Madrid: Castalia, 1969. Modernized version.
Dutton, Brian, ed. Gonzalo de Berceo, *Obras Completas*. 5 vols. London: Támesis, 1967–1981. (Vol. 1 published as *La vida de San Millán de la Cogolla*.)
García Turza, Claudio, ed. Gonzalo de Berceo, *Milagros de Nuestra Señora*. In *Obra Completa*, ed. Brian Dutton et al. Madrid: Espasa-Calpe, 1992.
Gerli, Michael, ed. Gonzalo de Berceo, *Milagros de Nuestra Señora*. Madrid: Cátedra, 1989.
———. "Poet and Pilgrim: Discourse, Language, Imagery, and Audience in Berceo's Milagros de Nuestra Señora." In *Hispanic Medieval Studies in Honor of Samuel G. Armistead*, ed. idem and Harvey L. Sharrer, 140–51. Madison: Hispanic Seminary of Medieval Studies, 1992.
Keller, John Esten. "Drama, Ritual, and Incipient Opera in Alfonso's *Cantigas*." In *Emperor of Culture: Alfonso X the Learned of Castile and His Thirteenth-Century Renaissance*, ed. Robert I. Burns, 72–89. Philadelphia: University of Pennsylvania Press, 1990.
———. *Gonzalo de Berceo*. Twayne's World Authors Series 187. New York: Twayne, 1972.
———, and Richard P. Kinkade. *Iconography in Medieval Spanish Literature*. Lexington: University Press of Kentucky, 1984.
Kinkade, Richard P. "A New Latin Source for Berceo's Milagros: MS110 of Madrid's Biblioteca Nacional." *Romance Philology* 25 (1971): 188–92.
———. "Sermon in the Round: The *Mester de Clerecía* as Dramatic Art." In *Studies in Honor of Gustavo Correa*, ed. Charles B. Faulhaber, idem, and T. A. Perry, 127–36. Potomac, MD: Scripta Humanistica, 1986.
Mount, Richard Terry, and Annette Grant Cash, trans. *Miracles of Our Lady* by Gonzalo de Berceo. Lexington: University Press of Kentucky, 1997.
Nelson, Dana. *Gonzalo de Berceo: "El libro de Alexandre." Reconstrucción crítica*. Madrid: Gredos, 1979.
Raby, F. J. E. *A History of Christian-Latin Poetry from the Beginnings to the Close of the Middle Ages*. 2nd ed. Oxford: Oxford University Press, 1966.

Sánchez, Tomás Antonio. *Colección de poesías castellanas anteriores al siglo XV.* Vol. 2. Madrid: A. de Sancha, 1779–1790.

Solalinde, Antonio G. *Milagros de Nuestra Señora.* 5th ed. Clásicos Castellanos 44. Madrid: Espasa-Calpe, 1958.

Stanton, Edward. *Road of Stars to Santiago.* Lexington: University Press of Kentucky, 1994.

Warner, Marina. *Alone of All Her Sex.* New York: Knopf, 1976.

Wilkins, Heanon. "Dramatic Design in Berceo's *Milagros de Nuestra Señora.*" In *Hispanic Studies in Honor of Alan D. Deyermond: A North American Tribute,* ed. John S. Miletich, 309–24. Madison: Hispanic Seminary of Medieval Studies, 1986.

THE MIRACLES OF OUR LADY

Introduction

1   Friends and vassals of Almighty God,
if it pleases you to listen to me,
I would like to relate a fortunate experience.
Afterwards you will truly consider it wonderful.

2   I, Master Gonzalo de Berceo,
while on a pilgrimage, happened to pause in a meadow,[1]
green and untouched, full of flowers —
a desirable place for a weary man.

3   The flowers there emitted a marvelous fragrance;
they were refreshing to the spirit and to the body.
From each corner sprang clear, flowing fountains,
very cool in summer and warm in winter.

4   There was a profusion of fine trees —
pomegranate and fig, pear and apple,
and many other fruits of various kinds.
But none were spoiled or sour.

5   The greenness of the meadow, the fragrance of the flowers,
the shade of the trees of soothing aromas
refreshed me completely and I ceased to perspire.
Anyone could live with those fragrances.

6   Never in this world did I find so delightful a place,
nor so soothing a shade, nor so pleasant a fragrance;
I removed my garment for a more comfortable repose
and lay under the shade of a beautiful tree.

---

[1] The meadow is an evocation of the medieval *locus amoenus* and symbolically associates the garden paradise with the Virgin Mary. As the allegory of the meadow unfolds, emphasis is placed on its perfection and perpetually pure or virginal state.

7   Lying in the shade, I forgot all my cares;
         I heard sweet, modulated bird songs.
         There never was heard music of organs so finely tuned,
         nor could more harmonious sounds be made.

8   Some birds carried the fifth, while others doubled;
         others held the basic melody, keeping everyone from erring.
         Upon resting and moving, they all waited for each other.
         No dull or raucous birds came near there!

9   There was no organist, *vihuela* player,
         nor *giga*, psaltery, or *rota*-player's hand,[2]
         nor other instrument, or tongue, or so clear a voice
         whose song would be worth a penny[3] in comparison.

10   Although we told you of all these virtues,
         rest assured we did not tell a tenth of them,
         for there was such diversity of splendors
         that neither priors nor abbots could count them.

11   The meadow I am telling you about had another fine quality:
         in neither heat nor cold did it lose its beauty;
         it was always green in its entirety.
         It did not lose its verdure in any storm.

12   As soon as I had stretched out on the ground,
         I was immediately freed of all suffering;
         I forgot all worries and past burdens.
         Anyone living there would be very lucky indeed!

13   No matter how many men or birds came there
         and gathered all the flowers they wished,
         there was never a lack of flowers in the meadow;
         for each one that they gathered, three and four would spring up.[4]

14   This meadow seemed like Paradise
         into which God put such great grace, such great blessing.
         He who created such a thing was a wise master;
         any man who should dwell here would never lose his sight.

15   The fruit of the trees was sweet and delicious;
         if Adam had eaten such fruit,

---

[2] The *vihuela*, the *giga*, and the *rota* are medieval stringed instruments. The *vihuela* is similar to the guitar. The *giga* is a kind of viola and the *rota* a kind of harp.

[3] *Dinero*, a coin of small value; therefore, the translation "penny" seems appropriate here and in strophe 324d.

[4] The spontaneous regeneration described here is in keeping with the "intactness" of the meadow mentioned in quatrains 2 and 11.

       he would not have been so badly deceived.
       Neither Eve nor her husband would have suffered such harm!

16   Gentle people and friends, what we have just said
       is an obscure parable and we wish to explain it.
       Let us remove the husk and get into the marrow.[5]
       Let us take what is within, and what is without, let us leave aside.

17   All we who live and stand upright,[6]
       even if we are in prison or bedridden,
       are pilgrims walking down the road.
       St. Peter says so — we prove it to you through him.[7]

18   As long as we live here, we dwell in a foreign land;
       the everlasting dwelling place, we await on high.
       Our pilgrimage, then, we finish
       when we send our souls to Paradise.

19   On this pilgrimage we have a good meadow
       in which any weary pilgrim will find refuge:
       the Glorious Virgin, Mother of the Good Son,
       the equal of whom has never been found.

20   This meadow was always green in purity,
       for her virginity never was stained;
       post partum et in partu,[8] she truly was a virgin,
       illesa, incorrupta[9] in her integrity.

21   The four clear streams flowing from the meadow
       signified the four Gospels,
       for the Evangelists,[10] the four who delivered them,
       talked with her as they wrote.

22   Everything they wrote, she emended.
       That which she praised was indeed true.
       It seems that she was the source from which all waters flowed
       while without her nothing received guidance.

---

   [5] The metaphor of the husk (*corteza*) and the marrow (*meollo*) is another common medieval metaphor referring to a real or symbolic meaning beyond the surface meaning.

   [6] Although the manuscript reads "en piedes andamos" (walk on our feet, or upright), Dutton corrects to "en piedes estamos" (stand on our feet, or upright) to avoid repetition of the rhyming word *andamos* that occurs again in 17c.

   [7] 1 Peter 2:11.

   [8] Latin: "after giving birth [to Christ] and during [his] birth."

   [9] Latin: "undefiled, incorrupt."

   [10] Matthew, Mark, Luke, and John.

23   The shade of the trees, good, sweet, and healthful,
        in which all pilgrims take respite,
        indeed are the prayers that Holy Mary says,
        she who prays for sinners day and night.

24   All who are in this world, the righteous and the sinful,
        regular and secular clergy, kings and emperors,
        we all hasten there, vassals and lords:
        all of us seek her shade to gather the flowers.

25   The trees that make sweet and blessed shade
        are the holy miracles that the Glorious One performs,
        for they are much sweeter than the delicious sugar
        given to the sick in their delirious suffering. [11]

26   The birds that sing in those fruit trees,
        that have sweet voices and sing devout songs,
        they are Augustine, Gregory, and others,
        who wrote about her true deeds.

27   These had love and loyalty for her
        and praised her deeds with all their might;
        they told of her, each in his own way;
        but, throughout it all, all held to one belief.

28   The nightingale sings with fine skill,
        and even the lark makes great melody,
        but Isaiah sang much better,[12]
        as did the other prophets, honored company.

29   The apostles sang in a most natural tone;
        the confessors and martyrs did likewise;
        the virgins followed the great and powerful Mother
        singing before her a very joyous song.

30   In all the churches, every day,
        the clergy sings lauds before her.
        All pay court to the *Virgo Maria*:[13]
        they are the most pleasing nightingales.

31   Let us turn to the flowers that comprise the meadow,
        which make it beautiful, fair, and serene.

---

[11] Sugar was a luxury item in the Middle Ages and used primarily in medicines.
[12] Especially Isaiah 7:14, "Behold a virgin shall conceive and bear a son …".
[13] Latin: "Virgin Mary."

The flowers are the names the book gives
to the Virgin Mary, Mother of the Good Son.[14]

32   The Blessed Virgin is called Star,
        Star of the Seas, Longed-for Guide;
        she is watched by mariners in peril,
        for when they see her, their ship is guided.

33   She is called, and she is, Queen of Heaven,
        Temple of Jesus Christ, Morning Star,
        Natural Mistress, Merciful Neighbor,
        Health and Cure of Bodies and Souls.

34   She is the Fleece that was Gideon's,
        on which fell the rain, a great vision;
        she is the Sling with which young David
        destroyed the ferocious giant.

35   She is the Fount from which we all drink,
        she gave us the food of which we all eat;
        she is called the Port to which we all hasten,
        and the Gate through which we all await entrance.

36   She is called the Closed Gate;
        for us she is open, to give us entrance;
        she is the Dove free of all anger,
        in whom lies no wrath; she is always pleased.

37   She rightfully is called Zion,
        for she is our watchtower, our defense;
        she is called the Throne of King Solomon,
        king of justice and admirably wise.

38   There exists no goodly name
        that in some way does not apply to her;
        there is none that does not have its root in her,
        neither Sancho nor Domingo, not Sancha nor Dominga.[15]

---

[14] These names, explained in quatrains 32–41, show the importance of the Virgin Mary in the medieval mind and especially are indicative of the interpretation of Old Testament figures as pointing to her and her role in the fulfillment of the divine plan.

[15] Berceo uses the common names Sancho and Domingo and their feminine equivalents to indicate that all Christian names in some way can be traced to the Virgin Mary. Sancho is derived from *sanctus* (holy) and Domingo from *dominicus* (belonging to the Lord).

39   She is called Vine, she is Grape, Almond, and Pomegranate,
       replete with its grains of grace,[16]
       Olive, Cedar, Balsam, leafy Palm,
       Rod upon which the serpent was raised.

40   The Staff that Moses carried in his hand,[17]
       that confounded the wise men esteemed by Pharaoh,
       the one that parted the waters and then closed them —
       if it did not signify the Virgin, it signified nothing.

41   If we think upon the other staff
       that settled the dispute concerning Aaron,[18]
       it signified nothing else — so says the text —
       but the Glorious One, and with good reason.

42   Gentlefolk and friends, in vain do we argue,
       for we enter a great well, whose bottom we cannot find;
       we would read more of her names
       than there are flowers in the largest field we know.

43   We have already said that the fruit trees
       in which the birds were singing their various songs
       were her holy miracles, great and outstanding,
       which we sing on the principal feast days.

44   But I want to leave behind those singing birds,
       the shade, the founts, and the aforementioned flowers
       and, about these fruit trees so full of sweetness,
       write a few verses, gentlefolk and friends.

45   I want to climb up into those trees for a little while
       and write about some of her miracles.
       May the Glorious One guide me so that I may complete the task,
       for I would not dare to undertake it otherwise.

46   I will take it as a miracle wrought by the Glorious One,
       if she should deign to guide me in this task.
       Mother Full of Grace, Powerful Queen,
       guide me in it, for you are merciful.

---

[16] The pomegranate is notable for the countless seeds in each of its fruits.
[17] Exodus 4:2–4; 4:17; 9:23; 10:13; 14:21; 14:27.
[18] Numbers 17.

Miracle 1

The Chasuble of Saint Ildephonsus

47   In Spain I desire at once to begin
in the great city of Toledo, a famous place,
for I do not know where else to begin,
because there are miracles more numerous than the sands of the seashore.

48   In fair Toledo, that royal city
which lies above the Tagus, that mighty river,
there was an archbishop, a loyal cleric
who was a true friend of the Glorious One.

49   According to the text,[1] they called him Ildephonsus,[2]
a shepherd who gave his flock good pasture,
a holy man who possessed great wisdom;
all that we may say, his deeds reveal.

50   He was always partial to the Glorious One;
never did man have more love for lady;
he sought to serve her with all his might
and did so sensibly and most prudently.

51   Besides his many other great services,
there are two in the writing which are most notable:
he wrote a book of beautiful sayings about her
and her virginity, contradicting three infidels.[3]

---

[1] Berceo refers to a written text, his Latin source, which in its turn derived the miracle story from Cixila's eighth-century Life of the saint. See *Patrologia cursus completes, series Latina*, ed. Jean-Paul Migne, 221 vols. (Paris, Garnier, 1884–1904), 96: 46–48. Hereafter this work is abbreviated in footnotes as *PL*.

[2] St. Ildephonsus (606–667) became Archbishop of Toledo in 657, unified the Spanish liturgy and is especially known for his devotion to the Blessed Virgin and his treatise on her perpetual virginity. See following note.

[3] This is a reference to the *Libellus de virginitate Sanctae Mariae contra tres infideles, more synonymorum conscriptus a beato Ildefonso, Toletanae sedis episcopo*, a treatise on the perpetual virginity of the Blessed Virgin Mary written by Saint Ildephonsus (*PL* 96: 53–110).

52   And the loyal cleric served her in another way:
        he changed her feast day to the middle of December,
        the one that falls in March, that most signal day
        when Gabriel came with his wonderful message.

53   When Gabriel came with the message,
        when sweetly he said, "Ave Maria,"
        and told her the news that she would bear the Messiah,
        remaining as virginal as she was on that day.

54   At that time of the year, as is well known,
        the Church does not sing a song of joy[4]
        and such a signal day does not get its rightful due;
        if we consider it well, he did a great favor.

55   Her loyal friend did a great and prudent deed;
        by placing that feast day near the Nativity,
        he joined a good grapevine to a good arbor —
        the Mother with the Son, a pair without equal.

56   The Lenten season is a time of affliction:
        no hallelujahs are sung nor are processions made.
        This wise man thought about all of this —
        and later, because of it, he earned an honorable reward.

57   St. Ildephonsus, loyal clergyman,
        prepared for the Virgin a general holy day;
        there were few in Toledo who stayed in their lodgings
        and did not go to Mass in the Cathedral.

58   The holy archbishop, that loyal cleric,
        was prepared to begin the Mass;
        he was seated on his precious throne
        when the Glorious One brought him a most honorable gift.

59   The Mother of the King of Majesty appeared to him
        with a book of great brightness in her hand;
        it was the book he had written about her virginity.[5]
        Ildephonsus was very much pleased!

---

[4] Berceo is referring to Lent, the penitential period before Easter, which he mentions specifically in 56ab. The feast of the Annunciation is 25 March, which usually falls during Lent.

[5] This is the book referred to in strophe 51cd.

60   She extended to him another favor, never before heard:
        she gave him a chasuble sewn without a needle;
        it was an angelic work, not woven by humankind;
        she spoke but few words to him, a good and perfect speech.

61   "Friend," she said, "know that I am pleased with you.
        You have sought for me not single but double honor:
        you wrote a good book about me and have praised me well;
        you have made me a new feast day, which was not the custom.

62   For your new Mass of this feast day,
        I bring you a gift of great value:
        a chasuble, a truly precious one, in which you may sing
        today on the holy day of the Nativity.

63 (64)[6] The throne upon which you now rest
        is reserved for your body alone;
        the vesting of this chasuble is granted to you;
        anyone else who wears it will not be well regarded."

64 (63) Having said these words, the Glorious Mother
        vanished from sight; he saw nothing more of her;
        the precious person had finished her mission,
        the Mother of Christ, His Daughter and Spouse.

65   This lovely feast day about which we have spoken
        was soon approved by the General Council;[7]
        it is observed and celebrated by many churches;
        as long as this world endures, it will not be forgotten.

66   When our Heavenly Lord Jesus Christ so willed it,
        St. Ildephonsus, that precious confessor, died;
        the Glorious One, Mother of the Creator, honored him;
        she did great honor to his body and even greater to his soul.

67   A foolish canon was elevated to archbishop;
        he was extremely proud and not very bright —
        he wanted to be the equal of the other; in that, he was wrong.
        And the people of Toledo did not consider it good.

---

[6] The inversion of verses [(64)(63)] here follows Dutton, who saw that the order in the manuscript [(63)(64)] makes little sense.

[7] In the year 656, the Tenth Council of Toledo officially moved the feast of the Annunciation from 25 March to 18 December.

68   He seated himself upon the throne of his predecessor
        and demanded the chasuble the Creator had given him;
        that foolish sinner said some unwise things
        which angered the Mother of God Our Lord.

69   He said some very foolish things:
        "Ildephonsus was never of greater dignity than I:
        truly I am just as well consecrated as he was,
        and we are all equal in our humanity!"

70   If Siagrio had not gone so far,
        if he had only held his tongue a little,
        he would not have fallen into the Creator's wrath
        where we fear — oh, woeful sin — he is lost!

71   He ordered his ministers to bring the chasuble
        so that he might go into Mass and lead the confessional prayer,
        but he was not permitted to do so, nor did he have the power,
        because that which God does not will to be can never be.

72   Although the holy vestment was ample in size,
        on Siagrio it was exceedingly tight;
        it held his throat like a hard chain,
        and he was suffocated right then because of his great folly.

73   The Glorious Virgin, Star of the Sea,
        knows how to reward her friends well;
        she knows how to reward the good for their goodness
        and how to punish those who serve her badly.

74   Friends, we should serve such a mother well:
        in serving her we seek our own benefit:
        we honor our bodies, we save our souls;
        and for only a little service we reap great rewards.

Miracle 2

The Fornicating Sexton

75   Friends, if you would wait a short while,
there is yet another miracle that I would like to tell,
which God deigned to reveal through Holy Mary,
whose milk He suckled with His own mouth.

76   A blessed monk was in a monastery;
where it was, I do not find in the reading,[1] so I cannot say.
He loved Holy Mary with all his heart,
and each day he bowed before her image.

77   Each day he bowed before her image;
he would bend his knees and say: "Ave Maria."
The abbot of the house gave him the sextonship,
for he considered him prudent and free from folly.

78   The wicked enemy, vicar of Beelzebub,
who always was and is the enemy of good people,
that wily adversary was able to stir things up so much
that he corrupted the monk: he made him a fornicator.

79   He took up a bad habit, that crazy sinner:
at night when the abbot was in bed,
he would go out of the dormitory, through the church;
thus the lewd man hastened to his wicked work.

80   Upon leaving, as well as upon returning,
he would have to pass by the altar,
and so accustomed was he to genuflecting and saying the "Ave"
that not a single time did he forget it.

81   There was a goodly river running near the monastery.
The monk always had to cross it;
once when returning from committing his folly,
he fell in and drowned, outside the abbey.

---

[1] Berceo refers to what he reads in his source text.

82   When the hour to sing matins[2] arrived,
        there was no sexton to ring the call;
        all the monks got up, each from his own place,
        and went to the church to awaken the friar.

83   They opened the church as best they could;
        they searched for the key-keeper but could not find him.
        They went everywhere looking high and low
        and finally found him where he lay drowned.

84   What could this be? They had not the slightest idea
        whether he had died or had been killed; they could not decide.
        The anxiety was great and even greater the sorrow,
        for the place, because of all this, would fall into disrepute.

85   While the body was lying in the river as if in a bath,[3]
        let us tell of the dispute in which the soul found itself:
        a great crowd of devils came for it,
        to carry it off to Hell, a place devoid of all pleasure.

86   While the devils were carrying it like a ball,
        the angels saw it and came down to it.
        The devils then made a very strong argument:
        that it did not belong to the angels and they should get away from it.

87   The angels had no grounds for reclaiming the soul,
        since the man had met a bad end; and that was so, without doubt.
        They could not wrest it from the devils even a little
        and had to withdraw sad-hearted from the fray.

88   The Glorious One, Queen of All, came to rescue the soul,
        for the devils were focusing on evil alone.
        She ordered them to wait and they dared not do otherwise;
        she took them to task very firmly and very well.

89   She presented an eloquent argument:
        "Against this soul, you fools," she said, "you have nothing.
        While it was in its body, it was my devotee;
        it would be wrong for me to abandon it now."

---

[2] One of the canonical hours sung before dawn.

[3] Berceo seems to be emphasizing the separation of the body from the spirit. Since the body is in the water, it is lying as if "in a bath" and coming to no real harm. In fact, the evocation of the bath implies that the body is quite content, experiencing true pleasure (see strophes 152, 448, and 609). The real harm or unpleasantness is awaiting the soul in hell, "a place devoid of pleasure."

90   The spokesman for the other side responded
       (he was a wise devil, clever and very precise),
       "You are Mother of the Son, the Just Judge,
       Who does not like force and is not pleased with it.

91   It is written that wherever a man dies,
       whether in good or in evil, he is judged accordingly;
       so if you break the law in this case,
       you will be undermining the entire gospel."

92   "You are speaking foolishly," said the Glorious One.
       "I will not challenge you, for you are a wretched beast.
       When the sexton left the monastery, he asked my permission;
       I will give him penance for the sin that he committed.

93   It would not be fitting for me to use force against you,
       but I appeal to Christ, to His court,
       to the One who is almighty and full of wisdom;
       I wish to hear this sentence from His lips."

94   The King of Heaven, Wise Judge,
       settled this dispute; you never saw it done better:
       the Lord ordered the soul returned to the body,
       then the sinner would receive whatever reward he deserved.

95   The company was sad and distressed,
       because of this terrible circumstance that had befallen them,
       but the friar, who was already dead, was resuscitated,
       and everyone was amazed that he was in good condition.

96   The good man spoke to them saying, "Friends,
       I was dead and now I am alive; you can be sure of it.
       Thanks to the Glorious One who saves her workers,
       she freed me from the hands of the evil warriors!"

97   He told them with his own tongue the whole litany:
       what the devils said, and what Holy Mary said,
       and how she freed him from their power.
       If it had not been for her, he would have had hell to pay.

98   They gave thanks to God, with all their hearts,
       and to the Holy Queen, Mother of Mercy, [4]
       who wrought such a miracle out of her own goodness
       and because of whom Christianity is stronger.

---

[4] This is a quotation of the prayer/antiphon beginning "Salve Regina, Mater misericordiae".

99   The monk confessed and did penance;
         he turned from all his wicked ways.
         He served the Glorious One while he could
         and, when God willed, died without remorse.
         Requiescat in pace cum divina clemencia.[5]

100   Many such miracles and many greater ones
         did Holy Mary work for her devotees.
         A thousandth of them could not be recounted by anyone;
         but, for those we can relate, be pleased with us.

---

[5] Latin: "May he rest in peace with divine clemency." The phrase "Resquiescat in pace" is from the Office of the Dead. The addition of "cum divina clemencia" emphasizes the importance of God's mercy in man's salvation. This is one of the few five-line stanzas in Berceo's works.

Miracle 3

The Cleric and the Flower

101 We read of a cleric who was crackbrained,
  and deeply absorbed in worldly vices,
  but even though he was foolish he had one saving grace:
  he loved the Glorious One with all his heart.

102 Even though he had bad habits in other things,
  in greeting her he was always very prudent;
  he would not go to church nor on any errand
  without first invoking her name.

103 I could not say what the circumstances were,
  for we do not know if he provoked it or not,
  but some enemies attacked this man
  and they killed him. May the Lord God forgive them!

104 The townspeople, as well as his companions,
  were not sure how this had come about;
  so, outside the town in some hills,
  they buried him, and not among Christians.[1]

105 The Virgin was saddened with this burial,
  for her servant lay excluded from his company.
  She appeared to a cleric of good understanding
  and told him they had erred in this.

106 Full thirty days had he been buried
  (in that length of time his body could be decayed);
  Holy Mary said, "You committed a grave injustice
  in that my scribe lies so far from you.

107 I, therefore, order you to report that my servant
  did not deserve to be barred from holy ground.
  Tell them not to leave him there another thirty days,
  but to place him with the others in the good cemetery."

---

[1] *Diezmeros*, tithers: faithful Christians. Thus they did not bury him among the faithful in the cemetery because they were not sure of the circumstances of his death.

108   The cleric, who had been sleeping, asked her,
       "Who are you who speak? Tell me, whom you command,
       for when I say this, I will be asked
       who the aggrieved one is, or who the buried one is."

109   The Glorious One responded, "I am Holy Mary,
       Mother of Jesus Christ, who suckled my milk.
       The one you excluded from your company,
       I held as a chancellor of mine.

110   The one you buried far from the cemetery,
       the one to whom you refused Christian burial:
       it is on his behalf that I tell all this to you.
       If you do not comply, consider yourself in peril."

111   The lady's command was then carried out.
       They opened the grave quickly and with despatch
       and beheld a miracle, not single but double;
       the one and the other were immediately well noted.

112   There issued from his mouth a lovely flower —
       of very great beauty and very fresh color.
       It filled the entire place with a wonderful fragrance;
       they did not smell any foul odor from the body.

113   They found his tongue so fresh and sound
       that it resembled the inside of a beautiful apple;
       it never had been fresher during midday rest
       when he would speak in the midst of the orchard.

114   They saw that this had come about because of the Glorious One,
       for no other could do such a great thing.
       They sang "Speciosa"[2] as they moved his body
       near the church to a more precious tomb.

115   Everyone in the world will do a great courtesy
       if he does service to the Virgin Mary.
       As long as he lives he will see contentment,
       and he will save his soul on the last day.

---

[2] Latin: "beautiful"; an antiphon in Latin sung in praise of the Virgin Mary.

Miracle 4

The Virgin's Reward

116   The book tells us of another cleric
        who loved the image of Holy Mary;
        he always bowed before her painting,
        and felt very great shame under her gaze.

117   He loved her Son and he loved her:
        he considered the Son as Sun and the mother as Star;
        he loved dearly both the Child and the maiden,
        but since he served them little, he was very troubled.

118   He learned five phrases, all phrases of joy,
        that speak of the Joys of the Virgin Mary;[1]
        the cleric recited these before her each day,
        and she was very well pleased with them.

119   "Joy to you, Mary, who believed the angel;
        Joy to you, Mary, who as a virgin conceived;
        Joy to you, Mary, who bore the Christ Child;
        the old law you closed and the new one you opened."

120   As many as there were wounds suffered by the Son,
        so many Joys did he recite to the one who bore Him.
        Indeed the cleric was good and very deserving,
        and he received a good reward, a good compensation.

121   In these five Joys we must understand more:
        five bodily senses that make us sin,
        sight, hearing, smell, taste,
        and that of the hands which we call touch.

122   If these five Joys that we have named,
        we offer freely to the Glorious Mother,

---

[1] Here, the five joyful events in the life of the Virgin Mary. Berceo makes specific reference to three: the Annunciation, the Incarnation, and the Nativity. The other two would most likely be the Resurrection and the Assumption.

for the error we commit due to these five senses,
we will earn pardon through her holy intercession.

123   This cleric fell gravely ill;
his eyes were about to pop out of his head;
he considered his journey to be complete
and his final hour to be drawing near.

124   The Mother of the Heavenly King appeared to him,
the one who in mercy is without peer;
"Friend," she said to him, "may the Spiritual Father save you,
you who were His mother's loyal friend.

125   Take heart, fear not, be not discouraged,
know that you will soon be relieved of this pain;
consider yourself at one with God, free from care;
your pulse now says that it has, indeed, ended.

126   With me near you, you need not fear;
consider yourself cured of all the pain;
I always received from you service and love,
and now I wish to repay you for your labor."

127   Indeed, the cleric thought he would rise from his bed
and walk through the country on his own feet,
but there is a big difference between thinking and knowing:
this matter was to end in another way.

128   Indeed, the cleric thought he would leave his prison
to make sport and laugh with his friends,
but his soul did not receive such an extension;
it forsook the body, it had to leave it.

129   The Glorious One, Queen of Heaven, took it.
The godchild went with the good godmother,
and the angels took it with divine grace;
they carried it to Heaven, where blessings never cease.

130   What the Glorious Mother promised him,
blessed may she be, she indeed fulfilled;
what she said, he did not understand,
but everything she said turned out true.

131   All who heard the voice and saw this happen
understood that the Glorious One performed a miracle;
they considered the cleric to be very fortunate,
and all glorified the precious Virgin.

Miracle 5

The Charitable Pauper

132   There was a poor man who lived off alms.
He had no other income or revenue
except on rare occasions when he worked;
he had in his bag very few pennies.

133   To win the favor of the Glorious One, whom he loved dearly,
he shared with the poor everything he earned;
in this he strove and in this he struggled;
to win her favor he forgot his own needs.

134   When this pauper had to pass from this world,
the Glorious Mother came to greet him;
she spoke to him very sweetly, she wanted to praise him;
everyone in the town heard her words.

135   "You have coveted our company a great deal
and have earned it with very good skill,
for you have shared your alms, you have said 'Ave Maria';
I, indeed, understood why you did it all.

136   Be assured that your job is well done:
this day that we are in is your last;
consider the 'Ite missa est' sung;[1]
the time has come to collect your wages.

137   I have come here to take you with me
to the kingdom of my Son who is, indeed, your friend,
there where the angels feed on good wheat bread;
the holy Virtues[2] will be pleased with you."

---

[1] Latin: "Go, mass is over," the final words of the mass, here used metaphorically to indicate the end of the poor man's life.

[2] The second choir of the second hierarchy of angels (according to one arrangement). See St. Thomas, *Summa Theologica*, trans. Fathers of the English Dominican Province (New York: Benziger Bros., 1947-48): I:108.

138   When the Glorious One had finished the sermon,
        the soul abandoned the fortunate body.
        An honored band of angels took it
        and carried it to Heaven — God therefore be praised!

139   The men who had heard the voice before
        at once saw the promise fulfilled.
        Each in his own way gave thanks
        to the Glorious Mother who is so prudent.

140   Unfortunate would be the one who heard such a thing
        without being extremely pleased with Holy Mary.
        If he did not honor her more, he would be impudent,
        for the one who parts from her is sorely deceived.

141   We wish to move on even further;
        a lesson such as this must not be cut short,
        for these are the trees in which we must take pleasure,
        in whose shade the birds are accustomed to sing.[3]

---

[3] Here Berceo pauses to refer back to the trees, shade, and birds of the allegorical introduction.

Miracle 6

The Devout Thief

142   There was a wicked thief who would rather steal
than go to church or build bridges;[1]
he knew how to maintain his house by theft,
a bad habit that he took up and could not quit.

143   If he committed other sins, we do not read about them;
it would be wrong to condemn him for what we do not know.
Let what we have said to you suffice;
if he did more, may Christ in whom we believe pardon him!

144   Among his other evils, he did have one good habit,
which availed him in the end and gave him salvation:
he believed in the Glorious One with all his heart;
he always greeted her facing her Majesty.[2]

145   He said, "Ave Maria" and more of the prayer;[3]
he always bowed before her image
and felt very great shame under her gaze;
in so doing, he felt his soul was more secure.[4]

146   As he who walks in evil, in evil must fall,
this thief was caught with stolen goods,
and as he had no way to defend himself,
he was sentenced to be hanged on the gallows.

147   The constable took him to the crossroads
where the gallows had been erected by council.

---

[1] Building and maintaining bridges was one of the civic duties of medieval man. See Alfonso el Sabio, *Siete Partidas* (1807; Madrid: Atlas, 1972), 1.6.54, 3.32.20.

[2] *Majestad*, majesty: a term used for the image of the enthroned Madonna and child.

[3] The "Ave Maria" was not a single fixed prayer during Berceo's time; rather, there were versions of different lengths. This remark indicates that the thief's devotion led him to pray a longer version.

[4] There are different versions of this strophe. We have followed Dutton's edition.

They covered his eyes with a well-tied cloth
and raised him from the ground with a tightly drawn rope.

148   They raised him from the ground as high as they could;
those who were nearby considered him dead.
If they had known before what they later learned,
they would not have done what they did to him.

149   The Glorious Mother, skilled in aid,
who is accustomed to helping her servants in trouble,
wished to protect this condemned man;
she remembered the service that he always rendered her.

150   As he was hanging, under his feet she placed
her precious hands and gave him relief;
he did not feel burdened by anything at all
and had never been more comfortable or more content.

151   Then on the third day his relatives came,
and with them his friends and acquaintances;
they came, with faces scratched[5] and grieving, to take him down,
but the situation was better than they thought.

152   They found him alive, happy, and unharmed.
He would not have been so comfortable had he been lying in a bath;
he said that under his feet there was a certain footstool
and that he would not feel any pain if he were to hang there a year.

153   When the ones who had hanged him heard this,
they thought that the noose had been faulty;
they regretted that they had not cut his throat:
that would have pleased them as much as what they later did do.

154   That entire band was of the same mind:
they had been foiled by the bad noose,
but they should now cut his throat with sickle or sword
so that their town would not be shamed by a thief!

155   The most agile young men went to cut his throat
with strong blades, long and sharp,
but Holy Mary interposed her hands,
and the gullet of his throat remained intact.

156   When they saw that they could do him no harm,
that the Glorious Mother wished to protect him,

---

[5] The scratching of the face in the Middle Ages was an outward indication of grief over loss through death. See Dutton *Obras Completas*, 2:73, n. 151c.

they withdrew from the dispute,
and until God willed otherwise, they let him live.

157   They allowed him to go his way in peace,
      for they did not wish to oppose Holy Mary.
      He bettered his ways and set folly aside,
      completed his life, and died when his time came.[6]

158   Mother, so compassionate, of such benevolence,
      who has mercy on the good and the bad,
      we should bless her with all our heart,
      for those who did bless her earned great riches.

159   The skills of the mother and those of Him whom she bore
      are exactly alike to the one who knows them well;
      He descended for all — the good and the bad;
      she came to the aid of all who called upon her.

---

[6] I.e., he died a natural death.

Miracle 7

St. Peter and the Proud Monk

160   In rich Cologne, a royal capital,[1]
       there was a monastery called St. Peter's;
       therein lived an undisciplined monk
       who cared little for what the rule[2] says.

161   He had very little sense; he committed much foolishness;
       although they punished him, he was incorrigible;
       because of this, a great misfortune befell him:
       a harlot bore a child by him.

162   For his body's sake and to live more soundly,
       he used electuaries[3] every day:
       in winter, warm ones, and in summer, cold.
       He should have been devout, but he was lustful.

163   In this life, he lived in great agitation
       and died of his sins, for his grave excesses;
       he neither took *Corpus Domini*[4] nor made confession,
       so the devils carried his soul off to prison.

164   St. Peter the Apostle took pity on him,
       for the monk had been ordained in his monastery,
       and he prayed to Jesus Christ with great devotion
       that He might extend to him a portion of His mercy.

165   Jesus Christ said, "Peter, My beloved,
       you know very well what David said in his book:

---

[1] Cologne was the capital of the electoral principality of the Rhine.

[2] Reference to the monastic rule (i.e., laws or regulations) by which the religious order was governed.

[3] Electuaries were medicines prepared in a base of honey. They were used in the Middle Ages to control the libido of the clergy (a double meaning).

[4] Latin: "body of the Lord," a reference to the Holy Eucharist.

that he shall dwell in the holy hill[5]
who enters without stain and free from sin.

166   That one for whom you pray on bended knee
       neither behaved righteously nor lived without stain;
       the monastery gained nothing from his company.
       He must sit in the chair he has earned!"[6]

167   St. Peter prayed to the heavenly Virtues,[7]
       that they might implore the Father of Penitents
       to remove this man from his mortal bonds.
       He responded in the same words as before.

168   He turned to the Glorious Mother of Our Lord
       and to the other virgins of her house;
       they went to Christ in great supplication;
       they prayed for the soul of the monk.

169   When Lord Christ saw His Glorious Mother
       and such a beautiful procession of her friends,
       He came out to receive them in a lovely way.
       The soul that beheld this would be blessed indeed.

170   "Mother," said Lord Christ, "I would like to know
       what matter brings you here with this company."
       "Son," said the Mother, "I have come to beg You
       for the soul of a monk from a certain monastery."

171   "Mother," said the Son, "it would not be right
       for the soul of such a man to enter into such delight;
       the entire Scripture would be discredited,
       but since it is your request, we will find a solution.

172   I will do so for love of you.
       Let it[8] return to the body in which it dwelt.
       Let him make penance as sinners do;
       thus, in a better way, can he be saved."

173   When St. Peter heard this sweet command
       and saw that his petition had ended happily,
       he turned to the devils, that malevolent band:
       he wrested from them the soul they were carrying.

---

[5] Psalms 15:1: "Lord, who shall abide in thy tabernacle? who shall dwell in thy holy hill?"

[6] He must be punished or rewarded according to his merits.

[7] The heavenly Virtues are one of the orders of angels (cf. quatrain 137).

[8] The soul.

174   He gave it to two children of great brightness,
             angelic creatures of great holiness;
             into their charge he willingly gave it
             to be returned to the body in all safety.

175   The children gave it to an honored friar
             who from childhood had been reared in the order.[9]
             The friar took it to the body which was laid out enshrouded,
             and the monk revived. May God be praised!

176   The guide, that is, the good friar I just mentioned,
             said to the soul of the monk,
             "I beg you for God's sake and Holy Mary's
             to pray for me every day.

177   Another thing do I request: that my grave,
             now all covered with trash,
             please be so kind as to have it swept clean.
             Do this and may God give you good fortune!"

178   The monk, the one who was dead, revived
             but for one whole day remained quite addled.
             However, he finally regained all of his wits
             and relayed to the community what had happened.

179   They offered thanks to God, to the Regal Virgin,
             and to the holy Apostle, keeper of Heaven's keys,
             who endured censure to save his monk.
             This was no miracle of ordinary value!

180   May no one harbor doubt within his heart
             nor say that this thing could or could not be.
             Let him fix his understanding on the Glorious One
             and he will comprehend that this does not defy reason.

181   Since the Glorious One is full of mercy,
             full of grace and free from sin,
             no request would ever be denied her;
             such a son would never tell such a mother "No."

---

[9] The friar-guide is dead; it is his spirit that ultimately delivers the monk's soul to his body.

Miracle 8

The Pilgrim Deceived by the Devil

182   Gentlefolk and friends, for God's and charity's sake,
hear another miracle, which is truly lovely;
St. Hugh, abbot of Cluny,[1] wrote it,
for it happened to a monk of his order.

183   A friar of his house, who was called Guiralt,
before becoming a monk was not very wise;
sometimes he committed the folly and sin
of an unmarried man without obligations.

184   He decided one day, there where he was,
to go on a pilgrimage to the Apostle of Spain;[2]
he arranged his affairs and looked for his companions;
they determined when and how they would make their way.

185   When they were about to leave he did a vile thing:
instead of keeping vigil, he lay with his mistress.
He did not do penance, as the law says,
and set out on the way with this stinging nettle.[3]

186   He had covered only a little of the journey;
it was perhaps about the third day,
when he had an encounter along the way
that appeared to be good, though in truth it was not.

187   The Old Devil was always a traitor
and is a skillful master of all sin;

---

[1] St. Hugh (1024–1109) became abbot of Cluny in 1049 at the age of twenty-five. Adviser to contemporary sovereigns and popes, he ruled over more than a thousand monasteries and dependencies. See *PL* 159: 845–984.

[2] St. James the Greater, whose shrine at Compostela was one of the leading pilgrimage destinations during the Middle Ages. See our Introduction.

[3] Literally, an "evil nettle" (*mala hortiga*), used figuratively to refer to his sin. The nettle is a plant armed with stinging or prickly hairs. Thus, the pilgrim sets out with the irritating "nettle" or "sin" since he did not repent and free himself of it.

sometimes he appears as an angel of the Creator,[4]
but he is a cunning devil, an enticer to evil.

188   The False One transformed himself into the semblance of an angel,
and stood before the pilgrim in the middle of a path.
"Welcome, my friend," he said to the pilgrim;
"you seem to me a little thing, innocent like a lamb.

189   You left your house to come to mine,
but upon leaving you committed a folly.
You intend to complete the pilgrimage without penance —
Holy Mary will not reward you for this!"

190   "Who are you, sir?" the pilgrim said to him.
And he responded, "I am James, son of Zebedee.
Be aware, friend, that you are wandering astray;
it seems you have no desire to save yourself."

191   Guiralt said, "Well, sir, what do you command?
I want to comply with all that you tell me,
for I see that I have committed great iniquities:
I did not do the penance that the abbots dictate."

192   The false James responded, "This is my judgment:
that you cut off the parts of your body that commit fornication;
then cut your throat; thus will you do service to God,
for you will make sacrifice to Him of your very flesh."

193   The ill-starred one, crazed and foolish, believed him;
he took out his knife that he had sharpened;
the poor crazy wretch cut off his genitals;
then he slit his own throat and died excommunicated.

194   When the companions with whom he had set out
arrived at where Guiralt was and saw him like that,
they were in greater affliction than they ever had been;
how this had come to pass they could not imagine!

195   They saw that his throat had not been cut by thieves,
since they had taken nothing from him nor robbed him.
He had not been challenged by anyone;
they did not know how this had come about.

196   They all quickly fled and scattered;
they thought they would be suspected of this death;
even though they were not guilty of the deed,
perhaps they would be taken prisoner and accused.

---

[4] 2 Cor. 11:14.

197   The one who gave the advice, together with his followers,
      big and little, small and large,
      falsehearted traitors, they shackled his soul
      and were carrying it to the fire, to the cruel sweats.

198   They were carrying it, and not gently;
      St. James, whose pilgrimage it was, saw it.
      He came out in great haste to the road
      and stood before them in the front rank.

199   "Free," he said, "oh evil ones, the prisoner that you carry,
      for he is not quite as surely yours as you think;
      hold him carefully; do not use force against him.
      I believe you cannot even if you try."

200   A devil retorted; he stood there obstinately:
      "James, you are trying to make mock of all of us.
      You want to go against what is right;
      you have some wicked scheme under your scapular.

201   Guiralt committed a sin: he killed himself with his own hand;
      he must be judged as a brother of Judas;[5]
      he is in all ways our parishioner;
      James, do not try to be villainous towards us!"

202   St. James said to him, "Treacherous tongue-wagger,
      your speech cannot be worth a bogus coin;
      using my voice, as a false advocate
      you gave bad advice, you killed my pilgrim!

203   Had you not told him that you were St. James,
      had you not shown him the sign of my scallop shells,[6]
      he would not have harmed his body with his own scissors
      nor would he lie as he lies, outside in the road.

204   I am greatly offended by your behavior;
      I consider my image mocked by you;
      you killed my pilgrim with a skillful lie.
      Moreover, I see his soul mistreated.

205   Let me await the judgment of the Virgin Mary;
      I appeal to her in this case;
      otherwise I will never be rid of you,
      for I see that you bring very great treachery."

---

[5] Judas Iscariot, who betrayed Christ, committed suicide (Matthew 27:5).

[6] An attribute of St. James the Greater, the scallop shell was also worn as a badge by his pilgrims.

206   They presented their arguments before the Glorious One;
        the matter was well stated by each party.
        The Precious Queen understood the arguments
        and the dispute ended appropriately.

207   "The deceit that he suffered must be held in his favor;
        he thought he was obeying St. James,
        and that, in so doing, he would be saved;
        the deceiver should suffer more."

208   She said, "I order this and give it as judgment:
        the soul over which you have the dispute
        shall return to its body and do penance,
        then as it merits shall it be judged."

209   This sentence was carried out; it was sanctioned by God.
        The wretched soul was returned to the body;
        even though it grieved the Devil and all his band,
        the soul went back to its former abode.

210   The body, which was lying there dazed, arose.
        Guiralt of the slit throat cleaned his face
        and stood there a short while like someone bewildered,
        like a man who is sleeping and awakens annoyed.

211   As for the wound he had from the throat-cutting,
        its scar barely showed,
        and all pain and fever had ended.
        Everyone said, "This man was indeed fortunate!"

212   Of everything else he was healed and mended,
        except for a tiny line that crossed him,
        but his private parts, all that were cut off,
        never grew back one bit and he remained in that condition.

213   He was completely sound, with everything healed over,
        and, for passing water, the hole remained.
        He requested those provisions that he had been carrying on his back.
        He prepared to go on his way, happy and content.

214   He gave thanks to God and to Holy Mary
        and to the holy Apostle whose pilgrimage he was making;
        he made haste and found his company;
        they had this miracle for comfort each day.

215   This great marvel was sounded throughout Compostela,
        and all the townspeople came out to see him
        saying, "Such a thing as this, we must write down;
        those who are yet to come will take pleasure in hearing it."

216   When he went back to his homeland, having finished the journey,
and people heard what had happened,
there was great commotion: they were moved
upon seeing this Lazarus[7] returned from death to life.

217   And this pilgrim pondered his fortune:
how God had delivered him from the wicked teeth.
He abandoned the world, friends, and relatives;
he entered the abbey of Cluny; he dressed in a penitent's habit.

218   Hugh, a good man, abbot of Cluny,
a religious man of very great holiness,
told this miracle that truly happened.
He put it in writing; he did an honorable thing.

219   Guiralt died in the order, leading a good life,
serving the Creator in word and in deed,
persevering in good, repenting of sin.
The Evil Enemy did not go off laughing at him.[8]
For all that he had sinned, he made good amends to God.

---

[7] Lazarus, the brother of Mary and Martha, was resuscitated by Christ after being dead for days (John 11:1–44).

[8] The evil enemy is the devil.

Miracle 9

The Simple Cleric

220   There was a simple cleric of little learning;
daily he said Holy Mary's Mass;
he did not know how to say any other, he said it each day;
he knew it more by habit than through understanding.

221   This officiant was denounced to the bishop
as an idiot, a plainly bad cleric.
He said only the "Salve Sancta Parens";[1]
the impaired dullard knew no other Mass.

222   The bishop was harshly moved to rage
and said, "Never did I hear such a deed of a priest."
He said, "Tell the son of the evil whore
to appear before me — do not postpone it through some ploy!"

223   The sinful priest came before the bishop;
with his great fear, he had lost his color;
from shame he could not look at his seigneur —
never was the wretch in such a bad sweat.

224   The bishop said to him, "Priest, tell me the truth,
is your stupidity such as they say?"
The good man responded, "Sir, for charity's sake,
if I said 'No,' I would be telling a lie."

225   The bishop said, "Since you do not have the knowledge
to sing another Mass — nor the wit or the ability —
I forbid you to sing, and I give you this sentence:
live as befits you, by some other means."

226   The priest went his way, sad and disheartened;
he felt very great shame and very great hurt;

---

[1] "Salve Sancta Parens," Latin: "Greetings, Holy Parent," the initial words of the introit sung on the feast days of the Blessed Mother.

weeping and moaning he turned to the Glorious One
so that she might advise him, for he was dismayed.

227 The merciful Mother, who never failed
anyone who fell at her feet in sincerity,
immediately heard the plea of her cleric;
she did not put it off and helped him at once.

228 The merciful Virgin, Mother free from sin,
appeared to the bishop immediately in a vision;
she spoke strong words to him, a very angry sermon;
she revealed the desire of her heart in it.

229 She said to him irately, "Imperious bishop,
why were you so harsh and villainous to me?
I never took a grain's-worth from you,
and you have taken a chaplain from me!

230 The one who sang Mass to me each day,
you held that he was committing an act of heresy;
you judged him a beast and a thing astray;
you took from him the order of chaplaincy.[2]

231 If you do not order him to say my Mass
as he was accustomed to say it, there will be a great quarrel,
and you will be dead on the thirtieth day.
Then you will see what the wrath of Holy Mary is worth!"

232 With these threats the bishop was terrified;
immediately he sent for the banned priest.
He begged his pardon for the error he had made,
for he was, in his case, badly deceived.

233 The bishop ordered him to sing as he had been accustomed to sing,
and to be the servant of the Glorious One at her altar;
should he lack anything in the way of clothing or shoes,
he would order it given him from his very own.

234 The good man returned to his chaplaincy;
he served the Glorious One, Holy Mother Mary.
He died in office, a death that I would like:
his soul went to Heaven, to the sweet society.

235 We could not write or pray enough,
even if we could endure for many years,
to be able to relate a tenth of the miracles
that, through the Glorious One, God deigns to show.

---

[2] To remove the order of chaplaincy is to prohibit from celebrating mass.

Miracle 10

The Two Brothers

236 In the town of Rome, that noble city,
  mistress and lady of all Christendom,
  there were two brothers of great authority:
  one was a cleric, the other a magistrate.

237 They called the cleric Pedro — that was his name —
  a wise and noble man, one of the Pope's cardinals.
  Among his vices, he had one that was unpardonable:
  he was very greedy, a mortal sin.

238 The second brother had the name of Estevan;
  among senators none was more proud.
  He was a very powerful Roman,
  and in *prendo prendis*[1] he had a well-practiced hand.

239 He was very covetous — he wanted very much to possess;
  he falsified judgments out of desire for property.
  He took from people what he could take;
  he valued money more than maintaining justice.

240 With the pronouncement of false judgments,
  he took three properties from St. Lawrence the Martyr;[2]
  St. Agnes[3] lost on his account goodly places,
  an orchard that was worth many pairs of coins.

241 The cardinal, Pedro the Honest, died
  and went to purgatory where he deserved to be taken.
  Within a few days Estevan died;
  he expected the type of judgment that he had given.

---

[1] *Prendo prendis*: first two elements of the Latin paradigm for *prendere* (to take): I take, you take . . . Use of the phrase indicates that Estevan stole from others.

[2] An early Christian saint, born near Huesca in Spain. Martyred in Rome in 258 and, according to legend, roasted alive on a gridiron in the presence of the emperor. He is the subject of Berceo's *Martyrdom of Saint Lawrence*.

[3] Fourth-century virgin martyr who died around 350 at the age of twelve.

242 St. Lawrence saw him and looked at him in an ugly way;
he squeezed his arm hard three times.
Estevan complained from way down in his belly;
iron pincers would not have squeezed so tightly.

243 St. Agnes saw the one who had taken her orchard:[4]
she turned her back on him; she looked at him with a wry face.
Then Estevan said, "This is little comfort;
all our profit has brought us to a bad port."[5]

244 God, our Lord, Just Judge,
the One from whom neither wine cellar nor pantry is hidden,
said that this man was a wicked crossbowman;
he blinded many men, not just one.

245 "He dispossessed many through false advocacy;
because of his sins, he always schemed treachery.
He does not deserve to enter Our company:
let him go lie with Judas in that infirmary!"[6]

246 The ancient warriors[7] took him in bonds,
those who always were our mortal enemies;
they gave him for his portion, not apples or figs,
but smoke and vinegar, wounds and pinches.

247 He saw his brother with other sinners,
where the wretch was in very bad sweats;
he let out cries and shouts, tears and lamentations.
He had a great abundance of evil servants.

248 (249) They had already carried the soul near to the dwelling place,
where it never would see a thing that would please it,
nor would it see sun or moon or goodly dew,
and he would be in darkness like an anchorite.

249 (248) He said to him, "Say, brother, I wish to ask you:
for what fault do you lie in such terrible misery,
for if God is willing and I can do it,
I will seek help for you in all the ways that I know."

250 Pedro said, "In life I had great avarice.
I had it, as though it were a mistress, along with covetousness;

---

[4] Estevan is the one who took the orchard.
[5] Our profit has brought us to a bad end, to ruin.
[6] Hell.
[7] The devils.

for that reason, I am now placed in such sadness.
'As one works, so let one be paid,' that is law and justice.[8]

251   But, if the Pope and his clergy
        sang Mass for me for just one day,
        I, trusting in the Glorious One, Holy Mother Mary,
        know that God straightway would improve my lot."

252   Although this man Estevan, about whom we speak so much,
        carried many injustices under his cloak,
        he had one good quality: he loved a saint
        so much that we could not show you how much.

253   He loved Projectus,[9] martyr of great worth:
        he kept his feast day well, as befitting a good lord;
        he gave him a splendid Mass and did him very great honor
        and, for the poor and for clerics, did as much good as he could.[10]

254   Lawrence and Agnes, although offended
        because he had earlier dispossessed them,
        were moved to pity and were mollified;
        they looked more to God than at his sins.

255   They went to Projectus, whose devotee he had been;
        they said to him, "Projectus, do not be caught napping.
        Think about your Estevan who is being scorned;
        give him a reward for having served you!"

256   He went to the Glorious One, who shines more than a star;
        he moved her with great pleading and went before God with her.
        He prayed for this soul, which they were carrying like a ball,
        that it might not be judged according to the complaint.

257   God, Our Lord, replied to this supplication,
        "I will grant such a favor because of your love;
        let the sinful soul return to the body;
        henceforth, it will receive whatever honor it deserves.

258   Let there be a time limit of thirty days,
        so that he may correct all his errors,
        and, indeed, I affirm to him by My words,
        that all his misdeeds will end."

[8.] One gets his just deserts. This is a motif seen in many of the miracle tales.

[9] Probably St. Projectus, Bishop of Imola (5th century).

[10] The Latin source indicates that Estevan (Stephanus) gave alms to the poor and fed the clergy. For the Latin see Dutton, *Obras Completas*, 2:101.

259   The petitioners rendered *gratias multas*[11] to God,
       because He had mercy on His sinners
       and freed this soul from wicked traitors,
       who are ever deceivers of the faithful.

260   When the diabolical band heard that,
       they let go the soul that they had bound;
       St. Projectus, who had won it back, took it
       and led it to its body, to its dwelling place.

261   The Glorious One, Mother of the Creator, said,
       "Estevan, give thanks to God the Good Lord.
       He has granted you a great favor, which could not be greater;
       if you do not watch yourself, you will fall from bad into worse.

262   Estevan, I still want to give you some advice,
       and, Estevan, it is advice that you must take.
       I order you to recite a psalm each day:
       'Beati inmaculati . . .'[12] which is very good to pray.

263   If you say this Psalm each morning
       and right the wrongs that you did to the churches,
       your soul will win glory when you die;
       you will avoid the punishment and the somber places."

264   Estevan revived — thanks be to Jesus Christ!
       He related to the Pope all that he had seen,
       what Pedro, his beloved brother, had said to him,
       and how he had lain in great torment, miserable and very sad.

265   He showed his arm that was bruised,
       the one that St. Lawrence had squeezed.
       With body prostrate, he asked a favor of the Pope:
       that he say Mass for the suffering Pedro.

266   So that they might believe and he might be believed,
       he said that after thirty days he would be dead;
       everyone said, "This is a certain sign;
       it will indeed be known if you are telling the truth or not."

267   He made rich restitution to the disinherited ones;
       he satisfied well those whom he had wronged.
       He confessed all his sins to the priest —
       all those he had done and spoken and thought.

---

[11] Latin: "Many thanks."
[12] Latin: "Blessed are the undefiled . . . ," first words of Psalm 118 (119 in King James Version).

268   When the four weeks were coming to an end
        and there were only a few mornings before the thirty days elapsed,
        Estevan bade farewell to the Roman people;
        he knew God's words would not prove to be vain.

269   On the thirtieth day he made his confession;
        he received *Corpus Domini*[13] with great devotion;
        he lay down on his bed, said his prayer,
        surrendered his soul to God and died blessed.

---

[13] Latin: "body of the Lord," a reference to the Holy Eucharist.

Miracle 11

The Greedy Farmer

270   There was in a certain region a farmer man
       who did more plowing than any other labor;
       he loved the land more than he did the Creator;
       in many ways he was a rebellious man.

271   He committed a sin, a truly dirty one:
       he changed the boundary markers to gain land;[1]
       in all ways did he commit injustice and deceit;
       he had a bad reputation in his region.

272   Although wicked, he loved Holy Mary;
       he heard her miracles and welcomed them;
       he always greeted her; each day he said,
       "'Ave gratia plena'[2] who bore the Messiah!"

273   The hayseed died owning much land;
       he was immediately captured by the devils' rope;
       they dragged him bound and thoroughly mauled,
       making him pay double for the bread that he had stolen.

274   As the devils carried this wretched soul away
       the angels took pity on it;
       they wanted to help it, to make it one of their own,
       but they did not have the flour for making such a dough.

275   If the angels gave them one good argument,
       the others gave a hundred bad arguments instead of good ones;
       the wicked ones had the good in a corner;
       the soul because of its sins did not come out of prison.

276   One angel got up and said, "I am a witness,
       and this that I tell you is the truth, not a lie:
       the body that had this soul with it
       was a vassal and friend of Holy Mary!

---

[1] Deut. 19:14, 27:17.
[2] Latin: "Hail to Thee, full of grace."

277   He always mentioned her at dinner and supper;
        he would say three words: 'Ave gratia plena';
        the mouth from which came such a hallowed song
        did not deserve to lie in so wicked a chain."

278   As soon as this name of the Holy Queen
        was heard by the demons, they promptly withdrew from there;
        they all dispersed like a mist;
        all abandoned the wretched soul.

279   The angels saw it being abandoned,
        its feet and hands well bound with ropes;
        it was like a sheep that lies trapped in brambles;
        they went and led it back to the fold.

280   O name so blessed and so virtuous
        that can chase and frighten away the enemy!
        Our hurting tongues and throats should not
        keep any of us from saying "Salve Regina Sancta."[3]

---

[3] Latin: reference to the antiphon "Salve Regina, mater misericordiae" ("Hail, Holy Queen, Mother of Mercy") (cf. quatrain 98).

Miracle 12

The Prior and Uberto the Sexton

281 In a good town that they call Pavia,[1]
a town of great wealth that lies in Lombardy,
there was a rich monastery
of many good men, a very holy company.

282 The monastery was erected in honor
of the One who saved the world, the Holy Savior;[2]
there happened to be a prior in it
who only wanted to live exactly as he pleased.

283 The good man had an erring tongue;
he said much filth, which is forbidden by the rule;[3]
he did not lead a very ordered life,
but did say his Hours[4] in serenity.

284 He had one custom that profited him:
he said all his Hours like a proper monk;
for those of the Glorious One he always stood;
and, for that reason, the Devil felt great animosity toward him.

285 Although in some things he seemed dull
and, as we told you, he was foul-mouthed,
in loving the Glorious One he was quite devout;
he said her office *de suo corde toto*.[5]

286 When God willed it, this prior died;
he fell into exile, in a harsh place;

---

[1] City in Lombardy, a region in the north of Italy, today capital of the province of Pavia.

[2] Reference to the monastery of San Salvador of Pavia, founded in the tenth century.

[3] Reference to the monastic rule.

[4] Canonical hours, times of day set for prayer.

[5] Latin: "with all his heart."

no one could tell you the misery
that the prior bore, nor could one imagine it!

287   There was a sexton in that abbey
who looked after the things of the sacristy;
he was called Uberto, a prudent man and without folly;
because of him, the monastery was worth more, not less!

288   Before matins, very early one morning,
this monk arose to say the matin prayer,
to ring matins, to awaken the company,
to set up the lamps, to light the dwelling.

289   The prior of the house, mentioned above,
had been dead for a year,
but his case was finally reviewed
as carefully as on the day he was buried.

290   The monk of the house who was the sexton,
before he began ringing the monitory bell,[6]
was cleaning the lamps to provide better light,
when he took great fright in a strange manner.

291   He heard a man's weak, tired voice;
it said "Friar Ubert" more than once;
Ubert recognized it and did not doubt at all
that it was the prior's; he took great fright.

292   He went out of the church, he went to the infirmary;
his spirit was not free of fear.
Were he going on a pilgrimage he would not have moved faster;
Sir Fear was driving him, by my head![7]

293   Being in such a state, out of his wits,
he heard, "Ubert, Ubert, why do you not answer me?
Look, have no fear; by no means be afraid;
consider how to speak to me and how to question me."

294   Then Ubert said, "Prior, in faith,
tell me about yourself, how you are,
so that the chapter will know
what state you are in or what state you expect."

295   The prior said, "Ubert, my servant,
know that up to now my state has been miserable;

---

[6] The "warning bell" that sounds the call for the canonical hours.
[7] A mild oath.

I fell into a place of exile, cruel and unpleasant.
The prince of the land[8] was called Smirna.[9]

296   I suffered great misery; I spent a very bad time.
I could not tell you the evil I have suffered,
but Holy Mary passed by there.
She felt grief and sorrow for the harm I was suffering.

297   She took me by the hand and carried me with her;
she led me to a serene and sheltering place.
She freed me from oppression of the mortal enemy;
she put me in a place where I will live without peril.

298   Thanks be to the Glorious One who is full of grace!
I am free from misery, I have come out of suffering;
I fell into a sweet garden near a sweet beehive,[10]
where I will see no lack of dinner or supper."

299   With that, the voice became silent and the monastery awoke;
they all went to the church with good will.
They said matins and prayers of intercession
in a manner that would please God.

300   Matins sung, the day dawned;
then they said prime[11] and afterward the litany;
the holy company went to the chapter house,
for this is the rule, the custom of monks.

301   Being in the chapter meeting and the lesson read,
the sexton made his genuflection;
he related to the assembly the entire vision,
weeping with very good reason.

302   All gave thanks to the Glorious Mother,
who to her vassals is always merciful.
They went to the church singing a beautiful hymn;
they had the whole story set down in writing.

---

[8] A name for the devil, the prince of darkness or prince of this world. (Cf. John 12:31.)

[9] The precise origin of the name Smirna is unknown. It appears in the Latin source, and there is reference to Smyrna in Revelation 2:8, where those who claim to be Jews but are not truly righteous are the "synagogue of Satan."

[10] The garden motif evokes the "garden paradise" of Berceo's introduction. Also, the bee symbolizes virginity since bees were thought to reproduce asexually, or by parthenogenesis.

[11] The second of the canonical hours, after matins.

303   After a little while, the sexton died;
        he died a death that God grants every Christian;
        he left harsh winter, he entered fair summer;
        he went to Paradise where he will be forever safe.

304   This is *summmum bonum*[12] to serve such a lady,
        who knows how to aid her servants in such an hour;
        this lady is a good shelter; she is a good shepherdess;
        she helps everyone who prays to her with a good heart.

305   All who heard of this vision
        gathered into their souls greater devotion,
        loving the Glorious One with a better heart
        and calling upon her in their tribulations.

---

[12] Latin: "the supreme or highest good."

Miracle 13

Jerome, the New Bishop of Pavia

306   In that same city,[1] there was a good Christian;
       he was named Jerome, he was a Mass-singer.[2]
       He did daily service to the Glorious One,
       day and night, winter and summer.

307   By chance, the bishop of the place died;
       another one could not be agreed upon at all.
       They held a triduum;[3] they wanted to pray to God
       so that He might show them whom they should elevate.

308   To a very religious and Catholic man,
       the Glorious One spoke and said in a vision,
       "Young man, why are you in such dissension?
       Give this election to my devotee."

309   The good man said to her, to be very sure,
       "Who are you who speak or who is the devotee?"
       "I am," she said, "the Mother of the True God;
       They call my key-keeper[4] Jerome.

310   Be my messenger, take this order:
       I command you to carry it out quickly.
       If the council does otherwise, they will be badly mistaken;
       my Son will not be pleased with their action."

---

[1] Pavia, the town in Italy in which the previous miracle (no. 12) takes place. St. Jerome of Pavia was its bishop (778–789).

[2] That is, a priest who officiates at mass.

[3] A religious exercise in which three days are spent in prayer, fasting, and other acts of devotion.

[4] Since one of the duties of the key-keeper, or keeper of the keys, is to defend the monastery with its sacred objects, the term may indicate that the Virgin sees Jerome in this light.

311   She said this and the electors believed it,
    but who Jerome was they did not know.
    They posted spies throughout the town;
    they were going to give a good reward to the identifiers.

312   They found Jerome, a parish priest,
    a man without great deeds but who knew little of evil.
    They led him by the hand to the cathedral seat;
    they gave him as his portion the bishop's throne.

313   Following the message that Holy Mary gave,
    they made him bishop and lord of Pavia;
    in that, everyone took great pleasure and joy,
    for they saw that it had come about in a good way.

314   He was a very good bishop and a just shepherd,
    a lion to the fierce and, to the meek, a lamb;
    he guided his flock well, not like a hireling,[5]
    but as a firm shepherd who takes the lead.

315   God our Lord guided his works;
    he had a good life, and a much better death.
    When he departed this world, he went to the greater one;
    the Glorious One led him, Mother of the Creator.

316   Mother so merciful, may she always be praised;
    may she always be blessed and ever adored,
    for she places her friends in such high regard.
    Her mercy can never be appreciated!

---

[5] John 10:12–13.

Miracle 14

The Image Miraculously Spared by the Flames

317   San Miguel de la Tumba[1] is a great monastery;
it lies surrounded, completely encircled by the sea,
in a perilous place where great hardships are suffered
by the monks who live there in that monastery.

318   In this monastery that we have named,
there were good monks, a well-proven community,
and a sumptuous and very honored altar of the Glorious One
that held a precious image of very great value.

319   The image was posed on her throne,[2]
with her Son in her arms, in the customary fashion;
with the kings[3] around her, she was well accompanied,
like a rich queen, sanctified by God.

320   Like a rich queen she wore a rich crown;
Over it was an elegant wimple instead of a veil:
it was beautifully cut and of very fine work,
and it brought honor to the town nearby.

321   There was hanging in front of it a lovely fan,
in the common tongue they call it a *moscadero*.[4]
Its craftsman had made it of peacock feathers;
it shone like stars, like the morning star.

---

[1] San Miguel de la Tumba refers to Mont-Saint-Michel, an island monastery in France located between Normandy and Brittany. The name was changed to Mont-Saint-Michel in the eighth century.

[2] For the general iconography see Ilene Forsyth, *Throne of Wisdom: Wood Sculptures of the Madonna in Romanesque France* (Princeton: Princeton University Press, 1972). See page 48 for the immunity of images to flames.

[3] Images of the Magi, the three kings who came from the East to worship the Christ child (Matthew 2:1 ff.)

[4] A fan for shooing flies (Spanish *moscas*).

322   A lightning bolt came out of the sky because of the grave sins;
           it burned the church on all four sides.
           It burned all the books and sacred cloths,
           and the monks themselves were almost burned.

323   It burned the cupboards and the frontals,[5]
           the beams, the cross braces, the rafters, the ridgepieces,
           the altar cruets,[6] chalices, and processional candlesticks.
           God suffered that calamity as He does others.

324   Although the fire was so strong and so scorching,
           it did not reach the lady nor did it reach the Child,
           nor did it reach the fan that was hanging in front;
           it did them not a penny's worth of damage.

325   The image did not burn nor did the flabellum[7] burn,
           nor did they suffer a hair's worth of harm.
           Not even the smoke reached it;
           it did not harm it any more than I would harm Bishop Tello.[8]

326   *Continens et contentum*[9] were completely ruined.
           Everything was turned to ash; it was all destroyed,
           but around the image for as much as an *estado*,[10]
           the fire had dared do no damage.

327   Everyone took this as an extraordinary marvel,
           that neither smoke nor fire reached her,
           that the flabellum remained brighter than a star,
           the Child very beautiful, and beautiful the maiden.

328   The precious miracle did not fall into oblivion;
           it was immediately well dictated and put into writing;
           as long as the world exists, it will be told;
           because of this, a calamity was converted into a blessing.

329   The Blessed Virgin, General Queen,
           just as she freed her wimple from this fire,
           so does she free her servants from the everlasting fire;
           she takes them to Heaven where they shall never know evil.

---

[5] Hangings for the front of the altar.

[6] Cruets for the wine and the water at mass.

[7] The fan.

[8] Tello Téllez de Meneses, bishop of Palencia, died in 1246. Berceo is thought to have studied in Palencia.

[9] Latin: "the container and its contents."

[10] *Estado*, Spanish: a linear measurement of approximately seven feet or a surface measurement of forty-nine square feet.

Miracle 15

The Wedding and the Virgin

330   In the town of Pisa, an illustrious city
that lies on a seaport[1] and is extremely wealthy,
there was a canon of good lineage;
the place where he was was called Saint Cassian's.

331   As did others about whom we have told above,
who were chaplains of Holy Mary,
this one loved her very much, more than many Christians,
and served her with his hands and his feet.

332   At that time the clergy did not have the custom
of saying any Hours to you, *Virgo Maria*,[2]
but he said them always and each day.
In the Glorious One he took pleasure and delight.

333   His parents had only this one son,
so when they died he was their heir.
They left him very valuable holdings in personal property,
so he had a fine, quite covetable inheritance.

334   When the father and mother were dead,
relatives came, sad and disheartened;
they told him he should produce some heirs
so that such valuable places would not be left barren.

335   He changed his intent from the one he previously had.
The ways of the world moved him and he said that he would do it.
They sought a wife for him who would be suitable,
and they set the day that the wedding would take place.

336   When the day to celebrate the wedding came,
he went with his relatives to take his wife;
he could not attend so well to the Glorious One
as he was wont to do in earlier times.

---

[1] The famous Tuscan city, west of Florence, is on the Arno River that flows into the Tyrrhenian Sea, a part of the Mediterranean.

[2] Latin: "Virgin Mary."

337   Going down the road to fulfill his pleasure,
        he remembered the Glorious One, whom he had offended.
        He considered himself wrong, and he held himself as dead;
        he pondered this matter that would lead him to a bad port.[3]

338   Reflecting on this matter with a changed heart,
        he found a church, a place consecrated to God;
        He left the other people outside the portico;
        the reformed groom entered to pray.

339   He went into the church, to the most remote corner,
        bent his knees, and said his prayer;
        the Glorious One, full of blessing, came to him,
        and angrily said these words to him:

340   "You ill-fated, stupid, crazy fool!
        What predicament are you in? What have you fallen into?
        You seem poisoned, as if you have drunk herbs
        or have been touched with St. Martin's staff.[4]

341   Young man, you were well married to me.
        I very much loved you as a good friend,[5]
        but you go around seeking better than wheat bread;[6]
        for that reason, you will not be worth more than a fig!

342   If you will listen to me and believe,
        you will not wish to cast aside the first life;[7]
        you will not leave me in order to have another;
        if you do, you will have to carry firewood on your back!"

---

    [3] Cf. quatrain 243.
    [4] St. Martin of Tours (ca. 315–387), patron saint of wine-bibbers and drunkards. To be touched by St. Martin's staff, then, would be to be drunk.
    [5] *Amigo*, Spanish: friend, or lover in the sense of "one who loves," a worshipful admirer and devotee.
    [6] The expression "to seek better than wheat bread" ("buscar major de pan de trigo") is proverbial and implies that someone is foolishly involved in a futile endeavor (since there is no bread better than that made of wheat). The phrase is found in the *Libro de Alexandre* (156d): "non quises[se]e buscar me[j] de pan de trigo" (ed. Dana Nelson [Madrid: Gredos, 1979]); in Juan Ruiz's *Libro de buen amor* (950d): "Quien mas de pan de trigo busca, syn seso anda" (ed. Julio Cejador y Frauca, 2nd ed. [Madrid: Espasa-Calpe, 1960]); and in Cervantes' *Don Quijote*: "¿No será mejor estarse pacífico en su casa y no irse por el mundo a buscar pan de trastrigo…?" (vol. 1, ed. Martín de Riquer [Barcelona: Editorial Juventud, 1965], 78). Compare *Miracles* 804 (759)c.
    [7] The religious life that the young man had promised the Virgin Mary he would follow.

343   The chastised groom left the church;
       everyone complained that he had delayed.
       They went on ahead to fulfill their mission;
       the whole business was quickly completed.

344   They had a splendid wedding and the wife was taken.
       Otherwise, if she had been disdained, it would have been an affront.
       The bride was well pleased with this groom,
       but she did not know where the ambush lay.

345   The aforementioned man knew well how to cover up;
       his tongue kept his heart's secret.
       He laughed and made merry, all quite appropriately;
       but the vision had him quite disturbed.

346   They had a lavish wedding and very great joy;
       perhaps they never had greater joy in one day,
       but Holy Mary cast her net around there
       and on dry land made a great catch.

347   When night came, at the time for sleeping,
       they made the newlyweds a bed in which to lie;
       before they had taken any pleasure with each other,
       the arms of the bride had nothing to hold.

348   The husband slipped from her hands, he fled from her;
       no one ever found out where he ended up.
       The Glorious One knew how to keep him well hidden;
       she did not consent for him to be corrupted!

349   He left a beautiful woman and very great possessions,
       which very few people would do nowadays;
       they never found out where he was — or was not.
       God bless anyone who does so much for Him!

350   We believe and imagine that this good man
       found some place of great religion[8]
       and hid there to say his prayers,
       for which decision his soul earned from God a good reward.

351   Surely we must believe that the Glorious Mother —
       because this man did such a great thing —
       would not forget him, for she is merciful;
       surely she had him dwell there where she dwells.

---

[8] *Lugar de gran religión*: "place of great religion" (a monastery).

Miracle 16

The Little Jewish Boy

352   In the city of Bourges, a foreign city,[1]
in another time there occurred a fine deed.
It is told in France and also in Germany;
indeed, it is similar and equal to the other miracles.

353   A monk wrote it down, a very truthful man;
he was a monk of the monastery of Sant Miguel de la Clusa.[2]
He was at that time hosteler[3] in Bourges;
Pedro was his name — of that I am certain.

354   In that city, since it was necessary,
a cleric had a school of singing and reading;
he had many pupils learning letters,
sons of good men who wanted to rise in esteem.

355   A little Jewish boy, native of the town, came
for the pleasure of playing with the children.
The others welcomed him, they caused him no grief;
they all took delight in playing with him.

356   On Easter Sunday, very early in the morning,
when the Christian people go to take *Corpus Domini*,[4]
a great desire to commune seized the little Jewish boy.
The woolless lamb took Communion with the others.

357   While they were taking Communion with very great zeal,
the little Jewish boy raised his gaze;
he saw over the altar a lovely figure,
a beautiful lady with a lovely Child.

---

[1] In central France, today the capital of the department of Cher.

[2] This is either St.-Michel-de-l'Ecluse in Bergerac, Dordogne (France) or San Michele de la Clusa in Susa, Piemonte (Italy).

[3] Monk in charge of a hospice maintained by his monastery.

[4] Latin: "body of the Lord," a reference to Holy Communion.

358   He saw that this lady who was seated
           gave communion to large and small.
           He was very pleased with her; the more he looked at her,
           the more he fell in love with her beauty.

359   He left from the church happy and pleased
           and went immediately to his house, as he was accustomed.
           Because he was late his father threatened him,
           saying he deserved to be whipped.

360   "Father," said the boy, "I will not deny anything,
           for I was with the little Christians early this morning;
           with them I heard Mass splendidly sung,
           and with them I partook of the Sacred Host."

361   This grieved the ill-fated man very much,
           as if the boy were dead or his throat had been cut;
           the bedeviled man in his great wrath did not know what to do,
           so he made evil faces like someone demon-possessed.

362   This treacherous dog had inside his house
           a large, fierce oven that instilled great terror.
           The mad sinner had it fired up
           so that it gave off an excessive great heat.

363   The false disbeliever took this little child,
           just as he was, shod and clothed;[5]
           he threw him into the raging fire.
           Ill come to such a father who does such to his son!

364   The mother shouted and clawed herself in despair;
           she had her cheeks torn with her nails.
           Many people came in a short time,
           for they were disturbed by such a loud plaint.

365   The fire, although raging, was very merciful;
           it did not harm him one bit: rather it showed him good will.
           The little boy escaped from the fire alive and well;
           the Almighty King wrought a great miracle!

366   The child lay in peace in the middle of the furnace;
           he could not have lain more peacefully in his mother's arms.
           He esteemed the fire no more than he would a young boy,
           for the Glorious One was giving him company and comfort.

---

[5] Cf. Daniel 3:21, typological reference for this story: Shadrach, Meshach, and
Abednego were cast fully clothed into the fiery furnace.

367 He came out of the fire without any injury;
     he felt no more heat than at any other time.
     He received no marks and no afflictions,
     for God had bestowed His blessing on him.

368 Everyone asked him, Jews and Christians,
     how he was able to conquer such mighty flames
     when he did not control his feet or his hands.
     Who protected him inside there? Make them certain.

369 The child answered with an outstanding response,
     "The lady who was in the golden chair,
     with her Son in her arms, sitting on the altar.
     She defended me and I felt nothing."

370 They understood that this was St. Mary,
     that she defended him from such a fierce storm.
     They sang great lauds; they had a lavish celebration.
     They placed this miracle among the other deeds.

371 They seized the Jew, the false disloyal one,
     the one who had done such great wrong to his little son.
     They tied his hands with a strong rope,
     and they cast him into the great fire.

372 In the time it would take for someone to count a few pennies,[6]
     he was turned into ashes and embers.
     They did not say psalms or prayers for his soul,
     rather they hurled insults and great curses.

373 They gave him dreadful rites; they made for him a vile offering:
     instead of "Pater Noster",[7] they said, "As he did so may he receive."[8]
     From this *comunicanda*[9] may the Lord God[10] defend us,
     and let such terrible payment be with the Devil.

---

[6] The original has "pipiones": a *pipión*, like *dinero*, is a coin of little value. We translate again "pennies." See also strophes 9d and 324d.

[7] Latin for "Our Father," i.e., the first words of the Lord's Prayer, thus the prayer itself.

[8] May he receive his just deserts.

[9] A Latinism indicating "Communion" (Dutton *Obras completas*, 2:128). A *comunicanda* is an antiphon sung during Communion: thus the term can be taken to refer to the service itself.

[10] Berceo combines the Latinate word *domni* (Lord) with the Spanish word *Dios* (God). We translate both to English: "the Lord God.".

374   Such is Holy Mary, who is full of grace;
          for service she gives glory, for disservice punishment;
          to the good she gives wheat, to the evil oats;
          the good go to glory, the others go in chains.

375   Whoever renders her service is fortunate;
          whoever rendered disservice was born in a harsh hour.
          The ones gain grace, and the others rancor;
          the good and the evil are revealed by their deeds.

376   Those who offend her or who disserve her
          won mercy if indeed they asked her for it;
          never did she refuse those who loved her,
          nor did she throw in their faces the evil they had done.

377   In order to prove this thing that we have told you,
          let us relate a beautiful example that we read;
          when it is told, we will believe it better;
          we will guard against causing her grief.

Miracle 17

Saint Mary's Church Profaned

378   There were three knights who were friends.
       They had a great dislike for another who was their neighbor;
       they would have gladly killed him if they could
       and sought zealously his cruel death.

379   So much did they discuss and scheme
       that one day, when they espied him alone,
       they ambushed him, for they intended to kill him.
       They wanted that more than great riches.

380   The man understood that they wanted to kill him,
       and did not dare to face them at all.
       He began to flee, for he wanted to escape.
       Then they made their move; they were going to catch up with him.

381   The one who was fearfully fleeing
       came upon a church and was greatly delighted.
       It was built in honor of the Glorious One;
       he hid himself inside it, the wretched sinner.

382   The ones who were following him, who wanted to kill him,
       had no respect for the sacred place.
       The Glorious One and God abandoned him;
       they took his soul from his body.

383   Inside the church consecrated to the Virgin,
       this person was mauled and killed.
       The Glorious One felt sorely offended;
       those who offended her gained nothing there.

384   The Queen of Glory considered herself insulted,
       because her church was violated.
       It weighed heavily on her heart; she was vexed by it.
       She quickly showed them that she was angry with them.

385   God sent upon them an infernal fire;
        it did not flame, yet it burned like St. Martial's fire.[1]
        It burned their limbs in a deadly way,
        and they cried out loudly, "Holy Mary, help!"

386   With this assault they were badly battered;
        they lost feet and hands and wound up deformed,
        their legs and arms drawn up to their chests.
        Holy Mary was collecting her due.

387   The people found out about it, and the men did not deny it;
        they deserved what they were suffering for it.
        They had not considered, when they committed the sacrilege,
        the angry Virtues that now battered them.

388   Neither male nor female saints would help them.
        Each day they got worse to the maximum degree.
        Finally, they took the path they should have taken before:
        they turned to the Glorious One who was making them burn.

389   They fell in supplication before her altar,
        sobbing as much as they could sob;
        they said, "Glorious Mother, deign to pardon us,
        for we find no other who can help us.

390   If we deserved harm, dearly have we suffered it;
        it will be in our minds as long as we live.
        Mother, if you pardon us, we promise
        never to use force again in your church.

391   Mother, you are greatly esteemed, for you are merciful;
        you always have mercy even when you are angry.
        Mother Full of Grace, pardon this sin;
        give us a good response, tempered and pleasing.

392   Mother, repentant are we of the error that we committed;
        we erred badly, we committed great madness;
        we took great punishment, we deserved even greater;
        we have paid for the share that we ate.

393   Mother, if you do not help us, we will not part from you;
        if you do not pardon us, we will not depart from this place;

---

[1] St. Martial's fire is the name of a disease also called St. Anthony's fire. It is a fever (ergotism) often confused with erysipelas. It is caused by the fungus *claviceps purpurea* that forms on rye, from which the common bread of the poor was made in the Middle Ages. The disease is gangrenous and results in the mortification and loss of limbs. Victims sometimes survive after losing all four limbs.

if you do not succor us, we will consider ourselves nothing;
without you, we will be unable to put an end to this fever."

394   The Glorious Mother, Solace of the Afflicted,
did not spurn the moans of the suffering men;
she did not look at their merits nor at their sins,
rather she looked to her temperance and helped the burned ones.

395   The Merciful Lady, who was irate before,
began losing her wrath and became more mild.
She delivered them from the wrath that she had raised against them;
all the malady was then abated.

396   The fires that were making them burn died down;
they had a greater cure than they were wont to have.
They felt that the Glorious One wanted to favor them;
they cried with great joy, they did not know what to do.

397   The fires died down; they felt no more pain,
but never again were they fully masters of their limbs;
they were forever deformed, forever beggars;
they always proclaimed themselves as great sinners.

398   With this relief that God wished to grant them,
they went immediately to the bishop to gain absolution;
they made confession as they should,
sobbing loudly, showing great remorse.

399   The bishop instructed them, he heard their confession.
He knew that they came truly contrite;
he gave them penance and absolution.
When all this was done, he gave them his blessing.

400   Besides the many pilgrimages that he ordered them to make,
and besides the many prayers that he ordered them to pray,
he ordered them always to carry on their backs
the weapons that they used to desecrate the church.

401   These penitents, when they had been instructed
and were absolved of all their sins,
departed immediately, sad and dismayed;
they went their separate ways, laden with their weapons.

402   Each went his own way, they did not stay together;
and, as for my belief, they never saw each other again.
Never again did all three lie under the same roof;
they complied honorably and well with what the bishop ordered.

403   If in committing the sin they were indeed reckless,
in doing penance they were very inspired;

their members did not hurt, but they went around very afflicted,
having bad nights and dark days.

404 If in committing the sin they were blind and stupid,
in correcting it they were steadfast and very devout;
however many days they lived, whether they were many or few,
they inflicted on their flesh misery and mortifications.

405 Of the three, one, skinny and very miserable,
came to Amfreville,[2] as the writing says;
he took shelter in the town, they put him up
with a holy woman where he was well lodged.

406 He told the lodgers his entire experience:
how in the church they had gone to excess,
how Holy Mary had been very angry with them,
and how they suffered from the vicious fever.

407 Thinking that what he had said would not be believed,
before many he removed his clothes;
he showed them a sword that he carried hidden,
girded to his flesh with a harsh strap.

408 It could have been about a half-palm in width,
and near the sword the flesh was very swollen.
That which lay under it was all burned.
The next day he left very early in the morning.

409 The people were all amazed,
for they heard strong words and saw damaged limbs;
wherever they gathered — single or married,
young or old — they all talked of this.

410 This miracle was immediately written and recorded
so that it would not be forgotten.
Many became afraid of committing such a sin,
of desecrating a church or a sacred place.

411 Such is Holy Mary, as you can comprehend:
she casts bad nets over those who walk in wickedness;
for believers she does great favors.
Many are the examples that you will find of this.

412 The examples are so many that they cannot be counted,
for they increase each day, so say the writings;
these with a hundred others would amount only to a tenth.
May she pray to Christ for the erring people.

---

[2] Amfreville-sur-Iton, France.

Miracle 18

The Jews of Toledo

413   In noble Toledo, an archbishop's see,
      on a great holy day in the middle of August,
      festival of the Glorious One,[1] Mother of the Good Son,
      there occurred a great and very signal miracle.

414   The archbishop, a loyal cleric,
      was in the middle of Mass at the sacred altar
      with important people listening, well-dressed people;
      the church was full, the choir packed.

415   The very devoted parishioners were in prayer,
      like people who want to win God's pardon.
      They heard a voice of great tribulation
      by which the entire procession was upset.

416   A voice from Heaven spoke, pained and angry.
      It said, "Hear, Christians, a remarkable thing!
      The Jewish people, deaf and blind,
      have never been so wicked to Lord Jesus!

417   As the Holy Scriptures tell us,
      they committed iniquities against Lord Christ;
      that sorrow cut to my heart,
      but all their madness had repercussions for them.

418   They felt nothing for the Son who deserved no harm,
      nor for His mother who saw such affliction.
      A people so vile, who would do such evil
      to such a one as they did, would commit any offense.

419   Those who in a bad hour were born, false and treacherous,
      are now reviving my former pains.
      They have me in a tight spot and in a great sweat!
      My Son, Light of Sinners, is on the Cross!

---

[1] The Day of the Assumption, 15 August, when the Virgin Mary was assumed into Heaven.

420   They are again crucifying my dear Son.
        Nobody could know how great is my sorrow!
        A bitter vine sprout is growing in Toledo —
        never was one so wicked nurtured on this earth!"

421   All the clergy heard this voice
        and many of the laymen in the Mozarab[2] congregation.
        They knew it was the voice of St. Mary;
        against her, the Jews were making folly.

422   The archbishop, who was singing the Mass, spoke,
        and the people who were round about heard him.
        He said, "Believe, O congregation, that the voice that spoke
        is greatly offended and therefore was complaining.

423   Be it known that the Jews are doing something
        against Jesus Christ, Son of the Glorious One.
        Due to this affliction the mother is displeased;
        thus, her complaint is neither idle nor false.

424   Clergy and laity, all who are gathered here,
        pay attention to this and do not scorn it;
        if you seek this thing out, you will find its trail.
        You will exact justice for this offense.

425   Let us not delay this; let us go to the homes
        of the chief rabbis, for we shall find something.
        Let us forego our meal; we will indeed recover it.
        Otherwise, the Glorious One will sorely challenge us."

426   The people and all the clergy moved.
        In great haste they went to the Jewish sector.
        Jesus Christ guided them and so did the Virgin Mary,
        and their treachery was soon discovered.

427   They found in the house of the most honorable rabbi
        a large body of wax shaped like a man.
        It was like Jesus Christ; it was crucified,
        held with large nails, and had a great wound in its side.

428   What outrage they committed against Our Lord.
        There they did it all to our dishonor!
        They executed them immediately, but not with pleasure.
        They got what they deserved, thanks be to the Creator!

---

        [2] In medieval Spain, the Mozarabs were Christians living in places under Muslim
control.

429   Those who could be caught were executed.
        They were given a bad meal, which they deserved.
        There they said "Tu autem";[3] they received a vile death.
        Afterwards they understood they had committed madness!

430   He who would affront Holy Mary
        should be rewarded as these were rewarded.
        So let us plan to serve and honor her,
        for her prayer will aid us in the end.

---

[3] Latin: the first words of the phrase "Tu autem Domine, miserere nobis" ("And Thou, O Lord, have mercy upon us") that indicates the end of the lesson read during meals in the monastery. Thus, the phrase "they said 'Tu autem'" means "they came to their end." Cf. *Life of Saint Aemilianus of La Cogolla*, strophe 482.

Miracle 19

The Pregnant Woman Saved by the Virgin

431   We wish to tell you of another miracle
that happened in another time in a seaport;
then you will hear it and you will be able to affirm
the virtue of Mary that is in every place.

432   You will hear in it what the Glorious One is like
on sea and on land, powerful everywhere:
how she quickly defends, for she is not lazy,
and never did anyone find such a merciful mother.

433   Near a salt marsh, Tumba[1] it was called,
there was an island close to the shore;
the sea would ebb and flow over it,
two times a day or sometimes three.

434   Well within the island, very near the waves,
there was a chapel that was St. Michael's;
great miracles always occurred there in that monastery,
but the entrance was somewhat difficult.

435   When the sea wished to flow out,
it would do so in a great rush; it could not restrain itself;
no one, no matter how nimble, could escape it;
if he did not get out before, he would have to perish there.

436   On the feast day of the precious archangel[2]
the sea was calmer; it was washing more slowly;
the people heard Mass, and not unhurriedly;
they fled immediately to safety with great speed.

---

[1] San Miguel de la Tumba (Mont-Saint-Michel), which is also the setting for Miracle 14.

[2] St. Michael, the Archangel, to whom San Miguel de la Tumba (Mont-St. Michel) is dedicated. His feast day is celebrated 29 September.

437   One day by chance, with the rest of the congregation,
        a frail pregnant woman set out;
        she could not protect herself as well on the return
        and regretted having entered there.

438   The waves were coming close; the people were at a distance;
        in her panic her legs became paralyzed;
        her companions dared not help her:
        in a short time, there were to be many crossings.

439   When they could do nothing else, the people fervently
        said in great haste: "Holy Mary, help!"
        The helpless pregnant woman, full-fraught with fright,
        remained in great trouble among the waves.

440   Those who got out, since they did not see anything,
        believed surely without a doubt that she had drowned;
        they said: "This poor woman was unfortunate;
        her sins laid a cruel ambush for her."

441   When they said this the sea withdrew;
        in a short time it returned to its place;
        Lord Christ wished to show them a great miracle,
        whence they might have something to tell about His mother.

442   They, all wishing to be on their way,
        extended their gaze; they looked toward the sand;
        they saw that a lone woman was coming,
        with her child in her arms, toward the shore.

443   The people were all amazed;
        they thought that fantasy had deceived them;
        but in a short time they were assured:
        they gave thanks to Christ with all hands uplifted.

444   They said: "Say, lady, for God and charity's sake!
        For God's sake, we beseech you, tell us the truth!
        Tell us all the facts of the matter
        and how you were freed from your pregnancy.

445   This thing happened through God, we do not doubt it,
        and through Holy Mary to whom we pray,
        and through St. Michael in whose honor we walk:
        this miracle is such that we must indeed write it down!"

446   "Listen," said the woman, "my good company,
        I believe that you never heard of a greater deed;
        it will be reported throughout foreign lands —
        in Greece and in Africa and in all of Spain.

447   When I saw that I could not wrest myself from death,
       since I was surrounded by the fierce waves,
       I commended myself to Christ and to Holy Mary,
       for I knew of no other help for me.

448   While I was in this situation, Holy Mary came;
       she covered me with the sleeve of her cloak;
       I felt no more danger than when I slept;
       if I lay in a bath I would not be happier!

449   Without care and without affliction, without any pain,
       I bore this little son — thanks be to the Creator!
       I had a good midwife,[3] there could be none better,
       she had mercy on me, a sinner!

450   She granted me a great boon, not single but double:
       were it not for her, I would be drowned;
       she aided me in the birth; had she not, I would be hurt.
       Never did a woman have such an honored midwife!

451   My situation was just as I tell you:
       Holy Mary had great mercy on me,
       whence we should all learn a lesson
       and beseech her to free us from the mortal enemy."

452   Everyone received great joy from the miracle;
       they gave thanks to God and to Holy Mary;
       all the community composed a good canticle,
       the clergy could sing it in the church:

453   "Christ, Lord and Father, Redeemer of the World,
       who in order to save the world suffered death and pain,
       Blessed be You, for You are a Good Lord:
       never did You feel repugnance for any sinner.

454   You freed Jonah from the belly of the fish,
       which held him three days closed up in his stomach;
       he received no injury because he was protected by You;
       the old miracle today is renewed.

455   The children of Israel obeyed your commandment
       and crossed the sea behind Moses;
       yet they suffered no harm beneath the waves,
       while all their pursuers drowned.

---

[3] Berceo uses the word *madrina* ("godmother" in modern Spanish) here and in 450d; however, the relationship is between the Virgin Mary and the pregnant woman (not between the Virgin and the newborn child). Thus "midwife" (*partera* or *comadrona* in modern Spanish) seems to be the more appropriate translation.

456   The ancient miracles, excellent and honored,
           with our own eyes we see them now renewed;
           Lord, your friends in the sea find fords;
           the others on dry land find themselves drowned.

457   Lord, your great and marvelous power
           saved Peter on the perilous sea;[4]
           Lord, You who became incarnate in the Glorious Virgin,
           in You alone do we trust and in nothing else.

458   Lord, blessed be Your sacred virtue;
           blessed be Your mother, Crowned Queen;
           blessed be You, praised be she:
           Lord, in her You had a blessed abode.

459   Lord, You who are without end and without beginning,
           in whose hand lie the seas and the wind,[5]
           deign to bestow Your blessing on this assembly,
           that we may all praise You with one will.

460   Men and women — all of us who are here —
           we all believe in You and we worship You,
           we all glorify You and Your mother:
           let us sing in Your name the 'Te Deum laudamus'."[6]

---

[4] Matthew 14:28–31.
[5] Cf. Mark 4:41, Luke 8:25.
[6] Latin: "We praise you O Lord!" A hymn of thanksgiving.

Miracle 20

The Inebriated Monk

461   I would like to tell you about another miracle
that happened to a monk of a religious order:
the Devil wanted to frighten him severely,
but the Glorious Mother knew how to prevent it.

462   Ever since he was in the order, indeed ever since he was a novice,
he always loved serving the Glorious One;
he guarded against folly, against speaking of fornication,
but he finally fell into a vice.

463   He entered the wine cellar by chance one day;
he drank a great deal of wine: this was without moderation.
The crazy man got drunk: he took leave of his senses;
until vespers he lay on the hard ground.

464   Then at the hour of vespers, the sun very weak,
he awoke badly; he walked around dazed.
He went out toward the cloister almost senseless;
everyone understood that he had drunk too much.

465   Although he could not stand up on his feet,
he went to the church as he was accustomed to do;
the Devil tried to trip him up,
because, indeed, he intended to conquer him easily.

466   In the form of a bull that is raging,
pawing the ground with his hooves, with changed countenance,
with fierce horns, angry and irate,
the proven traitor[1] stopped before him.

467   He made bad faces at him, the devilish thing;
he would put his horns in him, in the middle of his entrails.
The good man took a very bad fright,
but the Glorious One, Crowned Queen, helped him.

---

[1] The devil.

468   Holy Mary came with her honored garment,
which no living soul could fail to esteem.
She put herself in between him and the Devil;[2]
the oh-so-proud bull was immediately tamed.

469   The lady threatened him with the skirt of her mantle;
for him this was a very great punishment.
He fled and vanished, crying loudly;
the monk remained in peace, thanks be to the Holy Father!

470   Then a short time later, at a few paces
before he [the monk] began to climb the steps,
he attacked him again, making evil faces,
like a dog striking with fangs.

471   He came viciously, his teeth bared,
his countenance altered, his eyes open wide,[3]
to tear him to pieces, back and sides.
"Wretched sinner," said he, "grave are my sins!"

472   Indeed, the monk believed he would be torn to pieces;
he was in great trouble, he was badly disturbed.
Then the Glorious One helped him, that gifted one;
like the bull, the dog was driven away.

473   As he entered the church, on the highest step,
he attacked him again for the third time,
in the form of a lion, a fearsome beast,
bearing ferocity beyond imagination.

474   There the monk believed that he was devoured,
because in truth he saw a fierce encounter.
This was worse for him than all the past ones;
in his mind he cursed the Devil.

475   He said, "Help me, Glorious One, Mother, Holy Mary!
May your grace help me now, on this day,
because I am in great danger: I could not be in greater.
Mother, do not dwell upon my great madness."

476   Scarcely was the monk able to complete the words,
when Holy Mary came as she was accustomed to come.
With a stick in her hand to strike the lion,
she put herself in the middle and began to say,

---

[2] Berceo uses the name "*Peccado*" (Sin) for the devil.

[3] We follow Dutton (*Obras Completas*, 2:255) in rendering *ojos remellados* as "eyes open wide"; but José Baro (*Glosario*) and Daniel Devoto (*Milagros*) define *remellados* as "bloodshot."

477   "Sir false traitor, you do not learn a lesson,
        but I will give you today what you are asking for.
        Before you go away from here you will pay;
        I want you to know with whom you have waged war."

478   She began to give him great blows:
        the big blows drowned out the small;
        the lion suffered greatly;
        he never in all his days had his sides so beaten.

479   The good lady said to him, "Sir false traitor,
        you who always walk in evil belong to an evil master:
        if I catch you again here in these surroundings,
        of what you are getting today, you will get even worse."

480   The figure faded, it began to flee;
        never again did it dare to mock the monk;
        a long time passed before he healed;
        the Devil was glad when she ordered him to go.

481   The monk who had passed through all this
        was not fully recovered from the effects of the wine;
        both the wine and the fear had so punished him
        that he could not return to his customary bed.

482   The Precious Queen of precious deed
        took him by the hand, led him to his bed.
        She covered him with the blanket and with the bedspread;
        she put the pillow under his head just right.

483   Moreover, when she put him in his bed,
        she made the sign of the cross over him with her right hand; he was well
            blessed.
        "Friend," she said to him, "rest because you have suffered greatly;
        as soon as you sleep a little, you will be rested.

484   But this I order you, I tell it to you firmly:
        tomorrow morning look for a certain friend of mine;
        confess yourself to him and you will be in good standing with me,
        because he is a very good man and will give you good penance.

485   I shall go on my way, to save some other afflicted soul:
        that is my pleasure, my customary office;
        remain blessed, commended to God,
        but do not forget what I have commanded you."

486   The good man said, "Lady, truly
        you have shown me great mercy,
        and I want to know who you are or what your name is,
        because I will profit from it and you will lose nothing."

487   The good lady said, "So you may be well informed,
          I am the one who bore the true Savior,
          who suffered death and pain to save the world,
          to whom the angels do service and honor."

488   The good man said, "It is believable,
          Lady, that from you this deed could be born.
          Lady, let me touch your feet:
          never will I see such great pleasure in this world."

489   The good man insisted; he tried to get up,
          to get on his knees, to kiss her feet;
          but the Glorious Virgin did not wish to wait for him,
          She withdrew from his sight. He was very sad.

490   He could not see where she had gone,
          but he saw great lights shining around her.
          He could not at will take his eyes from her;
          he acted rightly because she had done him great favor.

491   The next morning with the bright light of day,
          he looked for the good man as she had commanded him.
          He made his confession with a humble face;
          he concealed nothing of what had happened.

492   When confession was made, the confessor
          gave the monk good advice, he gave him absolution.
          Holy Mary put such a blessing on him
          that the entire order was worth more because of him.

493   If he was good before, he was from then on better;
          he always loved the Holy Queen,
          the Mother of the Creator, very much and always did her honor.
          Happy was the one whom she received in her love.

494   The other good man, I do not know his name,
          the one whom Holy Mary ordered to confess him,
          felt such strong love from loving her so much
          that he would let his head be cut off for her.

495   All of the other people, lay and tonsured,
          clerics and canons and monks,
          were all in love with the Glorious One,
          who knows so well how to help the afflicted.

496   All blessed her and all praised her;
          they raised their hands and their eyes to her;
          they told her deeds, they sang her lauds.
          They spent their days and nights doing this.

497   Gentlefolk and friends, let this thing move us;
       let us all love and praise the Glorious One.
       We will not lay our hands upon anything so precious
       that helps us so much in time of peril.

498   If we will serve her well, whatever we may ask of her,
       we will gain it all, let us be very sure;
       here we will understand it long before we die
       that whatever we put there, we use well.

499   May she give us her grace and her blessing;
       may she keep us from sin and tribulation;
       may she win us remission of our sins,
       so that our souls may not go to perdition.

Miracle 21

The Pregnant Abbess

500   Gentlefolk and friends, excellent company,
since God wished to bring you to this place,
should you still like to wait on me a little,
I would like to tell you of another miracle.

501   I would like to tell you of another miracle
that the Glorious One did, Star of the Sea;
if you would hear me, you could indeed swear
that you could not taste a better morsel.

502   In righteous times when truth was valued,
when no one would tell a lie for anything,
back then they lived happily, reached old age,
and in their last years saw their great-grandchildren.

503   God did daily miracles for mankind,
for no one would lie to his Christian neighbor.
The weather was fair, both winter and summer;
it seemed all was simple in the world.

504   If men sinned, they did good penance,
then God pardoned them all ill will;
they placed all their affection in Jesus Christ.
I want to give you a good example of this.

505   I want to tell you a story about an abbess,
who sinned at a propitious time, so it seems to me.
Her nuns tried to slander her,
but they did not harm her worth a bean.

506   In that abbess lay much goodness;
she was very understanding and very charitable;
she guided her convent willingly,
and they lived according to the rules, in all chastity.

507   But the abbess fell one time;
        she did something crazy that is strictly forbidden.
        She stepped, by chance, on a strongly contaminated weed;[1]
        when she looked carefully, she found herself pregnant.

508   Her stomach was growing to her breasts
        and freckles were coming out on her cheeks.
        Some were big, others smaller;
        as in first pregnancies, these little things happen.

509   The affair was understood by her companions;
        the lit flame could not be hidden.
        It grieved some that she had fallen badly,
        but it pleased the others very much.

510   She oppressed them greatly, she held them cloistered,
        and she did not consent that they do forbidden things.
        They wanted to see her dead, the crazy, unhappy ones;
        this happens to superiors sometimes.

511   They saw that it was not something to be covered up:
        if so, the Devil could laugh at them.
        They sent a letter to the bishop to say
        that he had not visited them and ought to without delay.

512   The bishop understood in the letter
        that either there was a dispute, or they had committed some folly.
        He came to carry out his duty, to visit the convent;
        he had to understand the whole business.

513   Let us leave the bishop at ease in his house;
        let him be in peace and sleep, with his household.
        Let us tell what the pregnant one did,
        for she knew she would be harshly accused the next day.

514   Near her room where she was accustomed to lodge,
        she had a retreat, a convenient place.
        It was her oratory where she usually prayed;
        the altar was dedicated to the Glorious One.

---

[1] Dutton (*Obras Completas*, 2:174) explains that this is a folklore image and refers the reader to Daniel Devoto, "Notas al texto de los *Milagros de Nuestra Señora* de Berceo," *Bulletin Hispanique* 59 (1957): 5–25, here 12–16, and adds his own comments that this reference appears in the *romancero* and in traditional poetry in the La Rioja region of Spain where Berceo lived. See Harriet Goldberg, *Motif-Index of Folk Narratives in the Pan-Hispanic Romancero*, MRTS 206 (Tempe, AZ: MRTS, 2000), 153 (no. T514.1).

515   There she had the image of the Holy Queen,
        who was health and medicine for all.
        She had her adorned with a red curtain,
        for, in the end, she was Godmother for all.

516   She knew the next day she would be harshly accused;
        she had no excuse, it was proven fact.
        The fortunate one took good counsel;
        it was a marvel, how prudent she was.

517 (519) [2] She entered into her oratory all alone;
        she did not ask for any companion.
        Then she stopped helpless in first prayer,
        but God and her good fortune opened a way for her.

518 (517) She threw herself on the floor before the altar;
        she looked at the image, she began to cry.
        "Help me," she said, "Glorious One, Star of the Sea,
        because I have no other help that can help me.

519 (518) Mother, we read it well, the scripture says it,
        you are of such grace and such great temperance,
        that whoever willingly tells you his fear
        you immediately help him in all his anxiety.

520   You helped Theophilus[3] who was desperate,
        who with his blood made a pact with the Devil.
        Through your good counsel he was reconciled,
        whence all mankind gives thanks to you for it.

521   You helped, Lady, the Egyptian,[4]
        who was a great sinner because she was a loose woman.
        Blessed Lady from whom all good flows,
        give me some help before morning.

522   Blessed Lady, I failed to serve you,
        but I always loved to praise and bless you;
        Lady, I tell the truth; I do not intend to lie:
        I would like to be dead, if I could die.

---

[2] We have adopted the logic of Dutton's reordering of quatrains 517–519 and included the traditional numbers in parentheses.

[3] See Miracle 25 (The Miracle of Theophilus).

[4] Reference to Santa María Egipciaca or St. Mary of Egypt, famous as a penitent prostitute (354?-431?). See Miracle 25, n. 12 for fuller treatment.

523   Mother of the King of Glory, Queen of the Heavens,
        let flow some medicine from your grace;
        free from a harsh dishonor a wretched woman.
        This, if you wish it, can be quickly done.

524   Mother, for the love of your beloved Son,
        Son so spotless, so sweet and so perfect,
        let not this mercy that I ask of you be denied,
        for I see they are pursuing me closely with great shouting.

525   If you do not give me, Lady, some help,
        I am ill-prepared to come to the council;
        I want to die here in this little place,
        for if I go there they will do me great harm.

526   Crowned Queen, Temple of Chastity,
        Fountain of Mercy, Tower of Salvation,
        take some pity on this afflicted one;
        let your great pity not run out for me.

527   I want, before your Son, to give you as surety:
        nevermore will I commit this error.
        Mother, if I fail, take such vengeance upon me
        that everyone may speak of my disgrace."

528   So earnestly did she say her prayer
        that the mother full of blessings heard her.
        Like someone asleep, she saw a great vision;
        that ought to bring edification to all.

529   The lady remained asleep from a great weariness;
        God worked everything out of his pity.
        The mother of the King of Majesty appeared to her,
        two angels of very great brightness with her.

530   The lady was frightened and greatly terrified,
        for she was not accustomed to such a vision.
        She was very disturbed by the great brightness,
        but she was much relieved of her burden.

531   The Glorious One said to her, "Take courage, abbess,
        you are safe with me; do not complain;
        know that I bring you a good promise.
        Your prioress would not wish for better.

532   Do not be afraid of falling into dishonor:
        God has kept you from falling into that noose.
        Go to them without fear, keep the appointment with them;
        your back will not be broken because of that."

533   With the solace of the Precious Virgin,
the mother not feeling any pain,
the baby was born, a very beautiful little thing.
The Glorious One sent two angels to take it.

534   She said to the two angels, "I charge you both,
take this little boy to this friend of mine.
Tell him to rear him for me, so do I command you,
for he will indeed believe you; then return to me."

535   The two angels moved with great swiftness
and executed the order without delay.
It pleased the hermit more than great riches,
because truly it was a great honor.

536   The new mother regained consciousness, crossed herself,
and said, "Help me, Glorious One, Crowned Queen!
Is this true or am I deceived?
Blessed Lady, help this sinner!"

537   When she regained consciousness, she touched herself with her hands,
on her stomach, her sides, and along each loin.
She found her belly limp, her waist very thin,
as a woman who is freed from such a thing.

538   In no way could she believe it;
she thought it was a dream, not the real thing.
She felt herself and looked at herself a third time.
Finally, assured, she cast doubt away.

539   When the poor pregnant one felt herself delivered,
the sack emptied of the bad flour,
with great joy she began to sing, "Salve Regina,"[5]
the solace and medicine of the afflicted.

540   She wept profusely out of great joy,
and she said beautiful lauds to the Virgin Mary.
She did not fear the bishop nor her sisterhood,
because she was rid of the great malady.

541   She wept profusely, she offered prayers,
she said lauds and blessings to the Glorious One.
She said, "May you be praised, Mother: in all seasons
women and men must always praise you.

---

   [5] Latin: the initial words of the antiphon "Salve Regina, mater misericordiae" (Hail, Holy Queen, Mother of Mercy).

542   I was in great care and in great fear:
        I fell at your feet, I told you my anguish.
        Lady, your good remedy helped me:
        you must be praised by all creatures.

543   Mother, I above all ought to bless,
        praise, magnify, adore, and serve you.
        You deigned to save me from such great infamy
        for which everyone could always laugh at me.

544   Had this sin of mine gone to the council,
        I would have been the laughingstock of all women.
        How great and how good is your counsel, Mother:
        no one, neither great nor small, could imagine it.

545   For the mercy and the grace that you deigned to grant me,
        I would not know, Mother, how to thank you,
        nor could I ever deserve it, Mother,
        but I will never cease giving you thanks."

546   The lady remained in deep contemplation,
        praising the Glorious One, saying prayers,
        but an order came to her from those convened
        that she go to the council to answer the charges.

547   Since she did not fear being dishonored,
        she went immediately to kneel at the bishop's feet.
        She tried to kiss his hands as she should,
        but he refused to offer them to her.

548   The bishop began to rebuke her right away:
        she had done something for which she must pay.
        She should not be an abbess by any means,
        nor should she live with other nuns.

549   "All nuns who commit such great dishonesty:
        who do not safeguard their bodies or remain chaste,
        ought to be thrown out of the order.
        Elsewhere, wherever they wish, let them do such dirty business."

550   "Lord," she said, "why do you mistreat me?
        I am not, thankfully, what you think."
        "Lady," said the bishop, "why do you deny it?
        You will not be believed, for you will be proven guilty."

551   "Lady," said the bishop, "go to the common room.
        We will take counsel; afterwards we will do something."
        "Lord," said the lady, "do not say anything bad.
        I commend myself to God, who can and does protect."

552   The abbess went out of the assembly;
       as the bishop ordered, she went to the living quarters.
       Anger and hatred had their meeting;
       they kneaded their dough with barley flour.[6]

553   The bishop said to them, "Friends, we cannot
       condemn this lady unless we prove it."
       The convent said to him, "Given what we know well,
       sir, why shall we enter into another proof?"

554   The bishop said to them, "When she is convicted,
       you will be safer, she more ashamed.
       Otherwise, our judgment would be criticized;
       in the end she cannot be exonerated."

555   He sent his clerics, in whom he trusted most,
       so that they might prove how it was.
       They took off her skirt, although it grieved her.
       They found her so thin that she looked like a board.

556   They did not find on her any sign of pregnancy,
       neither milk nor trace of any evil-doing.
       They said, "This is nothing but a great illusion;
       never was there proffered such an extraordinary lie."

557   They returned to the bishop; they said to him, "Sir,
       know that the sister is accused without grounds;
       whoever tells you something else, other than your honor,
       tells you such a great lie that there could be none greater."

558   The bishop thought they were deceived,
       that the lady had promised them money.
       He said, "Evil men, you are not to be believed,
       because she is keeping something hidden under wraps."[7]

559   He said, "I will not believe you so quickly;
       either you are embarrassed or you took money.
       I want to see this with my own eyes;
       if it is not so, those who made the accusation must suffer for it."

---

[6] The metaphor of the barley dough (*massa de farina de ordio*) is in keeping with the hierarchy of bread and grains which Berceo has established. In this hierarchy, wheat is the grain *par excellence* and the others (oats and barley) are decidedly inferior. Compare strophes 137, 274, and 374.

[7] "She is keeping something hidden under wraps" captures the intent of Berceo's "otra quilma tiene de yuso los vestidos" ("she has another sack under her clothes").

560   The bishop got up from where he was seated,
        went to the abbess, angry and irate,
        made her, against her will, take off her habit,
        and found they denounced her for a crime falsely proven.

561   He returned to the convent, angry and very violent.
        "Ladies," he said, "you committed a great treachery;
        you said such evil about this woman
        that your religious order is greatly demeaned.

562   This cannot pass without justice;
        the blame you tried to cast on her,
        the *Decretum*[8] orders must fall on you;
        you must be thrown out of this place."

563   The abbess saw the ladies judged badly,
        that they were to be expelled from the house.
        She took the bishop aside, a good fifteen paces;
        "Sir," she said, "the ladies are not very guilty."

564   She told him her business, why it had happened,
        how she was deceived, because of her grave sins,
        how the Crowned Virgin helped her
        (were it not for her, she would be badly censured).

565   And how she ordered the child carried off,
        how she ordered the hermit to rear him;
        "Sir, if you wish you can prove it;
        for charity's sake, let not the sisters lose their place.

566   I would rather be shamed alone
        than see so many good nuns cast out.
        Sir, I ask you for mercy, pardon this time;
        may the penance for all be given to me."

567   The bishop was amazed; he changed his demeanor.
        He said, "Lady, if this can be proven,
        I will see that Lord Jesus Christ is pleased with you;
        as long as I live, I will do your bidding."

568   Then he sent two canons to the hermit,
        to prove if this was truth or deceit.
        They found the good man in a strange habit,
        holding the little boy wrapped in a cloth.

---

[8] The *Decretum* is a reference to *Decretum Gratiani* (*Gratian's Decree*), which was written with the title *Concordia discordantium canonum* (*A Harmony of Conflicting Canons*). The work appeared in 1140 and soon became the standard text for teaching canon law. Its author, Gratian, is believed to have been a teacher of canon law in Bologna. See *PL* 187.

569   He showed them the infant newly born that day;
he said that Holy Mary ordered that he be reared.
Whoever might doubt this would commit a great folly,
since it was the pure truth and not a barefaced lie.

570   They returned immediately to the bishop with the message;
they told him the news of what they had proven.
"Sir," they said, "be assured of this;
if not, you will commit a great error, you will acquire great sin."

571   The bishop considered himself mistaken regarding the abbess;
he fell to the floor, prostrate, at her feet.
"Lady," he said, "have mercy, for I have greatly sinned;
I pray that my sin may be pardoned by you."

572   "Lord," said she, "for God and the Glorious One,
consider your position: do not do such a thing.
You are a holy man; I, a grievous sinner.
If you do not return to your feet, I will be angry with you."

573   The abbess had this argument with the bishop,
but they ended completely in good agreement.
Forever they had both love and good will;
they cloistered their lives with great patience.

574   The bishop established peace in the convent;
he ended the disagreement and dissension.
When he took his leave, he gave them his benediction;
the visit was good for one and all.

575   He sent his greeting to the holy hermit,
as to a good friend, to a baptismal godfather,
that he rear the child until his seventh year.
Then he would strive to make him a good Christian.

576   When the time came, the seven years had passed,
he sent two of the most honored of his clerics
to bring the child from the forest to the town.
They fulfilled it as persons well instructed.

577   They brought him the child reared in the wilderness.
For his age, he was well taught;
it pleased the bishop, he was very satisfied.
He ordered him to study with a learned teacher.

578   He turned out to be a very good man, temperate in everything;
it seemed indeed that he was reared by a good master.
The whole town was very pleased with him:
when the bishop died, they gave him the bishopric.

579   The Glorious One, who had given him to be reared, guided him.
        With God, he knew how to govern his bishopric well;
        he guided the souls well, as he should.
        In all things he knew how to seek moderation.

580   The people loved him as did his clergy;
        the canons and all the nuns loved him.
        Everyone, wherever they were, prayed for his days,
        except some crazy ones who loved folly.

581   When the time came for him to die,
        his lady did not let him suffer long.
        She carried him to Heaven, to a safe place,
        where neither thief nor judge[9] can ever enter.

582   Let us all give thanks to the Glorious Virgin,
        of whom we read and prove so many miracles.
        May she give us grace so that we may serve her,
        and guide us to do things for which we may be saved.
        Amen.

[9.] Berceo expresses an intense distrust of judges (*merinos*). See Dutton's remarks in his edition (*Obras Completas*, 2:171) and idem, "The Profession of Gonzalo de Berceo and the Paris Manuscript of the *Libro de Alexandre*," *Bulletin of Hispanic Studies* 37 (1960): 137-45 for an explanation of this dislike.

Miracle 22

The Shipwrecked Pilgrim Saved by the Virgin

583   Gentlefolk, if you wish, while daylight lasts,
I will tell you even more of these miracles;
if you do not complain, I will not complain,
because Holy Mary is like a deep well.

584   Holy Mary is like a mighty river,
that everyone drinks from, beasts and people.
It is as great tomorrow as it was yesterday, and it is never empty;
it runs in all seasons, in hot and in cold.

585   She always helps in all places,
in valleys and mountains, on lands and seas;
those who know how to pray to her with a pure mouth
will not suffer severe pain in their loins.

586   We read a miracle of her holiness
that happened to a bishop, a man of charity;
a Catholic man of great authority,
he saw it with his own eyes; certainly he knew the truth.

587   Just as he saw it, so he wrote it;
he omitted nothing, nor did he add to it.
May God grant him Paradise, for he surely deserved it;
he said no Mass that helped him so much.

588   Some pilgrims went on a crusade to the Holy Land,
to salute the Sepulchre, to pray to the True Cross;
they embarked on ships to go to Acre,
if the Heavenly Father wished to guide them.

589   They had favorable winds immediately at the beginning,
a very delightful breeze, the whole sea tranquil;
the happy crowd was very joyful;
with such weather they would have crossed the sea quickly.

590   They had passed over a great part of the sea;
        they would have passed the other part quickly,
        but their destiny held for them a bad trap.
        Great joy was turned into sadness.

591   The storm moved in, a fierce wind;
        the pilot who guided the ship lost his wits.
        He gave no help, neither to himself nor to others:
        all of his skill was not worth one bean.

592   Another thing happened to them, a grievous harm:
        the ship broke apart down in its depths.
        They saw much water gush in, breaking into every corner;
        everything was going to ruin.

593   Near the big ship they had a smaller one
        (I do not know whether they call it a galley or a pinnace),
        so that if they were worried about a bad wind,
        in that small one they might escape the grave danger.

594   The captain, as would a loyal Christian,
        took the lord bishop by the hand.
        He put him, with other good men of very important status,
        in the boat; he lent good help.

595   One of the pilgrims, thinking he was wiser,
        jumped from the ship because he was very agile;
        he intended to enter the galley as a shipmate;
        he drowned in the water; he died, but not alone.

596   A half-hour could barely have passed,
        when God allowed the ship to be sunk.
        Of the people who had remained inside,
        not a single one escaped alive.

597   The bishop and the others who got out with him
        went to the closest land they could.
        They felt great pain for those who had perished;
        it grieved them because they had not died with them.

598   Feeling great sorrow and grief for the dead,
        they looked out afar: they looked at the sea,
        in case they might see some of the dead reach shore,
        for the sea never wants to conceal anything dead.

599   Looking to see if they could spot some of the dead,
        to give them burial, to put them under the ground,
        they saw little doves born from under the sea:
        as many as the dead, so many could they be.

600   They saw little doves come out from under the sea
        and fly whiter than snow against the sky.
        They believed they were the souls God wanted to take
        to holy Paradise, a glorious place.

601   With justified envy, they were beside themselves;
        they were sorely grieved that they were alive;
        since they believed very firmly, there was no doubting
        that the doves were the souls swallowed by the sea.

602   They said, "Alas, pilgrims! You were lucky:
        you are now passed *per ignem et per aquam*;[1]
        we remain in the wilderness as helpless ones;
        we keep vigil while you sleep securely.

603   Thanks to the Holy Father and to Holy Mary,
        you now wear the palm of your pilgrimage;[2]
        we are in sadness and you in joy;
        we intended to act prudently and we committed folly."

604   Having great grief from the harm that came to them,
        they wanted to go on, to start their journey.
        They saw a traveler come out of the sea;
        it seemed that he was a wretched pilgrim.

605   When he came to them, it was on the shore.
        All knew him; he was the one who had jumped.
        They all crossed themselves saying, "How, in what way
        did he remain alive in the sea one whole hour?"

606   The pilgrim said, "Hear me and may you live!
        I will assure you of that which you doubt.
        I want you to know how I escaped alive;
        you will say 'Deo gratias'[3] as soon as you hear it.

607   When I tried to jump out of the big ship,
        for it was clear it was going to sink,
        I saw I could not save myself from death;
        I began to say, 'Help me, Holy Mary!'

---

[1] Latin: "through fire and through water." See Psalms 66:12 and Luke 3:16. The phrase is also used to signify trial by ordeal.

[2] The palm is the badge worn by the pilgrim (or palmer [Spanish *palmero*]) who has made the journey to Jerusalem, just as the scallop shell is that of the pilgrim to Santiago de Compostela. The palm is also the reward for martyrdom and symbol of the same.

[3] Latin: "Thanks be to God."

608   I said these words, 'Help me, Holy Mary!'
        I could not say more for there was no time.
        She was immediately ready, since it pleased her;
        if it were not for her, I would be drowned.

609   She was immediately ready; she brought a good cloth:
        it was a cloth of value, never did I see its equal.
        She threw it over me and said, 'No harm will come to you;
        believe that you fell asleep or lay in a bath.'

610   Never did a man of flesh see such exquisite work;
        it was the work of angels rather than material.[4]
        I lay as comfortable as if under a canopy,
        or as someone who falls asleep in a green meadow.

611   Happy will be the soul and fortunate
        that under so rich a shade finds rest;
        neither cold nor heat nor wind nor ice
        will bother it and make it uncomfortable.

612   Under this cloth rest, happy and satisfied,
        the glorious virgins, beloved of Lord Christ,
        who sing multiple lauds to His mother.
        and have precious and honorable crowns.

613   The shade of that cloth is so soothing
        that one who is hot finds coolness beneath it,
        and one who is cold finds tempered warmth;
        God, what magnificent help in times of anguish!"[5]

614   So many are her mercies, so many her charities,
        so many her virtues, so many her kindnesses,
        that neither bishop nor abbot could count them,
        nor could kings nor very rich men imagine them.

615   The grief that they felt for those who had perished,
        they forgot it all with the pleasure of the miracle;
        they rendered thanks to God; they chanted the "Te Deum";[6]
        then they finished sweetly with "Salve Regina."[7]

---

[4] Ildephonsus's chasuble is also of heavenly workmanship (Miracle 1).

[5] See also Miracle 19, quatrain 448, where the Virgin's cloak protects the pregnant woman and Miracle 24 (25), quatrain 716 (880) ff., where she causes her wimple to capture and hold one of the thieves.

[6] Latin: abbreviated title of the hymn "Te Deum laudamus" (We praise you, O God).

[7] Latin: the initial words of the antiphon "Salve Regina, mater misericordiae" ("Hail, Holy Queen, Mother of Mercy").

616   The pilgrims then completed their pilgrimage;
        they arrived at the Sepulchre with very great joy.
        They adored the Cross of the Son of Mary;
        never in this world did they see such a good day.

617   They related the miracle of the Glorious Mother,
        how she freed the man from the perilous sea.
        They all said it was a wondrous thing.
        About it they had a story written, a delightful tale.

618   However many heard this holy miracle,
        all to the Glorious One said their prayers;
        they had better devotion in serving her,
        since from her they hoped for mercy and reward.

619   The fame of this deed flew over the seas.
        The wind did not stop it; it dwelt in many homes.
        They put it in books in many places,
        where it is praised by many mouths today.

620   As many as bless the Glorious Mother,
        by the King of Glory! do the right thing,
        since through her we came out of the harsh prison,
        the dangerous abyss in which we all lay.

621   We, who because of Eve had fallen into damnation,
        through her, recovered our lost paradise;
        were it not for her, we would lie dead,
        but her Holy Fruit redeemed us.

622   By her Holy Fruit that she conceived,
        who for the world's salvation suffered passion and death,
        we came out of the pit that Adam opened for us,
        when, against the proscription, he bit the bad bite.

623   Since then she always strives to help the afflicted,
        to guide the wretched, to call back the sinner;
        on land and sea, she does great miracles,
        like those that have been told and even greater ones.

624   May she who is abundant and full of grace
        guide our actions, our suffering lives;
        may she, in this world, guard us from evil attack,
        and, in the other, win for us a dwelling with the saints.
        Amen.

Miracle 23

The Merchant from Byzantium

625   Friends, if you would pay a little heed,
I would read a beautiful miracle to you.
When it has been read, you will be very pleased;
you will prize it more than an average meal.

626   In the city that is named for Constantine
(for Constantine founded it in earlier times,
the one who gave Rome to St. Peter as a home),[1]
there was a good man of great wealth.

627   This burgher had a very big heart;
in order to increase his importance, he went to great expense.
He spent his fortune, he gave it freely;
no matter who asked of him, he would not say no.

628   To enhance his fame, to increase his importance,
he shared without regret all the money he could;
if his own dwindled, to gain still greater fame,
he willingly took loans from his neighbors.

629   He spread his wealth generously and without prudence;
his riches diminished, but not his good will;
one always would find many people in his house,
at times twenty, at times thirty, sometimes a hundred.

630   Since he made great expenditures, expenses without moderation,
his money gave out, and he found himself in a bind;
he did not find a loan, nor did he find credit,
neither among strangers nor among his acquaintances.

---

[1] According to the *Donatio*, a document attributed to the Emperor Constantine (4th century), the city of Rome and all the West were given to the Pope and his successors. This document was proven to be false by the Italian Lorenzo Valla in the fifteenth century, but at the time of Berceo it was still thought to be authentic.

631   Everyone understood that he was impoverished;
        he did not find a loan nor money on credit.
        The good man had fallen into dishonor;
        he considered what was past to be all lost.

632   The man with great complaint went before the altars;
        he uttered his prayers aloud:
        "Lord, who art one God and three equal Persons,
        be merciful and do not abandon me.

633   Lord, until now You have sustained me;
        now, due to my sins, I have fallen in need.
        I have lost all the esteem I had;
        it would have been better had I not been born.

634   Lord, give me help in some way,
        send me Your grace by some path;
        for You, such an act is a very easy thing.
        I swam the whole sea, will I die on the shore?"

635   While he was praying, God wished to help him.
        The burgher thought of a good recourse;
        it did not come from his own head, rather
        the One who rules the world wished to guide him.

636   There was in the city a very rich Jew;
        there was no richer man in that vicinity.
        He decided to go to him,
        to ask him for help for God and charity's sake.

637   Then he went to the Jew and was well received;
        the Jew asked him how he was and why he had come,
        for he had known him in other times
        and had indeed heard of his situation.

638   The burgher told the Hebrew his business:
        "Mr. Fulano,[2] I believe that you indeed know my situation;
        I would like very much to obtain a loan from you,
        since I never thought I would see myself in this predicament.

639   When God willed me to have wealth,
        as my neighbors know, I helped everyone.
        I had the doors of my house open;
        whatever God gave me, I shared with all.

[2] *Don Fulano*: Berceo uses one of the given names for anonymity; similarly, in English one might say "Mr. So-and-so" to avoid revealing a subject's name or to use when the subject's name is unknown.

640   I would like, if I could, to continue doing that,
         but I have fallen on hard times and am diminished in riches;
         but if you would lend me some of yours,
         I will pay you back at a fixed time."

641   The Jew said to him, "I will gladly do it.
         I will lend you however much you want of my riches,
         but give me a guarantor who is reliable.
         If you do not, I would fear being deceived."

642   The Christian said to him, he spoke to him aptly:
         "Sir, I cannot give you any other guarantor,
         but I will give you Christ, my God and my Lord,
         Son of the Glorious One, Savior of the world."

643   The Jew said to him, "I could not believe
         that He of whom you speak, born of Mary,
         is God, but that He was a wise man and not foolish,
         a true prophet; I would not believe anything else.

644   If He will back you, I, for His love,
         will give you a loan without any other guarantor,
         but it seems to me a despicable, vile thing,
         and you seem to me almost a mocking man.

645   I do not know how He could do it,
         because He is not in this world, as I believe;
         do not hope that He is coming to help you,
         whence it behooves you to get other aid."

646   The Christian responded; he said to the Jew,
         "I understand that you consider me mad and foolish,
         that I do not have any sense, and that I am a fool,
         but I trust after this you will see otherwise."

647   The Jew said to him, "If you demonstrate such a thing,
         I will give you the loan, however much you ask,
         but if this is a trick, with what you get from me,
         you will not be paying either troubadours or minstrels."

648   The burgher said to the renegade rogue,
         "If you will come with me to my sacred place,
         I will show you Mary with her good Son."
         The Jew said to him, "I will do it gladly."

649   He took him to the church; with God and His guidance,
         he showed him the image of Holy Mary,
         with her Son in her arms, her sweet Companion.
         Those of the Jewish quarter were ashamed.

650   The good man said to those of the synagogue,
          "This is our Lord and this our lady.
          Whosoever calls on them is always very fortunate;
          whosoever does not believe in them will drink fire and flames."

651   He said to the Jew who was the most important,
          the one who promised to lend him money,
          "These are my lords and I their servant.
          Let these be my surety, for I can offer nothing else."

652   The Jew said to him, "I will take them,
          I will not ask you for other guarantors;
          but if you fail me, I will challenge them,
          and I will make known what kind of loyalty you bring."

653   The Christian gave the guarantors to the rogue;
          he put in his hand mother and Son.[3]
          They agreed on a certain date for his payment;
          the citizen burgher received the money.

654   When the burgher had received the money,
          he was joyous and considered himself saved;
          he returned to the Glorious One; he went there prudently;
          he went to give thanks to God with all his heart.

655   He bent his knees before the Majesty,
          he raised his eyes to God with great humility;
          "Lord," he said, "You showed me mercy and charity;
          You have taken me out of very great poverty today.

656   Lord, yesterday I was poor and in debt;
          today, because of Your grace, I am rich and affluent.
          I gave You for a guarantor, but I did it unwillingly;
          it would be a great injustice if You were challenged because of me.

657   Lord, I would not want to go back on my word;
          what I proposed before You I want to fulfill,
          but if I cannot come by the appointed day,
          I will send the money to You.

658   Lord, if by chance I am far away,
          so that I cannot come by the time agreed,
          I will put it before You, my guarantor,
          and You, however You wish, make the payment to him.

---

[3] Having an icon as guarantor was the custom in Byzantium. The touching of the images is the formal gesture symbolizing the sealing of the contract.

659   Queen of Heaven, mother of wheat bread,[4]
        by whom the mortal enemy was defeated,
        You are my guarantor, I say the same thing to you
        that I have told to the One you have with you."

660   When the burgher had said his prayer,
        and had placed his contract with the rogue,
        he arranged his affairs and readied his departure;
        he went to foreign lands, to a distant region.

661   He went to foreign lands, to Flanders and France,
        with much merchandise and he made great profit;
        with God and the Glorious One his worth grew;
        he rose to great wealth and great excellence.

662   With the large business in which he was occupied,
        he was very distant from his country.
        He did not return on the agreed day;
        due to his grave sins, he had forgotten it.

663   The day that he was to pay was approaching;
        only one day more was to pass.
        The burgher remembered the business;
        the good man wanted to kill himself with his own hands.

664   He said, "I have failed badly, wretched sinner;
        I cannot help the guarantor at all;
        my Redeemer will be challenged because of me,
        and so will His holy mother, she of Rocamadour.[5]

665   Lord, you understand it and you know the truth,
        how very grieved I am in my heart;
        Lord, give me help for pity's sake,
        so that Your great Majesty may not be challenged."

666   He took all the money, tied in a sack;
        not even a worn-out penny[6] was missing;

---

[4] The wheat bread is the best and from it the host is made. Therefore the *pan de trigo*, or wheat bread, is Christ. See Dutton (*Obras Completas*, 2:196) and R. T. Mount, "Levels of Meaning: Grains, Bread and Bread Making as Informative Images in Berceo," *Hispania* 76 (1993): 49–54.

[5] The image of the Virgin of Rocamadour (Lot, France) was highly revered in the Middle Ages and the chapel that held it was an important pilgrimage destination. According to legend, the image was carved by Zaccheus the Publican, who went from the Holy Land to France, where he lived as Amadour.

[6] The *pugés* (here translated as "penny") is a coin of infinitesimal value of the archbishopric of Puy.

> he took it to the shore, carried on his back;
> he threw it into the waves where there was no ford.

667 He turned to Jesus Christ with great devotion;
     weaping bitterly, he said his prayer.
     "Lord," he said, "You know this whole matter,
     because You are the guarantor of our agreement.

668 Lord, since I cannot pay the moneylender,
     because between us there lies a very rough path,
     Lord, who art called the true Savior,
     put this money in his coffer tomorrow.

669 Glorious Lady, my Holy Mary,
     you indeed are in the midst of this business;
     when you look at it carefully, it is yours more than mine.
     I give you the money, Lady, you guide it.

670 Both you and your Son were in the agreement;
     you are both guarantors to the renegade rogue.
     Let it be your will that he be paid tomorrow;
     because of a bad servant let not the good Lord be challenged.[7]

671 I entrust it to you, I consider that I have paid;
     I hold myself as free of obligation, because I have given it to you.
     I, Mother, pray to you; you beseech your Son.
     However you wish, tomorrow let the rogue be paid."

672 It pleased the Glorious One, also her beloved Son;
     the next morning when the sun was up,
     the chest that was carrying the loaned money
     floated to the door of the infidel rogue.

673 The town where the Jew made his home,
     the one who had lent the burgher the money,
     lay inhabited, so we read, near the sea;
     the waves sometimes beat against its walls.

674 On that morning, at about the hour of prime,
     those of the Jewish quarter, a useless lot,
     went to entertain themselves on the shore;
     they saw this box floating near the beach.

675 Some frivolous youths went to get it
     and many times made vain attempts;
     it slipped away and escaped their hands;
     many people saw this, Jews and Christians.

---

[7] Cf. Matthew 18:23–85.

676   Some wise Christians came at the noise,
        with grapples, hooked poles, swift boats.
        It was all to no avail, for they were all knaves;
        never did men exude more useless sweat.

677   By chance the true owner came by;
        the chest came to his hands right away.
        He carried it to his house; inside, in his larder,
        he made a great pile of gold and silver.

678   When the rogue had put away the money,
        the chest that it came in was carefully examined;
        he put it under his bed greatly lightened;
        everyone was envious of the renegade rogue.

679   The treacherous rogue, greedy by nature,
        the despicable one, thought of nothing else;
        he considered that his good fortune was marvelous;
        he called the burgher "the Lying Mouth."

680   The Jews, that evil race, reproached him,
        for he had lost his money due to his own foolishness;
        never had anyone accepted so senseless a surety,
        for he took as guarantor a hard statue.

681   Let us leave the Jew, greedy and usurious.
        Let God not take him out of there; let him guard his larder.
        Let us talk instead about the merchant's situation;
        let us take him the news from where the chest reached shore.

682   The burgher of Byzantium lived in great grief,
        for he could not pay the Jew by the appointed time.
        The good man could not brighten his face;
        his men could not comfort him no matter what.

683   A long time passed; he earned a great deal of money,
        buying and selling according to the law of merchants.
        When the time came, he left those paths;
        he returned to his province with other companions.

684   The news spread through Constantinople
        that the burgher, don Valerio, had come.
        It pleased the Jew; he considered himself lucky;
        he thought he would double the money lent.

685   Then he went straightaway to the [merchant's] house, for he knew where
        he lived.
        The Jew vilified him because he had not paid;
        the good man told him he was mad,
        for he owed him nothing of what he demanded.

686   The Jew said to him, "I am in the right,
        for I have good witnesses for what I demand of you.
        If you say you paid, show the where and the when,
        for in the end, I believe I will not go away singing.[8]

687   I trusted in your Christ, a great trickster,
        and in His little mother who was scarcely better.
        I will get the satisfaction that corresponds to the guarantor I took;
        whoever trusts in you again, may he receive the same or worse."

688   The Christian said to him, "You are speaking nonsense.
        good mother, good Son, you have little respect for them;
        never in this world did such a lady don such a wimple,
        nor was a child ever born with so gifted a mouth.

689   The money you gave me, I am very certain,
        and I have good witnesses, that I have repaid you.
        If you still say no, I will make you a better offer:
        let the guarantors that you took say so."

690   The rogue was happy, he considered himself protected;
        he said, "I am in agreement, you will not be challenged."
        He thought that the image, which lacked the power of reason,
        could not say a word by which he would be defeated.

691   They went to the church, these two litigants,
        to make the inquiry as to who had the money.
        Many went behind them and many in front,
        to see if the wooden figures would have the ability to speak.

692   They stopped before the crowned Child,
        whom the mother sweetly embraced.
        The burgher said to Him, "Lord so perfect,
        judge this suit, for I am sorely challenged.

693   You are informed of how I did it:
        whether he got it or not, you know it, Lord.
        Lord, shed Your grace over me, a sinner;
        say whether he received it, since You were the guarantor."

694   The Crucifix spoke; it gave him a good response:
        "He is lying because he received payment on the designated day:
        the basket in which the carefully counted money came,
        he has hidden under his own bed."

---

[8] *Non iré cantando*: in saying "I will not go away singing," the Jew indicates that he will likely not be pleased with the outcome.

695   The whole town went, as it wished;
        they went to the house; they were quite correct to do so.
        They found the chest where it lay under the bed;
        the evil rogue was confused and in a sorry state.

696   Whether he, sad and scared, liked it or not,
        the whole affair was made known.
        He and his companions were immediately converted;
        he died in the good faith, wrested from the bad one.

697   Always on that day when this thing happened,
        when the image spoke, due to its excellent virtue,
        they held a noble festival with kyries and sequences,
        with great exultations to God and to the Glorious One.

698   The people of the town, paupers and wealthy,
        made great exultation, all with instruments;
        they prepared banquets, they gave *ad non habentes*[9]
        their meat and fish, salted and fresh.

699   The bottles of strong wine went round,
        and marvelously prepared dishes;
        whoever wanted to partake did not do without;
        no one felt scorned at this time.

700   A rich archdeacon, from very foreign lands,
        was present at this feast among that company;
        he saw great dances, huge processions,
        the likes of which he had never heard or seen.

701   He asked how this festival was started,
        for it was a great event, nobly celebrated.
        A Christian told him its origin in depth
        and that he should know this was a proven truth.

702   It pleased the archdeacon, who considered it a great thing;
        he said, "Laudetur Deus e la Virgo gloriosa."[10]
        His fine hand put it in writing.
        May God grant him Paradise and delightful rest.
        Amen.

---

[9] Latin: "to the have-nots," i.e., to the poor.
[10] Latin-Spanish macaronic: "May God and the Glorious Virgin be praised!"

Miracle 24 (25)

The Robbed Church

703 (867)[1] I would like to tell you of yet another miracle
 that the Glorious One did; it is not to be forgotten.
 She is a perennial fountain from which the sea flows,
 which in no season ever ceases to flow.

704 (868) Indeed I believe that whoever hears this miracle
 will not want to take off the wimple that covers her,
 or snatch away by force what she holds.
 He must remember this as long as he lives.

705 (869) This very beautiful miracle happened
 in the time of the king of good fortune,
 Don Fernando by name,[2] lord of Extremadura,
 grandson of King Alfonso, a person of great temperance.

706 (870) Some thieves set out from around Leon,
 from that bishopric, from that region.
 They came to Castile in great confusion
 led by the Devil, who is a wicked guide.

707 (871) One was a layman born in a bad hour;
 the other a cleric ordained by the bishop.
 They arrived in Çohinos;[3] the Devil led them,
 the one who led Judas to do his evil business.

708 (872) Outside the town, in a plain
 not very far away, there was a church.
 Near the church, there was an inhabited convent.
 A Benedictine nun lived therein.

---

[1] As indicated in the introduction to the translation, we have followed Dutton's suggestion for reversing the traditional order of Miracles 24 and 25. This requires renumbering the quatrains in each miracle tale as well. The traditional numbers for the tales themselves and for their quatrains are given in parentheses.

[2] This king is Fernando III el Santo, who died in 1252. He was the grandson of Alfonso VIII. This reference sets the tale in the time of Berceo.

[3] Ceinos de Campo in the province of Valladolid.

709 (873) Both these thieves planned the thing.
           They moved by night, each one with a pickax.
           They unhinged the doors and looked in the corners.
           They discerned that indeed the convent was without men.

710 (874) The nun who kept the convent was poor.
           She had little food, very few clothes,
           but she had a cloth, which was very good.
           For a woman of the order, it was a seemly covering.

711 (875) What was in the convent was all emptied out,
           badly handled, placed in a sack.
           The layman was a man of rather bad judgment,
           but of worse was the cleric, who had read more.

712 (876) When what was in the convent was put in a sack
           (it would all be worth very little in money),
           the miserable ones, ministers of the Devil,
           believed that everything valuable was locked up in the church.

713 (877) With the pickaxes the lock was yanked off;
           the doors unhinged, the church robbed.
           Nothing remained of what was there.
           They committed great sacrilege for very slight gain.

714 (878) They stripped the cloths that covered the altar,
           the vestments and books with which they [the clergy] would chant.
           The precious place, where sinners would pray
           to the Creator, was badly damaged.

715 (879) When they had committed this great madness,
           they both raised their faces upward.
           They saw the image of the Glorious Virgin
           with her Child in arms, her sweet Infant.

716 (880) She had a most honored crown on her head,
           covered with a white and very sheer wimple.
           To the left and right she had it beautifully draped.
           They intended to take it from her, but they gained nothing at all.

717 (881) The cleric hurried and became more daring,
           for in ecclesiastic things he was more versed.
           The unfortunate man went to snatch the wimple,
           since with that action they would finish their business.

718 (882) The Glorious One considered herself affronted,
           since they had despoiled her so villainously.
           She showed that she was not very pleased with the service.
           Never did anyone see a wimple so disputed.

719 (883) As soon as the evildoer snatched the wimple,
            it stuck to him so firmly on his closed fist
            that it would not be so stuck with glue
            or with a nail driven by a hammer.

720 (884) They lost their memory and they well deserved to;
            the layman and the cleric lost all their wits.
            They went for the door; they could not find it.
            Those born for evil went wandering in circles.

721 (885) They could not let loose of what they had taken.
            Now they wanted, willingly, to turn it loose if they could.
            They would turn it loose with pleasure. They did not wish to carry it off,
            but they did not know how to judge where the door was.

722 (886) They went groping from corner to corner
            as Sisinnio[4] did, the jealous man,
            husband of Theodora, a woman of great renown,
            who was converted by Pope Clement.

723 (887) The mad, star-crossed ones, abandoned by God,
            were going around like drunkards all dazed.
            Now they fell on their faces, now on their sides;
            they were badly prepared to go on a pilgrimage.

724 (888) The anchoress, with the loss she had suffered,
            came out as best she could from where she had lain hidden.
            She shouted and cried out, and she was soon helped;
            the fastest people came immediately.

725 (889) Then a great crowd of people came.
            They entered the church; they found the thieves.
            Then they attacked them, for they came infuriated,
            giving them hard blows with very big sticks.

726 (890) They hit them with great sticks and great blows to the face,
            giving them very many kicks and many blows with rods.
            They got so many of the great blows over their bodies
            that the small ones were forgotten.

---

[4] St. Clement, pope and martyr of the first century, converted a Roman lady, Theodora, wife of Sisinnio, to Christianity. One day Sisinnio and his servants followed his wife to the church where she heard Clement say mass. They lost their sight and hearing when they tried to leave, but the prayers of Theodora and Clement restored their senses and Sisinnio was converted. This information is given by Michael Gerli in his edition of the *Milagros de Nuestra Señora* (190). See also Devoto, "Notas al texto," 23-25.

726 (891) They made them tell the whole story:
from what land they came or by what pilgrimage,
and how Holy Mary had caught them,
because they had done her a great villainy.

728 (892) Before dawn they were well imprisoned;
when the sun rose it found them well subdued.
Everyone called them proven traitors,
for against the Glorious Lady they were so bold.

729 (893) After Mass was said, the council met.
All felt like giving them bad treatment.
They made a harsh decision concerning the evil layman.
They raised him from the ground with a strong cord.

730 (894) When a devout canon who led a holy life,
who had his love well kindled in God,
saw the wimple sewed to the hand,
he said that such justice was unheard of.

731 (895) The good man wished to take the wimple,
to kiss the veil instead of the Glorious One,
but God wanted to honor the good Christian,
and the wimple right then was loosened from the thumb.

732 (896) A few days later (God wished to guide him),
it happened that the bishop came to the place.
They led the cleric to present him to the bishop,
to see whether he would order the cleric held or freed.

733 (897) They led the cleric with hands well tied,
his shoulders well thrashed from the blows.
They told him the news of his late-night deeds
and how he did the things that God had forbidden.

734 (898) He himself confessed with his own mouth
his whole story, his crazy conduct:
how they had stolen the wimple from the Glorious Lady.
Never did they do anything of such little profit.

735(899) The bishop got him and took him to Leon,
hands tied behind him as appropriate for a thief.
Everyone who saw him and knew the story
said, "God confound such a crazy man!"

736 (900) The bishop did not dare to judge the case.
He called all the clergy to council.
When they arrived on the assigned day,
he presented the cleric to them and told them of his madness.

737 (901) He asked them for advice. What should be done with him?
No one knew how to respond to that.
The bishop indeed knew how to get justice.
He wanted to convict the cleric by his [own] admission.

738 (902) The bishop said, "Cleric, did you do such evil?
Do you admit to what they attribute to you?"
"Sir," said the cleric, "my spiritual father,
for my wickedness I never found a match.

739 (903) However much they tell you of me, it all is very true.
They do not tell you a tenth of my wickedness.
Sir, for God's sake and for charity,
do not consider my merit, but rather your goodness."

740 (904) "Friends," said the bishop, "this is appropriate;
he is not our cleric or of our bishopric.
It is not right for him to be condemned by us.
Let his bishop judge him, his goodness and his sin.[5]

741 (905) He has declared himself to belong to the Bishop of Avila.
He claims to be his cleric and of his bishopric.
The law forbids one [bishop] to judge another's cleric;
for that, I could be denounced later.

742 (906) But I pronounce this sentence: that he be banished.[6]
If he is found in any part of this bishopric,
he is to be strung up immediately, hanged in a tree,
and anyone who pardons him is to be excommunicated."

743 (907) Never more did they see him after they sent him off;
never did they report him in the entire bishopric.
They zealously guarded the new miracle well
and put it in the book with the others.

744 (908) May you, Glorious Mother, always be praised,
for you know how to give to the evil ones a bad punishment.
As a judicious person, you know how to honor the good.
For this you are called "Mother Full of Grace."

745 (909) You took the evil ones who came to affront your convent
as prisoners inside your chapel.
For the good man who wanted to kiss your wimple,
you duly unfastened it for him, as the document tells.

---

[5] See the trial in *El libro de buen amor*, vv. 321-71.

[6] Many scholars, including John E. Keller, read this word as *açotado*, meaning "beaten."

746 (910) Blessed Lady, Consummate Queen,
           crowned by the hand of Christ, your Son,
           free us from the Devil, from his trap,
           for he sets an evil ambush for the soul.

747 (911) Guide us, Lady, in the lawful life;
           win for us, in the end, a good and perfect destiny.
           Guard us from evil blows and from falling into sin,
           so that in the end, our souls may have a good departure.
           Amen.

Miracle 25 (24)

The Miracle of Theophilus

748 (703)[1] I wish to speak to you about the case of Theophilus;
    so beautiful a miracle is not to be forgotten,
    for in it we can understand and believe
    that the Glorious One protects those who know how to pray to her.

749 (704) I would not want, if I could, to prolong the story,
    for you would be bored and I could err.
    God is usually pleased with the short prayer;
    may the Creator allow us to make use of it.

750 (705) There was a good man of great wealth
    who was called Theophilus, as the text says.
    He was a peaceful man; he did not like contention.
    He knew very well how to control his carnal nature.

751 (706) In the place where he was, he held great authority;
    he was vicar to his lord the bishop.[2]
    He had superiority over those in the church,
    except that the bishop had the command.

752 (707) He was in himself of good bearing;
    he knew how to be at peace and in good agreement with everyone.
    He was a temperate man, a man of great knowledge;
    he was well endowed with intelligence and wisdom.

753 (708) He clothed the naked; he fed the hungry.
    He welcomed the pilgrims who came cold.
    He gave good instruction to those who erred,
    that they might repent of all their failings.

754 (709) The bishop did not have a burden or care,
    except singing his Mass and praying his Psalter;

---

[1] The numbering of this miracle tale follows Dutton.

[2] As vicar, Theophilus was second in command in the bishopric and was empowered to act in behalf of the bishop in administrative matters.

he [Theophilus] excused him from all his work;
to tell of all his goodness would make a long story.

755 (710) The bishop loved him very much,
for Theophilus freed him from all obligation.
Ordinary people and the gentlefolk considered him a beacon,
for he was everyone's leader and guide.

756 (711) When the time came for him [the bishop] to die,
the bishop could not live beyond the appointed moment;
he became ill and died; he went to rest with God.
May God give him Paradise, one should so pray.

757 (712) The people of the land, all the clergy,
everyone said, "Let Theophilus have the bishopric;
we understand superiority lies in him.
It is fitting that he have the command."

758 (713) They sent their letters to the archbishop:
for God's sake, let him not change his mind from Theophilus,
for they all considered that the soundest advice.
Anything else would be winter; this would be summer.[3]

759 (714) Those of the archbishopric sent for him.
They said to him, "Theophilus, take this bishopric,
since the whole council grants it to you,
and you are requested by all the people."

760 (715) Theophilus responded to them with great simplicity,
"Gentlemen, change your mind, for God's sake and for charity,
for I am not so worthy of such an office;
to make such a choice would be a great blindness."

761 (716) The archbishop said, "I want you to speak;
I want you to accept this election."
"Sir," Theophilus said to him, "you will not insist so much
as to bring me to it willingly."

762 (717) Those of the canonry, whether it pleased them or not,
had to make another selection.
The bishop whom they ordained
put another vicar in the position.

---

[3] This metaphor based on the seasons is typical of Berceo and reflects his life and times. The long, bright, and warm summer days are good; they allow one to accomplish a great deal. The short, gloomy, and cold days of winter, in comparison, are bad; they are physically less pleasant and do not allow one to accomplish as much.

763 (718)   All cases were taken to the new vicar;
the people served Theophilus, but they served him more.
Theophilus became jealous; the young man was furious.
He who was Abel became Cain.[4]

764 (719)   In the bishop's house, he was not so favored
as he used to be with the former one.
He was greatly disturbed in his mind;
he was beside himself with envy.

765 (720)   He considered himself mistreated and ill-fated;
he saw himself disdained by the great and the small.
He was blinded by indignation and was badly disturbed;
he conceived a wild madness, a truly outrageous error.

766 (721)   In that bishopric where Theophilus lived,
there was a Jew in that Jewish quarter.
He knew evil things, every treachery,
for he had his brotherhood with the Old Enemy.[5]

767 (722)   The false trickster was full of evil vices;
he knew enchantments and many curses.
The evil one drew circles[6] and did other tricks;
Beelzebub guided him in all his work.

768 (723)   He was very knowledgeable in giving bad advice.
The false traitor destroyed many souls,
as he was the vassal of a very evil lord;
if ordered to do evil, he did even worse.

769 (724)   People thought that he cured by knowledge;
they did not understand that Satan guided it all.
When by chance he guessed something right,
the crazy people almost adored him.

770 (725)   The Devil had put him in a prominent place:
all came to him asking advice.
What he told them, he made it seem true.
He knew how to deceive people in an evil way.

---

[4] Theophilus, who formerly was favored like Abel, becomes envious and resentful (like Abel's brother Cain). See Genesis 4.

[5] *Uestantigua*: from Latin *hostis antiquus*: "old enemy," one of the names for the devil. The etymon *hostis* (horde, throng) may also be interpreted as referring to the devil's army, thus "Ancient Horde."

[6] Magic circles, alluding to the reputation of Jews as magicians.

771 (726) All considered him a prophet, young and old;
           all ran to him like pigs to acorns.
           Those who were sick, they carried on litters;
           all said, "We will do whatever you command."

772 (727) Wretched Theophilus, without God's protection,
           was conquered by his madness and the promptings of the Devil.
           He went to ask advice from the diabolical trickster:
           how could he return to his previous status?

773 (728) The Jew told him, "If you will believe me,
           you can easily return to what you want.
           Have no doubt, if you are steadfast,
           all is recovered, if you do not repent."

774 (729) Theophilus answered him like someone drugged,
           "For that I came to you, to follow your command."
           The Jew said to him, "Be assured,
           consider your business all done.

775 (730) Go to your bed to rest, return to your house.
           Tomorrow early, while everyone sleeps,
           steal away from your men, from all your household.
           Come knock at my door and do nothing else."

776 (731) Theophilus was happy and pleased with this;
           he considered his whole business well done.
           He returned home greatly deceived;
           it would have been better had he stayed there.

777 (732) Then, the next evening, with everyone asleep,
           he stole away from his men; he went out of his house.
           He went to knock at the door, for he knew the entrance.
           The trickster was ready; he opened for him without delay.

778 (733) He took him by the hand, in the middle of the night;
           he led him out of the town to a crossroads.
           He told him, "Do not cross yourself or fear anything,
           for your whole situation will be improved tomorrow."

779 (734) In a short time, he saw many great people come,
           with candelabra and burning candles in their hands;
           ugly and not radiant, with their king in their midst.
           Now Sir Theophilus wished he were with his kin!

780 (735) The treacherous trickster took him by the hand;
           he led him to the tent where the master was.
           The king received him with sufficient great honor,
           as did the princes who were around him.

781 (736) Then the king said to him, "Don Fulano, what do you seek?
          I want you to say what present you bring me
          or what man is this that you present to me?
          I want to know right away, this you can indeed believe."

782 (737) The Jew said to him, "Lord, crowned king,
          this used to be the vicar of the bishopric.
          Everyone loved him very much; he was an honored man.
          Now they have taken it away, whence his standing is reduced.

783 (738) Therefore he comes to fall at your feet,
          so that you may recover for him what he used to have.
          If he does do you service with all his might,
          you will have a good vassal in him, in my opinion."

784 (739) The Devil said to him, "It would not be very just
          for me to seek such profit for another's vassal;
          but if he denies Christ who makes us much despised,
          I will have his benefice restored completely.

785 (740) Let him deny his Christ and Holy Mary,
          write me a contract to my liking,
          put his seal there at the end,
          and he will return to his rank with great improvement."

786 (741) Theophilus, wishing to rise in importance,
          had to consent to the pleasure of the Devil.
          He made his contract with him and validated it
          with his own seal, which he could not deny.

787 (742) He left him with this; he went back to his house:
          it was almost cockcrow when he returned.
          No one was aware of this journey of his,
          except God from whom alone nothing is hidden.

788 (743) But he lost his shadow,[7] he was always shadowless.
          He lost his good color, he remained pale.
          Not due to the power of the Devil, but as God willed,
          the unfortunate one returned to his [former] post.

789 (744) The treacherous one returned to his post;
          the bishop knew that he had badly erred.
          He had removed him from the vicarage.
          "Sir," said Theophilus, "may you be pardoned."

---

[7] Dutton (*Obras Completas*, 2:234) tells us that according to Menéndez Pidal, it was a general belief that those who had made a pact with the devil lost their shadow. Dutton suggests that *sombra*, or shadow, might also signify peace or well-being.

790 (745)   If before Theophilus had been well liked and loved,
            he was afterwards more served and much more esteemed.
            God alone knows, He who is well informed,
            whether it came to him through God or through the Devil.

791 (746)   He lived some days in this happy state,
            enjoying the bishop's love and great favor,
            receiving from the people many good gifts,
            but in the end Christ wounded him with His lance.

792 (747)   This vicar, being in this vicarage,
            became very boastful and very daring.
            He took to vainglory and great pride;
            everyone understood that he was proud.

793 (748)   The Lord, who does not want the death of sinners
            but, rather, that souls be saved and errors amended,[8]
            inflicted mortal pains on this sick man,
            the one who was deceived by evil traitors.

794 (749)   The good he had done in past times,
            the good Lord did not want lost to him.
            He resuscitated his mind that lay as dead,
            then he opened his eyes, which were asleep.

795 (750)   He breathed a little, he regained consciousness,
            he considered his case, he saw himself badly manipulated;
            he considered more deeply what he had promised.
            There Theophilus fell as dead to the ground.

796 (751)   He said to himself, "Wretched, ill-fated one,
            from the height where I was, who has knocked me down?
            I have lost my soul, scorned my body;
            the good that I have lost, I will not see recovered.

797 (752)   Wretched sinner, I do not see where to come ashore.
            I will not find anyone who will pray to God for me.
            I will die as one who lies in the middle of the sea,
            who does not see land to which he can escape.

798 (753)   Wretch, poor me, I was born in a bad hour.
            I killed myself with my own hands: my madness killed me.
            God had put me in a good position;
            now I have lost all good fortune.

---

[8] Ezekiel 33:11: "… I have no pleasure in the death of the wicked; but that the wicked turn from his way and live: turn ye, turn ye from your evil ways; for why will ye die, O house of Israel?"

799 (754) Wretch, although I may wish to return to the Glorious One,
           who the scripture says is so merciful,
           she will not want to hear me, for she is angry with me
           because I denied her; I did such a contemptible thing.

800 (755) Judas, the traitor, had no greater blame,
           he who sold his Lord for a few coins.
           I sinned over all others, wretched sinner,
           so for me no one will be a petitioner.

801 (756) I am lost to God and to Holy Mary,
           lost to the saints because of my treachery.
           I cut all the tree limbs where I had my feet;[9]
           had I not been born, it would have been much better.

802 (757) On Judgment Day, I, false traitor,
           with what face will I come before our Lord?
           Everyone will talk about me, wretched sinner.
           No one worse than I will come to the assembly.

803 (758) I saw that vicarage in a bad hour;
           I listened to the Devil, I sought my own dark day.
           The trickster, the one of the Jewish quarter, destroyed me,
           the one who destroyed many others with bad advice![10]

804 (759) I had no needs, nor did I go as a beggar;
           everyone did me honor and was pleased with me;
           but I went to ask for better than wheat bread.
           I looked for my own knife; I was my own enemy.

805 (760) I had something to wear and something to put on my feet.
           I had enough for myself; I had enough to give
           but I went bargaining for a black day.[11]
           I ought to kill myself with my own hands.

806 (761) Indeed I know that I will not be able to end this fever.
           There is no doctor or physician who can help me,
           save Holy Mary, Star of the Sea,
           but who would dare go beseech her?

---

[9] Compare *Duelo* 204 b-d. This is similar to the English expression "to saw off the branch one is sitting on." See also *Milagros* 796 (751) where Theophilus laments having been brought down from great heights.

[10] Spanish *matar*: normally "to kill," used here in the sense of "destroy." See *Milagros* 768 (723) b and 798 (753) b.

[11] "Mas fui pora mercado día negro buscar": in this context, the implication is "I went for a deal, to look for what turned out to be a black [fatal] day."

807 (762) I, stinking wretch who stinks more than a dog,
           a dog that lies rotting, not one that eats bread.
           She will not want to hear me, this I know full well,
           since I was, toward her, stupid and villainous.

808 (763) Though I would like to have the saints as intercessors,
           as they are all informed of my bad action,
           the martyrs and all the confessors are angry with me;
           much more angry are the apostles who are much greater.

809 (764) I do not want to abandon the head for the feet;
           I want to approach the Glorious Mother.
           I will fall at her feet, in front of her altar;
           waiting for her grace, I am willing to die there.

810 (765) There I will fast, I will do penance.
           I will weep, I will say prayers,
           I will mortify my flesh, food for worms,
           so that she will take notice of me in some season.

811 (766) Although I denied her like a crazy fool,
           for I was deceived by a false Jew,
           steadfastly I believe; I trust in her mercy,
           for of her was born Christ who was my Savior.

812 (767) If I go to her temple tomorrow, very early,
           it will happen to me as it happened to the Egyptian,[12]
           who suffered great scorn as a bad woman,
           until the Glorious One acted as intermediary for her.

813 (768) Although God in his mercy may allow me
           to enter to see the Majesty,[13]
           lightning or fire or some other storm will come;
           it will do harm to many because of my evilness.

814 (769) Although God may allow me to do all this,
           although He may allow me to relate my affliction in peace,
           I cannot imagine with what words to begin,
           nor do I imagine how I can open my mouth."

[12] Santa María Egipciaca (354?-431?), known in English as St. Mary of Egypt. A penitent harlot who became a saint, she—like St. Mary Magdalene—is a model of the repentent sinner.
[13] Spanish *majestat*: *Majestat* designates the typical image of the enthroned Virgin with the Christ child on her lap.

815 (770) He abandoned his house and all he had;
he did not tell anyone what he wanted to do.
He went to the church in the town where he lived,
weeping as much as he could.

816 (771) He threw himself at the feet of the Holy Queen,
who is godmother and counsel of sinners.
"Lady," he said, "help my wretched soul;
to your mercy I come seeking medicine.

817 (772) Lady, I am lost and I am abandoned.
I wrote a bad contract and I am badly deceived.
I gave, I know not how, my soul to the Devil:
now I understand that I made a bad bargain.

818 (773) Blessed Lady, Crowned Queen,
you who always pray for wayward people,
do not have me go rejected from your house,
otherwise some will say that you no longer have power.

819 (774) Lady, you who are the Door of Paradise,
in whom the King of Glory put so many blessings,
Lady, turn your beautiful face to me,
for I am very repentant of the contract.

820 (775) Turn towards me, Mother, your precious face:
if you are angry with me, you are justified in being so.
Let not this affair grow any worse than it already is;
turn to Theophilus, Glorious Queen."

821 (776) Forty days he continued this plea;
he suffered great tribulation day and night.
Only of this was he mindful, not of any other thing:
to call on the Glorious One with a steadfast heart.

822 (777) Because Theophilus persisted in his determination,
it pleased the King of Heaven on the fortieth day;
the Holy Virgin Mary appeared to him at night.
She said harsh words to him as one who is angry.

823 (778) She said to him, "What are you doing, ill-fated man?
You are writing on ice, you are pleading in madness.
I am fed up with your case: you cause me great bitterness,
you are very persistent, you vex beyond measure.

824 (779) You make crazy and vain petitions;
you have denied us, you looked for another lord.
Sir, evil renegade, much worse than Judas,
I do not know who will petition the Creator for you.

825 (780) I would be ashamed to petition my Son;
I would not dare to begin the speech.
The One whom you denied and sought to grieve
will not want to hear us or pardon you."

826 (781) "Mother," said Theophilus, "for God and charity,
do not look to my merit, look to your goodness.
In all that you say, you tell the whole truth,
for I am dirty and false, full of evil.

827 (782) I am repentant, Lady, may penitence avail me;
it saves souls, such is our belief.
It saved Peter[14] who committed a great wrong
and cleansed Longinus[15] of a very great violence.

828 (783) Holy Magdalene,[16] sister of Lazarus,
sinner beyond measure, for she was a loose woman;
I tell you the same thing about the Egyptian:[17]
it cured them both, it cures all evil.

829 (784) All at once, David committed three mortal sins,[18]
all ugly and dirty and all cardinal.
He made his penitence with heartfelt moans;
the Father of the penitents pardoned him.

830 (785) The towns of Nineveh[19] that were condemned
did penance crying for their sins.
All their failings were pardoned;
many who were spared would have been destroyed.

831 (786) This speech, Lady, is yours to consider:
doing penance thus should help me.
Mother, if you wished and it were your pleasure,
this doctrine ought not come to an end with me."

832 (787) He was quiet after all this. Then Holy Mary spoke,
and she said, "Theophilus, you have a very complicated plea.
Indeed, I would pardon easily my dishonor,
but that of my Son, I truly would not dare to.

---

[14] Reference to the denial of St. Peter (Matthew 27:67-75).

[15] Longinus is traditionally the centurion present at the crucifixion.

[16] St. Mary Magdalene.

[17] See *Miracles* 812 (767) b.

[18] David's three sins were the killing of Uriah, his adultery with Bathsheba, and his ordering of the census of the Hebrews (2 Samuel 24).

[19] See Jonah 3, Matthew 7:41, and Luke 11:32.

833 (788) Although you denied me and did a vile deed,
     I wish to advise you with true counsel.
     Turn to my Son, for He is angry with you,
     since He considers Himself very mistreated by you.

834 (789) Pray to Him constantly with very great fervor,
     deny the Devil, confirm your belief.
     He is very merciful and very knowledgeable;
     He kills, He gives life, for His is such power."

835 (790) "Mother," said Theophilus, "may you always be praised.
     It was like Easter, a great day when you were born.
     My soul is greatly comforted with this;
     your word brings proven medicine.

836 (791) I would not dare to implore your Son.
     To my misfortune, I sought to grieve Him greatly,
     but I trust in Him as I should trust,
     and I want to demonstrate my belief to you.

837 (792) I believe that there is one God and that He is Trinity,
     Trinity in Persons, one the Deity;
     there is no diversity in the Persons:
     Father, Son and Spirit, They are truly One.[20]

838 (793) I believe in the incarnation of Jesus Christ,
     who was born of you, Mother, for our redemption.
     He preached the Gospel, then He suffered the Passion;
     on the third day He was resurrected.

839 (794) I believe completely in His Ascension,
     that He sent the grace of consolation.[21]
     I believe in the last regeneration,[22]
     when good and bad will receive their reward.

840 (795) Mother, I believe it all, I am very certain of it,
     of everything Christ orders a Christian to believe,
     but I am in great shame, in very great fear,
     for I was, my Lady, very villainous to Him.

---

[20] The doctrine of the Holy Trinity was defined at the Council of Nicea (335) and the Council of Constantinople (381). Theophilus's words are an expression of faith according to the Nicene Creed and, especially with his insistence on "Trinity in unity," the later so-called Athanasian Creed.

[21] The descent of the Holy Spirit at Pentecost.

[22] The General Resurrection and Last Judgment.

841 (796) He will not want to hear me, a bad, dirty,
and discredited man, because it is not fitting.
Mother, I fear so much that I would be rejected,
that our case would end up much worse.

842 (797) If it is to turn out well, or you want to help me,
you must work on this case, Mother.
Do not tell me to search for another advocate,
for even if I searched, I could not find one.

843 (798) You are helpful in everything, thanks to the Creator!
In beseeching your Son, your Father, your Lord,
whatever you say and wish,
He will do it all for you with great love.

844 (799) What you never did for another sinner,
do it not for Theophilus, but for Our Lord.
Return me to the grace of your Holy Flower,
the Flower that you bore without stain or pain.

845 (800) Blessed Lady, Illustrious Queen,
calling still upon your boldness, I wish to tell you something else:
If I do not recover the letter I wrote to my ruin,
I will not consider myself free from the evil noose."

846 (801) Holy Mary said, "Sir Dirt, Sir Evil,
the letter you wrote with your wicked leader,
that later you sealed with your own seal,
lies in a small corner of Hell.

847 (802) My Son will not want, on account of your plight,
to undertake such a pilgrimage, descending to Hell,
for it is a stinking place, with a stinking brotherhood.
It would be very daring just to suggest it to Him."

848 (803) "Lady, blessed among all women,
your Son will want what you want.
He will give you everything that you request;
the letter will come to me if you so wish.

849 (804) Wherever the Devil has put it,
if He only wishes, then it will be returned.
Lady, you are the health and life of all;
I cannot beg you more, nor do I know what more to ask of you."

850 (805) Holy Mary, Proven Good Comfort, said to him,
"Be in peace, Theophilus. I see you quite tormented.
I will go, if I can, to carry out the mission.
May God have it carried out quickly!"

851 (806) The Blessed Mother, having given this speech,
vanished from before him; he could not see anything,
but his will was comforted,
for her solace is proven medicine.

852 (807) If Theophilus was very devoted before,
after this he was more remorseful.
Three days and three nights he was in prayer;
he neither ate, nor drank, nor left off Scripture reading.

853 (808) His eyes resembled two perennial fountains;
he hit his head against the hard stones;
his fists gave his chest great blows.
He said, "Help me, Mother, as you help others!

854 (809) Help me, Holy Mother, hear my cries,
you who do such things and others even greater.
You know my affliction; you understand my pain;
do not forget me, Mother, Solace of Sinners."

855 (810) Theophilus suffered much during this three-day period,
lying on the ground praying continuously.
Never did a Christian suffer more in as many days;
in the end, his suffering was not in vain.

856 (811) The Queen of Glory, Mother, Holy Mary,
visited him again on the third day.
She brought him greetings, joyous news,
which anyone who lies in sickness would want.

857 (812) "Know, Theophilus," She said, "that your prayers,
your great moans, your afflictions,
have been carried to Heaven with great processions.
The angels carried them, singing sweet sounds.

858 (813) My Son is pleased with your efforts;
the wrong that you did, you have amended well.
If you persevere as you have begun,
your case is well placed and very well assured.

859 (814) I spoke about your case willingly,
I bent my knees before the Majesty.
God has pardoned you, a great charity has He done;
it is necessary that you be firm in your goodness."

860 (815) "Mother of God, Our Lord," said Theophilus,
"because of you this comes to me; I am well aware of it.
You freed from condemnation a sinful soul
that would lie in Hell with Judas the traitor.

861 (816) But with all this that you have done,
           still I am unsure, still I remain unsatisfied,
           until I recover the letter
           which I wrote when I had denied your Son.

862 (817) Mother, if I recovered the letter
           and saw it burned in a fire,
           even if I were then to die, I would not care,
           for my soul, Lady, is badly entangled.

863 (818) Mother, indeed I know that you are exasperated with this matter,
           but if you fail me, I have nothing to rely on.
           Lady, you who have begun this matter,
           have the letter returned to me; it will indeed be in good keeping."

864 (819) "It will not stay there for that reason," said the Glorious One,
           "let the matter not be damaged for so little."
           The Precious Queen disappeared from him;
           She went hurriedly to search for this letter.

865 (820) Theophilus, who was discouraged, took heart
           and no wonder since he was so distressed;
           he returned to his study as was his custom.
           Never was there in this world a more troubled confessor.

866 (821) He returned to his study to do his penance,
           to be very abstinent in eating and drinking;
           he had all his faith in the Glorious One,
           that God through her would give him His love.

867 (822) On the third night he lay asleep,
           for he suffered great torment; he was scarcely conscious.
           The Glorious One came to him with the errand completed,
           quietly and without any noise, his letter in hand.

868 (823) The Wife of Christ, maiden and mother,
           cast it down to him and it struck him.
           Sir Theophilus awoke, from death he returned to life;
           he found in his lap the ill-conceived letter.

869 (824) With this Theophilus was happy and heartened:
           he saw the letter returned to his hand.
           There he found that he was well cured of the fever.
           He held tight to the letter and fulfilled his three days of prayer.

870 (825) Theophilus, the confessor, was very happy
           when he held the letter in his power.
           He gave thanks to Christ and to Holy Mary,
           for she had taken care of his situation.

871 (826) He said, "Good Lady, may you always be praised,
may you always be blessed, always glorified.
To sinners you are well proven,
for never was there born another so sweet or so helpful.

872 (827) May you always be blessed, may your Fruit be praised.
Holy is your name, holier is His.
You took me, Mother, out of the diabolic pit,
where always, *sine fine*,[23] I would lie suffocated.

873 (828) Blessed Lady, Mother, Holy Mary,
I cannot tell you how much I thank you.
Mother, give me intelligence, wisdom, and knowledge
with which I may praise you, for I would do so very gladly.

874 (829) Powerful Queen of honored deeds,
who always works to save the wayward,
attain for me, Lady, pardon from my sins,
so that I may worthily praise your great good.

875 (830) Mother of the King of Glory, out of compassion,
purify my lips and my will,
so that I may worthily praise your goodness,
for you have done exceedingly great charity for me."

876 (831) The next day, after this had occurred,
when the Glorious Mother had brought the letter,
it was Sunday, a wonderful day
when all the Christian people go about happily.

877 (832) The entire population came to hear Mass,
to take the blessed bread, to receive the holy water.
The bishop of the town wanted to say Mass;
the good man wanted to fulfill his office.

878 (833) Theophilus, the confessor, a penitent Christian,
went to the church with his letter in hand.
He prostrated himself at the feet of the good celebrant;
he confessed the whole story from beginning to end.

879 (834) He made his confession, pure and true,
how he led his life from an early age,
then how he was taken from the path by envy,
which blinded him in a strange way.

---

[23] Latin: "without end", eternally.

880 (835) How he went to the Jew, a renegade rogue,
           how he had given him dirty and unsound advice,
           how he had made a pact with the Devil,
           and how the pact was confirmed by a letter.

881 (836) How, through the Glorious One, he had recovered that document,
           the one he had sealed with his seal.
           He did not leave out a thing, small or large,
           until he had told all he had been through.

882 (837) He showed him the letter that he held in his fist,
           in which all the vigor of the bad pact lay.
           The bishop who saw this thing crossed himself;
           the matter was so enormous that he hardly believed it.

883 (838) "Ite missa est"[24] said, the Mass ended
           and everyone was eager to leave.
           The bishop made a sign with his holy hand;
           all the people remained as they had stood.

884 (839) He said, "Hear, gentlefolk, of a great event:
           never in this world did you hear of one so great.
           You will see how the Devil, who uses evil tricks,
           badly deceives those who do not guard themselves from him.

885 (840) This our canon and our companion,
           moved by his madness and a false adviser,
           went to seek the smart and crafty Devil
           to recover an office he held before.

886 (841) He knew how to deceive him, the false traitor;
           he told him to deny Christ, his Lord,
           and Holy Mary, who was a good sister,
           and then he would return him to all his honor.

887 (842) This wretched sinner agreed to it;
           he made his pact with him, this was the worst.
           He corroborated that work with his own seal.
           Lord, Our God, guard us from such a friend.

888 (843) God, who always desires the health of sinners,
           who suffered great pains to save us,
           did not want such works to be fruitful,
           for they were cultivated by evil farmers.

---

[24] Latin: "Go, Mass is over," the final words of the mass.

889 (844) If the Glorious Virgin had not defended him,
the unhappy one would surely have been led astray,
but her holy grace has now helped him.
She has recovered the letter; if not, he would be lost.

890 (845) I hold it in my fist, you can see it;
there is no doubt here; you must believe it.
We must then all render thanks to God
and to the Holy Virgin who deigned to defend him."

891 (846) All rendered thanks, women and men;
they proffered many lauds and great processions,
weeping greatly, saying prayers
to the Glorious Mother, good in all seasons.

892 (847) The "Te Deum laudamus"[25] was sung loudly,
"Tibi laus, tibi gloria"[26] was repeated well.
They said "Salve Regina";[27] they sang it with gusto
and other songs sweet of sound and word.

893 (848) Then the bishop ordered a great fire built;
with the people who were in the church seeing him,
he threw that letter into the flames.
It burned; parchment and wax turned into ash.

894 (849) As soon as the people had acclaimed their invocation,
the letter was burned. Thanks to the Creator!
The holy confessor received *Corpus Domini*,[28]
with all the people who were around seeing him.

895 (850) As soon as Theophilus, a mortified body,
received *Corpus Domini* and was fully confessed,
he was surrounded by brightness within sight of the people,
a splendor so great it could not be imagined.

896 (851) The people were certain that he was a holy man
and that he, for whom God did so much, was of great merit,
and God covered him with such a precious cloak,
from which the Devil took great affliction.

---

[25] Latin: "We praise thee O God"; the opening words of the hymn generally known as the "Te Deum".

[26] Latin: "Praise to thee, glory to thee."

[27] Latin: "Hail, Queen." First words of a prayer or hymn to the Virgin Mary traditionally sung as an antiphon.

[28] Latin: "the body of the Lord"; Theophilus receives Holy Communion. The phrase is repeated in 895(850) b.

897 (852) His face was shining, emitting rays of light,
           like that of Moses when he carried the Law,[29]
           or like St. Andrew when he was on the cross;
           with this the Creator was giving him no small honor.

898 (853) When the people and the gentlefolk saw this,
           that such shining rays were issuing from his face,
           they sang other lauds and other new songs.
           All were ardent in praising the Glorious One.

899 (854) Theophilus so persisted in his contemplation
           that vainglory did not move him, nor did he become proud.
           He returned to the church where he had seen the vision;
           never at any time was he more devout.

900 (855) The good man understood, God made him certain,
           that his last day was drawing quite near.
           He divided what he had; no money was left;
           he gave it all to the poor; he made a good planting.

901 (856) He asked for pardon from those of the neighborhood;
           they all pardoned him willingly.
           He kissed the hand of the bishop; he acted correctly;
           he died on the third day; God granted him mercy.

902 (857) He lived only three days after receiving communion,
           after the document had turned to ash.
           He died in the church where he had been visited;
           in this same place, his body was buried.

903 (858) Thus died Theophilus, the fortunate.
           The error he committed, may God be praised,
           he completely amended it; he pleased God.
           The Glorious One helped him; may she be much thanked.

904 (859) Gentlefolk, such a miracle as we have heard,
           we must never cast into oblivion.
           Otherwise, we will all be of bad conscience,
           for we have no common sense or acquired wisdom.

905 (860) So says St. Paul,[30] the good preacher,
           who was a loyal vassal of God, Our Lord,
           that all things written that are of the Creator,
           all preach the salvation of man the sinner.

---

[29] Exodus 39:29-30, 35.
[30.] See Romans 15:4.

906 (861) From this story, understand and appreciate
how much penitence is worth to the one who knows how to use it.
If not for it, you could swear
Sir Theophilus would have gone to a bad place.

907 (862) Had the Glorious Mother, who deigned to help him,
not understood him, she would not have come to see him.
Whoever wishes to listen and to believe me,
let him live in penitence, and he may be saved.

908 (863) Friends, if you wish to save your souls,
if you wish to take my advice,
make your confessions, do not delay,
and take penance and think about how to keep it.

909 (864) May Jesus Christ will it, as may the Glorious Virgin,
without whom no good thing is done,
that we endure this sorrowful life,
so that we may gain the lasting and luminous one.
Amen.

910 (865) The Glorious Mother, Queen of Heaven,
who was for Theophilus such an excellent godmother,
may she be a help for us in this wretched world,
so that we cannot fall into evil ruin.
Amen.

911 (866) Mother, be mindful of your Gonzalo
who was the versifier of your miracles.
Pray for him, Lady, to the Creator,
since your privilege helps the sinner.
Win for him the grace of God, Our Lord.
Amen.

Bibliography

Editions and translations

Baños, Fernando, ed. *Milagros de Nuestra Señora*. Barcelona: Crítica, 1997.

Beltrán, Vicente, ed. *Milagros de Nuestra Señora*. 3d ed. Barcelona: Planeta, 1990.

Bolaño e Isla, Amancio, ed. *Milagros de Nuestra Señora. Vida de Santo Domingo de Silos. Vida de San Millán de la Cogolla. Vida de Santa Oria. Martirio de San Lorenzo*. Modern version with prologue. Mexico: Porrúa, 1965.

Devoto, Daniel, ed. *Milagros de Nuestra Señora*. Modern version. Odres Nuevos. Madrid: Castalia, 1969.

Dutton, Brian, ed. *Los Milagros de Nuestra Señora de Gonzalo de Berceo*. 2d ed. Vol. 2 of *Obras completas* of Gonzalo de Berceo. London: Támesis, 1980.

Dutton, Brian, et al., ed. Berceo, *Obra completa*. Madrid: Espasa-Calpe, 1992.

Gerli, Michael, ed. *Milagros de Nuestra Señora*. 4th ed. Madrid: Cátedra, 1989.

Hamel, A., ed. *Milagros de Nuestra Señora*. Halle: Niemeyer, 1926.

Janer, Florencio, ed. *Los Milagros de Nuestra Señora*. In *Biblioteca de Autores Españoles* 57, 103–31. Madrid: Real Academia Española, 1852.

Matus Romo, Eugenio, ed. *Milagros de Nuestra Señora*. Modern version with prologue and notes. Santiago de Chile: Universitaria, 1956.

Montoya Martínez, Jesus, ed. *El libro de los Milagros de Nuestra Señora*. Granada: Universidad de Granada, 1986.

Mount, Richard Terry, and Annette Grant Cash, trans. *Miracles of Our Lady by Gonzalo de Berceo*. Lexington: University Press of Kentucky, 1997.

Narbona, A., ed. *Milagros de Nuestra Señora*. Madrid: Alce, 1984.

Sánchez, Tomás Antonio. *Colección de poesías castellanas anteriores al siglo XV*. Vol. 2. Madrid: A. de Sancha, 1779–1790.

Studies

Ackerman, Jane E. "The Theme of Mary's Power in the *Milagros de Nuestra Señora*." *Journal of Hispanic Philology* 8 (1983): 16–31.

Alonso, Dámaso. "Berceo y los 'topoi'." In idem, *De los Siglos Oscuros al de Oro*, 74–85. 2a ed. Madrid: Gredos, 1964.

Alvar, Manuel. "*Tienllas* (Berceo, *Mil.*: 246a, 273c)." In *Romanica Europae et Americana: Festschrift für Harri Meier*, ed. Hans Dieter Bork, Artur Greive, and Dieter Woll, 22–26. Bonn: Bouvier, 1980.

Andrachuk, Gregory Peter. "Berceo and the *Clérigo simple*." *La Corónica* 15 (1987): 264–67.

Arnold, Harrison H. "Irregular Hemistichs in the *Milagros* of Gonzalo de Berceo." *PMLA* 50 (1935): 335–51.

———. "Synalepha in Old Spanish Poetry: Berceo." *Hispanic Review* 4 (1936): 141–58.

Artiles, Joaquín. *Los recursos literarios de Berceo*. 2a ed. Madrid: Gredos, 1968.

Baldwin, Spurgeon. "Narrative Technique in Gonzalo de Berceo." *Kentucky Romance Quarterly* 23 (1976): 17–28.

Baro, José. *Glosario completo de los "Milagros de Nuestra Señora" de Gonzalo de Berceo*. Boulder: Society of Spanish and Spanish-American Studies, 1987.

Bartha, J. K. "Four Lexical Notes on Berceo's *Milagros de Nuestra Señora*." *Romance Philology* 37 (1983): 56–62.

———. *Vocabulario de los "Milagros de Nuestra Señora" de Gonzalo de Berceo*. Normal, IL: Applied Literature Press, 1980.

Beltrán, Luis. "Between Poetry and the Play: Possible Traces of a Lost Theatre." In *Los hallazgos de la lectura: Estudio dedicado a Miguel Enguídanos*, ed. John Crispin, Enrique Pupo-Walker, and Luis Lorenzo-Rivero, 11–27. Madrid: Porrúa Turanzas, 1989.

Bermejo-Cabrero, José Luis. "El mundo jurídico en Berceo." *Revista de la Universidad de Madrid* 70–71 (*Homenaje a Menéndez Pidal* 2) (1969): 33–52.

Boreland, Helen. "Typology in Berceo's *Milagros*: The *Judiezno* and the *Abadesa preñada*." *Bulletin of Hispanic Studies* 60 (1983): 15–29.

Boubée, Joseph. "La poésie mariale. Gonzalo de Berceo (1198?–1260?)." *Etudes des Pères de la Compagnie de Jésus* 90 (1904): 512–36.

Buceta, Erasmo. "Un dato para los *Milagros* de Berceo." *Revista de Filología Española* 9 (1922): 400–2.

Burkard, Richard. "Narrative Art and Narrative Inconsistency in Berceo's *milagro* of the Shipwrecked Pilgrim." *Romanistisches Jahrbuch* 40 (1989): 280–91.

———. "Revenge of a Saint or Revenge of the Deity? Ambiguousness in Five of Berceo's Mary Legends." *Romanistisches Jahrbuch* 37 (1986): 251–63.

———. "Two Types of Salvation in Berceo's *Milagros de Nuestra Señora*." *Hispanic Journal* 9 (1988): 23–35.

Burke, James F. "The Ideal of Perfection: The Image of the Garden-Monastery in Gonzalo de Berceo's *Milagros de Nuestra Señora*." In *Medieval, Renais-*

sance and Folklore Studies in Honor of John Esten Keller, ed. Joseph R. Jones, 20–38. Newark, DE: Juan de la Cuesta, 1980.

Cabada Gómez, Manuel. "La metafábula." *Senara: Revista de Filoloxia* 1 (1979): 151–70.

Campo, Agustín del. "La técnica alegórica en la introducción de los *Milagros de Nuestra Señora*." *Revista de Filología Española* 28 (1944): 15–57.

Capuano, Thomas. "Agricultural Elements in Berceo's Descriptions of Hayfields." *Hispania* 69 (1986): 808–12.

———. "*Semencero* in Berceo's *Milagros*." *Journal of Hispanic Philology* 8 (1984): 233–38.

Carrizo Rueda, Sofía. "Textos de la clerecía y de la lírica cortesana y la cuestión de 'lo oficial' y 'lo popular'." *Revista de Dialectología y Tradiciones Populares* 44 (1989): 27–39.

Castro, Américo. "Gonzalo de Berceo." In idem, *La realidad histórica de España*, 341–50. Mexico: Porrúa, 1954.

Cirot, Georges. "L'expression dans Gonzalo de Berceo." *Bulletin Hispanique* 44 (1942): 5–16.

Darbord, Michele. "Los *Milagros de Nuestra Señora* de Berceo: Rhétorique et poésie." *Iberia* 1 (1977): 71–79.

Devoto, Daniel. *Gonzalo de Berceo et la musique. Etudes sur deux mots espagnols anciens*. Paris: La Sorbonne, 1955.

———. "Notas al texto de los *Milagros de Nuestra Señora* de Berceo." *Bulletin Hispanique* 59 (1957): 5–25.

———. "Los ojos de Berceo." *Realidad* [Buenos Aires] 14 (1949): 68-78.

———. "Tres notas sobre Berceo y la historia eclesiástica española." *Bulletin Hispanique* 80 (1968): 261–99.

———. "Tres notas sobre Berceo y la polifonía medieval." *Bulletin Hispanique* 82 (1980): 293–352.

Diz, Marta Ana. "Berceo: La ordalía del niño judío." *Filología* 23 (1988): 3–15.

———. *Historias de certidumbre: los "Milagros" de Berceo*. Newark, DE: Juan de la Cuesta, 1995.

Drayson, Elizabeth. "Some Possible Sources for the Introduction to Berceo's *Milagros de Nuestra Señora*." *Medium Aevum* 50 (1981): 274–83.

Duarte, Sergio. "Elementos dramáticos en cinco *Milagros de Nuestra Señora* de Berceo." *Duquesne Hispanic Review* 11 (1972): 35–52.

Dutton, Brian. "Berceo's *Milagros de Nuestra Señora* and the Virgin of Yuso." *Bulletin of Hispanic Studies* 44 (1967): 81–87.

———. "The Profession of Gonzalo de Berceo and the Paris Manuscript of the *Libro de Alexandre*." *Bulletin of Hispanic Studies* 37 (1960): 137–45.

Dyer, Nancy Joe. "A Note on the Use of *verso agudo* in the *Milagros de Nuestra Señora*." *Romance Notes* 18 (1977): 252–55.

Fernández y González, Francisco. "Berceo, o el poeta sagrado de la España cristiana del siglo XIII." *La Razón* 1 (1860): 222-35, 300-22, 393–402.

Ferrer, José. "Berceo: *Milagros de Nuestra Señora*. Aspectos de su estilo." *Hispania* 33 (1950): 46–50.

Finke, Wayne H. "La imagen de la mujer en *Los Milagros* de Berceo." In *Festschrift for José Cid Pérez*, ed. Alberto Gutiérrez de la Solana and Elio Alba-Buffill, 211–15. New York: Senda Nueva de Ediciones. 1981.

Foresti Serrano, Carlos. "Sobre la Introducción de los *Milagros de Nuestra Señora*." *Anales de la Universidad de Chile* 107 (1957): 361–67.

García de la Fuente, Olegario. "Sobre el léxico bíblico de Berceo." In *Actas de las III Jornadas de Estudios Berceanos*, ed. Claudio García Turza, 73–89. Logroño: Instituto de Estudios Riojanos, 1981.

Garci-Gómez, Miguel. "La abadesa embargada por el pie." *Revista de Dialectología y Tradiciones Populares* 44 (1989): 7–26.

Gariano, Carmelo. *Análisis estilístico de los "Milagros de Nuestra Señora" de Berceo*. 2a ed. Madrid: Gredos, 1971.

———. "El género literario en los *Milagros* de Berceo." *Hispania* 49 (1966): 740–47.

Garofoli, Bruna. "L'aggettivazione nei *Milagros* di Berceo: L'uomo." In *Actas del Congreso Internacional sobre la lengua y la literatura en tiempos de Alfonso X*, 239–56. Murcia: Universidad, 1985.

Garrido Gallardo, M.A. "Una clave interpretativa para tres 'recursos literarios' fundamentales en los *Milagros de Nuestra Señora*." *Revista de Filología Española* 59 (1977): 279–84.

Gerli, E. Michael. "Poet and Pilgrim: Discourse, Language, Imagery, and Audience in Berceo's *Milagros de Nuestra Señora*." In *Hispanic Medieval Studies in Honor of Samuel G. Armistead*, ed. idem and Harvey L. Sharrer, 140–51. Madison: Hispanic Seminary of Medieval Studies, 1992.

———. "La tipología bíblica y la introducción de los *Milagros de Nuestra Señora*." *Bulletin of Hispanic Studies* 62 (1985): 7–14.

Gicovate, Bernard. "Notas sobre el estilo y la originalidad de Gonzalo de Berceo." *Bulletin Hispanique* 62 (1960): 5–15.

Giménez Resano, Gaudioso. "Cómo vulgariza Berceo sus fuentes latinas." *Berceo* 94-95 (1978): 17–29.

———. *El mester poético de Gonzalo de Berceo*. Logroño: Instituto de Estudios Riojanos, 1976.

Gimeno Casalduero, Joaquín. "Homenajes I: Elementos románicos, y su función, en el milagro XIV de Berceo: 'La imagen respetada'." In *Estudios en homenaje a Enrique Ruiz–Fornells*, ed. Juan Fernández Jiménez, José Labrador Herraiz, and L. Teresa Valdivieso, 259–66. Erie: Asociación de Licenciados y Doctores Españoles en Estados Unidos, 1990.

Girón Alconchel, José Luis. "Sobre la lengua poética de Berceo (y II): El estilo indirecto libre en los *Milagros* y sus fuentes latinas." *Revista de Filología* 4 (1988): 145–62.

Goldberg, Harriet. "The Voice of the Author in the Works of Gonzalo de Berceo and in the *Libro de Alexandre* and the *Poema de Fernán González*." *La Corónica* 8 (1980): 100–12.

González-Casanovas, R. J. "Marian Devotion as Gendered Discourse in Berceo and Alfonso X: Popular Reception of the *Milagros* and *Cantigas*." *Bulletin of the Cantigueiros de Santa María* 4 (1992): 17-31.

Guillén, Jorge. "Lenguaje poético: Berceo." In idem, *Lenguaje y poesía*, 13–39. Madrid: Revista de Occidente, 1962.

Gutiérrez-Lasanta, F. "Gonzalo de Berceo, cantor de la Gloriosa." *Berceo* 5 (1950): 733–47.

Gybbon-Monypenny, G. M. "The Spanish *mester de clerecía* and Its Intended Public: Concerning the Validity as Evidence of Passages of Direct Address to the Audience." In *Medieval Studies Presented to Eugene Vinaver*, 230–44.. Manchester: Manchester University Press, 1965.

Kantor, Sofía. "Un Récit à dominante modale-illocutoire: 'El clérigo simple' de Gonzalo de Berceo." *Strumenti Critici* 41 (1980): 60–91.

Keller, John E. "The Enigma of Berceo's *Milagro XXV*." *Symposium* 29 (1975): 361–70.

———. *Gonzalo de Berceo*. Twayne World Authors Series 187. New York: Twayne, 1972.

———. "A Medieval Folklorist." In *Folklore Studies in Honor of Arthur Palmer Hudson*, special issue of *North Carolina Folklore* 13 (1965): 19–24.

———. "On the Morality of Berceo, Alfonso X, don Juan Manuel and Juan Ruiz." In *Homenaje a don Agapito Rey*, ed. Josep Roca Pons, 117–30. Bloomington: Department. of Spanish and Portuguese, Indiana University, 1980.

———. *Pious Brief Narrative in Medieval Castilian and Galician Verse: From Berceo to Alfonso X*. Lexington: University Press of Kentucky, 1978.

Kelley, Mary Jane. "Spinning Virgin Yarns: Narrative, Miracles and Salvation in Gonzalo de Berceo's *Milagros de Nuestra Señora*." *Hispania* 74 (1991): 814–23.

Kelly, Edith L. "'Fer', 'far', 'facer', 'fazer', in Three Works of Berceo." *Hispanic Review* 3 (1935): 127–37.

Kinkade, Richard P. "Sermons in the Round: The *Mester de Clerecía* as Dramatic Art." In *Studies in Honor of Gustavo Correa*, ed. C. B. Faulhaber et al., 127–36. Potomac, MD: Scripta Humanistica, 1986.

Kirby, Steven D. "Berceo's *descanto*." *Hispanic Review* 43 (1975): 181–90.

Lanchetas, Rufino. *Gramática y vocabulario de las obras de Berceo*. Madrid: Rivadeneyra, 1900.

Landa, Luis. "'La deuda pagada' de Rasi a Gonzalo de Berceo." *Sefarad: Revista de Estudios Hebraicos, Sefardíes y de Oriente Próximo* 47 (1987): 81–86.

Lewis, Julie. "La estrella, la sombra y el centro en los *Milagros* de Berceo." *Abside* 37 (1973): 110–19.

Lida, María Rosa. "Estar en (un) baño, estar en un lecho de rosas." *Revista de Filología Española* 3 (1941): 263–70.

Lope Blanch, Juan M. "La expresión temporal en Berceo." *Nueva Revista de Filología Hispánica* 10 (1956): 36–41.

López García, A. "Los códigos sintagmáticos de la narración (a próposito de la originalidad del Teófilo de Berceo)." *Berceo* 91 (1976): 147–66.

López Morales, H. "Los narradores de los *Milagros de Nuestra Señora*." In *Actas de las III Jornadas de Estudios Berceanos*, ed. García Turza, 101–11.

Loveluck, Juan. "En torno a los *Milagros* de Gonzalo de Berceo." *Atenea* 108 (1951): 669–84.

Lugones, N. A. "A los bonos da trigo, a los malos avena." *Berceo* 93 (1977): 171–79.

Marechal, Leopoldo. "El epíteto peyorativo en Berceo." *Kentucky Romance Quarterly* 21 (1974): 309–16.

Menéndez Peláez, J. "La tradición mariológica en Berceo." In *Actas de las III Jornadas de Estudios Berceanos*, ed. García Turza, 113–27.

Molina, R. A. "Gonzalo de Berceo y el lenguaje oral." *Quaderni Ibero–Americani* 37 (1969): 8–12.

Montoya Martínez, Jesús. "El alegorismo, premisa necesaria al vocabulario de los *Milagros de Nuestra Señora*." *Studi Mediolatini e Volgari* 30 (1984): 167–90.

———. "El milagro literario hispánico." In *Proceedings of the 10th Louisiana Conference on Hispanic Languages and Literatures*, ed. Gilbert Paolini, 211–20. New Orleans: Tulane University, 1989.

———. "El prólogo de Gonzalo de Berceo al libro de los *Milagros de Nuestra Señora*." *La Corónica* 13 (1985): 175–89.

Mount, Richard Terry. "Levels of Meaning: Grains, Bread, and Bread Making as Informative Images in Berceo." *Hispania* 76 (1993): 49–54.

———. "Light Imagery in the Works of Gonzalo de Berceo." In *Studies in Language and Literature, Proceedings of the 23rd Mountain Interstate Foreign Language Conference*, ed. Charles Nelson, 425–30. Richmond: Department of Foreign Languages, Eastern Kentucky University, 1976.

Nelson, Dana. "Generic vs. Individual Style: The Presence of Berceo in the *Alexandre*." *Revue de Philologie* 29 (1975): 143–84.

Nykl, Alois R. "Old Spanish Terms of Small Value." *Modern Language Notes* 42 (1927): 311-33; 46 (1931): 166–70.

Perry, T. Anthony. *Art and Meaning in Berceo's "Vida de Santa Oria".* New Haven: Yale University Press, 1968.

Prat-Ferrer, Juan José. "Estructura y función de los *Milagros de Nuestra Señora* de Gonzalo de Berceo." Ph.D. diss., University of California at Los Angeles, 1989.

Resnick, Seymour. "The Jew as Portrayed in Early Spanish Literature." *Hispania* 34 (1951): 54–58.

Rey, Agapito. "Correspondence of the Spanish Miracles of the Virgin." *Romanic Review* 19 (1928): 151–53.

Rozas, Juan Manuel. "Composición literaria y visión del mundo: *El clérigo ignorante* de Berceo." In *Studia Hispanica in honorem Rafael Lapesa*, 3:431–52. Madrid: Gredos, 1975.

Ruiz y Ruiz, Lina A. "Gonzalo de Berceo y Alfonso El Sabio: *Los Milagros de Nuestra Señora* y *Las Cantigas*." *Revista de la Universidad de San Carlos* [Guatemala] 24 (1951): 22–90.

Salmón, Josefa. "El paisaje en Berceo, Garcilaso y Balbuena: Tres concepciones del universo." *Prismal/Cabral* 7–8 (1982): 57-73.

Saugnieux, Joël. *Berceo y las culturas del siglo XIII.* Logroño: Instituto de Estudios Riojanos, 1982.

Scholberg, Kenneth R. "Minorities in Medieval Castilian Literature." *Hispania* 37 (1954): 203–8.

Snow, Joseph T. "Gonzalo de Berceo and the Miracle of Saint Ildefonso: Portrait of the Medieval Artist at Work." *Hispania* 65 (1982): 1–11.

Sobejano, Gonzalo. "El epíteto en Gonzalo de Berceo." In *El epíteto en la lírica española*, 185–91. Madrid: Gredos, 1956.

Solalinde, Antonio García. "Gonzalo de Berceo y el obispo don Tello." *Revista de Filología Española* 9 (1922): 398–400.

Suárez Pallasá, Aquilino. "El templo de la 'Introducción' de los *Milagros de Nuestra Señora* de Gonzalo de Berceo." *Letras* (Organo de la Facultad de Letras y Ciencias Humanas de la Universidad Nacional Mayor de San Marcos) 21–22 (1989-1990): 65–74.

Vicente García, Luis Miguel. "El milagro XVI de los *Milagros de Nuestra Señora* y la versión latina: Transformación de algunos temas." *Mester* 17 (1988): 21–27.

Vila, Claudio. "Estudio mariológico de los *Milagros de Nuestra Señora* de Berceo." *Berceo* 8 (1953): 343–60.

Wilkins, Heanon. "Dramatic Design in Berceo's *Milagros de Nuestra Señora*." In *Hispanic Studies in Honor of Alan D. Deyermond: A North American Tribute*, ed. John S. Miletich, 309–24. Madison: Hispanic Seminary of Medieval Studies, 1986.

————. "La función de los diálogos en los *Milagros* de Berceo." In *Actas del Sexto Congreso Internacional de Hispanistas* (1977), ed. Alan M. Gordon and Evelyn Rugg, 798–801. Toronto: Department of Spanish and Portuguese, University of Toronto, 1980.

————. "Los romeros y las romerías en *Milagros de Nuestra Señora*." In *Studia Hispanica Medievalía. II Jornadas de Literatura Española*, 139–52. Buenos Aires: Editorial Ergon, 1987.

Zamora, Silvia Rosa. "La estructura bipolar y tripartita del milagro XXV de Berceo." *Mester* 17 (1988): 29–37.

INTRODUCTION TO *THE PRAISES OF OUR LADY*

TRANSLATED BY JEANNIE K. BARTHA

The genres of medieval literature written explicitly in praise of the Blessed Virgin Mary flourished and reached a peak in thirteenth-century Spain in the works of Berceo and in the Galician-Portuguese *Cantigas de Santa María*.[1] In the fourteenth century, praises of Our Lady continued to be written. Juan Ruiz, Archpriest of Hita, included many in his *Libro de buen amor*,[2] and Don Juan Manuel of the same century composed a tract on her assumption to heaven in which praises were inserted.[3] Across the ages such praises rang out, some in prose, others in poems, and many set to music.

Berceo, who had been steeped in the ecclesiastical writings of the period, drew upon the vast corpus of the literature of praises and hymns written in Our Lady's honor. His own *Praises* are deeply colored by earlier praises set down in Latin and in the vernacular, as well as by the considerable body of medieval hymns. They will strike certain familiar chords in the minds of his readers today, just as they must have struck such notes in the thirteenth century. How could it be otherwise? Anyone who wrote in those times, or who writes today in praise of the Virgin, must perforce fall back upon the ancient formulas: Full of Grace, Star of the Sea, Fountain of Piety, Temple of Christ, and the like, if he hopes to gain and hold the sympathetic attention of his readers or listeners. Tradition demands it. And so Berceo wholeheartedly followed this convention. A deep sense

---

[1] The edition of Florencio Janre, *Loores de Nuestra Señora*, Biblioteca de Autores Españoles 57 (Madrid: Real Academia, 1951), 92–103 is the only available text in Spanish. Kathleen Kulp-Hill's translation of the *Cantigas: Songs of Holy Mary by Alfonso X, The Wise: A Translation of the* Cantigas de Santa María, MRTS 173 (Tempe: Arizona Center for Medieval and Renaissance Studies, 2000) is the only available English translation of this work.

[2] Julio Cejador y Frauca, ed., Juan Ruiz, *El Libro de Buen Amor: Edición y Notas* (Madrid: Clásicos Castellanos, 1913).

[3] See the edition of Pascual de Gayangos, Biblioteca de Autores Españoles 51 (Madrid: Real Academia, 1952), 439–42. The full title of the work by Don Juan Manuel is *Tractado en que se prueba por razón que Santa María está en cuerpo et alma en parayso*.

of devotion and spiritual sincerity as well as beautifully crafted poetic imagery characterize this work. The poet experimented occasionally in his *Praises of Our Lady* with what might be called poetic acrobatics not usually found in his repertoire. He created in at least two separate quatrains (24 and 97) a species of internal rhyme. Ordinarily, it will be recalled, his *mester de clerecía* was couched in monorhymed quatrains. In the places mentioned, however, he presents not only lines rhyming in the final syllable, but within the line at the end of each hemistich. The three internal rhyming lines (quatrain 97) are worth recalling in Spanish:

> *Si tú nunca moriesses / vivir yo no podría*
> *si tú mal non sofriesses / yo de bien non sabría;*
> *si tú non decendiesses / yo nunqua non subría,...*

Abbreviations

Dutton	Dutton, Brian, ed. *Los Loores de Nuestra Señora*. In Gonzalo de Berceo, *Obras Completas*, 3: 69–117. London: Tamesis, 1975.
Logroño	*Loores de Nuestra Señora*. In Gonzalo de Berceo, *Obras completas*, intro. Rufino Briones, 255-88. Logroño: Instituto de Estudios Riojanos, 1971.
M.P.	Menéndez Pidal, Ramón, ed. *Cantar de Mío Cid. Texto, gramática y vocabulario.* 4th ed. Madrid: Espasa-Calpe, 1969.
Montgomery	Montgomery, Thomas, ed. *El Evangelio de San Mateo. Texto, gramática, vocabulario.* Madrid: Aguirre Torre, 1962.
Salvador Miguel	Salvador Miguel, Nicasio, ed. *Loores de Nuestra Señora*. In Gonzalo de Berceo, *Obra completa*, with Isabel Uría, 859–931. Madrid: Espasa-Calpe, 1992.

THE PRAISES OF OUR LADY

1   I commend myself to you, Virgin, Mother of Mercy,
who truly did conceive through the Holy Spirit,[1]
and in your virginity begot your precious Son,
serving your Spouse with absolute fidelity.

2   Lady, I would like to praise and court you,
and touch the hem of your ample skirts,
for I feel unworthy to appear before you:
I hope I may not lose your confidence.

3   Confident in you, Mother, I wish to tell
of how God came to redeem the world through you;
give me a good start and give me a good ending,
how and what to pursue concerning your subject.

4   When the serpent deceived our first parents,
and deprived them of sense with cunning words,
the deceitful flatterers were fearful of you then,[2]
but they were not certain of the time or the hour.

5   All the patriarchs and prophets told of you,
for through the Holy Spirit they perceived your power;
all made their prophecies and signs because of you,
for those fallen through Adam would recover through you.

6   The burning bush that appeared to the shepherd[3]
and remained intact and as perfect as before,
signified you who were incorrupt,
unshaken from the firmness of your vow.

7   Mother, you were seen in the sign of the staff
that resolved the dispute concerning Aaron;[4]

---

[1] See Luke 1:35.
[2] Traditional Marian interpretation of Gen. 3:15.
[3] See Exod. 3:2.
[4] See Num. 17:16–21.

a staff that was rootless and dry, bore fruit,
and, Virgin, you gave birth entirely unscathed.

8   The word of Isaiah[5] was fulfilled in you, Lady,
that a shoot would sprout from the root of Jesse,
and a bud would blossom such as never seen before,
upon which the Spirit would rest with seven gifts.

9   Mother, you were the shoot, your Son the blossom
that raises the dead with His sweet odor;
healthful to the sight and vital to the taste,
filled with the seven gifts and sole giver of them.

10   You were the chamber in the words of the psalmist,[6]
whence the bridegroom issued with radiant appearance;
a giant with great tidings who made a great conquest,
he was learned and wise, a king and bishop.

11   Mother, you are the figure that brought the fleece,
whence a new miracle occurred through Gideon;[7]
through him came the dew, through you the Divine King:
you opened the way to victory in the battle.

12   In the words of Ezekiel,[8] the gate securely closed
signified you who were always faithful;
the Lord of Israel passed through you alone,
and the angel Gabriel is witness to that.

13   Mother, those and others were your messengers,
and they had many suchlike companions;
for they came from all peoples, not from just one,
and all were true in their words about you.

14   All were awaiting the time of your Son:
because He came late, they were sorely distressed;
but even though late, they did not doubt He would come:
great was their joy in spite of their suffering.

15   Jacob and Daniel[9] decreed a time limit
for the Jews to lose both scepter and unction.
O hardhearted people, both deaf and blind,
who will not believe the Word or even listen to reason!

---

[5] See Isa. 11:1–3.
[6] See Ps. 19:6.
[7] See Judg. 6:36–40.
[8] See Ezek. 44:1–3.
[9] See Deut. 9:25–27.

16   The famous Jeremiah who claimed he was too young,[10]
    the equal of whom could not be imagined,
    behaved to Jacob[11] like a son who loved him;
    he agreed to serve him after coming on earth.

17   Moses[12] spoke about him to that hard people:
    "A prophet is rising from among your descendants
    who must be obeyed by every last creature,
    for he who heeds him not shall suffer immensely."

18   Zechariah, the father of him who was precursor,[13]
    spoke of him when he recovered his speech;[14]
    Elizabeth his wife was the one who bore him:[15]
    all of this later was confirmed by the Son.

19   A long time passed before this was fulfilled,
    but God's divine grace cast it not into oblivion;
    help for salvation was prepared in heaven
    for Adam to recover the good he had lost.

20   You must have known that very great secret:
    that is why God made you to be born of kings;[16]
    you were pleased to promise the vow of chastity;[17]
    you took great care not to break it.

21   Gabriel[18] was sent with the message
    to you, my Lady, in the town of Nazareth;
    he found you all alone in a small chamber;
    he greeted you sweetly; he said: "Ave María."[19]

22   You were called blessed and full of grace:
    by divine grace you conceived and gave birth without pain;
    through you the deadly chain came to be loosened;
    through you the hundredth sheep recovered his place.[20]

---

[10] See Jer. 1:6.

[11] Probably meaning that Jeremiah served the people of Israel as a son who loved them.

[12] See Deut. 18:15–20.

[13] John the Baptist.

[14] For Zechariah's reference to the prophets, see the Canticle of Zechariah in Luke 1:67–79.

[15] See Luke 1:5–25.

[16] See Luke 2:4–5.

[17] In the Apocryphal Gospels, Mary as a child takes the vow of chastity.

[18] See Luke 1:26–33.

[19] 'Hail Mary.'

[20] For the Parable of the Lost Sheep, see Matt. 18:12–14.

23   To your blessed fruit called Jesus Christ,
        to Him the kingdom of David was granted;[21]
        His power is eternal and beyond all telling;
        through Him light was made and the earth created.

24   You received the message with great humility;
        you acknowledged that what he spoke was the truth;
        you questioned the manner in which you would conceive,
        and the words he replied were completely reassuring.

25   Nine months He rested in your holy womb,
        until the time came for Him to be born;
        when the days were completed and the moment arrived,
        you gave birth to Son and Father on a bed of hay.

26   Holy was your childbirth, holy your offspring;
        you were virgin before and virgin you stayed;
        you gave birth and remained completely unscathed,
        and thus you fulfilled the word of Isaiah.[22]

27   You were sorely distressed, for there was no room,
        and you placed the babe in a manger for cattle;[23]
        Habakkuk had told of that in his writings:
        he was afraid that it would happen in that way.[24]

28   Mother, at the birth new signs occurred:
        shepherds who were watching saw new lights;
        they heard new songs of joy and of peace;
        it was then they understood the truth of the matter.

29   Plenty of other marvelous signs occurred:
        oil flowed from a rock,[25] a new star was born;[26]
        time came to a halt when the virgin gave birth:
        there was peace throughout the world as never before her.

30   After seven days when the eighth day dawned,
        you circumcised the child as the Law commanded;[27]
        you performed the ritual but He guided it;
        you nourished Him but He governed you.

---

[21] See Luke 1:32.
[22] See Isa. 7:14 and Matt. 1:23.
[23] See Luke 2:7.
[24] See Hab. 3:2 (in Spain, quoted in the Nativity liturgy).
[25] See Job 29:6 and Deut. 32:13.
[26] See Matt. 2:2 and 10.
[27] See Luke 2:21.

31   A new star appeared then in the east,
        although not a believer, Balaam[28] told of it;
        . . . .[29]
        they knew it was a sign of the Almighty King:
        they came to seek Him, they bore Him gifts.

32   Three gifts were offered Him, each one symbolic:
        gold for His kingship of royal ancestry,
        frankincense as was befitting to God,
        and myrrh for embalming His mortal flesh.

33   On the fortieth day from the time of His birth,
        you offered Him in the temple, Simeon received Him;[30]
        he was greatly pleased with Him; he gave Him the blessing:
        never was there offered such a noble oblation.

34   Mother, the prophet Malachi foretold of that step,[31]
        how the beloved Messiah would come to the temple,
        and as you knew the laws and the prophecies,
        you went to fulfill them when the time came.

35   News of that King was spreading far and wide;
        the kings of Judea were withdrawing;
        they were not of the ancestry[32] and so they were worried;
        though famous for their valor, He would reign someday.

36   Herod above all was terribly angered:
        he was worried and afraid of losing his kingdom;
        a wicked thought occurred to him — it came from the devil;
        he was destroyed by evil when he went to extremes.

37   To find the Child he imposed a wicked edict:
        to slay every male child of two years and under;[33]
        warned by the angel, Joseph arose with Him;[34]
        may a king of such justice be confounded by God!

---

[28] See Num. 24:15 and 17.

[29] Dutton, 3:78, note 31a, remarks that even though the two manuscripts do not indicate it, lines are missing here since the subject of the verb *sopieron* in 31c and the two plural verbs in 31d is missing. Dutton believes that as many as four lines could be missing, and that perhaps 31ab belong to one quatrain and 31cd to another. He suggests that the subject here might be the three kings who came from the east.

[30] For the Presentation of our Lord in the temple, see Luke 2:22–32.

[31] See Mal. 3:1.

[32] King Herod was not from the royal house of David.

[33] See Matt. 2:16–18.

[34] See Matt. 2:13–15.

38   When they slit their throats, we can each imagine
       how great could have been the cries of the mothers;
       according to Jeremiah, who is bound to be believed,
       in Rama there was heard the weeping of Rachel.[35]

39   When Herod realized that he had been deceived,
       that the wise men were gone and the Child had escaped,
       he was covered and afflicted by deadly sores;
       he took his own life and died in despair.

40   He died alone like a wicked traitor;
       then the angel[36] informed you of his death;
       you returned from Egypt where you were staying;
       Joseph helped you like a faithful servant.

41   Mother, you pondered each one of those matters:
       you forgot not a single word or deed;
       you helped your Son in human affairs;
       you entrusted eternal matters to Him.

42   When He was twelve, although a child in years,
       He was already beginning to speak about justice;[37]
       He made clear the prophecies, He surpassed the teachers:[38]
       they dared not speak immoderately before Him.

43   When the time was fulfilled and He reached the age,
       He received baptism with great humility;
       not that there was any stain of sin on Him,
       but His receiving the water gave it authority.[39]

44   St. John the Baptist, when he saw Him come,
       pointed Him out and began to say,
       "That is the lamb who must redeem the world:
       He should be giving what He just received from me."[40]

45   After the baptism He endured the forty days;[41]
       He feared the devil who lay in wait to trap Him;

[35] See Matt. 2:17–18 and Jer. 31:15.
[36] See Matt. 2:19–21.
[37] See Luke 2:46–50.
[38] See Luke 2:46–47.
[39] For the baptism of Jesus, see Mark 1:9–11 and John 1:29–34.
[40] For the reaction of St. John the Baptist to Jesus asking that he baptize Him, see Matt. 3:13–15.
[41] The forty days when Christ withdrew and fasted in the desert after His baptism. See Luke 4:1–2.

on the fortieth day, His body hungered for food;
when he perceived His hunger, the devil doubted.

46   The devil was striving to get Him in his power,
        but he was hindered from accomplishing his aim;
        he tried plenty of times but he did not breach the wall;
        he thought he was crafty but proved to be unlucky.

47   We derived great benefit from that temptation:
        there we were avenged for the first offense;[42]
        the evil was conquered by His very deed;
        your Son, Mother, was obtaining His justice.

48   Once out in the world He made Himself known:
        He made wine from water,[43] He multiplied the loaves;[44]
        He instructed the people who willingly heard Him;
        He certainly knew how to respond to John's message.

49   He chose His followers from a humble background:[45]
        He did not want those who were high and mighty;
        He taught them the *Pater Noster,*[46] He put them on the path;
        He widened the scope of forgiveness for Christians.

50   Among all the many things that He did and said,
        He commanded us to feed the poor[47] and to render good for evil;[48]
        He changed Simon's name and put him in charge;[49]
        He did not deny His tribute to His earthly lord.[50]

51   He revealed His splendor[51] to three of His own,
        that they might believe in His divine nature;
        they were men in His confidence and witnesses to Him:
        Peter erred a little, but he did so with great piety.[52]

---

[42] The Original Sin committed by Adam and Eve.
[43] See John 2:1–11.
[44] See Matt. 14:15–21, Mark 6:35–44, Luke 9:12–17, and John 6:5–13.
[45] Jesus chose Peter and Andrew, James and John, who were fishermen. See Matt. 4:18–22, Mark 1:16–20, Luke 5:1–11; cf. Ps.113:7.
[46] The prayer the "Our Father".
[47] See Luke 18:22.
[48] See Luke 6:27, 35.
[49] See Matt. 16:18–19, Mark 3:16, and John 1:42.
[50] Refers to the passage in Matt. 22:15–21 and Mark 12:13–17 where Jesus utters the famous words "Render to Caesar what is Caesar's and render to God what is God's."
[51] Refers here to the Transfiguration of our Lord before His three disciples Peter, James, and John. See Matt. 17:1–8, Mark 9:2–8, and Luke 9:28–36.
[52] See Matt. 16:22–23.

52   He heard the Canaanite woman[53] and saved the one condemned,
        the woman whom they judged should be stoned for adultery;[54]
        He never rejected the pious female sinner;[55]
        He brought three dead back to life, including one from his tomb.[56]

53   Who could possibly number His great works of mercy?
        Mother, it would be folly to even think of doing so;
        fear of passing away is beginning to seize me,
        for man's day of reckoning is bound to come.

54   On the sixth day before suffering the Passion,
        He entered the Holy City in procession;[57]
        the crowds that followed Him, shouting "Salvation,"
        were announcing beforehand His great Resurrection.

55   The great feast of the Passover was approaching;
        the value of your Son above all was rising;
        envy was greatly corrupting the scribes:
        like the wicked, they were taking bad advice.[58]

56   He ate the Passover meal[59] with His friends;
        He established new laws and eliminated the old ones;
        those He held[60] to be brothers turned out to be foes:
        such as they were, their deeds bear witness.

57   While at supper He made His solemn covenant,
        of the bread and the wine He made a great sacrament;
        He laid upon us a strong remembrance of His death:
        after the washing of the feet He gave a new commandment.[61]

58   When all the rituals of the supper were completed,
        the betrayal[62] was accomplished and the people were stirred;
        Judas was the ringleader who had sold Him:

---

[53] See Matt.15:21–28.

[54] See John 8:3–11.

[55] See Luke 7:37–50.

[56] The son of the widow of Nain (Luke 7:11–15), Jairus's daughter (Luke 8:41–42 and 49–56), and Lazarus, the "one from his tomb" (John 11:17–44).

[57] For the Entry of Jesus Christ into Jerusalem when we celebrate Palm Sunday, see Matt. 21:1–11 and Mark 11:9–11.

[58] For the conspiracy against Jesus, see Luke 22:1–6.

[59] For The Last Supper, see Matt. 26:20–29 and Luke 22:14–20.

[60] Here I read *tenie/tenia* with Salvador Miguel, 883, 56c and Logroño, 263, 56c rather than *credie* with Dutton, 3:82, 56c.

[61] See John 13:34.

[62] For the Betrayal of Jesus, see Matt. 26:47–56, Mark 14:43–50, Luke 22:47–53, and John 18:1–8.

for him it would be better if he had never been born.[63]

59   They got a terrible shock the moment He was captured;
through His divine grace we can understand
that He could certainly defend Himself from them without arms,[64]
but He willingly surrendered Himself to the Passion.

60   He only said to them, "I am He Whom You seek,"
and they fell in a faint as if from great blows;[65]
in the end He allowed them to have their way,
and the wicked secrets were revealed.

61   Jesus Christ was captured when and as He willed;
Judas repented of having betrayed Him;
he returned to the council the money he had gotten:
he hanged himself[66] and died a shameful death.

62   Meanwhile, the Lord was tightly bound,
and just as foretold[67] His disciples fled;[68]
undeserving of evil, He was sentenced to death;
He remembered Peter even though he had denied Him.[69]

63   They tied His hands and scourged Him with a whip;[70]
many people bore false witness against Him;[71]
they rejected Him and called for Barabbas;[72]
now it is apparent how mistaken they were.

64   Pilate was deeply disturbed by this captive,
and, as he said, he was glad to be rid of Him;[73]
the Jews took the sin upon themselves,[74]
and they shall never grab their beards over that bargain.[75]

---

[63] See Matt. 26:24 and Mark 14:21.
[64] See Matt. 26:53–54.
[65] For the arrest of Jesus, see John 18:6.
[66] For the death of Judas, see Matt. 27:3–5 and Acts 1:18.
[67] For the prophecy, see Zech. 13:7.
[68] See Matt. 26:56 and Mark 14:50.
[69] For Peter's denial of Christ, see Matt. 26:69–75, Mark 14:66–72, Luke 22:54–62, and John 18:17, 25–27.
[70] See John 19:1 and Matt. 27:26.
[71] For Jesus before the Sanhedrin, see Matt. 26:57–68 and Mark 14:53–65.
[72] Concerning Barabbas who was released instead of Jesus, see Matt. 27:16–21, Mark 15:7–15, Luke 23:18–19, and John 18:39–40.
[73] See Matt. 27:24.
[74] See Matt. 27:25.
[75] According to M.P. *Cantar II*, 494 under *barba* ('beard') the expression in O. Sp. *prenderse a la barba* meaning 'to put one's hand on one's beard' was an attitude in frequent use in the Middle Ages to express satisfaction.

65   Justice miscarried and truth was destroyed there;
injustice and falsehood wielded the power;
the whole wicked band lined up against Him:
that is why He had previously wept for the city.[76]

66   That day, Friday, will always be mentioned:
on a day such as that[77] Adam was deceived;
Christ was crucified to save the world,
between two thieves, each on either side of Him.[78]

67   His eyes were blindfolded,[79] his face all bruised;[80]
a crown of sharp thorns[81] was jammed on His head;
He was given a very thin reed for a scepter;[82]
they tried to give Him the most shameful of deaths.

68   And with all that, the wicked were not satisfied,
for our mortal sins were still upon Him;
they bowed before Him on bended knee,[83]
and the proven infidels told Him, "Ave Rex."[84]

69   We should not be silent about His great patience,
for everything He did we have as an example;
He endured words and deeds whereby we learn
how He made no reproach, so neither should we.

70   Mother, you were dreadfully crushed by His suffering:
the sword of your Son pierced your soul;[85]
the words of the ancient proved to be true:[86]
why marvel if such a Mother grieved for such a Son?

71   Amidst all His suffering He did not forget you:
He reminded you there of the words at the wedding;[87]

---

[76] For the lament of Jesus over Jerusalem, see Matt. 23:37–39 and Luke 19:41–44.

[77] Here I read *en tal mesmo día* as in Ms. IS, with Logroño, 264, 66b and *en atal mesmo día* with Salvador Miguel, 885, 66b rather than *en essi día misme* with Dutton, 3: 84, 66b.

[78] See Luke 23:32–33 and John 19:18.

[79] See Luke 22:64.

[80] See Mark 15:19 and John 19:3.

[81] See Matt. 27:29, Mark 15:17, and John 19:2.

[82] See Matt. 27:29.

[83] See Matt. 27:29 and Mark 15:19.

[84] "Hail, King." For the mockery of Jesus by the soldiers, see Mark 15:16–20.

[85] See Luke 2:35.

[86] Berceo is referring here to the words of the prophet Jeremiah (Jer. 31:15) as cited in Matt. 2:17–18.

[87] See John 2:4 for the words Jesus said to His mother at the Wedding at Cana.

He entrusted you to the one He loved best;[88]
you were well entrusted, for he took great care of you.

72   While on the cross He said He was thirsty:
He said that because He desired our good;[89]
the deceitful bystanders who were near Him
gave Him the worst and bitterest of drinks.

73   He willed to suffer the Passion in every limb of His body,
otherwise every one of our limbs would be lost;
a Lord who makes such reparation for His subjects
ought to be served with great devotion.

74   The most important thing yet to be told
is what your Son, Mother, willed to endure:
to conquer death and to regain life,
above all else He willed to die on a cross.

75   There was dreadful lamentation the moment He died:
the veil was torn and the sun was darkened;[90]
Dimas was saved and Gestus was condemned;[91]
Lady, you were sick and brokenhearted.

76   The hardest rocks split open with grief;
many holy dead came back to life;[92]
some knew that the Son of God had been killed,[93]
but the unfortunate Jews acknowledged nothing.

77   Yet the infidels did something even more:
with a dreadful blow, they pierced His right side,
from which there flowed blood and water,[94] our salvation and life,
and thus Holy Church was healed from the morsel.[95]

---

[88] For Jesus entrusting His mother to the care of St. John, His most beloved disciple, see John 19:26–27.

[89] See John 19:28–30.

[90] For what happened at the moment of Christ's death, see Matt. 27:45 and 51, Mark 15:33 and 38, and Luke 23:44–45.

[91] The two thieves who were crucified on either side of Jesus. According to Dutton, 3:113, note 75c, although their names do not appear in the New Testament, they were known in the Middle Ages and can be found in apocryphal gospels such as the *Acts of Pilate*.

[92] See Matt. 27:51–53.

[93] See Matt. 27:54.

[94] See John 19:34.

[95] The bite of apple taken by Adam and Eve through which they committed Original Sin. See Gen. 3:6.

78   I have come to the part that I was greatly dreading,
        to the wicked offense where I feared to stumble;
        I see that I am guilty for my Lord's maltreatment,
        I see Him die for me, so that I should not be lost.

79   How can I, a wretched sinner, be held without blame,
        when I see such a great ruler die for me?
        He was the Creator of heaven and earth,
        and the wise ordainer of the four elements.

80   On the first day, He created light;[96]
        on the second, He placed the dome between the waters;
        on the third, He gathered the seas and made the plants,
        and now I see Him dead, with total meekness.[97]

81   From the fourth day on, merely by His command
        the firmament was furnished with new lights;
        on the fifth day, He made the birds and the fish;
        now I see Him dead, and because of my sin.

82   On the sixth day, He made man, His principal creation,
        and made other animals different in kind;
        He rested on the seventh day, but not from fatigue:
        now He hangs on the cross for my folly.

83   He put the man and woman He had made in His garden;
        He showed them all things and how not to go astray;
        He banished them from there when they disobeyed Him:
        I see Him dead on the cross, to erase that sin.

84   The people were growing in greater disorder;
        Noah built the Ark[98] to serve them as a warning;
        in the end He took vengeance saving Noah and the seven;[99]
        He finally died for me, bearing much suffering.

85   He did other deeds much greater than those:
        I dare not tell the major ones but only the minor:
        He created the rainbow with its different hues,
        and now for my life, He suffers great anguish.

---

[96] For the Story of Creation, see Gen. 1.
[97] Quatrains 80–94 recall the *Improperia* or Reproaches of the Good Friday liturgy.
[98] For the story of Warning of the Flood, see Gen. 6–8.
[99] The *seven* is a reference to the seven pairs of clean animals God allowed Noah to take into the ark. See Gen. 7:2.

86   He gave Abraham victory and taught him faith;
        He skillfully brought His people out of Egypt;[100]
        He gave David a kingdom[101] and wisdom to his son;[102]
        now He suffers death, and because of my sins.

87   He gave the Jews the ten commandments of the Law[103]
        which are being recited today, I believe;
        there were other decrees[104] attached to those;
        the author of all this suffers for my sins.

88   The first commandment was to believe in one God;
        in the second, the sin of blasphemy was forbidden;
        in the third, He ordered the Sabbath to be kept;
        now I see him crucified for my sins.

89   The fourth commandment is to honor our parents;
        the fifth above all forbids us to kill,
        the sixth, to fornicate, the seventh, to steal;
        He Who commands all this, I see suffering for me.

90   The eighth forbids the bearing of false witness,
        the ninth, the coveting of our neighbor's goods;
        the tenth, the coveting of our neighbor's wife;
        God Who came for all, hangs on the cross for me.

91   From the bear and the lion[105] he freed David,
        a mighty champion who slew the Philistine;[106]
        through Him was Judea freed from Babylon;[107]
        now to grant me pardon, He allowed Himself to die.

92   You know He saved Susanna[108] from her accusers;
        you can be sure He saved the three young men from the fire;[109]
        He showered great favors on the Maccabees;[110]
        now you see how He died on the cross for us.

---

[100] For the Exodus from Egypt and the Journey to Sinai, see Exod. 12:37–51.
[101] See 2 Sam. 2:4.
[102] For the wisdom of Solomon, King David's son, see 1 Kings 3.
[103] For the Ten Commandments, see Exod. 20.
[104] The rest of the Law, for example in Leviticus.
[105] See 1 Sam. 17:34–36.
[106] For the story of David and Goliath, see 1 Sam. 17.
[107] Berceo refers here to the years when the Jews lived in captivity in Babylon. See Daniel and Jeremiah.
[108] For the story of Susanna's virtue, see Dan. 13.
[109] For the story of Shadrach, Meshach, and Abednego, see Dan. 3.
[110] For the story of the Maccabees, see 1 Macc. 3–9:22.

93   Everything in the whole world that could be imagined,
          whatever we can discover and whatever is concealed
          was all made by Him, with the exception of sin:
          now for my trespasses, I see Him offended.

94   In great shame I lie, a wretched sinner,
          when I see such a good Lord die so poorly served;
          I broke His commandments, He dies for love of me:
          in great shame I lie, a wretched sinner.

95   Lord, although I see You dead, indeed I know You live;
          even though dead, I firmly believe that You live;
          in this I do not waver: You die that I may live;
          I greatly desire Your Resurrection.

96   All the degradation that I see You endure,
          I believe that I heard Isaiah[111] tell of;
          when Jeremiah wept he saw this coming;[112]
          Lord, may You be praised for having willed to die.

97   If You had never died, I could not live;
          if You had not suffered evil, I would not know good;
          if You had not descended, I would never rise;
          may You be praised, Christ, and you, Virgin Mary.

98   Lord, I accept whatever You reproached me for:
          You did so much for me that You should not do more;
          Lord, I beg You as a favor since You did so much,
          not to weary of me since You have loved me so greatly.

99   Let us return to the story, let us not postpone it:
          let us follow the path that we began;
          let us adore the cross and let us believe in Christ,
          that we may be worthy to see the Resurrection.

100   Joseph[113] was granted his request for the body,
          but not the Joseph, Mother, who was Your spouse;
          he placed it in a tomb that had never been used;
          though made for himself it was put to good use.

101   There are two things no one could possibly tell of:
          how such a great treasure lay in such a mean place,

[111] For Isaiah's prophecies about the death of the Messiah, see Isa. 53:1–10.
[112] See Jer. 9:1.
[113] Joseph of Arimathea, who requested from Pilate the body of Jesus for burial. For the burial of Jesus, see Matt. 27:57–61, Mark 15:42–47, Luke 23:50–56, and John 19:38–42.

or, Mother, how deep was the anguish of your sorrow;
no one could possibly tell of those two things.

102   Divine grace from this dead man was never at rest:
He breached the precincts of hell, as He fervently desired;
He removed His friends from there, a thing He always sought;
there was such great rejoicing in a land of sadness.

103   Let us change the subject and sing another tune:
we will hear[114] such tidings as to make us rejoice;
the Lord came back to life, we do not know what time,
on a Sunday morning according to Scripture.[115]

104   Sunday is the sacred day of the week,
a day that is favored with many privileges;
only that day takes its name from the Lord:[116]
it is a day to be observed above all others.

105   On a Sunday, no doubt the world was created;
on such a day heaven and earth were formed;
before them, that day was made and illumined;
go and sleep on Saturday for it is no longer fated.

106   Sunday was the day greatly loved by Christ,
for He willed to come back to life on Sunday;
let us keep Sunday as we are commanded:
let us stay the course determined for us.

107   He visited His friends, God, such great a joy!
two suns, thank God, were born that day.[117]
May the whole wicked band get no thanks;
Christ was resurrected, God, what great joy!

108   Some good women[118] came from the tomb;
it is they who gave us those very good tidings;

---

[114] Here I read *oiremos/oyremos* (Ms. I) with Salvador Miguel, 895, 103b and Logroño, 270, 103b rather than *dizremos* with Dutton, 3:90, 103b.

[115] For the day of Christ's resurrection, see Matt. 28:1, Mark 16.1, Luke 24:1, and John 20:1.

[116] The Spanish word *domingo* 'Sunday' is derived from the Latin words *dies dominicus* 'the day of the Lord'.

[117] Berceo refers to the fact that both Christ and the Virgin Mary came back to life that day. See Berceo's *El Duelo de la Virgen* lines 196b,c, in Dutton, 3:45; also below, 211.

[118] See Matt.28:1 (Mary Magdalene and the other Mary), Mark 16:1 (Mary Magdalene, Mary the mother of James, and Salome), Luke 24:10 (Mary Magdalene, Joanna, and Mary the mother of James plus others), and John 20:1 (only Mary Magdalene).

they looked in the tomb and saw the shroud;[119]
they carried a special greeting to Peter.[120]

109   Woman grew prodigiously in grace through that:
       she completely redressed the wrong she did against us;[121]
       through that and other things she obtained great favor:
       great joy increased for the women of this world.

110   If we were lost through woman and the tree,[122]
       through woman and the tree[123] we are now redeemed;
       through those same steps by which we were confounded,
       ancient ground has been restored to us.

111   Mother, your ancestry is highly exalted;
       if Eve sinned you have made amends for it;
       indeed it is obvious that Christ was your advocate;[124]
       your ancestry, Lady, is irreproachable.

112   Rejoice, Lady: you should be joyful,
       for good news is spreading and you see new times;
       now you have obtained what you always hoped for:
       rejoice, Lady: you should be joyful.

113   We who sin against Him were greatly encouraged
       that He forgave Peter after he repented;
       by that, He showed us how He never rejected
       a single sinner, if he asked Him for forgiveness.

114   Those who were entrusted to guard the tomb
       were bribed into telling a colossal lie;
       they said, "His disciples came while we were sleeping;
       they robbed us of the body and put it somewhere else."[125]

115   Who ever beheld greater false witness?
       Who could possibly see the thief if he were sleeping?
       They must have been afraid to admit they did not not see him.
       Such confusion in the witnesses may be from God![126]

---

[119] See John 20:7.
[120] See Mark 16:7.
[121] Berceo refers here to Gen. 3:6 where Eve eats the apple and gives some of it to Adam, thus causing original sin to the human race.
[122] The forbidden tree in the Garden of Eden.
[123] The cross Christ was crucified upon.
[124] See 1 John 2:1.
[125] See Matt. 28:11–15.
[126] Meaning that "[God] brings them down by their own tongues". See Ps. 64: 7–9.

116   Let them tell us this, if they say He was stolen:
how is it they did not take the shroud along with Him?
They will say, "They were lazy and that is why they left it."
They lie! — for thieves do not go in for such laziness.

117   Let us leave off there and tell the best part:
let us firmly believe that Christ was resurrected;
as Scripture tells us, He appeared to Peter,[127]
Christ was resurrected, in good time we were freed!

118   When He came back to life we were all resurrected,
we came out of prison and recovered our freedom;
let us all render thanks to the Virgin Mary
through whom we sinners gain such great favor.

119   There is something in Scripture that we must not forget,
it is why we should put our trust in your Son:
all His opponents who sought Him harm
in the end had to die a frightful death.

120   Herod the First,[128] unlucky to be born,
we have already heard about how he died;
Judas died a wicked death just as he deserved;[129]
fortunate indeed was he who truly believed in Him.

121   Herod the Second was struck down by the angel,[130]
a few days later he died all decayed;
Pilate took his own life,[131] for he went crazy;
so far as we have heard, that is how they all died.

122   The Jews quarreled on the feast of the Passover:
thirty thousand of them died there killing each other;[132]
the remainder of those who escaped from there
were uprooted by the leaders of the Romans.

---

[127] See Luke 24:34 and 1 Cor. 15:5.

[128] Herod the Great, King of Judea, the same Herod referred to in lines 36a and 39a, died in 4 B.C.

[129] See Matt. 27:3–8 and Acts 1:18.

[130] Herod Agrippa, 39–44 A.D. See Acts 12:23.

[131] See above, line 64a. Pontius Pilate was procurator of Judea from 26–37 and apparently committed suicide in the year 40 A.D. See Dutton, 3:114, note 121c.

[132] In the year 70 A.D., a few days before the Jewish Passover, Titus arrived before the walls of Jerusalem with a large Roman army. The different political factions among the Jews began to fight each other, and that, combined with the hunger they were suffering, caused thousands of deaths (Dutton, 3:114, note 122a).

123   Titus and Vespasian[133] fought against them:
eleven times a hundred thousand Jews died there;
we should not mourn their death, for indeed they deserved it;
we reaped all the benefit of the good they lost.

124   Once the time was fulfilled for the Resurrection,
before the time came for the Ascension,
He appeared ten times to His followers:
we can give account of all ten occasions.

125   The first time of all was to St. Magdalene,
when she stood confused before the tomb;[134]
the second time He appeared to two of the women,[135]
when they had returned to the sacred sepulcher.

126   He appeared third to St. Peter wherever he was,[136]
and fourth to those on the road to Emmaus,[137]
fifth, in the chamber when Thomas was not there,[138]
and the sixth time with Thomas there,[139] which benefited us.[140]

127   The seventh time on the Sea[141] where the seven were fishing,[142]
the eighth on the mountain where all were awaiting Him,[143]
the ninth to the eleven when they were at table,[144]
the tenth when they watched Him ascending to Heaven.[145]

128   During the time of the forty days,[146] Mother,

---

[133] Vespasian and his son Titus were entrusted with the war in Judea in the year 66
A.D. In 68, when Nero died, Vespasian became emperor and returned to Rome. Titus at-
tacked Jerusalem in 70 and when the city fell there was a dreadful massacre during which
more than a million Jews died and the Temple was burned to the ground. (See Dutton,
3:115, note 123a.)

[134] See Mark 16:9–10 and John 20:14.

[135] See Matt. 28:9.

[136] See Luke 24:34 and 1 Cor. 15:5.

[137] See Mark 16:12 and Luke 24:13–16.

[138] Luke 24:36 and John 20:19.

[139] See John 20:26–27.

[140] Here Berceo refers to the words Christ said to St.Thomas: "Have you come to be-
lieve because you have seen me? Blessed are those who have not seen and have believed."
(John 20:29).

[141] The Sea of Tiberias also called the Sea of Galilee.

[142] See John 21:1–24.

[143] Matt. 28:16–20.

[144] See Mark 16:14.

[145] See Mark 16:19 and Luke 24:50–51.

[146] See Acts 1:3.

the news spread everywhere bit by bit;
those who were wise believed the truth;
those who disbelieved doubled their sin.

129   The core companions were confirmed in the faith;
they were well advised what to do and what not to:
once they were inspired by the Holy Spirit,[147]
every evil argument was proven to be false.

130   Everything else having come to pass, on the fortieth day
Jesus Christ gathered all His companions together;
He loved them like brothers, He gave them great authority;
He paid regard to you above all, Virgin Mary.

131   He ordered them to preach to the ends of the earth;[148]
He showed them the way that they should baptize;[149]
He commanded them not to disperse from the city,[150]
for there they should wait for the gift that was promised.[151]

132   He entrusted His perfect disciples to the Father;
He gave them the blessing with His glorious hand;
He returned in His precious body to whence He had come;[152]
the entire heavenly court rejoiced over Him.

133   A short while later, two men came there:
they were angels of God clothed in white garments;[153]
they said, "Why do you men stand here watching?
Have faith that He will return just as He ascended."

134   He secured freedom for many who were captives:
those captives are mentioned by David in his psalm;[154]
grace and dignity increased in us greatly;
our human nature is highly ennobled.

135   If we should doubt, we could certainly doubt
whether Christ could show us greater mercy;
a good Lord for a bad servant let Himself be crucified,
then He placed him with Him and made him reign.

---

[147] See John 20:22.
[148] See Acts 1:8.
[149] See Matt. 28:19.
[150] See Acts 1:4.
[151] The gift of the Holy Spirit. See Acts 1:4–5.
[152] See Acts 1:9.
[153] See Acts 1:10–11.
[154] See Ps. 126.

136   While the angels were observing all of that,
        they saw our group standing above them;[155]
        they showed amazement as if at something new;
        from that time on they were more in awe of us.

137   Lucky the moment you were born, Blessed Lady,
        for you gave birth to something so sublime;
        fortunate the hour when you sheltered the Messiah:
        that is why all peoples call you highly exalted.

138   The companions of Christ, sad and confused,
        returned to the city[156] with you, Mother;
        they awaited the divine grace granted to them;
        they reaped such reward for serving such a Lord.

139   Peter spoke some words which were wise,
        that Judas' place should not stay vacant;
        how before it was prophesied by David[157]
        that someone better should get the bishopric.[158]

140   They were somewhat troubled over that;
        of the two that pleased them they doubted which to choose;[159]
        they left it to God and could not have done better,
        for they would be happy with whichever one He commanded.

141   It was well that they did this and indeed He welcomed it;
        they fervently entreated Him and indeed He heard them;
        it pleased Him that the lot should fall to Matthias:[160]
        thus they filled the void that was left by Judas.[161]

142   It is demanded of us here, and we cannot keep silent,
        about the ancient custom which we read in the Law;
        do not be annoyed even though it may delay us,
        for because of that we will understand this better.

143   The numeral seven is indeed very holy,
        always advantageous from ancient times;

---

[155] According to Salvador Miguel, 904, note 136b, Berceo is referring to Hebrews 1:5 and 1 Cor. 6:3 in which Jesus is exalted above the angels, but Berceo is reinterpreting the lines here and placing the eleven apostles also above the angels.

[156] See Acts 1:12.

[157] See Acts 1:20 and Ps. 109:8.

[158] Here Berceo uses church language describing as a "bishopric" the office of the apostle who will be chosen to replace Judas.

[159] See Acts 1:23–25.

[160] See Acts 1:26.

[161] Meaning that Matthias made up the number of twelve apostles.

God invested its meaning with such importance,
for it is a numeral that is entirely perfect.

144   God Himself willed to consecrate this number
when it pleased Him to rest on the seventh day;[162]
seven times a day He wants us to praise Him;[163]
He got the world moving in seven days.[164]

145   According to the Law, any debt owed by man
might not be claimed in the seventh year;[165]
neither captive nor servant was to be coerced,[166]
until that year was entirely over.

146   And what is more, in that year[167] they did no work,
for in the sixth year they gathered all they needed;
and in the eighth year they suffered no shortage,
for they had grain and victuals from the sixth year.

147   At the end of fifty years[168] came greater pardon,
and every captive was released from prison;
Judea in such a year departed from Babylon,
in the time of Cyrus,[169] a praiseworthy man.

148   Debts were absolved, their payment never required;
those who were exiled returned to the land;
every enemy was made welcome there;
past injustices would not be reproached.

149   It was legally recognized above all the others,
and it was desired above all the others;[170]
because of this joy it was called Jubilee:
good use would be made of such a year now.

---

[162] See Gen. 2:3 and Exod. 20:11.

[163] Here Berceo is referring to the canonical hours. Also see Ps. 119:164.

[164] The seven days of the Creation.

[165] See Deut. 15:1–2.

[166] See Deut. 15:1–2 and Lev. 25:39–41.

[167] No work on the land was to be done during the seventh or sabbatical year. See Lev. 25:1–7.

[168] For the Jubilee Year, see Lev. 25:8–10.

[169] Cyrus the Great, King of Persia (559–529 B.C.), conquered Babylon in 539 B.C. and in 536, a Jubilee Year for the Jews, he allowed them to return to Judea from their captivity in Babylon. He died in 529 B.C.

[170] Here I read *e era sobre todos los otros deseado* with Salvador Miguel, 909, 149b rather than *sobre todos los otros era bien deseado* with Dutton, 3: 97, 149b.

150   The greatest prayer[171] asks for only seven things,
        seven gifts of the Spirit[172] from the Lord our God;
        out of homage to that, the Creator commanded
        that the seventh day should be held in honor.

151   When the sons of Israel departed from Egypt,
        they received the Law after seven weeks;
        but they never understood this figure of theirs,
        and like straw on water they sank to the bottom.

152   So much time had duly passed[173]
        since the Lord Jesus Christ had broken camp;[174]
        thus, that appointed day had arrived,
        when the Holy Spirit was expected to be sent.

153   Such a thing was fitting for the Holy Spirit,
        because of the seven holy gifts He brought with Him;
        who would ordain such a wise thing, Mother,
        if not your Son through Whom everything came?

154   All the disciples were gathered together,[175]
        as instructed by Jesus when He went away;[176]
        they were prepared to receive the grace;
        all were assembled close by you, Lady.

155   According to Scripture, it was probably terce,[177]
        but concerning the time we should have faith in the Person;[178]
        they heard a noise[179] that descended from heaven:
        the Holy Spirit came with great power and might.

156   The room where they were became all illumined;
        the light appeared to be scattered in tongues;[180]

---

[171] The prayer the "Our Father."

[172] For the seven gifts of the Spirit, see above, line 8d and footnote 5.

[173] Berceo refers here to the Pentecost, the 50 days that had to pass between the Passover and death of Jesus and the time when the Holy Spirit descended upon the apostles. See Acts 2:1–2.

[174] Here Berceo employs a military term to express Jesus' departure from the earth and His Ascension to Heaven.

[175] See Acts 2:1.

[176] See Luke 24:49.

[177] The third hour, terce, was nine o'clock in the morning since the first hour was six o'clock in the morning. See Acts 2:15.

[178] Berceo means here the Third Person of the Blessed Trinity, the Holy Spirit, and may be drawing a correspondence between the third hour and the Third Person.

[179] For the Descent of the Holy Spirit see Acts 2:2.

[180] See Acts 2:2.

each one of them received the grace that was sent;
never in this world was there a room with finer people.

157   They became very strongly imbued with wisdom:
       they spoke in languages they had never heard;[181]
       they preached the faith in a daring way;
       they were so enkindled that they feared no threats.

158   Judea, ever evil, thought they were drunk,[182]
       for little did they remember the words of Joel;[183]
       Peter countered them with words from Scripture;
       Judea could not possibly compete against Peter.

159   People from everywhere were gathered there,[184]
       and every last one of them was totally amazed;[185]
       they spoke every language, they recited them by memory
       as sharp as a knife that had just been ground.

160   They grew in courage and lost all fear;
       each on his own went forth to the nations;
       they preached a new law and conquered the world;
       they gladly endured whatever befell them.

161   How courageous Peter proved himself to be:
       he who spoke the words of denial to the woman,[186]
       later spoke without fear in the presence of Nero,[187]
       caring not in the least for any of his threats.

162   Twelve men were highly favored,
       the twelve who were named apostles by Christ;
       but drawn from among them were only four
       through whom the Gospels were revealed.

163   John and Matthew were the first,
       and after them came Luke and Mark;
       all were sincere and faithful workers:
       the Lord of the vineyard paid them good wages.[188]

---

[181] See Acts 2:4.

[182] See Acts 2:13.

[183] See Acts 2:16–21 and Joel 3:1–5.

[184] See Acts 2:5–11.

[185] See Acts 2:12.

[186] See note 69 above.

[187] Nero was emperor of Rome between 54 and 68 A.D. Traditionally, the date of St. Peter's martyrdom in Rome is placed in the year 64.

[188] Here Berceo compares the four Evangelists to workers in a vineyard who earn their daily wages. He is making a parallel to the parable of the Workers in the Vineyard in Matt. 20:1–16.

164   Matthew began with the Incarnation,
       that is why he is depicted with the face of a man;[189]
       Luke has the image of an ox for narrating the Passion,
       about how your Son, Lady, became an oblation.

165   Mark above all of them narrates the Resurrection,
       so his voice roars with the strength of a lion;
       John begins his text with the Trinity,
       that is why he is subtly compared to an eagle.

166   Brothers and sisters, let us all resolve
       to extend our hands to those men;
       let us entreat them to be our intercessors,
       that our fickle deeds may not hinder us.

167   They hold the keys to open and close,
       they have the power to bind and to loosen;[190]
       we men and women must gain their favor,
       so they will know us when our time comes to enter.

168   Here the entire Holy Church began;[191]
       from here it was shaped and completely ordained;
       but, Mother, your Son was the cornerstone:
       the entire edifice was raised upon Him.[192]

169   Those men have yet another great privilege:
       on Judgment Day they will judge the cases;[193]
       together with Your Son they will distribute the rewards;
       the shares will be determined once and for all.

170   There, we shall all come to the fullness of age;
       there, your Son will come in His majesty;
       there, the cross and humanity will come;
       there, truth will part from falsehood forever.

---

[189] The symbolic depiction of the faces of the four Evangelists proceeds from Ezek. 1:10. Matthew is depicted with a man's face because his narration begins with the geneology and human side of Christ. Mark's face is that of a lion because like a lion's roar, he began his Gospel with the voice of one crying in the desert. Luke has the face of an ox because he began his Gospel with Zechariah who was a priest. John is depicted with the face of an eagle because he told of the Word of God like one on eagle's wings. (See T. Montgomery, *El Evangelio de San Mateo* [Madrid: Aguirre Torre, 1962], 22–23.)

[190] See Matt. 16:19, 18:18.

[191] Here I read *ovo comienço/comienzo* with Salvador Miguel, 913, 168a and Logroño, 279, 168a rather than *ovo cimiento* with Dutton, 3:100, 168a.

[192] See Matt. 21:42, Mark 12:10, Luke 20:17, quoting Ps. 118:22; also 1 Pet. 2:7.

[193] See Luke 22:30.

171   All the good and the bad will be gathered there together:
the good will indeed be separated from the bad;
each one's heart will be revealed:[194]
both righteous and sinful will be put to shame.

172   The Lord Jesus Christ will show us all His wounds,
the ones He received on the cross for us;
there, every careless act will be rebuked,
and the good will be thanked for the alms they gave.[195]

173   We shall find ourselves terribly mortified,
when we witness the blood flowing from His wounds;
we shall see the heavenly virtues tremble;
indeed we should now be fearing that day.

174   Indeed we should now be fearing that day,
and arranging our affairs while we have time;[196]
confessing our sins and doing penance,
parting from evil and persevering in good.

175   God will invite the just to reign with Him;
He will take the wheat and reject the chaff;[197]
He will send those who are wicked to the devil,
from whose hand may God protect all my friends.

176   How will I, a sinner, appear on that day,[198]
whose words and deeds were always vain and foolish?
I never said a good thing or did a worthwhile deed:
what shall I, a wretched sinner, do on that day?

177   A lover of folly, I never heeded the Gospels;
I focused immoderately on sensual delights;
I was never concerned about shunning evil;
how shall I, a wretched sinner, stand in His sight?

178   I kept without faith the promise sworn
and given at the moment when I was baptized;
I was always involved in forbidden things;
I, a wretched sinner, never thought of such an ambush.

---

[194] See 1 Cor. 14:25; cf. Luke 2:35.
[195] Cf. Matt. 25:40.
[196] Cf. Isa. 38:1.
[197] See Matt. 3:12; Luke 3:17.
[198] This passage recalls the *Dies Irae*, the Sequence for the dead.

179   When I saw the things of the world flourish,
        and the vainglory of it reflected there,
        my friends and relatives all around me,
        I never thought that I should focus on that.

180   I was bored by the hours I spent in church:
        my mind was distracted by shallow thoughts;
        there I was occupied by everything trivial;
        wretched sinner, how badly deceived I was!

181   Gentlefolk and friends, let us guard against guile,
        for those humiliations and those fears
        could be much greater than what you hear:
        the pleasures of this world can turn into sorrows.

182   There is one matter that should break our hearts,
        wherefore sinners ought to be frightened:
        those who that day will be judged to be punished
        will have the devil to contend with forever.

183   They will lie forever in the power of the devil:
        they will suffer many pains that will never end;
        they will always increase and never diminish;
        those who escape them will indeed be lucky.

184   Although they repent, it will do them no good,
        for they will feel loathing and disgust for themselves;
        they will see how God does justice to the wicked,
        for as they sowed, so shall they reap.[199]

185   They will ask each other, "What shall we wretched do?
        We shall lie here forever, we shall never get out;
        if we cry for mercy, we shall not be heard.
        What shall we wretched do? We shall live eternally in death."

186   The devil will reply, "You have realized too late,
        you did not think of that when you still had power;
        I promised you that, when you became mine;
        now accept whatever you earned at that time."

187   My friends, while we are here, let us give it some thought:
        let us put no faith in the deadly enemy;
        let us restrain our bodies; let us serve the Creator;
        let us not lose our souls for our pitiful bodies.[200]

---

[199] See Gal. 6:7.
[200] Cf. Matt. 16:26, Mark 8:36, and Luke 9:25.

188   If we knew the good things God has in store for us,
then we would acknowledge how deceived we are;
they could not be described or much less imagined,
worth more than an empire, more than a kingdom.

189   What could be as great as seeing His face,
or understanding how the Son is born of the Father,
or knowing how the Spirit proceeds from them both,
or coming to know how all three are one God?

190   I know indeed that this is true and not false:
all three are equal and have no beginning;
they are one in nature and indivisible:
this is the foundation of our holy faith.[201]

191   It is not for us to say what are His riches;
neither gold nor silver can compare with His jewels;
of[202] His ever new and extraordinary treasures,
the sum of their wealth could never be imagined.

192   Eternal life and everlasting salvation,
a sun more dazzling, solid peace and stability,
a wind more marvelously light and fine:
such a good King's kingdom is very desirable!

193   We come to the end here of all our digressions:
let us entrust ourselves to God, let us flee the devil;
let us conclude this part here although we go further;
may we never fall into choosing evil.

194   Let us firmly believe everything we have heard;
all this is our faith, we will sin if we doubt it;
if we will not not believe this, we will not be saved;
let us never forget to fear the Last Judgment.

195   In the end it is mercy that has to help us,
for no good deed of ours could possibly save us;
yet we should keep on doing good until we die,
for mercy will proceed from the deeds that we do.

196   It is in God that we have our greatest hope,
but in you, Lady, we have great confidence,
for in you we place all our courage;
help us, Lady, before we are in danger.

---

[201] Refers to the "Nicene Creed".

[202] Here I read *de* with Salvador Miguel, 919, 191c and Logroño, 282, 191c rather than *da* with Dutton, 3: 104, 191c.

197   That is why you are called Star of the Sea,
        because in such danger you are meant to help us:
        by your guidance we are meant to reach the shore,
        and to escape from those most powerful waves.

198   Mother, in the experience of the first coming,[203]
        you were the path that led to our salvation;
        at the second one,[204] Mother, strive for us,
        that we may not be caught in the deadly trap.

199   Mother, you are called Fountain of Mercy;
        you were a reliquary filled with holiness;
        all of Christendom awaits your mercy,
        for it believes through you it will gain salvation.

200   Anyone who courted you was never disappointed;
        everything he put in you he got back double;
        the ungodly Theophilus[205] indeed discovered it,
        for through your guidance, Mother, he recanted.

201   Mary the Egyptian,[206] a grievous sinner,
        was reconciled before your image;
        in you she found help for all her suffering:
        you alone undertook to be her guarantor.

202   Great is your mercy and great your power,
        precious your name and solid your affection;
        devotion to you brought honor to Ildephonsus;[207]
        disagreement with you brought harm to Julian.[208]

203   Of such examples as those and others more important,
        a hundred thousand or so would hardly be a tenth;
        so numerous are they as to be beyond telling:
        we reap great benefit from that for our sins.

204   Sweet is your name and everything about you:
        at your birth a rose issued from a thorn;

---

[203] The first coming when Christ was born.
[204] The second coming of Christ.
[205] For the Miracle of Theophilus, see Berceo's *Milagros de Nuestra Señora*, above, 123–141.
[206] St. Mary of Egypt (354?–431?), a penitent harlot who became a saint.
[207] St. Ildephonsus (606–667), Archbishop of Toledo. See Berceo's *Milagros de Nuestra Señora*, "The Chasuble of St. Ildephonsus," above, 19–22.
[208] Julian, the Apostate, Roman emperor from 361 to 363. (Dutton, 3:117, note 202d.)

you opened up the mysteries as something natural,[209]
and Christ welcomed[210] you as His spouse.

205   Flowers are as nothing compared to your beauty,
       for such a Master painted your colors;
       your features are noble, your virtues the best,
       wherefore your suitors praise you so greatly.[211]

206   Mother, everything about you is so greatly gifted
       that once a person has been in your company,
       everything about him is forever made straight,
       and his soul in the end is protected from the devil.

207   Mother, the preferring and the mention of your name
       bring pleasure to the ears and sweetness to the heart;
       the soul is greatly pleased when it hears your words;
       Mother, God has bestowed on you His full blessing.

208   Mother, you were filled with every goodness;
       you were generously imbued with the Holy Spirit;
       you gave birth and suckled and remained incorrupt;
       Judea is lost for it does not believe that.

209   One could think of this matter like a piece of crystal,
       pierced through unharmed by the ray of the sun;[212]
       that is how you engendered without corruption,
       as if you yourself passed through a vision.

210   Crystal, no doubt, is cold by nature,
       but we observe heat issuing from it;
       so it was not irreverent when God was willing,
       that you, being Virgin, should bring forth a child.

211   We can give yet another positive reason
       to prove the truth of what we say:
       a star casts a ray and remains unchanged;
       in that same way you as a virgin begot.

---

[209] Here I read *como natural cosa* with Salvador Miguel, 923, 204c and Logroño, 284, 204c rather than *con natura donosa* with Dutton, 3:106, 204c.

[210] Here I read *recebió* with Salvador Miguel, 923, 204d and Logroño, 284, 204d rather than *priso* with Dutton, 3:106, 204d.

[211] Berceo uses the style of a Provençal troubadour here.

[212] According to Salvador Miguel, 924, note 209, the metaphor of the ray of the sun passing through glass as applied to the virginity of Mary had a long previous history in Spanish literature.

212   Tell me, then, if that does not satisfy you,
        how did Habakkuk[213] pass through the closed gate?
        How did the fire abate for the young men?[214]
        Disprove it or believe it or say, "I know nothing."

213   We wholly acknowledge everything we tell of you;
        we do not doubt that you were virgin and mother;
        it is to you, Blessed Lady, that we have recourse,
        for we have never found any suchlike intercessor.

214   Mother, entreat your Son for us, your sinners:
        you have a Son and Father Who will hear your prayers;
        He will want to please you, His mother and daughter:
        protect us, Lady, from evil cares and worries.

215   Peace and well-being were reestablished by you;
        all previous anger was forgiven by you;
        be pleased, Lady, to lend us your help,
        for our troops lie in grave danger.

216   Through you the people parted from original sin;
        through you the sin against heaven was redressed;
        royal are you and everything about you:
        that is why you are peerless, according to the text.[215]

217   There is another privilege that we know of by habit:
        we invoke your name whenever we are in trouble;
        you are ready before we even ask you;
        were it not for you we would often fall.

218   We men and women look to you as our Mother;
        you guide us, Lady, as if we were your children;
        righteous and sinners, we await your mercy;
        we trust that through you God will grant us His.

219   Angels and archangels, cherubim and seraphim,
        apostles and martyrs, righteous and confessors,[216]
        with stoles and maniples[217] sing praises to you;
        those with most zeal are considered as best.

---

[213] See Dan. 14:33–38.

[214] See Dan. 3.

[215] The source used by Berceo.

[216] People who confess Christianity; also a category of non-martyr saint.

[217] A eucharistic vestment consisting of an ornamental band or stripe worn on the left arm near the wrist.

220   Virgins follow you as their mistress;
      all of them glorify and praise your person;
      Queen, invested with such a noble crown,
      we make you our advocate:[218] plead for us.

221   He who can praise you does so justly and rightly,
      but we great sinners may not do so;
      Glorious Empress, deign to glance our way,
      that we may worthily sing your glory.

222   Lady, we are pursued by great hostilities:
      the world with its adversities is against us;
      the devil's many falsehoods aid and abet it;
      with them he keeps our bodies falsely minded.

223   Amidst so many perils, who could protect us?
      We may be lost, Mother, if you do not help us;
      Queen of Heaven, be ready to aid us:
      we lie in danger, they hasten to betray us.

224   No human force could possibly think and speak
      of all the great gifts God's will bestowed on you;
      for you Christ willed to conquer His kingdom,
      where men and angels are expected to serve you.

225   Your subject, Lady, is just like the sea
      which all your narrators will have to dip into;
      if the world should last a hundred thousand years,
      no man's tongue could finish telling one-tenth of it.

226   Lady and Queen so worthy and powerful,
      take pity on us who are your sinners;
      extend your mercy to all of Christendom,
      for God, through your prayer, will show us compassion.

227   Help the living, pray for the dead,
      comfort the sick, convert the sinner,
      counsel the unfortunate, visit the afflicted,
      preserve the peaceful, reform the angered.

228   Uphold the Orders, Mother, save the clergy,
      broaden the faith, protect the monasteries;
      we always have need of you night and day,
      for our minds are wholly devoid of goodness.

---

[218] An allusion to the antiphon "Salve Regina: Advocata nostra."

229   Strengthen the weak, shield the strong,
        deliver the traveler, raise the downhearted,
        sustain those who stand, awaken those who sleep,
        establish in each of us appropriate habits.

230   Mother, for my followers I beg your mercy;
        for my dearest friends I beseech you always;
        take into your charge family relatives and elderly;
        all of us sinners entrust ourselves to you.

231   For I, who have sinned above all, I beg mercy:
        Mother, turn to me, let me not be forgotten;
        take away the sin that I lie steeped in;
        captive in Egypt I am beguiled by my pleasures.[219]

232   Again I beg mercy for your troubadour
        who composed this poem and was your suitor:
        intercede for him to your Son;
        obtain for him alms in the house of the Lord.

233   Pray for peace, Mother, and for clement weather;
        obtain our salvation and protect us from evil;
        guide us through mortal life in such a way
        that in the end we may gain the kingdom of heaven.
        Amen.

---

[219] Exod. 16:3.

Bibliography

Secondary Works and Sources of Reference

Andrés Castellanos, María S. de, ed. *La Vida de Santa María Egipciaca.* Madrid: Aguirre Torre, 1964.

Baró, José. *Glosario completo de los "Milagros de Nuestra Señora" de Gonzalo de Berceo.* Boulder: Society of Spanish and Spanish-American Studies, 1987.

Bartha, Jeannie K. "Four Lexical Notes on Berceo's *Milagros de Nuestra Señora.*" *Romance Philology* 37 (1983): 56–62.

———. *Vocabulario de los "Milagros de Nuestra Señora" de Gonzalo de Berceo.* Normal, IL: Applied Literature Press, 1980.

Blecua, J. M., ed. *El Conde Lucanor.* Madrid: Castalia, 1969.

Cejador y Frauca, J. *Vocabulario medieval castellano.* Orig. 1929; repr. New York: Las Américas, 1968.

Corominas, Joan, ed. *Libro de Buen Amor.* Madrid: Gredos, 1967.

———, and José A. Pascual. *Diccionario crítico etimológico castellano e hispánico.* 6 vols. Madrid: Gredos, 1980–1991.

Covarrubias Orozco, Sebastián de. *Tesoro de la lengua castellana o española.* Orig. 1611; repr. Madrid: Turner, 1977.

Deyermond, Alan. "Observaciones sobre las técnicas literarias de los *Loores de Nuestra Señora.*" In *Actas de las III Jornadas de Estudios Berceanos,* ed. Claudio García Turza, 57–62. Logroño: Instituto de Estudios Riojanos, 1981.

Dutton, Brian. "A Chronology of the Works of Gonzalo de Berceo." In *Medieval Hispanic Studies Presented to Rita Hamilton,* ed. A. D. Deyermond, 67–76. London: Tamesis, 1975.

———. *A New Berceo Manuscript, Biblioteca Nacional Ms. 13149. Description, Study and Partial Edition.* Exeter Hispanic Texts 32. Exeter: University of Exeter Press, 1982.

Goicoechea, Cesáreo. *Vocabulario riojano.* Madrid: Aguirre Torre, 1961.

Gulsoy, J. "The -i Words in the Poems of Gonzalo de Berceo." *Romance Philology* 23 (1969–1970): 172–87.

Honnorat, S. J. *Dictionnaire Provençal-Français.* 3 vols. Orig.1848; repr. Marseille: Laffitte Reprints, 1971.

Keller, John Esten. "The Blessed Virgin as a Patron of the Arts and Letters." In *Models in Medieval Iberian Literature* ed. Judy B. McInnis, 3-7. Newark, DE: Juan de la Cuesta, 2002.

———. *Gonzalo de Berceo.* Twayne World Authors Series 187. New York: Twayne, 1972.

———. *Pious Brief Narrative in Medieval Castilian and Galician Verse: From Berceo to Alfonso X.* Lexington: University Press of Kentucky, 1978.

Koberstein, G., ed. *Gonzalo de Berceo, "Estoria de San Millán": Textkritische Edition.* Münster: Aschendorff, 1964.

Kulp-Hill, Kathleen, trans. *Songs of Holy Mary by Alfonso X, The Wise: A Translation of the* Cantigas de Santa María. MRTS 173. Tempe: Arizona Center for Medieval and Renaissance Studies, 2000.

Lanchetas, Rufino. *Gramática y vocabulario de las obras de Gonzalo de Berceo.* Madrid: Sucesores de Rivadeneyra, 1900.

Lappin, Anthony. *Berceo's Vida de Santa Oria: Text, Translation and Commentary.* Oxford: Legenda, 2000.

Latham, R. E. *Revised Medieval Latin Word-List.* London: Oxford University Press, 1965.

Lazar, Moshé, ed. *La Fazienda de Ultramar.* Salamanca: Cervantes, 1965.

Levy, Emil. *Petit Dictionnaire Provençal-Français.* Orig. 1909; 5th ed. Heidelberg: Carl Winter, 1973.

Marden, C. Carroll, ed. *Libro de Apolonio.* Orig. 1922; repr. Millwood: Kraus Reprint Co., 1976.

Menéndez Pidal, Ramón, ed. *Cantar de Mío Cid. Texto, gramática y vocabulario.* 4th ed. Madrid: Espasa-Calpe, 1969.

Montgomery, Thomas, ed. *El Evangelio de San Mateo. Texto, gramática, vocabulario.* Madrid: Aguirre Torre, 1962.

Mount, T., and Annette G. Cash, trans. Gonzalo de Berceo, *Miracles of Our Lady.* Lexington: University Press of Kentucky, 1997.

Nebrija, Antonio de. *Vocabulario de Romance en Latin.* Orig. 1516; transcr. Gerald J. MacDonald. Philadelphia: Temple University Press, 1973.

Ramoneda, Arturo M., ed. Gonzalo de Berceo. *Signos que aparecerán antes del Juicio Final, Duelo de la Virgen, Martirio de San Lorenzo.* Madrid: Castalia, 1980.

Real Academia Española. *Diccionario de la lengua española.* 19th ed. Madrid: Espasa-Calpe, 1970.

Solalinde, A. G., ed. *Milagros de Nuestra Señora.* 8th ed. Madrid: Espasa-Calpe, 1972.

Walsh, John K., ed. *El Libro de los Doze Sabios o Tractado de la Nobleza y Lealtad.* Madrid: Aguirre, 1975.

Willis, Raymond S., ed. *El libro de Alexandre.* Orig. 1934; repr. Millwood: Kraus Reprint Co., 1976.

———. *Libro de Buen Amor.* Princeton: Princeton University Press, 1972.

Introduction to
The Lamentation of the Virgin

Translated by Jeannie K. Bartha

In 197 moving quatrains and 13 unusual couplets noted below, Berceo presents to his audience the events connected with Christendom's most awesome episode: the Crucifixion of our Lord Jesus Christ. He does so by following an account ostensibly written by St. Bernard of Clairvaux. This account takes the form of a dialogue between the saint and the Blessed Virgin (e.g. Sermon 43 on the Song of Songs, PL 183. 993–995). Using contemporary language, imagery, and popular turns of phrase, Berceo depicts Our Lady as a warm and all-too-human suffering mother. Berceo's technique is what a modern reader would describe as an interview between Bernard the monk, as the reporter, and the Virgin, who is a victim herself, as the witness. The poem, like a good reportage, sets the stage, gives the background of the story, quotes verbatim here and paraphrases there. The drama is projected through questions and answers, drawing listeners into the circle of bystanders, as it were, to hear the unfolding of events. Of course, none of the details of the "interview" can be found in Holy Writ, and many of the descriptions that Berceo attributes to the Virgin originate in the poetic imagination. There is a long tradition of this in both East and West, from Romanos Melodes's "Mary at the Cross" to the *Stabat Mater dolorosa* attributed to Jacopone da Todi. Berceo's poem is a representative piece of writing for the Middle Ages in topic, style, language, and characterization.

After quatrain 177 Berceo breaks away from the *cuaderna vía* of the *mester de clerecía* to insert a peculiar *cántica* ('chanty'), the so-called *Eya velar* ('Keep Watch') in the form of 13 lyric couplets. The exact source of the *Eya Velar* is unknown. It is believed to be a watchman's song, and indeed, a version in Latin that was apparently sung by watchmen has been discovered (see note ad loc.). Ultimately the source may be folkloristic, even in the Latin version. Berceo either knew the Latin and rendered it into Spanish, or he knew the Spanish version and simply borrowed it from oral lore or from a written source and inserted it into the *Lamentation*. It is a strange yet highly dramatic element in the poem.

Its rhythmic pattern suggests that it may have been sung to a tune lost over time. As a poetic device, it broke the Virgin's lament and permitted the listener or reader to alter the relentless flow of the drama. Viewed from a contemporary perspective, it might even be that the powerfully effective repetition of the words *eya velar* was designed for audience participation whereby listeners would have chanted the words, possibly accompanied by a rhythmic drumbeat-like pounding on tables or like objects.

Abbreviations

Dutton   Dutton, Brian, ed. *El Duelo de la Virgen*. In Gonzalo de Berceo, *Obras Completas*, 3: 17–58. London: Tamesis, 1975.

Logroño   *Duelo que fizo la Virgen María el día de la pasión de su fijo Jesu Christo*. In Gonzalo de Berceo, *Obras completas*, intro. Rufino Briones, 427–55. Logroño: Instituto de Estudios Riojanos, 1971.

Orduna   Orduna, Germán, ed. *Duelo de la Virgen*. In Gonzalo de Berceo, *Obra completa*, with Isabel Uría, 797–857. Madrid: Espasa-Calpe, 1992.

Ramoneda   Ramoneda, Arturo M., ed. *Duelo de la Virgen*. In Gonzalo de Berceo, *Signos que aparecerán antes del Juicio Final, Duelo de la Virgen, Martirio de San Lorenzo*, 159–227. Madrid: Castalia, 1980.

THE LAMENTATION OF THE VIRGIN

1   In the precious name of the Holy Queen,
the one who bore healing and salvation to the world,
if she were to guide me by divine grace,
I would like to compose a poem of her sorrow.

2   The sorrow she suffered over her Holy Child,
in Whom the devil never gained any entry;
when He was abandoned by His disciples,
He Who did no evil and was judged so unjustly.

3   St. Bernard, a fine monk and good friend of God,
tried to discover the anguish of the sorrow I relate to you,
but he could never seek any other entrance
but the one to whom Gabriel said, "The Lord is with Thee."[1]

4   Over and over again the devout gentleman,
while shedding lively and heartfelt tears,
made this petition to the Glorious Lady:
that she should send him her consolation.

5   The good man would say with all his heart,
"Great and powerful Queen of the Heavens,
with whom the Messiah shared every secret,
do not be stinting of your mercy.

6   The entire Holy Church will reap the benefits;
greater respect will be shown to your person;
greater news of your excellency will be known
than all the masters of France announce."

7   The monk so earnestly pressed the matter
that his cry was to rise up to the heavens;
"Let us prepare to return," said Holy Mary;
"this monk will not give us any peace."

---

[1] See Luke 1:28.

8   The Glorious Lady descended to the house
        where the monk was praying with his cowl thrown back;
        she said, "God save you, my suffering little soul:
        I have made a great call to bring you comfort."

9   "Lady," said the monk, "if you are Mary,
        the one who suckled the Messiah at her breast,
        then you are the one I was persistently seeking,
        for all my hope lies entirely in you."

10   "Friar," said the Lady, "do not doubt about the matter,
        I am Mary, the spouse of Joseph;
        I am drawn here swiftly by concern for your request;
        I want us both to compose a poem together."

11   "Lady," said the monk, "I know very well
        that neither sadness nor grief can touch you,
        for you dwell in the glory of the Lord our God,
        but please do me the favor of seeking help.

12   I beg you to tell me right from the beginning,
        when Christ was taken if you were with Him,
        how you gazed at Him or with what suffering eyes;
        I beg you to tell me one way or another."

13   "Friar," said the Lady, "it is difficult for me
        to recall my suffering, for I am glorified;
        but I have not forgotten that arrow of mine,
        for I have it deeply imbedded in my heart.

14   Neither old nor young nor married woman
        suffered such pain or died pierced by such a lance,
        for I was boiled twice and doubly grilled;
        the anguish of Mary could never be imagined.

15   The night of the Supper, when we ate,
        we consumed sweet morsels of the body of Christ;
        and then came a clatter of men bearing arms:
        they entered the house as if possessed by the devil.

16   The Shepherd stood firm and held His ground;
        the flock of sheep were scattered all around;[2]
        they seized the Lamb, those false crusaders,
        guided by the wolf that reaped the reward.

17   At this sudden surprise that had befallen us,
        my blood ran cold and I lay in a faint;

[2] See Matt. 26:31.

I would rather have died than endure such a life:
if they had killed me they might have cured me.

18   When I came to my senses, I looked all around:
I saw neither the Shepherd nor His disciples;
first and foremost I was frantic with worry;
I had no desire to get any help.

19   I pursued the wolves who bore the Shepherd away,
while firmly reproaching them for leaving me behind;
they paid not the slightest heed to my cries,
for they had already accomplished what they came for.

20   My dear little sisters were weeping loudly,
both beating their breasts over their cloaks;
they went wailing outside into the wilderness;
they were both aunts of my very sweet Son.

21   Mary of Magdala never left His side,
for apart from me, she of all women loved Him best;
her bitter mourning could not have been greater;
we women were all shocked by what she did.

22   With all the other women so greatly distressed,
who would imagine the anguish of the one that bore Him?
I knew all about Who He was and where He came from,
for it was I who nursed Him with my very own milk.

23   They stripped Him of His clothing leaving Him in undergarments;
they all shouted together at Him, "Get moving, get moving!
He Who broke the Sabbath deserves such a tree:
He shall be hanged by the sixth hour."

24   The infidels acted with great cruelty,
whipping Him[3] severely with knotted ropes;
rivulets of blood flowed down His bare shoulders,
and during all this I suffered deadly trembling.

25   But those vile people did something even worse:
they jammed a crown of thorns[4] right down on His skull,
and placed in His hand a scepter made of cane,
shouting, "Hail to our King" — which is just what He was.

26   No one could ever die so greatly afflicted.
I begged for death, but it would not come;
I only desired not to go on living,

[3] See Matt. 27:26.
[4] See Matt. 27:29.

but the Lord God would not accept my request.

27   The good Lord willingly suffered His martyrdom,
       for that was the reason the Father had sent Him;
       in spite of the outrage, He prayed for them
       that the Lord God should pardon them their sin.

28   I in my misery was gazing at my Son,
       while smiting my cheeks and bending low to the ground;
       there were other good women loudly lamenting
       with both of my sisters already mentioned.

29   I gazed at Him for He was suffering so greatly:
       He gazed at me in my deep distress;
       amidst all the anguish He never forgot me;
       at my every cry He gazed at me intently.

30   My precious Son, Lord of the universe,
       suffered more over me than He did for Himself;
       He carried all His ministry through to completion,
       just as the Holy Gospel shows us.

31   The Jews refused to have blood on their hands,
       for their law forbade them to commit such a sacrilege:[5]
       since it was almost or already noon,
       they handed Him over to the pagans to be hanged.

32   The pagans led Him, bound with a rope,
       out of the city well away from the market;
       they threw on His back a heavy piece of wood
       from which was made His cross of crucifixion.

33   Hurriedly the pagans laid Him on the cross,
       nailing His hands and His feet to the wood;
       He was treated savagely by the cruel villains
       who weep today while the Christians laugh.

34   Outraged for my Son I stayed right near Him,
       my head hanging sadly, my hands on my cheeks;
       the wicked crowd was swirling all around me,
       but not a single one of them pushed me aside.

35   I stood there stunned and unable to speak;
       outraged for my Son I could find no rest,
       for the morsel was bitter and hard to swallow,
       worse than a green serbal,[6] a really sour fruit.

---

[5] See John 18:31.

[6] A type of wild pear found in Spain. See Ramoneda, 302, s.v. *sierva*.

36 The Holy Child, while hanging on the cross,
    cast His sweet gaze everywhere around Him;
    He saw me wretched, deeply saddened with grief,
    crying out in anguish: "My Son! My Son!"

37 He saw His disciple whom He loved so much,
    saw how the son of Zebedee was weeping;
    He gave him to me as a son,[7] for He greatly cherished him,
    and me to him as a mother, thus binding us together.

38 While on the cross with outstretched arms,
    — not for anything He had done, but for our sins,
    for He ardently desired to save sinners —
    His lips being dry, He said He was thirsty.[8]

39 When they heard His words, those good-for-nothings
    who were more rabid than carnivorous curs
    opened their jaws like nasty hound dogs,
    and like wicked cupbearers they gave Him a foul brew.

40 They gave Him a terribly bitter concoction,
    a coarse blend of gall mixed with vinegar
    that He would not swallow, for it was harsh;
    everything remained on them and on their descendants.

41 Those low-down characters did many terrible things:
    I witnessed it all, every one of their tricks;
    the Master was suffering and Mary was weeping;
    it was a bitter day for the two of them together.

42 Those ungodly people mocked Him even more:
    they bandaged His eyes so He could not see anything;
    each young punk gave Him his slap
    saying, "Tell us, Christ, who is the one that just hit you?"[9]

43 Friar, let us not continue in such a long digression,
    for you can read every twist and turn for yourself:
    it is all written down in St. Matthew's Gospel,
    and in the Gospel of John, the son of Zebedee.

44 It is best that we speak in our private conversation
    of the matter of my sorrow and my misfortune,
    of the martyrdom I suffered without sword or spear,
    if God would only help us to recall it to mind.

---

[7] See John 19:26–27.
[8] See John 19:28.
[9] See Matt. 26:68.

45   Friar, I tell you true and you must believe me,
        I would rather have died than to go on living,
        but it was not the will of the Heavenly King:
        we had to drink the absinthe down to the dregs.

46   Outraged for my Son, my Lord, my Father,
        my Light, my Comfort, my Salvation, my Shepherd,
        my Life, my Help, my Glory, my Sweetness,
        I had no pleasure or interest in living.

47   I had no pleasure or interest in living,
        my soul was so burdened down with sadness;
        anyone who tried to speak to me lightly
        would be out of his senses or unaware of justice.

48   Seeing my Son in such a state,
        crucified between two wicked men,
        and He so undeserving of such a wicked judgment,
        my heart could never be peaceful again.

49   I witnessed the blood flowing from His holy hands,
        and from His feet which were also wounded,
        His side pierced, and the fickle crowd appearing,
        and Jews and pagans jeering at Him.

50   Jews and pagans jeering at Him,
        kicking Him wickedly like worthless old nags
        who had manes and tails that were badly groomed,
        chanting horrid evensongs and even worse matins.

51   With their terrible betrayal and killing of my Son,
        how could my heart ever be peaceful?
        They purchased Him first from one of His disciples;
        they put Him through a dreadful Passion and killed Him in the end.

52   From His hands and feet fresh blood flowed
        which stained the cross of palm and olive wood;
        those wicked men were spitting in His face,
        while His sorrowful mother stood seething with anger.

53   The blood gushed down in great spurts from His body,
        and His mother caught it on scraps of pure white linen;
        they were left as a heritage for future generations
        so their descendants will taste bitter fruits forever.[10]

---

[10] Cf. Matt. 27:25.

54   As to further suffering meted out to my Lord,
my own poor soul suffered greater affliction;
time after time I besought the Almighty
to grant me death which would suit me better.

55   Time after time I repeated my prayer;
I never could endure such a death that many times;
I would rather sustain severe blows to my head
than to suffer so many terrible afflictions.

56   I said to the pagans, "People, by your faith,
kill me first rather than Christ;
if you kill the mother you will be shown greater mercy:
by God, do not kill such a beautiful child."

57   I said to the Jews, "Relatives and friends,
all of us come from the same ancestry;
accept my request and these cries of mine:
kill me, and thus you may see your children's children.[11]

58   Thus you may see your future generations,
and you shall gain the bodies you have suffered so much for;
only free the body you purchased from Judas:
you do harm to the mother since you did not kill her.

59   If only you had killed or buried me before,
or had thrown me in the fire or down a well,
you would have cured me, for I would not feel anything:
I would not be so boiled or so grilled today."

60   Happy are the mothers and fortunate are those
who do not see their sons suffer such evil;
but none could imagine the extent of my sorrow,
for no mother ever bore a son of such nature.

61   No mother ever bore a son of such nature
who never did evil or ever deserved it,
who always did right and desired only justice;
no such infant was ever baptized.

62   No human eyes ever saw such a child:
He always sought to please and benefit all;
He never took a thing from the good or the bad,
nor would He ever reply to any wicked words.

---

[11] Cf. Ps. 128:6.

63   Although they insulted Him He showed moderation;
        He never answered back, He stayed very quiet;[12]
        no one was ever insulted by His lips;
        no one was ever refused His grace.

64   He never turned away any just man or sinner,
        or refused him help as His perfect Lord;
        and those who were hungry or desired to eat,
        He fed with love in His own special way.

65   The sick who came to Him seeking health
        He sent away healed, joyful and happy;
        in word and in deed He gave such comfort
        that they ardently desired to return to His presence.

66   His holy sermons were so gifted
        that they healed the sick and freed them from sin,
        they sustained the needy and guided the erring;
        all who heard them were made content.

67   Even if the Pharisees would not believe Him,
        they still could not answer any of His questions;
        if they tried to trap Him on any matter,
        how well He could protect and defend Himself against them!

68   Mary Magdalene would indeed tell you
        how He received her when He was at supper;
        He never focused on her multitude of sins:
        He forgave them all and freed her from suffering.[13]

69   No one in distress who came to see Him
        ever failed to find the help that he needed;
        those wanting food got help from Him:
        even with no money they lacked for nothing.

70   The merciful Lord, above everything else,
        the perfect Lord brought the dead back to life;
        those He was good to, like a loyal Father,
        were the very ones who sought His downfall.

71   Instead of looking to serve Him with love,
        they sought for Him trouble and complete dishonor;
        and what is even worse, they finally sought His death:
        it was the sheep who had the Shepherd destroyed.

[12] See Matt. 27:12, 14.
[13] See Luke 7:37–50.

72   The sheep caused the Shepherd to be hanged;
        they asked for Barabbas who deserved the sentence;
        they brought condemnation on their own good King,
        and that is the reason I had to suffer so harshly.

73   'O beloved Son, Lord of Lords,
        I suffer the sorrow, You suffer the pains;
        betrayed by Your subjects who paid You wicked service,
        You suffer the agony, I the dreadful effects.

74   My beloved Son so abundant in mercy,
        why is Your mother left abandoned by You?
        I would be pleased with You if You would take me,
        for I will be desolate here alone without You.

75   Son, I would like to die near You,
        I would not like to return to the world without my Son;
        Son, Lord and Father, deign to look at me:
        a son should not refuse a request from his mother.

76   Sweet and protective Son, Temple of Charity,
        Ark of Wisdom, Fountain of Mercy,
        do not leave your mother among such people,
        for they cannot even recognize kindness or goodness.

77   Son, You show wisdom in all things;
        You are a wise mediator in a conflict;
        do not leave Your mother in such a shameful place,
        where they hang the saint and save the traitor.

78   Son, we always made our lives together;
        our love for each other was deep and intense;
        You and I always had faith in each other;
        Your abundant mercy now forsakes me.

79   Son, do not forget me, and take me with You.
        I have only one good friend left in this world,
        John, whom You gave me as a son, weeps here with me:
        I beseech You to grant me what I ask You.

80   I beseech You to grant me what I ask You,
        a request small enough from any mother;
        Son, indeed I implore You and I urge You
        not to let this request be forgotten.'

81   The Lord replied, and these are His words:
        'Mother, your terrible anguish deeply grieves me;
        I am moved by your tears and your eloquent words,
        more bitter to me than mortal blows.

82   Mother, I surely told you, — but you have forgotten,
        distracted by your great and terrible grief —
        why I was sent by the Father from heaven,
        to endure the martyrdom of crucifixion.

83   Mother, you of all people certainly know
        of how our first parents committed the sin,
        of how the devils so cunningly deceived them,
        and the lies the wicked flatterers told them.

84   They lost paradise and then they lost life,
        and all their descendants were lost through them;
        then the door to the fine garden[14] was closed,
        never more to be opened until my coming.

85   By universal sentence they all went to hell,
        where they lay entrapped in a terrible stench,
        unable to escape it through any penance,
        but some among them were true believers.

86   The Heavenly Father, God the Almighty,
        in abundant mercy and very great wisdom
        remembered the souls of His devout brethren,
        and would not leave them lying in such an infirmary.

87   He would not leave them lying in such a stinking vale,
        where the devils do a great deal of filthy work;
        He sent His Son, the Angel of great help,[15]
        to move them from there to another place.

88   Mother, you were the first to know the secret:
        you received the message from the angel Gabriel;
        you safely concealed it in your fine storeroom,
        and tied the keys firmly to your noble waist.

89   Mother, our moment of triumph is at hand,
        for our foes are now trying to reach the hill;
        Mother, take courage, do not be dismayed:
        your lamentations may hinder our progress.

90   Mother, you are full of spiritual grace;
        you are the mother of a perfect and precious Son;
        endure the fact that I suffer such evil,
        for no other salt can possibly cure it.

---

[14] The Garden of Eden.
[15] Cf. Isa. 9:6 (Vulgate).

91   There is no other way to cure this evil,
no magic solution or greater wisdom,
apart from this cup that we must drink,[16]
and you and I, dear Mother, may not spill it.

92   You and I, dear Mother, both must taste it,
I enduring the pains and you the dreadful grief;
from this time on all peoples must praise you
for suffering together with your Son to save souls.

93   Mother, very soon the cup will be drained;
what the Father commanded will soon be accomplished;
all the living and the dead will be grateful to us,
and your great lamentation will be turned to great joy.[17]

94   If I drink the cup as I have been commanded,
Satan will be vanquished and my Father pleased;
Adam and Eve will emerge in famous company
from the depths of hell, to the great regret of those there.

95   The words from the poisonous mouth of Caiaphas,[18]
utterly lacking in peace and good will,
this is the time for us to fulfill them,
but Caiaphas shall reap no great reward from them.

96   I myself must descend into hell
to remove any doubt from John the Baptist;[19]
I intend to give them such a mouthful to eat
that they will always grieve and have reason to weep.

97   I will move from there those who truly loved me,
to a better home which they so richly deserved,
and reopen the holy gates that were closed,
and mingle humans with angels who never mixed before.

98   Mother, temper your lament and be more moderate;
for God's sake, Mother, do not upset yourself so;
you are upsetting us all with your affliction:
Mother, do this for God the holy Father.'

99   'Son,' said the mother, 'with the words that You speak,
it is as if You bring me back from death to life;
those words that You utter comfort me greatly,
for I certainly see that You suffer for us all.

---

[16] Cf. Matt. 26:39,42; Mark 14:36; Luke 22:42.
[17] Cf. John 16:20.
[18] See John 11:49–50 and 18:14.
[19] See Matt. 11:2–6 and Luke 7:18–23.

100   For the sake of us all, Son, You suffer immensely;
        for all peoples You drink sour wine and bitterness;
        You do it to save the whole human race
        so sorely afflicted down through the ages.

101   Scripture tells us that all through the ages,
        surely five thousand and two hundred years,
        that the just and unjust lay all mixed together,[20]
        but not all of them endured the same suffering.

102   Lord, You know those who are meant to be released,
        and those who are lost and have to stay there;
        Lord, You Who know how to judge all things,
        go and help Your own whom You came to get.

103   Son, go quickly where You want to go,
        that You may not suffer so long in this martyrdom;
        gather Your sheep, Your little ones, together,
        but in all Your hurry do not forget me.

104   Help Your mother, do not leave her forgotten,
        for You know very well the anguish she suffers;
        Son, if I am abandoned thus by You,
        those ungodly people will take vengeance on me.

105   Son, we may not hinder Your departure,
        for then Your crucifixion would be terribly wasted;
        for all of us hope to gain life through You,
        but do not keep us waiting too long for Your coming.

106   If You do not come back quickly
        and respond to Your disciples,
        they may possibly find me drowned in sorrow,
        for I will not sleep well until Your return.'

107   'Mother,' said the Son, 'three days from today
        I will be with you alive; you will witness great joy:
        I will visit you first of all, Virgin Mary,
        and afterwards Peter with all his companions.

108   And with that, Mother, I will take my leave;
        I have told you everything I have to say.'
        He bowed His head like one who wants to sleep;
        He gave His soul up to God and let Himself die.

---

[20] Cf. Matt. 5:45.

109   When the Glorious Lord gave up His soul,
        the glorious and most precious Mother
        fell dead on the ground as if violently ill,
        forgetting the words of her Holy Spouse.

110   Forgetting the words of her Holy Spouse,
        so severely afflicted and grieved was she,
        for she had never had such a horrible shock,
        or ever received such a scorching blow.

111   She had never received such a scorching blow,
        or ever been so seared by a sudden assault;
        those who were near her, in order to revive her,
        splashed her with cold water, but she did not come to.

112   They splashed cold water on her eyes and face,
        but no matter how they shouted Mary did not respond,
        for she was stricken by a dreadful illness
        that no doctor's medicine could possibly help.

113   It was not surprising that she who bore Him
        should faint like that in her grief for such a Son;
        in the signs from heaven similar things occurred:
        all made lamentation the moment that He died.

114   The angels in heaven kept them company:
        they grieved over Christ and grieved over Mary;
        the sun lost its light, the day became darkened,
        but the Jews refused to heed the warning.

115   The veil that separated the temple from the altar,
        was torn in two since it could not weep;
        even the rocks split open with grief;[21]
        the wretched Jews were unable to breathe.

116   From old sepulchers of ancient times,
        where many holy people were lying imprisoned,
        and which opened by themselves without any digging,
        people of great ancestry came back to life.

117   Many pious people came back to life,
        the perfectly faithful righteous and just;
        it is a well-known fact that they appeared to many,
        for St. Matthew in his wisdom tells us so.[22]

---

[21] See Matt. 27:51–52.
[22] See Matt. 27:52–53.

118   While that news spread throughout the world,
        the whole of nature lay in a swoon;
        and I in my misery responded to their cries,
        for everyone thought they would be destroyed.

119   Then Centurio,[23] a noble gentleman, spoke;
        he bore testimony indeed great and true:
        'People, this unfortunate man was just:
        He was sent from God, He was His messenger.

120   He was the greatly beloved Son of God,
        an angelic being and perfect in goodness;
        He never should have been hanged by us,
        and that is the reason for these terrifying things.'

121   I replied in my misery a good hour later,
        crying: 'Son, Son, my Salvation and my Life,
        my Light, my Help, my Goodness and my Refuge,
        You no longer speak to me and now I am lost.

122   Now I am wretched and I am unfortunate,
        when my dear Son does not answer me at all;
        now I am stricken by a terribly evil blow;
        now I consider myself poor and forlorn.

123   Son, You are alive though I see You dead,
        and even though dead I believe You are alive;
        but I am really dying of longing for You,
        for I am terribly dazed and out of my wits.

124   Through the holy nature You got from Your Father.
        You live forever, for You cannot die;
        but through the meager traits You received from me,
        from them You get hunger, thirst, and death.[24]

125   Son, why do You let Your mother live,
        when You have placed Yourself on the cross to die?
        Son, You should not be willing to allow
        that I should suffer to the point of begging for death.

126   Son, I felt no pangs at Your birth,
        no stabbing pains or other discomfort;
        when the false traitors killed the male children,[25]
        we went off to Egypt like fine gentlefolk.

---

[23] Dutton, 3:49, note 119a states that as it frequently happened in the Middle Ages, Berceo misinterpreted the Latin word *centurio* as a proper name.

[24] This refers to the theological doctrine according to which the divine deeds stemmed from Christ's divine nature while the human deeds come from his human nature.

[25] The killing of the Holy Innocents. See Matt. 2:16.

127   Son, You have always shielded me from evil attacks,
        for You never allowed any suffering to touch me;
        You have always had compassion for Your mother,
        but now You have become very cruel to me.

128   When You refused to save Yourself from death,
        Son, You should have taken me away before You;
        that I should not witness Your terribly great suffering,
        Son, only for that have I reason to reproach You.

129   Son, only for that could I possibly reproach You,
        but even though I say so I would not dare to do so;
        but with all my heart I would really love to,
        for no one knows the evil that I would avoid.'

130   No one could possibly conceive or imagine,
        even I cannot convey the depths of my suffering;
        my heart is too crushed to be able to express it;
        my Son understands it if He cared to speak.

131   My Son knows, and keeps to Himself
        the suffering and agony I endure for my child;
        may He be blessed as a noble Son
        Who was unwilling to displease His Father.

132   After midday on Friday afternoon,
        about the ninth hour, the sun on the wane,
        Joseph,[26] a good man, went to the governor
        to request the holy body that was dead by then.

133   He requested the holy body to give it a tomb
        as is naturally required for any dead person;
        Pilate prudently granted his request,
        and so, God bless me, he did the right thing.

134   He who requested it did the right thing,
        but not less Pilate who willingly gave it;
        the two of them together deserved a reward,
        but He thanked the former more than the latter.

135   May the Lord our God thank them both,
        for both were good, but the former was better;
        the provider of the tomb made a greater gesture
        than the other, whom I believe deserved less credit.

136   While Joseph was arranging everything else,
        I was suffering miserably and could not stop weeping;

---

[26] Joseph of Arimathea. See Matt. 27:57–61.

I was scolding my Son for not speaking to me;
I was well aware that I was out of my wits.

137   I never left my place right by the cross:
I saw every scheme that they were hatching;
I observed them all and they all observed Mary;
my lamentation made them think I was out of my wits.

138   I embraced the cross as high as I could,
and consoled myself by kissing His feet;
His mouth was too high for me to reach,
and so were His hands which I ardently longed for.

139   I cried, 'O wretched me! What I had to witness!
I never thought I would fall into such a trap.
I have lost help, courage, and wisdom;
weep well, my eyes, do not stop your tears.

140   Weep well, my eyes, keep shedding tears;
my heart is outraged, it can give me no peace;
indeed we must remember that this day is ill-fated,
and those who serve my Son must unfailingly keep it.

141   May those in our party remember this day,
a day so painful, so terribly unjust,
a day when I, Virgin Mary, lose my sunshine:
a day when the sun dies is a day uncompleted.

142   A day when I am deprived of every brightness,
the light of my eyes and every mercy,
when all the elements heartily weep;
I commit no sin if I weep in my misery.

143   If in my misery I weep or faint,
or if in such great anguish I sicken of life,
it is because I do not know why I deserve this,
but still I thank God through Whom it came.

144   Son Who shines brighter than the sun or the moon,
Who governed all things right from the cradle,
Lord, You Who desire to save every soul,
remember this river of tears that I am weeping.

145   Remember the many tears that I shed,
and my unconcealed groaning and moaning;
Your suffering and my agony I cannot convey,
for the depths of my grief leave me speechless.

146   Grief overwhelms me and hinders my speech;
whoever hears me should not blame me,

for so great are my sorrow and my heartbreak,
only she who has lost such a son can imagine.'

147   When Joseph had obtained that perfect body,
he said to Pilate, 'May God give you thanks.'
Then he returned to the body that was hanging,
striking his forehead with his clenched fist.

148   Those of us there made great lamentation,
renewing our weeping as best we could;
our great lamentation was no surprise,
for bitter and evil were our morsel and drink.

149   All were earnestly weeping and wailing,
but the most unrestrained was she who bore Him;
I in my misery ran and leaped among them,
tearing my garments with outrage for my Son.

150   The Arimathean who had obtained the body
summoned Nicodemus, a very fine gentleman;
one held the body clasped in his arms,
the other withdrew the driven nails.

151   From the Lord Who never does anything in vain,
they removed the nail from His right hand first;
He lowered Himself a little and made Himself lighter:
it seemed to me that He descended to the earth.

152   He bent towards me in this first coming,
and witnessing this I experienced healing;
although I was dazed I grasped His hand,
saying, 'O my sweet and perfect Son!'

153   I took His right hand, the one I could reach:
I was still unable to get to the other;
I was kissing that one and suffering over it,
while I was continuing to help Joseph.

154   Those two gentlemen both took down the body;
they covered it with cloth and laid it on the ground;
they anointed His body with a precious ointment,
treating it with the greatest possible reverence.

155   Both of them gave Him a worthy tomb
which Joseph had previously made for himself:
they wrapped him in linen according to the law;[27]
I in my misery witnessed bitter entrails.

---

[27] See John 19:39–40.

156   I in my misery witnessed bitter entrails,
        bitter cooks and bitter food;
        an inscription written in Hebrew and Latin,
        and thirdly in Greek,[28] bread from evil flour.

157   I read the letters as they were written,
        but did not understand them, for they were obscure;
        those cunning people were up to their tricks
        making short letters long, and narrow letters wide.

158   I was speechless with outrage for my Son;
        they made me move from there to elsewhere,
        so that I might have some relief from my sorrow,
        for I was on the point of laying down my soul.

159   They made me go and stay with John in his home,
        for he would give me bread and water for supper,
        that on the morrow I might keep the sabbath there,
        for I could have died from such great affliction.

160   John took me along to stay in his home,
        for my Son had already entrusted me to him;
        I did not get a wink of sleep that night,
        nor did I chew a single bite of food.

161   Friday night until early next morning,
        I suffered great bitterness, a dark, dreadful night,
        crying: 'Son, Son, where is Your home?'
        I never thought I would see the light of day.

162   The sabbath dawned, a miserable day:
        we suffered great sadness and nothing of joy;
        we composed a long litany of our sorrow;
        both John and Mary made great lamentation.

163   We women that day were completely crushed,
        more than if we had all been viciously beaten;
        we were much too weary even to move,
        but I, above all, ached deep down inside me.

164   We were all unrestrainedly weeping and wailing,
        but she who had borne Him suffered greater anguish;
        she was more afflicted and more distressed,
        for she had as her pittance bitter entrails.

165   She gnawed a green apple, such a sour pittance,

---

[28] See John 19:19–20.

more bitter for her than a sharp blow from a lance,
except for the fact she could not die without grief,
for she sought no other satisfaction from God.

166   To add even more to my sorrow and affliction,
all the Jewish people stirred from their quarter;
they went to Pilate to take counsel,
to be sure the disciples could not steal Him from them.[29]

167   'Sir,' they said, 'that impostor
stirred us all up like a great scoundrel;
He said some things that made us afraid,
for the company He kept was no better than Himself.

168   He boasted to those who were His disciples,
that He had to die by the Passion and the cross,
but that on the third day He would come forth from the tomb,
and He would come back to life in better condition.

169   Sir, we are afraid His disciples will come
since we will all be observing the Sabbath;
they will steal His body and we will be tricked;
they will laugh at us: we will be taken for fools.

170   Sir, it is essential that you post a guard,
that we may not suffer even further mockery;
all of us would much sooner be dead
than to suffer such mockery from vile men.

171   They would ridicule us and make up songs,
for His men are a pack of worthless scoundrels;
they would fill the whole world, every mountain and valley:
they would use the lie to tell stories and sermons.'

172   Then Pilate replied to those fellows,
for he had no trouble seeing through them:
'You have plenty of guards and enough bold men,
guard the tomb well, and invent songs about Him.

173   Some tell psalms and others, stories,
some say Glorias and others, blessings;
. . . .[30]
you shall spend the whole night making such music.

174   Do not let any other company near you,

---

[29] For all this see Matt. 27:62–66.
[30] A line is missing here from the manuscript. See Dutton, 3:42, note 173c.

none of His disciples or any strangers;
speak to them harshly, threaten them angrily,
tell them you will make their wives[31] into widows.

175   Surround the tomb with excellent watchmen:
may they not be drunkards or sleepyheads;
may they not care about doing other jobs tomorrow,
or going tonight to visit their wives.'

176   They returned to the tomb suited in armor,
shouting out many foul and filthy things,
inventing songs that were utterly worthless,
playing their instruments, zithers, *rotas* and *gigas*.[32]

177   The scoundrels sang some tunes they made up
that were very bitter and harsh for his mother:
'Jews of the district, let us be watchful and wise,
or else we shall be mocked and insulted by them.

178   Heigh keep watch! Heigh keep watch! Heigh keep watch![33]
Keep the watch, you Jews from the district, heigh keep watch,
lest they steal their God from you, heigh keep watch.

179   For they will try to steal Him from you, heigh keep watch,
Andrew and Peter and John, heigh keep watch.

180   You do not know enough magic spells, heigh keep watch,
to get you out from under the stone, heigh keep watch.

182 (181)   Your tongue was so talkative, heigh keep watch,
that it led you down an evil path, heigh keep watch.

184 (182)   Your tongue was so careless, heigh keep watch,
that it brought you to an evil end, heigh keep watch.

181 (183)   They are all petty thieves, heigh keep watch,
who lurk by the bolts of the doors, heigh keep watch.

183 (184)   They are all beggars, heigh keep watch
a mixture of flotsam from the river, heigh keep watch.

---

[31] Here I have read *nañas/nanas* respectively with Orduna, 849, 174d and Logroño, 450, 174d rather than *putannas*, with Dutton, 3:42, 174d.

[32] Medieval stringed instruments. The *giga* is a kind of viola and the *rota* is a kind of harp.

[33] See Dutton, 3:8–16 for a detailed treatment of verses 178–190 and for the order of verses 182–190. Compare the anonymous poem "O tu qui servas armis ista moenia" with its repeated "eja vigila": in *The Penguin Book of Latin Verse*, ed. F. Brittain (Harmondsworth: Penguin, 1964), 156–57.

185 (185) You do not know enough tricks, heigh keep watch,
           to get you out of this in a year, heigh keep watch.

186 (186) You do not know enough tales, heigh keep watch,
           to get you out of the prison, heigh keep watch.

188 (187) The disciple sold Him, heigh keep watch,
           the Master was unaware, heigh keep watch.

187 (188) Both Matthew and Thomas, heigh keep watch,
           really want to steal Him, heigh keep watch.

189 (189) Philip, Simon, and Judas, heigh keep watch,
           seek help to steal him, heigh keep watch.

190 (190) If they want to accomplish it, heigh keep watch,
           today seems to be the day, heigh keep watch.'

191 While capering about they shouted their taunts,
     things most unseemly and terribly wicked;
     they insulted the Heavenly King with such folly,
     by the way they referred to Christ and His disciples.

192 Above all else He felt sorrow for His mother,
     for they uttered great blasphemy and evil before her;
     He turned their sport into something else again,
     converting their singing from loud to sepulchral.

193 They got a huge and terrifying shock,
     and not from any weapons or human strength,
     but it befell them through God, the Spiritual Lord
     Who would not suffer them as His equals.

194 Such a fright and such evil fortune befell them,
     they lost their consciousness and all their wits:
     they all tumbled dead upon the bare ground;
     they all lay entangled around the tomb.[34]

195 Much later the unfortunate men came to,
     unable to see from their eyes all injured;
     they bumped into each other as if in a spell,
     and all their laughter turned to agonized weeping.

196 Christ returned to life, God, such great joy!
     Two suns, thank God, were born that day;
     Christ and the Virgin Mary came back to life:
     all the bitterness was turned into joy.

---

[34] See Matt. 28:4.

197   The swaggering and jeers of the wicked scoundrels
        who loped around in a fury like starving dogs,
        were not worth a single tail of an evil hawk,
        worth less than yipping curs, those yapping hound dogs.

198   The wits of humans are weak and flawed,
        as useless as any cracked pot against God;[35]
        all else lacks root and fades away quickly,
        but what God ordains is truly established.

199   Herod[36] indeed firmly tried to work
        to shorten the life of the young King;
        he ordered every male child of Bethlehem slaughtered,
        but he never could find the One that he sought.

200   Let those who began the tower of Babylon[37]
        receive no thanks, for they never completed it;
        those foolish young men who put God to the test,
        manfully struggled, but never succeeded.

201   Saul[38] labored hard against the kingdom of Christ,
        to prevent the spreading of the Gospel faith,
        but truth refused to yield to the lie,
        and heavenly grace to be trampled under foot.

202   It is useless for the ox to kick against the goad,[39]
        for he only succeeds in injuring his hoof;
        he who foolishly spits saliva upwards
        has it fall back down on his bearded face.

203   He who challenges God gets what he asks for:
        thus says the psalter and thus says Scripture,
        for the foot is in trouble if it strikes a stone,[40]
        an injury to the toe goes straight to the heart.

204   He who will hear me and will believe me
        should never cut the branch from under his feet;
        when he cuts it and then he moves,
        his feet will not stay where he wanted them to be.

---

[35] Cf. Isa. 45:9.
[36] King Herod the Great (40–4 B.C.) ordered the slaughter of the innocents. See Matt. 2:16.
[37] See Gen. 11.
[38] For the conversion of Saul (St. Paul), see Acts 9:1–9.
[39] See Acts 9:5, 26:14.
[40] Cf. Ps. 91 (90):12.

205 Queen of Glory, Mother of Mercy,
Lady of the Angels, Gate to Salvation,
Aid to Souls, Most Chaste Flower,
I learn from you about holy charity.

206 You are the Blessed Pathway of the Sea,
where pilgrims cannot be in danger;
You guide them, Lady, so they may not sin,
while guided by you they can gain salvation.

207 Mother Full of Grace, may you be greatly lauded,
may you be thanked and may you be exalted;
may you be welcomed and your praises sweetly sung,
you who endured so much suffering and anguish.

208 I entrust to you, Mother, my life and my endeavors,
my soul and my body and the Orders I took,
my feet and my hands, though already consecrated;
may my eyes not see anything improper.

209 Lady of the Heavens, full of blessings,
open your ears and hear my petition:
I cannot offer you any oblation,
but may your holy grace accept my poem.

210 Mother, for Theophilus[41] who was so desperate,
You gained grace from your Holy Child.
Lady, please arrange the same for me,
so I may never see myself crushed by the devil.

[41] See Dutton, 2, *Milagros*, 703–866 and Ramoneda, 211, note 210; also above, 117-141.

Bibliography

Secondary Works and Sources of Reference

Andrés Castellanos, María S. de, ed. *La Vida de Santa María Egipciaca*. Madrid: Aguirre Torre, 1964.

Baró, José. *Glosario completo de los "Milagros de Nuestra Señora" de Gonzalo de Berceo*. Boulder: Society of Spanish and Spanish-American Studies, 1987.

Bartha, Jeannie K. "Four Lexical Notes on Berceo's *Milagros de Nuestra Señora*." *Romance Philology* 37 (1983): 56–62.

———. *Vocabulario de los "Milagros de Nuestra Señora" de Gonzalo de Berceo*. Normal, IL: Applied Literature Press, 1980.

Blecua, J. M., ed. *El conde Lucanor*. Madrid: Castalia, 1969.

Cejador y Frauca, J. *Vocabulario medieval castellano*. Orig. 1929; repr. New York: Las Américas, 1968.

Corominas, Joan, ed. *Libro de Buen Amor*. Madrid: Gredos, 1967.

———, and José A. Pascual, *Diccionario crítico etimológico castellano e hispánico*. 6 vols. Madrid: Gredos, 1980–1991.

Covarrubias Orozco, Sebastián de. *Tesoro de la lengua castellana o española*. Orig. 1611; repr. Madrid: Turner, 1977.

Devoto, Daniel. "Sentido y forma de la cántica *Eya velar*." *Bulletin Hispanique* 65 (1963): 206–37.

Dutton, Brian. "Berceo's Watch-Song 'Eya velar'." *Modern Language Notes* 89 (1974): 250–59.

———. "A Chronology of the Works of Gonzalo de Berceo." In *Medieval Hispanic Studies Presented to Rita Hamilton*, ed. A. D. Deyermond, 67–76. London: Tamesis, 1975.

———. *A New Berceo Manuscript, Biblioteca Nacional Ms. 13149. Description, Study and Partial Edition*. Exeter Hispanic Texts 32. Exeter: University of Exeter Press, 1982.

———, ed. Gonzalo de Berceo, *Obras Completas*. 5 vols. London: Tamesis, 1967–1984.

Goicoechea, Cesáreo. *Vocabulario riojano*. Madrid: Aguirre Torre, 1961.

Gulsoy, J. "The -i Words in the Poems of Gonzalo de Berceo." *Romance Philology* 23 (1969–1970): 172–87.

Honnorat, S. J. *Dictionnaire Provençal-Français*. 3 vols. Orig. 1848; repr. Marseille: Laffitte Reprints, 1971.

Keller, John Esten. "The Blessed Virgin as a Patron of the Arts and Letters." In *Models in Medieval Iberian Literature*, ed. Judy B. McInnis, 5-7. Newark, DE: Juan de la Cuesta, 2002.

———. *Gonzalo de Berceo*. Twayne World Authors Series 187. New York: Twayne, 1972.

———. *Pious Brief Narrative in Medieval Castilian and Galician Verse: From Berceo to Alfonso X*. Lexington: University Press of Kentucky, 1978.

Koberstein, G., ed. *Gonzalo de Berceo, "Estoria de San Millán": Textkritische Edition*. Münster: Aschendorff, 1964.

Kulp-Hill, Kathleen, trans. *Songs of Holy Mary by Alfonso X, The Wise: A Translation of the* Cantigas de Santa María. MRTS 173. Tempe: Arizona Center for Medieval and Renaissance Studies, 2000.

Lanchetas, Rufino. *Gramática y vocabulario de las obras de Gonzalo de Berceo*. Madrid: Sucesores de Rivadeneyra, 1900.

Lappin, Anthony. *Berceo's Vida de Santa Oria: Text, Translation and Commentary*. Oxford: Legenda, 2000.

Latham, R. E. *Revised Medieval Latin Word-List*. London: Oxford University Press, 1965.

Lazar, Moshé, ed. *La Fazienda de Ultramar*. Salamanca: Cervantes, 1965.

Levy, Emil. *Petit Dictionnaire Provençal-Français*. Orig. 1909; 5th ed. Heidelberg: Carl Winter, 1973.

Marden, C. Carroll, ed. *Libro de Apolonio*. Orig. 1922; repr. Millwood: Kraus Reprint Co., 1976.

Menéndez Pidal, Ramón, ed. *Cantar de Mío Cid. Texto, gramática y vocabulario*. 4th ed. Madrid: Espasa-Calpe, 1969.

Montgomery, Thomas, ed. *El Evangelio de San Mateo. Texto, gramática, vocabulario*. Madrid: Aguirre Torre, 1962.

Mount, T., and Annette G. Cash, trans. Gonzalo de Berceo, *Miracles of Our Lady*. Lexington: University Press of Kentucky, 1997.

Nebrija, Antonio de. *Vocabulario de Romance en Latín*. Orig. 1516; transcr. Gerald J. MacDonald. Philadelphia: Temple University Press, 1973.

Orduna, Germán. "La estructura del *Duelo de la Virgen* y la cántica *Eya velar*." *Humanitas* (Tucumanán) 4.10 (1958): 175–204.

Real Academia Española. *Diccionario de la lengua española*. 19th ed. Madrid: Espasa-Calpe, 1970.

Scarborough, Connie L. "Narrative Voices in Berceo's *El duelo de la Virgen*." *Romance Notes* 34 (1993): 111–18.

Solalinde, A. G., ed. *Milagros de Nuestra Señora*. 8th ed. Madrid: Espasa-Calpe, 1972.

Walsh, John K., ed. *El Libro de los Doze Sabios o Tractado de la Nobleza y Lealtad.* Madrid: Aguirre, 1975.

Willis, Raymond S., ed. *El libro de Alexandre.* Orig. 1934; repr. Millwood: Kraus Reprint Co., 1976.

———. *Libro de Buen Amor.* Princeton: Princeton University Press, 1972.

II: The Hagiographical Poems:

The Life of Saint Dominic of Silos,
The Life of Saint Aemilianus of la Cogolla,
The Life of Saint Oria,
and The Martyrdom of Saint Lawrence

INTRODUCTION TO
THE LIFE OF SAINT DOMINIC OF SILOS

TRANSLATED BY JEANNIE K. BARTHA

Among Berceo's Lives of saints, his longest work is *The Life of St. Dominic of Silos* which he wrote in 777 monorhymed quatrains, employing the numeral 7, so symbolic since ancient times. It seems that Berceo may have had more than one reason for writing this work. There is some evidence to suggest that he wrote *The Life of St. Dominic* at the behest of the monks of San Millán for reasons of propaganda, to attract more donations and pilgrims to the monastery of Silos, and also for reasons of piety and dedication to the revered saint. Berceo himself attests to another highly personal motivation: his desire to serve God and thus garner favor from Him.

Berceo used a known source, a Latin prose work, *Vita Sancti Dominici*, written shortly after St. Dominic's death in 1073 by a certain Grimaldo who was a monk at Silos. Grimaldo's acquaintanceship with the saint enabled him to give a vivid account of Dominic's life, so much so, in fact, that his *Vita Sancti Dominici* departed from the established tripartite form of presentation followed by medieval hagiographers. When Berceo transformed Grimaldo's original Latin prose into the vernacular Spanish of the day and versified it in the *mester de clerecía* style, he reintroduced the traditional tripartite form. Hence the work has the familiar divisions: (i) the saint's birth, childhood and early life; (ii) the series of miracles worked by him during his lifetime; and (iii) the miracles wrought through his intercession after his death and elevation into heaven. Berceo clearly indicates the beginning and ending of each part of the *Life* and provides definite yet effortless transitions between the parts.

Writing for a largely untutored audience, Berceo maintains a close affinity with his public. One finds the same techniques as those in *The Life of San Millán*: diminutives common to Berceo's native region of la Rioja, local expressions and turns of phrase, all of which in fact are a sophisticated way of establishing a rapport with the listener. Reaching and holding the audience was of utmost importance to Berceo, who saw this work as a didactic tool for the education, edification, and inspiration of the general public. To achieve this, Berceo had to introduce lyrical passages, dramatic episodes, stirring images, terrifying scenes, and emotional fervor. Herein lies much of his originality as a poet.

The Life of St. Dominic of Silos by its sheer size and impact might well have established the author's reputation as an authority on local saints and as a troubadour of pious subject matter. Such Lives could well have attracted the groups of pilgrims who wandered the roads leading to the many shrines of Spain. Recited skillfully or read with feeling, Berceo's works could have been as attractive as were the secular narratives and epics originating in earlier times. In the "Age of Faith" — as the thirteenth century could justly be called — the accounts of the lives of holy men and women were popular entertainment. Berceo's long saints' Lives might have been too extended for continuous recitation or reading, but, recited part by part with intermissions, they would have exercised fascination upon the listener.

The Lives constitute both a poetic and an ethnographic treasure-house. Their rich vocabularies, their wealth of idiomatic and proverbial expressions, and their imagery all contribute to the development of the Spanish language and the unfolding of Spanish literature. Similarly, their depiction of daily life, customs, folkways, and beliefs all help the modern reader to gain a better understanding of the medieval mind and medieval poetic art.

Abbreviations

Dutton   Dutton, Brian, ed. La Vida de Santo Domingo de Silos. In Gonzalo de Berceo, Obras Completas, 4. London: Tamesis, 1978.

Logroño   Vida del glorioso confesor Sancto Domingo de Silos. In Gonzalo de Berceo, Obras completas, intro. Rufino Briones, 7–123. Logroño: Instituto de Estudios Riojanos, 1971.

Orduna   Orduna, Germán, ed. Vida de Santo Domingo de Silos. Salamanca: Anaya, 1968.

Ruffinatto   Ruffinatto, Aldo, ed. Vida de Santo Domingo de Silos. In Gonzalo de Berceo, Obra completa, with Isabel Uría, 251–453. Madrid: Espasa-Calpe, 1992.

THE LIFE OF SAINT DOMINIC OF SILOS

1   In the name of the Father Who created all things,
and the Lord Jesus Christ, Son of the Glorious Lady,
and the Holy Spirit seated equal to them,
I will compose a poem about a holy confessor.

2   I will compose a poem in the plain language
used by the people for speaking to their neighbors,
for I am not so learned as to create another text in Latin.
I believe it will indeed be worth a glass of fine wine.[1]

3   I want you to know right from the start,
and to set you straight, whom this story is about:
it is the whole truth indeed about St. Dominic,
the one from Silos who guards the border.[2]

4   In the name of God Whom we mentioned first,
may His be the fame, and I be His laborer;
for my pains I await my reward from the One
Who gives generous reward for small service.

5   The worthy St. Dominic, according to what is written,[3]
was a native of Cañas, of no mean parentage;
he was made faithful and just in every way,
completely righteous and free of any fault.

6   He had good parents, friends of the Creator,
who followed the examples of the Fathers;[4]
indeed they knew how to avoid making enemies,
and they kept good advice firmly in mind.

---

[1] The reward usually earned by the troubador. (See Dutton, 4:156, note 2d.)

[2] Traditionally, Spanish saints from the period of Berceo were outstanding for their qualities of protecting or guarding the borders between the territories occupied then by the Christians and those occupied by the Moors. (See Ruffinatto, 258, note 3d.)

[3] Berceo frequently uses words such as *dizlo la escriptura* or *dizlo el cartelario*, or *como diz el escripto* etc., 'according to the text' or 'according to what is written' etc., when he refers to the source he uses, which is the Latin text of the Saint's life written by the monk Grimaldo. (See Dutton, 4:156, note 5a.)

[4] Referring to the Church Fathers.

7   His distinguished father was named Juan,
         a man of remarkable ancestry and habits,
         a lover of justice and perfectly prudent:
         he would not be bribed into falsifying judgment.

8   I would not know the name of his mother:
         as it was not written I would not guess it,
         but may God and Holy Mary keep her soul;
         let us pursue the course and hold to our path.

9   The stock was good, it produced a fine sprout,
         it was no slight reed that was swayed by the wind,[5]
         for he was from the start a prudent child, firmly planted,
         and he was unwilling to hear any foolish talk.

10   He served his parents with all his heart,
         and towards them he showed complete humility;
         though only a child, he had such great candor
         that he was astonishing to all those around him.

11   He cared very little for laughter and games,
         and took little pleasure in those who indulged in them;
         though very young, he was very discreet;
         he was greatly beloved by young and old.

12   He directed his tightly-closed eyes towards the ground:
         he had them well trained not to see any nonsense;
         his mouth and his lips he kept well sealed,
         so as not to say anything foul or foolish.

13   The daily bread that his parents gave him,
         he would not put all of it into his mouth;
         he shared it with the youngsters whom he knew;
         he was a perfect young person of proper habits.

14   One thing I do believe and I know that it is true,
         is that he was being guided by the King of Glory,
         for His goodness does accomplish such things
         as endowing dumb animals with the power of speech.[6]

15   That divine grace was working in this pupil of His,
         and through that seasoning he became so enlightened,
         else he would not have been so bright for his years,
         for the one loved by God is always very wise.

---

[5] Allusion to Matt. 11:7.
[6] See Num. 22 for the story of Balaam and his talking ass.

16   If he heard a good story he could certainly retain it,
        he always remembered it and never forgot it;
        he blessed his food when he wanted to eat,
        and did the same to whatever he had to drink.

17   He said the *Pater Noster*[7] a great many times,
        and the *Credo in Deum*[8] pausing after each clause,[9]
        with other prayers he was used to reciting,
        and these were unwelcome tidings for the devil.

18   The holy child lived with his parents,
        his mother and father loved him dearly;
        he was untroubled by anything else,
        he was wholly concerned with honoring them.

19   When old enough to walk and to follow orders,
        he was sent by his father to keep the sheep;
        the son obeyed, for he did not wish to sin;
        he departed with his flock, ready to guide them.

20   He guided his flock like a good shepherd,
        no one any older would do it so well;
        he would not let them graze in another's pasture;
        the sheep were extremely delighted with him.

21   He gave them fine grazing and kept them from harm,
        for fear of getting a good scolding from his father;
        he would not deceive either rich or poor:
        he would rather lie with fever for a whole year.

22   He was sure to take them right out in the morning;
        he kept a sharp lookout for their needs;
        he was skillful and wise in walking close by them;
        in neither sun nor rain did he ever flee for cover.

23   He returned home with them in the evening,
        with his shepherd's crook and shaggy cape;
        as soon as he came in to his mother and father,
        he would kneel down and kiss their hands.

24   The Shepherd Who never sleeps at any time,
        and Who created the deep and bottomless abysses,
        kept those animals safe from all injury:
        neither wolf nor thief did them any harm.

---

[7] The prayer the "Our Father".
[8] The prayer the "Creed".
[9] Spaces for pausing when the official, liturgical *Creed* is recited in chorus (Ruffinatto, 262, note 17b).

25   With the excellent keeper the Shepherd gave them,
        and the help they obtained from God's sacred grace,
        the flock prospered and improved every day,
        to such an extent that it was envied by some.

26   Abel was the first of all shepherds and martyrs:
        he offered his best sheep in sacrifice to God;[10]
        that is why God gave him his share in heaven:
        let us give him for a like companion him from Silos.

27   The holy patriarchs all were shepherds
        who were the keepers of the ancient Law;
        even from that which we read and know,
        San Millán[11] and other confessors were shepherds.

28   Many fine stories we read about shepherds
        who turned out to be wise and holy men;
        indeed we find in many of the texts
        that this occupation leads to good ends.

29   It is a worthy occupation and not degrading,
        free of any fault and entirely meaningful;
        David, a bold spear[12] and such a noble king,
        started out no doubt by being a shepherd.[13]

30   Our Lord Jesus Christ, so highly powerful,
        called Himself a Good Shepherd,[14] which He truly was;
        bishops and abbots and all those in high office
        are called shepherds over Christian people.

31   The worthy St. Dominic at first was a shepherd,
        and then became a father and guider of souls;
        he was good to begin with and afterwards better;
        may the King of Heaven give us his love.

32   For four years he was a shepherd of animals,[15]
        and many were bred from all those he was given;
        his father thought he was a lucky man
        that God had lent him such a good child.

---

[10] See Gen. 4:4.

[11] See Dutton, 1, *San Millán*, quatrains 5–8.

[12] Meaning 'a bold warrior', an epithet commonly used in epic poetry.

[13] See 1 Sam. 16:11–13.

[14] See John 10:14.

[15] According to Dutton, 4:157, note 32a, St. Dominic was about fourteen or fifteen years old when he began to pasture his father's sheep; therefore he was about eighteen or nineteen when he left this occupation.

33   Let us move ahead, let us not tarry;
there is a great deal of material, let us not delay,
for although we cover many of his merits,
we cannot tell even a thousandth of them.

34   The holy little shepherd and child[16] of good habits,
while walking with his flock on the outskirts of Cañas,
thought to become a priest, to know heroic deeds,
to live a life of virtue among more chaste companions.

35   His parents were pleased when they heard this;
they exchanged his clothing for something better;
they sought for him the best possible teacher;
they took him to the church and offered him to God.

36   They gave him a primer[17] befitting an acolyte;
he sat down on the ground and removed his hood;
he took up his stylus[18] in his right hand,
and in no time at all he had learned the title.

37   The boy came to his school early in the morning,
never needing to be told by his mother or sister;
he would not nap for long during the day;
he had learned something the very first week.

38   In a very short while the boy knew the Psalms,
and nicely recited hymns and canticles by memory;
he quickly learned the Gospels and the Epistles;
it took him more time[19] to learn something longer.

39   He read and sang well without any slackness,
since he had a mind that was very sharp,
for he knew that therein lay his advantage,
and he would not miss the core of the tree for its bark.[20]

40   The youngster was raised filled with blessing;
he left youth behind and became a holy man;
God heard his prayer and favored him greatly;
the light from his heart was shining forth.

---

[16] Here I have read *niño* with Ruffinatto, 267, 34a; Orduna, 57, 34a; and Logroño, 14, 34a rather than *pleno*, with Dutton, 4:40, 34a.

[17] Meaning his first reading book.

[18] Used by a student learning to write on wax.

[19] Here I have read *tiempo* with Ruffinatto, 269, 38d; Orduna, 58, 38d; and Logroño, 14, 38d rather than *mosto* with Dutton, 4: 41, 38d.

[20] He went beyond the surface meaning (the bark), to discover the deeper meaning of the text (the core).

41   He imposed on his body grave sentences,
        fastings and vigils and other abstinences;
        he guarded himself from every sin and failing,
        and strictly adhered to prescribed rules.[21]

42   The bishop of the area heard of this good Christian,
        and he was content that he belonged to him;
        he commanded him to take Orders,[22] himself laying hands on him,
        and in no time at all he was made a priest.

43   The new priest celebrated holy Mass;
        he performed his whole office with great virtue:
        he watched over his church and did service to God,
        displaying no slackness or any bad habits.

44   Such a youth who received the four ranks[23] was like silver
        that turned to gold when he became Epistle reader;[24]
        gold to pearls when he became Gospel reader,[25]
        and when he rose to priesthood[26] he was like a morning star.

45   The entire holy Church was exalted with him,
        and all the earth was made brighter by him;
        Cañas would forever have been rich and prosperous,
        if he had not moved from its see.[27]

46   The famous father instructed the people;
        he brought folks together and parted them from sin;
        he did not hold back from visiting the sick,
        and if he could he gave alms willingly.

47   He persevered in doing good both summer and winter,
        and to anyone who asked he gave sound advice;
        while the bread lasted his hand was never idle:
        you can take it for a fact he was a good Christian.

48   He was far superior to everything we say:

---

[21] The rules for religious observance.

[22] The sacrament conferred on a candidate to become a deacon or priest. St Dominic was ordained by the bishop himself.

[23] The four minor ranks are ostiary or doorkeeper (one who opens and closes the church and who calls those worthy to receive communion and rejects those unworthy to do so), lector, exorcist, and acolyte. (See Dutton, 4:157, note 44a.)

[24] Corresponding to the rank of subdeacon. (See Dutton, 4:157, note 44b.)

[25] Corresponding to the rank of deacon, aged twenty-five or over. (See Dutton, 4:157, note 44c.)

[26] The final rank, minimum age of thirty. (See Dutton, 4:157, note 44d.)

[27] Meaning 'the bishop's diocese', i.e. 'if he had not moved from the diocese of Cañas.'

that is how he was held along the whole riverbank;[28]
he certainly knew how to stave off the devil
who could find no way at all to deceive him.

49   The blessed priest, from the time he was ordained,
      remained for a year and a half where he had been raised;
      he was loved and cherished by all the people,
      but there was one matter that did disturb him.

50   The good man was musing on the things of the world:
      he could see them all going from bad to worse;
      falsehood and avarice had linked up together,
      with many other evils drawing close to them.

51   He said, "Woe is me! If I do not move from here,
      I will have to contend against what I would not like;
      it is bad to keep flax close to the fire:
      great dangers usually result from that.

52   If I sin against someone God will reproach me;
      if someone sins against me I fear I will be blamed;
      I had better seek a more remote place:
      it will be better for me than living in town.

53   Those who wished to give God perfect service,
      to be able to protect themselves from every fault,
      adopted that life which I ardently desire,
      if the Lord Who said 'I thirst'[29] be willing to guide me.

54   In the early times those who preceded us,
      who were the founders of the holy Church,
      wished to make themselves endure such a life:
      they bore hunger and thirst, heat and cold.

55   St. John the Baptist, when his childhood was over,
      gave up wine and cider, meat and fish;
      he fled to the desert where he earned such fame
      as could not be told by any man high or lowborn.

56   The good father Anthony, and Paul[30] his counterpart
      who as they say, was the first hermit,

---

[28] The bank of the River Tuerto which passes through Cañas. (See Dutton, 4:157, note 48b.)

[29] Christ, who said "I thirst." (See John 19:28.)

[30] St Anthony Abbot (251–356), one of the founders of monasticism in Egypt, and St. Paul of Thebes, the first Christian hermit who died around 347, and known to the former. (Dutton, 4:158, note 56a)

both lived in the desert, a strange wilderness,
neither eating fine bread nor wearing fine clothing.

57   Mary the Egyptian,[31] an immoderate sinner,
        dwelled a long while in the fearsome wilderness;
        by leading a harsh life she was saved from her sins:
        he who lives such a life is extremely lucky.

58   The worthy confessor who is our neighbor,
        the faultless San Millán,[32] advocate of the poor,
        while walking through the desert, opened the path there
        that led him up to Heaven where no judge enters.[33]

59   His good teacher by the name of St. Felices,[34]
        he who lay enclosed in the cave at Billivio,
        was a true hermit, perfect in goodness;
        the teacher was fine and he trained a fine pupil.

60   Without any doubt those were very wise men
        who abandoned the town in order to save souls;
        they lived in the wilderness in misery and suffering:
        that is how they work miracles for which they are adored.

61   Many were the fathers who led such lives:
        a portion of them lie in the *Vitae Patrum*;[35]
        they shunned all the glory of the world
        in order to gain perfect happiness in Heaven.

---

[31] St. Mary the Egyptian, born in the middle of the fourth century, a prostitute who withdrew to the desert to do penance. (Ruffinatto, 272, note 57a)

[32] San Millán, the hero of Berceo's work the *Vida de San Millán*, holy patron saint of the Monastery of San Millán de la Cogolla. (See Dutton, 4:158, note 58b, and Ruffinatto, 272, note 58b.)

[33] Here Berceo displays his own attitude and that of the people of the Middle Ages who had antipathy for judges in the provinces who had executive power, monitoring the execution of sentences passed by ordinary judges, and who could be appealed to concerning those sentences. (See Ruffinatto, 272, note 58d.)

[34] St. Felices of Billivio was San Millán's teacher (see *San Millán*, quatrains 13–25). He was a hermit in the castle at Billivio, an ancient place near Haro situated high on a cliff on the right of the River Ebro, where he died around the fifth century and was buried and venerated there until the year 1090 when his relics were transferred to San Millán where they continued to be venerated. (See Dutton, 4:158, note 59ab, and Ruffinatto, 272, note 59ab.)

[35] The *Lives of the Fathers* or *Vitae Patrum*, a collection of stories and maxims on the lives of the Fathers of the desert and other saints which began to be written up in the sixth century. (See Ruffinatto, 272 note 61b.)

62   The Savior of the world Who for us became human,
when He wanted to fast after being baptized,
to give us an example He went off to the desert
where the devil came forth but greatly repented it.[36]

63   The monks in Egypt, blessed companions,
to break their bodies became hermits;
they anchored their wills more closely to their hearts.
There is much that has been written[37] about such men.

64   What shall I, a wretched sinner, do in town?
I will eat and drink and dress and live well;
God knows that to live like that does not please me,
for that life leads to ill-fated pleasure."

65   The worthy priest, who was trusted by all,
abandoned Cañas where they loved him greatly,
his parents and friends and those whom he cherished;
he withdrew to the wilderness where no man lived.

66   When he found himself alone and away from the people,
he rejoiced as though he had recovered from a fever;
he gave thanks to Christ Who had been his guide —
rest assured that he had no fish for his supper.

67   The new hermit gave himself to great suffering,
making many supplications and praying his Psalter,
and strictly reciting his hours and all his office:
he was giving his body mighty little rest.

68   Enduring a harsh life and lying on a hard bed,
the good man gained control of his body;
the devil was lying in wait to attack him,
and was highly annoyed by all this suffering.

69   Despite bad weather and freezing frost,
or very cruel and intemperate winds,
or noxious mist and jagged rocks,
all these torments were as nothing to him.

70   He endured cruel suffering day and night,
such as you have heard of and can only imagine,
but to that good Christian and successor of Elijah,[38]
all that suffering mattered not in the least.

---

[36] See Luke 4:1–13.
[37] Yet another reference to the *Vitae Patrum*. See note 35 above.
[38] For the life of Elijah in the wilderness, see 1 Kings 17:5.

71   It was very remiss of those who knew
        not to put in writing[39] the place where he stayed;
        or I think that perchance they did not know
        and thus they did not say, for it was always changing.

72   Wherever he stayed, in valley or town,
        the place was more famed due to his merit,
        for by the good man, as the saying goes,
        and by the confessor the place is made holy.

73   He lived as a hermit for a year and a half:
        so says the text though I did not know it;
        if I had not read it I would not say it,
        for to state something doubtful would be a great sin.

74   All his sufferings and all his temptations
        could never be told by any learned priest,
        except by those who endured such afflictions
        and passed through them with a steadfast heart.

75   The good man prayed with all his heart
        for God to protect the whole of Christendom,
        to give bread and peace and truth to the people,
        love and charity and clement weather.

76   He prayed that He should give healing to the sick,
        that He should give freedom to those in captivity,
        that He should remove the power of the infidel
        to oppress Christians and treat them cruelly.

77   He prayed most earnestly to his divine Lord
        that deceitful heretics who sow wicked poison
        should be hemmed in and repulsed by Him,
        that the dregs of their wicked wine should not blunt the faith.

78   He prayed to God often for his very own self,
        that He Who was Father and light of Christianity
        should protect him from error and deadly cunning,
        so he would not betray his baptismal promise.

79   He did not forget to pray for the dead,
        for those who were loyal and confessed before dying;

---

[39] Dutton, 4:158 note 71b comments that the Latin text of Grimaldo from which Berceo obtained his material on the life of St. Dominic does not give the location of the place.

and for other friends of his whom he indicated,
the good man said twice as many *Pater Nosters*.[40]

80 The worthy St. Dominic, accustomed to suffering,
gave no rest or relief to his body;
he lived that life a good year and a half:
be assured, he had little pleasure during that time.

81 So that he should live in even greater hardship,
and not do a single thing without permission,
he thought to be a monk and practice obedience,
to be restricted indeed beyond his powers.

82 Let no one consider this as a whim,
or belittling in any way of his sanctity,
for within himself he always had perfect charity,
this man who placed his will in the power of another.

83 The famous confessor came down from the wilderness,
and went to San Millán,[41] a well-established place;
his request to be a monk was gladly granted:
he would end up well if he died in that state.

84 The new knight took well to the Order,
turning out to be a fine monk in the community,
a mild and agreeably delightful companion,
humble and true in word and in deed.

85 With a good many thanks to God and Holy Mary,
there happened to be no better monk in the monastery;
he would always follow the Rule[42] to the letter;
he protected the Order indeed with no nonsense.

86 The worthy St. Dominic, a faithful cleric,
went about in the Order like a good priest,
his hood drawn about him, his eyes tightly closed,
with sallow complexion, like one who is suffering.

87 Any order at all from his father abbot,
or the prior or superior in the community,
he was most willing to instantly obey;
the good men judged him to be a fine Christian.

---

[40] See note 7 above.

[41] St. Dominic arrived at the monastery of San Millán in the year 1033 at thirty-three years of age, and the abbot of San Millán who clothed him in the Benedictine habit was Bishop Sancho de Nájera, who died around 1034 (Dutton, 4:159, note 83b, and Ruffinatto, 278, note 83bc).

[42] The Rule of St. Benedict.

88   In the cloister or choir, or any other place
        where the Rule forbade, he would not talk;[43]
        anyone at all who really wished to find him
        went to the church right near the altar.

89   If ordered to go out and do manual labor,[44]
        the good man knew very well to agree to it;
        they could not make him laugh at any minstrel's verse,[45]
        or get him to say a single frivolous thing.

90   Because the friar was so good and virtuous,
        and was found so ready to practice obedience,
        and his whole behavior was likewise so good,
        there were some among them who were peeved by this.

91   While his other brothers were trying to endure it,
        he never would want to come out of the church;
        he would want to spend his days and nights there,
        to save his soul and to serve the Creator.

92   All of them looked to him as to a mirror,
        for under his fine skin there lay a great treasure;
        that holy council looked to him as a father,
        except for some malicious, worthless persons.

93   We told you before, if you will recall,
        that the tale of his merits would make a long string;
        let us move forward if you will allow us,
        for there still remains much more than you think.

94   The abbot of the monastery spoke with his community;
        they thought about the matter and made a decision:
        to put the will of this man to the test,
        to see if indeed he was all that he seemed.

95   They said, "Let us test him and see what we have:
        when we discern him we will be more certain,
        for, according to the words we usually read in Scripture,
        we hear the tongue but we cannot know the heart.[46]

----

[43] The Rule of St. Benedict forbids talking during meals, afternoon rest, and other occasions (Dutton, 4: 159, note 88b, and Ruffinatto, 280, note 88b).

[44] The Rule of St. Benedict dictates that each monk must carry out a certain amount of manual labor every day (Dutton, 4:159, note 89a, and Ruffinatto, 280, note 89a).

[45] Profane verses.

[46] Berceo may be referring here to Mark 7:6.

96   Let us order him to go to some deaconry[47]
        that is just as poor as the meanest hovel;
        if he will not do it or displays some anger,
        then we will understand that he is deceitful."

97   There was near Cañas and there is today,
        a house that was named for Holy Mary;
        it was very poor and indeed very empty:
        they ordered him to go and take charge of that place.

98   With no hesitation the good man agreed;
        he instantly bowed and received the blessing;
        he prayed briefly before the holy body;[48]
        his words were few, but very wise.

99   "Lord," he said, "You Who are all-powerful,
        Who will not let Your truly beloved ones fall,[49]
        may it please You, Lord, to give me Your protection,
        that what I have suffered may not go to waste.

100   I have always ardently desired and I still am eager
        to withdraw from the world and all its turmoil,
        to live under Your Rule and die in Your service;
        Lord, I implore Your mercy and Your favor.

101   To gain Your grace I practiced obedience,
        to live a life of suffering and die as a penitent;
        out of fear of You, Lord, I will not sin,
        or else I would not[50] leave this cloistered life.

102   Lord, I will do this insofar as I have to,
        or else I would make myself fodder for the devils;
        I dare not kick against the goad;[51]
        You know this cup[52] which I drink without pleasure.

---

[47] According to Dutton, 4:160, note 96a, Chapter 21 of the Rule of St. Benedict speaks of the deacons who governed ten monks. The office was called the "deaconry" and Dutton concludes on this basis that "deaconries" were small monastic dwellings.

[48] According to Dutton, 4:160, notes 98c and 118a, and also according to Ruffinatto, 288, note 118a, by the words "holy body" Berceo means the body of San Millán, or the relics of the saint.

[49] Allusion to Matt. 10:29–31.

[50] Here I read *non* with Ruffinatto, 283, 101d; Orduna, 70, 101d; and Logroño, 24, 101d rather than *luego* with Dutton, 4:51, 101d.

[51] See Acts 9:5 and 26:14.

[52] Referring here to the words of Christ during his Agony in the Garden. See Matt. 26:42.

103   I want to do some service to the Glorious Lady,
       for I believe and acknowledge[53] that she is virtuous,
       for she was mother and spouse of the Lord of the world:
       I am pleased to go to the house where she dwells."

104   With reluctance, the gentleman left the monastery;
       he bid farewell to all his cherished friars;
       those who truly loved him were very sorry;
       those who schemed against him now were contrite.

105   The blessed man went to the house named for Holy Mary:
       he found neither bread nor any other food in it;
       he went begging alms like a persistent pilgrim:
       all gave him something: here a crust of bread, there a measure of flour.

106   With God and the Glorious Lady and his solid faith,
       good things came to him from the daily offering;
       he was poor at night and rich in the morning;
       he indeed shared his gains with those Christian people.

107   To adhere to the Rule,[54] the man of good sense,
       wishing to suffer by working with his hands,
       to stop begging, began to do manual labor
       which was something very hard for him to bear.

108   He improved the buildings, he extended the properties,
       he embellished the church, you may certainly believe it,
       with some books and vestments and many good things;
       during this time he suffered many adversities.

109   I, Gonzalo, who compose this in his honor,
       I saw it,[55] just as I shall see the face of God,
       a small and really rather simple kitchen
       that they say was built by that good confessor.

110   In just a few years the house was restored,
       and plenty well provisioned with grain and animals;
       the poor already found themselves a home there;
       through him, thanks to God, the church was made holy.

111   He confessed[56] his father and made him a friar
       who was to end up by dying in his arms;

---

[53] Here I read *creo bien e entiendo* with Ruffinatto, 285, 103b; Orduna, 71, 103b; and Logroño, 24, 103b rather than *ca lo yo bien* with Dutton, 4:51, 103b.
[54] See note 42.
[55] This is quite probable because Berceo's native town is about two kilometers from Cañas (Ruffinatto, 284, note 109b).
[56] Meaning 'converted him to the monastic life.'

his son buried him in that same ossuary:
I regret we are not certain of the location.

112   His mother, who refused to be received in the Order,
her son did not want to bring to the house;
the old lady died persisting in her stubbornness;
may God receive her soul if she is willing to hear Him.

113   Let us leave the good man resting in his house,
and serving the poor with his companions;
let us return to the monastery of San Millán,
for the whole story is not yet completed.

114   The abbot[57] of the house, like a wise man,
reflected on this matter and considered it wrong
that a man such as this should be so far away,
when through him the monastery would be in better order.

115   He assembled his community to deal with this matter:
they saw that it neither looked well[58] nor was appropriate
for such a perfect Christian leading such a worthy[59] life
to be made into a deacon of a wretched deaconry.[60]

116   All said, "We will be pleased if he comes to the monastery;
all of us are happy and glad about this;
we recognize in him the perfection of goodness;
we never had a single bit of trouble with him."

117   His companions sent for him right away:
those carrying the message needed little persuasion;
he instantly obeyed their very first words;
the porters gladly opened the doors to him.

118   He went to pray before the holy body,[61]
then ascended to the choir to obtain the blessing;
they all showed very great sympathy for him,
as towards a companion of such perfection.

119   The perfect and very patient Christian
obtained such great love through obedience,

---

[57] In 1036, the abbot was García (Dutton, 4:160, note 114a, and also Ruffinatto, 286, note 114a).

[58] Here I read *fermosa* with Ruffinatto, 287, 115b; Orduna, 73, 115b; and Logroño, 26, 115b rather than *primosa* with Dutton, 4:53, 115b.

[59] Here I read *preciosa* with Ruffinatto, 287, 115c; Orduna, 73, 115c; and Logroño, 26, 115c rather than *fermosa* with Dutton, 4:53, 115c.

[60] See note 47 above.

[61] See note 48 above.

for through all that prompted him and all his suffering,
he would never be moved to commit any sin.

120   The Heavenly King endowed him with such grace
       that he no longer seemed to be a mortal creature,
       but either an angel or a spiritual being
       who lived with them in human form.[62]

121   Instead of the Rule[63] they all looked to him;
       in cloister and in choir they were led by him;
       the words that he uttered seemed to be honeyed,
       like those that flowed from the lips of Gregory.[64]

122   Because he was so good and better than all,
       the abbot of the monastery gave him the priorate;[65]
       if he could he would rather have gracefully declined,
       but he considered it a sin to say, "I will not."

123   According to the text, he held the post of prior,
       not like a hireling but like a righteous shepherd;
       and the wicked wolf, the enemy of souls,
       was driven by him out of the sanctuary.[66]

124   Many matters that were in terrible confusion
       were restored to order by this prior;
       when at times the abbot used to go away,
       he found things none the worse on his return.

125   Blessed is the cloister guided by such a leader,
       blessed is the flock kept by such a shepherd;
       fortunate the castle that has such a lord,
       happy the gate that has such a keeper.

126   There is one thing I wholeheartedly regret:
       that we have to digress a little from our story;
       a dispute which occurred around the worthy man,
       why he crossed the mountains and the Gatón Spring.[67]

---

[62] A truism, the monastic life being called the 'angelic life'.

[63] See note 42 above.

[64] St. Gregory (540–604) (Dutton, 4:160, note 121d).

[65] The abbot made him prior, a superior officer in a monastic order or religious house next in rank below an abbot.

[66] Cf. John 10:11–13.

[67] The Gatón Spring (in the mountain range called the "Sierra de San Lorenzo") is the source of the Gatón River in the region of La Rioja Alta. That little river flows into the Najerilla near Mansilla. (See Ruffinatto, 290, note 126d, and Orduna, 75, note 126d. See also Dutton, 4:161, note 126d, in which he refers to the mountain range as the "Sierra

127   King García, lord of Nájera,
        was the son of King Sancho the Great,[68]
        a loyal knight and a noble warrior,
        but he could have acted better towards San Millán.

128   He was a man of good habits, physically handsome,
        of very sound mind and fortunate in battles;
        he widowed many Moorish women of their husbands,
        but he had one flaw, which was that he was greedy.

129   Among his many other deeds of chivalry,
        he conquered Calahorra, seat of the bishopric;[69]
        he won back her church for the Virgin Mary:
        on that day he gave great service to God.

130   King Fernando,[70] who governed León,
        Burgos and Castile, Castro and Carrión,
        was his brother: they had the same parents;
        Monte d'Oca[71] was the border of their kingdoms.

131   He came to San Millán, moved by the devil;
        whatever was his trouble, he came in bitter mood;
        once he was lodged he summoned the community:
        indeed they understood that he was discontented.

132   "Abbot," said the king, "I want you to hear me,
        you and your community, those who dwell here.
        I wish you to know why I have come;
        I want you to help me and I cannot excuse you.

---

de la Demanda.") According to Ruffinatto, this is the first allusion made by Berceo to the route St. Dominic will have to take in order to reach the monastery of Silos.

[68] King García Sánchez, son of Sancho the Great (1000–1035), reigned from 1035 to 1054, when he died fighting his brother Fernando I of Castile in the Battle of Atapuerca. From then on, Nájera became part of Castile (Dutton, 4:161, note 127a; Ruffinatto, 290, note 127a; and Orduna, 76, note 127a).

[69] García de Nájera conquered Calahorra and reestablished its bishopric and the Cathedral of Santa María in April of 1045. The thirtieth of the same month, he gave Abbot Gómez de San Millán several possessions in Calahorra. The following year, when Abbot Gómez was consecrated Bishop of Nájera and Calahorra, the king gave him a monastery which was to pass to San Millán upon his death. The following episode took place in 1040, that is, quite a bit before the reconquest of Calahorra (Dutton, 4:161, note 129b, and Ruffinatto, 290, note 129b).

[70] Fernando I, King of Castile and León 1032–1065, was also the son of Sancho the Great (Dutton, 4: 161, note 130a).

[71] Monte d'Oca was the ancient border between Castile and Navarra, 30 kilometers east of Burgos (Dutton, 4:161, note 130d).

133   It would take a long time to tell my business,
           and lengthy stories are always tedious;
           I wish to be brief and not draw this out:
           I want you to give me some treasures as a gift.

134   The truth is that my ancestors[72] gave them,
           those and everything else in the early times;
           it is right that they be of benefit to me now:
           we will even pay for them one way or another."

135   The abbot and his friars were terribly frightened;
           not one of them replied, they were so bewildered;
           the prior understood that they were overwhelmed;
           he replied and said some unwelcome words to him.

136   "King," he said, "I beg you the favor of listening to me,
           may you not be offended by what I mean to tell you;
           although I am most limited of all in brains,
           I shall not say willingly anything improper.

137   Your ancestors built this sacred hospice,
           you are the patron and native lord of it;
           we would do great wrong if we denied this to you:
           in so doing, we would commit grievous sin.

138   Those who built it gave it to the Order;
           they gave properties and offered treasures;
           they did it in order to give service to God;
           since putting them there, they have never come back for them.

139   What has once been offered to God
           must never be put to any other use;
           he who changed that would take leave of his senses:
           on Judgment Day he would be rebuked for it.

140   You are very unwise if this happens through you;
           you are poorly counseled if someone so advises you.
           King, protect your soul, do not commit such a sin,
           for it would be a sacrilege, a most forbidden crime.

141   I advise you indeed, sir, to take nothing from here;
           live from your rightful rents and taxes;
           do not sell your soul for goods that do not last;
           take care *ne ad lapidem pedem tuum offendas.*"[73]

---

[72] From the year 920 to 1031, many donations made by the ancestors of King García de Nájera can be found in the Monastery of San Millán (Dutton, 4:161, note 134a).

[73] Meaning 'not to dash your foot against the stone' or 'lest you dash your foot against the stone.' See Ps. 91 (90):12 and Matt. 4:6.

142   "Monk," said the king, "you are terribly out of order:
        who made you so bold as to speak before the king?
        It seems that you are unaccustomed to silence:[74]
        I think you will indeed be found wanting there.

143   You have poor sense and you speak like a fool.
        I will have your eyes put out[75] if you chatter so much;
        but I want to advise you to keep your mouth shut:
        you speak without leave, you cause much confusion."

144   The prior stood firm; he paid no attention:
        "King," he said, "I am telling the solid truth about this;
        it would not be falsified by laws or decrees,
        yet you promise to reward me with mighty poor wages.

145   I am undeservedly reproached by you, King;
        you threaten me unjustly while I speak correctly;
        you should not be outraged against me for such a thing;
        may God protect you, King, from doing such a deed."

146   "Monk," said the king, "you are a man of sound mind;
        you seem an expert in law, but not a cloistered monk;
        I will not think I am truly avenged of you,
        not until I have had your tongue cut out."[76]

147   All of these threats enumerated by the king
        mattered not in the least to the blessed man;
        the more words he uttered, the stronger he became;
        he was sorely grieved because the king was sinning.

148   "King," he said, "you do wrong to insult me so:
        you utter unsuitable words in great anger;
        you throw a great load of sin on your back
        in wanting to slice up the limbs of others.

149   The mistaken words that you utter with such wrath,
        and the other sins that you commit every day,
        may Christ, the Son of Mary, forgive you for them,
        but I would not change a word of everything I told you."

150   The king spoke the words: "You reckless monk,
        you speak as one safely ensconced in a castle;

---

[74] Meaning that St. Dominic is sinning against the Benedictine Rule of silence.

[75] The supreme punishment for the crime of lèse majesté (Dutton, 4:162, note 143b).

[76] Another punishment of mutilation for the crime of lèse majesté (Dutton, 4:162, note 146d).

but if I can get you outside of this sanctuary,[77]
you may be very sure that you shall be hanged."

151   St. Dominic, friend of the Creator, spoke:
        "King, for God's sake, heed what I tell you;
        the deadly enemy has you in chains:
        that is why he incenses you to quarrel with me.

152   Your words and anger bring you great harm:
        the devil, who is immensely deceitful, is plotting this;
        I am deeply disturbed, King, by your reproaches;
        all of us here are sorely distressed.

153   You can kill the body and maltreat the flesh,
        but you have no power, King, over the soul;[78]
        the Gospel, which indeed we must believe, says
        that He who judges souls is the One to be feared.

154   Indeed I advise such a lord as you, King,
        do not try to take a thing from the holy confessor;
        do not take a thing back of what you have offered,
        or else you may not see the face of God.

155   But if it is your will to remove the treasures,
        we will not give them to you: go take them yourself;
        if the patron of the place[79] does not protect[80] them,
        we will be unable, King, to quarrel with you."

156   The king was angry beyond measure and reason;
        he fastened his cloak and departed from the monastery;
        he thought he had been dealt a treacherous blow;
        he felt only rage and ill will towards the prior.

157   The worthy confessor stayed on in his monastery;
        he remained unaffected by all the rumors;
        he protected the office entrusted to him:
        should they make him a martyr he would be very pleased.

158   He went before the holy body and said to San Millán,
        "Listen, father of the many who eat your bread,[81]

---

[77] As is well known, monasteries and churches usually had the privilege of serving as places of asylum for those persecuted by the law (Ruffinatto, 296, note 150c).

[78] See Matt. 10:28 and Luke 12:4–6.

[79] Meaning San Millán, patron saint of the region.

[80] Here I read *amparare* with Ruffinatto, 297, 155c; Orduna, 81, 155c; and Logroño, 32, 155c rather than *rencurare* with Dutton, 4:59, 155c.

[81] Formula used in epic poetry to express the relationship of the vassal to his lord (Ruffinatto, 298, note 158b).

you see how meanly the king acts towards me:
he pays me no greater honor than he would to a dog.

159   Worthy sir and father, protector of the land,
I beg you to deal with this terribly great blow,
since I bear it for you, worthy sir and holy father,
yet I am but little frightened by his threats.

160   Confessor who shared your cloak with the poor,[82]
leave me not unprotected, guide me where to go;
because of me may your monastery not fall on evil;
because of me may this angry lion not maltreat it.

161   It is certainly apparent that he is furious with me,
and will seek entry through some evil crack;
not fearing to sin, he will do harm to the house,
for I believe indeed that he is incensed with wrath."

162   Everything happened just as he suspected:
he seemed to have guessed correctly on the matter,
that he would have to eat bread from flour milled elsewhere,
and he would not be around San Millán much longer.

163   He kept very quiet; he knew how to keep hidden;
he would not reveal his heart to anyone;
he waited to see how this thing might turn out,
but he never desisted from serving God.

164   The devil did not stay around there for nothing;
he had quickly hatched a wicked piece of advice:
he showed the king down a rotten path,
towards avenging the outrage he had imagined.

165   King García spoke with the abbot:
"Abbot," he said, "I am mistreated in your abbey;
nothing in the world could have made me believe
that I would be rebuffed in this house.

166   I tell you firmly, and I want you to know,
if you do not give me justice over that babbling prior,
I will take away the treasures and even the lands,
and all of you here will be shown the door."

167   The abbot was swayed; he quickly changed:
we think that he must have been touched by jealousy;
he granted he would gladly do the king's will,
that the prior would not remain in the house or the priory.

---

[82] See Dutton, 1, *San Millán*, quatrain 240.

"I will be pleased with you," said the king, "if you do that."

168   What St. Dominic had suspected before
       was already being plotted by the devil;
       he was stripped of the priorate that he had,
       and was most unjustly cast out of the house.

169   They used the excuse that they did it reluctantly,
       because they saw that the king was displeased with him,
       and this was the way for them to appease him,
       and have him forget the outrage he had suffered.

170   They gave the monk a wretched hovel to live in,
       where he could find mighty little help;
       all of this trouble he regarded as trifling:
       he gazed upon it as through a looking glass.

171   There were three places,[83] according to what we read,
       but where and what they were we do not know;
       we can suppose that all of them were miserable;
       we do not imagine that the wealthy provided them.

172   God gave him fine grace, for[84] he deserved it,
       and everyone gave him all that he needed;
       if allowed, he would have lived on what he had,
       but the wicked enemy did not want that.

173   The king was unable to forget the outrage;
       he was lying in wait, looking for a pretext;
       before half a year he slapped a huge tax on him:
       he thought in this way he would have justice from him.

174   "King," said St. Dominic, "why do you persist?
       It seems that you are much more incensed every day;
       I want you to hear, in case you do not realize,
       you seem to be frittering your time away.

175   King, you know well you never gave me a thing,

---

[83] Apparently Berceo misunderstood the reference in his Latin source (see note 3 above) to *Tres Cellulas*: a place called 'Tres Celdas' ('Three Cells') where there was the small monastery of San Cristóbal de Tobia (no longer in existence), about six kilometers to the southeast of San Millán. The three disciples of San Millán, Citonato, Sofronio, and Gerontio, withdrew to spend their last years in the wilderness and they were buried in the three cells where they had lived. The monastery of San Cristóbal was built around them and was granted to San Millán by King Sancho el Mayor in 1014. (See Dutton, 4:163, 171a, and Ruffinatto, 300, note 171a.)

[84] Here I read *ca* with Ruffinatto, 301, 172a; Orduna, 85, 172a; and Logroño, 34, 172a rather than *qual* with Dutton, 4:62, 172b.

nor am I entrusted with the money of another;
nor would I be wanting to keep such a thing:
I would rather share it with the poor and the needy.

176   By God, do not try so hard to pursue me;
       you should know that you cannot get a thing out of me;
       even if I wanted I would have nothing to give;
       who could possibly squeeze blood from a turnip?"

177   "Monk," said the king, "you are not to be believed:
       we know you have piled up plenty of money;
       when you held the abbey in your power,
       they all tell me indeed what you used to do."

178   "King, this grieves me more than anything else:
       you accuse me of theft, a mortal sin;
       I never did such a thing as to keep another's goods.
       I bring as a witness the spiritual Father."

179   "My fine monk," said the king, "you know plenty about evil:
       you are simply denying what all of us know;
       that hypocritical behavior of yours
       will lead you, I believe, to a bitter end."

180   "King," said the monk, "if such is my fate,
       that I may not live in safety under you,
       to flee from bitterness I will leave your land;
       I will seek where to live in Extremadura."[85]

181   He commended himself to the Father who gives and takes;[86]
       he took his leave of all and left his native soil;[87]
       he set out on the highway; he crossed the mountains
       for the region of Nájera: he was done a dreadful wrong.[88]

182   When that gentleman was descending the mountains,
       drinking the cold waters and prodding with his staff,
       he arrived at the court of King Fernando:[89]
       the king was pleased and said his party was enhanced.

---

[85] Extremadura meant the farthest territory of the Christian kingdom, that is, the territory closest to the Moors. Until the middle of the eleventh century, the name of Extremadura was given to the region which bordered on Castile, the basin of the River Duero (Dutton, 4:163, note 180d, and Ruffinatto, 302, note 180d).

[86] Cf. Job 1:21.

[87] St. Dominic went to Castile around 1040 or 1041 (Ruffinatto, 302, note 181b).

[88] A comment here about the travails of St. Dominic due to having been persecuted by King García.

[89] See note 70 above.

183   "Prior," said the king, "you are most welcome:
        I am heartily pleased that I have met you;
        through acquaintance with you, I consider myself protected."
        All were pleased and he was cordially welcomed.

184   "King," said the monk, "I thank you very much
        for paying me such great and undeserved honor;
        but by God whom I obey, I implore you
        to accept a request that I submit to you.

185   I have left my abode and the realm of my birth,
        because I was unable to agree with your brother;
        I beg you to provide me with a hermitage,[90]
        where I may serve the One born of the Virgin Mary."
        "By my faith," said the king, "this pleases me."

186   Let us leave the good man resting with the king:
        it behooves us to digress a little from the subject,
        or else we could not make sense of the story;
        though we prolong it we can surely to return to it.

187   If you have heard, in the region of Caraço,[91]
        an important capital and famous fortress,
        there was a monastery that was a fine place,
        but so run-down that it was to be abandoned.

188   A fine community of black monks[92] used to live there,
        and God was pleased with the way they served Him;
        but the winds of change blew in such a way
        that they scarcely had any sustenance at all.

189   The entire downfall and extent of the failure
        came about due to carelessness and great neglect,
        or else God imposed such a sentence on the house
        in order to bestow great honor on St. Dominic.

190   But there still were quite a few monks in the house
        who led a good life and were holy men;
        indeed they were poor in cloaks and mantles,
        and when they had eaten they were not very full.[93]

---

[90] According to tradition, St. Dominic was granted a hermitage near the church of San Andrés de Burgos (Dutton, 4:163, note 185c, and Ruffinatto, 304, note 185c).

[91] The Carazo plateau seven kilometers east of Silos, which the River Ura or Mataviejas crosses (Dutton, 4:163, note 187a and Ruffinatto, 304, note 187a).

[92] Benedictine monks, whose habit is black.

[93] Here I read *non muy fartos* with Ruffinatto, 307, 190d; Orduna, 88, 190d; and Logroño, 37, 190d rather than *pocos cantos* with Dutton, 4:65, 190d.

191   There was among them a perfect Christian:
        according to the text he was called Liciniano;
        such extreme evil grieved and concerned him,
        for it always grew worse in winter and summer.

192   He entered the church and approached the altar;
        he went down on his knees and began to pray:
        "Lord God, Who are feared by the winds and the sea,
        cast Your glance upon this place.

193   Lord, look not upon us who are sinners,
        for we are careless and poor providers;
        remember those good men who came before us,
        and who were the keepers of this monastery.

194   Lord, from somewhere send us a shepherd
        who will put this house into better order;
        we suffer from want, and worse, from shame.
        You are the One Who knows why this happens.

195   Worthy St. Sebastian whose name this place bears,[94]
        beloved martyr of God, hear my prayer;
        remove this affliction from this monastery:
        may your house not fall into such great ruin.

196   Give us someone to govern us, servant of God,
        you who suffered great martyrdom to gain His love;
        even though we are bad and really quite worthless,
        may your house not fall into such great dishonor.

197   A house so noble that achieved such perfection,
        where counsel was found more than thousands of times,
        where a great community of fine monks lived,
        soon will become the dwelling place of serpents.

198   Sir, I beg you the favor of hearing me:
        may such a famous monastery be not destroyed;
        seek for some help, martyr of good sense.
        I hereby take leave of you with this petition."

199   His devout prayer was heard and granted by God,
        for it was uttered by the monk with perfect sincerity;
        it inspired in the good-living sovereign and king
        something that had not occurred to him before.

---

[94] The monastery and church of Silos was originally named after San Sebastián of Silos until the death of St. Dominic in 1073, after which it was called Santo Domingo de Silos (Dutton, 4:164, note 195a, and Ruffinatto, 306, note 195a).

200   It suddenly entered the mind of the king
         to give the monastery to the worthy man;
         God would bestow His sacred blessing on the house,
         and perchance that curse would finally be lifted.

201   The king spoke most tactfully with his gentlemen,
         with his nobles and those who were wise;
         "My friends," he said, "hear a few words of speech,
         and open your hearts to what I mean to say.

202   We all acknowledge the well-known fact
         of how ruined the church of Silos has become;
         an estate so great has become so impoverished
         that hardly three monks can even subsist there.

203   All of this comes about due to our sins,
         for we are sinners and we do not mend our ways;
         we simply do not put our minds on this:
         rest assured that here we most grievously err.

204   A kingdom is upheld by a monastery,
         for God is served in it night and day;
         likewise a kingdom can suffer from evil
         if such a fine place falls into ruin.

205   Should it please you all, I would think it good
         for us to have a man who is devout and virtuous,
         and it is my belief that I have one at hand
         whom I understand to be of flawless behavior.

206   The prior of San Millán has fallen among us,
         a man of holy living and perfect goodness;
         he is exiled from his land for some reason or other,
         and in my view this has come about through God.

207   He would be a most appropriate man for such a thing:
         he is very cautious and also very strict;
         as far as we can see he is beloved by God:
         through him the monastery would regain its state."

208   "King," they said, "your words to us are very timely,
         and all of us gratefully thank you for them;
         we believe what you say to be suitable advice,
         and if it pleases you we are all in agreement."

209   They dealt with the bishop[95] over this whole decision:
         the bishop thought it was absolutely excellent;

---

[95] Don Julián, bishop of Burgos from 1026 to 1043 (Dutton, 4:164, note 209a).

> no man high or low said a word against it;
> no council or town had any trouble with it.

210   When the monks of the house heard all about it,
     there never was a day of such great rejoicing;
     they went to the church and gave thanks to God;
     they recited wholeheartedly the "Te Deum laudamus."[96]

211   The bishop confirmed him and gave him the ministry,
     and then he blessed and consecrated him;
     he gave him his seat, his crook, and all he needed;
     the community gladly paid him obeisance.

212   When all the religious rites were completed,
     the blessed abbot[97] came to the monastery;
     not until he actually set foot in the abbey
     did the monks forget the suffering they had endured.

213   King Fernando, may God love him,
     acted as usual with great common sense;
     he did not send him alone, but in fine company,
     for he sent along with him many worthy men.

214   He sent fine men and those in high positions,
     priests and canons and blessed abbots,
     young men and old of various ages:
     blessed be a king who does such good things.

215   That gentleman was seated in the abbey;
     he was greatly distressed by its impoverished state,
     but God soon changed it into better condition,
     and sorrow was turned into great rejoicing.[98]

216   Right from the start the Order was reformed,
     which had become slack through the evil of sin;
     he gathered discreet companions around him:
     those that he saw were thoughtful in manner.

217   Day and night that gentleman suffered,
     toiling by day and praying by night;
     he shaped his friars indeed by his example,
     giving equal treatment to both young and old.

---

[96] The well-known hymn of thanksgiving which begins with the words "We praise You, God" (Ruffinatto, 310, note 210d).

[97] St. Dominic was made abbot of Silos in January of 1041 (Dutton, 4:164, note 212c).

[98] Allusion to John 16:20.

218   The monks were good men; they loved their shepherd;
       God established between them love and harmony;
       there was no entry there of the evil disturber
       who set Adam and Eve against their Lord.

219   King Fernando, may he rest in paradise,
       already saw what he desired in the house;
       he saw his new shoot graft naturally to the vine:
       thank God, he did not need to regret what he had done.

220   The king and the people gave them their help,
       some in the church, others in the refectory,[99]
       some in the vestry, others in the dormitory,
       some in the office,[100] others in the responsory.[101]

221   He saw his whole monastery well taken care of,
       the church well served, the community in good order,
       a holy abbot living a life of perfect goodness;
       he said to himself, "May God be praised."

222   I would rather not greatly detain you on this;
       I would like to press on and move ahead,
       to progress in this work while God gives me strength,
       for we have many other matters to deal with.

223   If you remember rightly, you have already heard
       how this blessed abbot, inspiration of abbots,
       endured so many troubles and adversities,
       and the paths he had to pass through from early on.[102]

224   Because he was always chaste and very patient,
       meek and humble and embracing obedience,
       in word and in deed keeping from sin,
       God had tremendous affection for him.

225   The King of Kings for Whom he suffered so much
       held everything he did in safekeeping for him;
       to give him the good comfort that he deserved,
       He wanted to show him what reward he would gain.

---

[99] The dining hall of a convent or monastery.

[100] The religious services.

[101] The response recited or sung in a religious service after a reading.

[102] Here I read *orto ya* with Logroño, 42, 223d rather than *Ortoya* with Dutton, 4:70, 223d. For theories about the meaning in Spanish of the problematical line 223d see Dutton, 4:164, note 223c (sic); Orduna, 94, note 223d; Ruffinatto, 314, note 223d; and Logroño, 530 under the word *rade*.

226   The glorious confessor who suffered so greatly
        was asleep in his bed, for he was sorely fatigued;
        he had a vision through which he was consoled
        for his suffering in the future and even in the past.

227   According to what we read, those who wrote it
        heard it straight from his very own mouth;
        we know that they told the whole truth about this,
        without adding or subtracting a single word.

228   He drew aside the monks closest to him,
        those who held the highest ranks in the house;
        "My friends," he said, "I beg you as good monks
        not to relate a word of what I will tell you.

229   In a dream I saw myself in a dreadful place,
        by the shore of a river as terrible[103] as the sea;
        anyone at all would be afraid to approach it,
        for it was wild and terrifying to cross.

230   Two rivers[104] with abundant waters flowed from it,
        not small streams, but very deep rivers;
        the one was just as white as crystal pebbles,
        the other more crimson than wine from a grapevine.[105]

231   Over the first river I saw a bridge
        that was not any wider than a palm[106] and a half,
        made of nothing whatsoever but solid glass:
        to tell you the truth it was a terrifying path.

232   Clothed in white dalmatics[107] with fine brocaded silk,
        two gentlemen were standing at the end of the bridge,
        with gold braid on their fronts, their sleeves and their collars:
        loquele nec sermones[108] could describe their adornment.

---

[103] Here I read *fiero* with Ruffinatto, 315, 229b; Orduna, 95, 229d; and Logroño, 43, 229b rather than *fuerte* with Dutton, 4:71, 229b.

[104] For the geography of these two rivers, see Dutton, 4:164, note 230a.

[105] Here I read *parrales* with a small *p*, with Ruffinatto, 317, 230d; Orduna, 95, 230d; and Logroño, 43, 230d rather than *Parrales* with a capital *p* with Dutton, 4:71, 230d. However, Dutton may be correct in concluding that Berceo was referring to the place-name *Parrales* rather than the word *parral*, 'grapevine.' (See Dutton, 4:165, note 230d.)

[106] A measurement of length equal to about twenty-one centimeters or the span of a man's hand stretching from the thumb to the little finger.

[107] A dalmatic is a sleeved liturgical vestment worn by officiating deacons and bishops.

[108] 'No word or speech.' Berceo is alluding to the words in Ps. 18:4.

233   One of those two most illustrious persons
        was holding in his hands two exquisite crowns,
        in a finely-wrought gold never seen by man:
        no human ever gave such noble gifts to another.

234   The other held a crown six times more gorgeous,
        encircled all around with many precious stones;
        it was so brilliant that it shone even brighter than the sun:
        no human ever saw such a beautiful thing.

235   I was summoned by the first one who held the two crowns
        to cross over to them by taking the steps;
        I told him that the steps presented a danger;
        he said I should take them without fear or hesitation.

236   I stepped onto the bridge although it was narrow;
        I passed as easily along it as on a wide road;[109]
        they welcomed me in a cordial manner,
        coming halfway towards me along the path.

237   'We are pleased with you, Friar,' said the one clothed in white;
        'Be welcomed and highly praised by us;
        we have come to tell you a delightful piece of news
        that you will be pleased with when we have told you.

238   These two crowns so noble that you see
        are held in safekeeping by our Lord for you;
        take care not to lose them since you have earned them,
        for the devil would like to steal them away from you.'

239   'Gentlemen,' I said to them, 'for God's sake hear me.
        What is the reason for what you are telling me?
        I have not led such a life or done such good things;
        do make known to me the reason for this.'

240   'You do right to ask the reason,' said the messenger,
        'and we will certainly give you a correct reply;
        the one is for being a good and chaste monk,
        and for showing no reticence in practicing obedience.

241   The other one my Lady, Holy Mary, won for you,
        for her church[110] was sanctified under your guidance;
        you made great improvements to her monastery:
        she sends it because she is greatly pleased with you.

---

[109] Here I read *carrera* with Ruffinatto, 317, 236b; Orduna, 97, 236b; and Logroño, 44, 236b rather than *rarera* with Dutton, 4:72, 236b.

[110] The church of Santa María de Cañas. See quatrains 97–110.

242 This third one, so gorgeously wrought,
   is because of your being entrusted with this monastery
   that was wandering in sin like a beast with no reins,
   and which you have rescued from poverty and strife.

243 If you persevere in your customary habits,
   the crowns are yours, consider that you have earned them;
   many suffering people will find refuge in you;
   they will come needing help and will go away counseled.'

244 Immediately after they had said these words,
   they vanished from sight and I could see nothing;
   I awoke and raised my hand to bless myself;
   God knows I experienced a change of heart.

245 Friars and companions, let us look after souls,
   let us be true both to God and to man;
   if we will be upright and faithful to God,
   we will earn crowns that are worth more than money.

246 For this miserable world that will only last briefly,
   let us not lose the other one that will never end.
   Who will not exchange poverty for riches?
   He who will seek shall easily find.[111]

247 Furthermore, I beg you and ask you as a favor,
   to keep this confession of mine a secret;
   may it not be revealed until a later time,
   until my soul departs from this bodily prison."

248 The worthy St. Dominic, inspiration of Hispania,
   saw other strange visions aside from this one,
   but the friars in his communities did not hear them,
   for he kept them hidden deep down inside him.

249 Because of those visions that God showed him,
   no boasting of self ever entered his flesh;
   he endeavored more fervently to serve the Lord Jesus;
   he did not turn his head towards anything foolish.

250 His flesh and the devil were only too willing
   to take his good seat from him and stir him up;
   there was great strife between them because they could not do it,
   for this star stood so close to the sun.

[111] See Matt. 7:7 and Luke 11:9.

251   Concerning the request he made to his companions,
          they acted correctly in not revealing it;
          indeed they kept the secret for as long as he lived;
          they did not want to make any trouble for their father.

252   The worthy St. Dominic, such a noble confessor,
          should be compared to the holy St. Martin,[112]
          who saw the Lord Jesus Christ wrapped up in the cloak
          that he had given to the poor suffering man.

253   The glorious confessor, worthy of adoration,
          God wished to honor in all his ways;
          in all his offices to make him His heir,
          in order to give him greater glory in heaven.

254   In his earliest years he was a shepherd,
          an office that was customary at that time;
          then he studied and was ordained a priest,
          a discreet and moderate director of souls.

255   Then he was a hermit who suffered greatly,
          living in the wilderness away from the people,
          seeing vile faces and encountering much evil,
          where he suffered greater martyrdom than any martyr.

256   After entering the Order he practiced obedience,
          placing all that concerned him in the power of another;
          he proved how good and how patient he was,
          as if he had taken a penance on himself.

257   Even in the monastery he rose higher in rank:
          the abbot of the house gave him the priorate;
          our words have made known to you all of that,
          about what fire he was in and how he was scorched.

258   In the end, the good and very holy man,
          because he had carried out every high office,
          was willed by God to be elected as abbot;
          in truth his elector made no mistake there.

259   Aside from all these honors that he had received,
          God gave him further noble and perfect graces:
          to see visions, and persons richly clothed,
          to hear such promises as I have read to you.

---

[112] St. Martin of Tours (316–397). When he was a young officer in the Roman army, he gave half of his cape to a poor naked person. He was named bishop of Tours in 370 (Dutton, 4:165, note 252b).

260 Even without all that very long litany,
he was further rewarded by God and Holy Mary:
they invested his tongue with the gift of prophecy,
for it is certainly known that he prophesied.

261 So that you may believe that I tell you the truth,
I will give some authority to this for you,
of how he was a prophet and spoke with certainty,
through which his great holiness was affirmed.

262 St. Vincent was the name of an ancient martyr
who was the brother of both Sabina and Cristeta;[113]
they all died for God by a violent hand;
they all lay in Avila:[114] I tell you no lie.

263 King Fernando, who always loved goodness
and who strove with all his heart to accomplish it,
thought of transferring them to greater sanctity,
and of placing them in more honorable tombs.

264 That bold spear[115] thought it most advisable
to bring them to the place called San Pedro de Arlanza;[116]
they would have a better resting place with that fine community,
and no doubt at all they would be better served.[117]

265 Opposite a place around the region of Lara,[118]
in a bend that is taken by the River Arlanza,

---

[113] Sts. Vincent, Sabina, and Cristeta were martyred around the year 304 during the reigns of the emperors Diocletian and Maximian. (See Dutton, 4:165, note 262ab, and Ruffinatto, 324, note 262ab.)

[114] The Arabs destroyed the city of Avila around 715 and it was not repopulated until the year 1090. This transfer was verified in 1061. (See Dutton, 4:165, note 262ab, and Ruffinatto, 324, note 262d.)

[115] See note 12 above.

[116] San Pedro de Arlanza in the province of Burgos, where there is a Benedictine monastery situated about 12 kilometers to the northeast of Silos, on the north shore of the river Arlanza, between the mountains and the river. It seems to have been in existence previous to the year 912 when it was endowed and restored by Fernán González and his wife doña Sancha. It was reduced to ruins by a fire in 1894 (Ruffinatto, 324, note 264b, and Dutton, 4:165, note 264b).

[117] Here Berceo is emphasizing the strong ties that existed between the monasteries of Silos and San Pedro de Arlanza (Ruffinatto, 324, note 264cd, and Orduna, 101, note 264b).

[118] The district of Lara where San Pedro de Arlanza is found. The town of Lara is about nine kilometers to the north of San Pedro (Dutton, 4:166, note 265a, and Ruffinatto, 324, note 265a).

there lies a monastery, a very noble house
called by the name of San Pedro de Arlanza.

266   It had a holy abbot, a servant of God,
García by name, a lover of goodness;
he was the head and superior of the monastery:
the flock gave proof of what the shepherd was like.

267   In a vision he saw he should perform a service:
the very precious bodies of those holy martyrs
he should have exhumed from the old cemetery,
and have them brought to his monastery.

268   He spoke to that king, God give him sweet repose,
the one called Fernando, a very noble prince;
he considered it a sensible and very fine deed,
and the abbot lost no time at all in performing it.

269   He invited the bishops and the provincials,[119]
the abbots and priors and other cloistered monks,
the deacons and priests and other such persons,
and all those senior and high-ranking people.

270   Gentry and higher nobility gathered there,
men and women from the common folk;
there were processions of all different types:
some sang praises and others sang hymns.

271   They brought the body of the worthy St. Vincent,
and the bodies of his famous and noble sisters;
all were singing praises to Almighty God
Who shows everlasting mercy towards sinners.

272   They crossed the abundant waters of the Duero,
together with such others as the Duratón and Esgueva;[120]
they arrived in Arlanza close to the house;
the people would not enter any of its premises.

273   The worthy St. Dominic, native of Cañas,
born at a lucky moment,[121] full of good habits,

---

[119] Religious superiors of an Order in a given district.

[120] The trip from Avila to San Pedro de Arlanza would involve crossing the Duratón tributary, the Duero River and the Esgueva tributary in that order (See Dutton, 4:166, note 272ab; Orduna, 103, note 272b; and Ruffinatto, 326 note 272b).

[121] The expression in Spanish *nasció en bon punto* 'he was born at a lucky moment' is typically found in epic poetry when describing epic heroes such as the Cid in the *Cantar de Mío Cid* (ed. Menéndez Pidal, 812–813 s.v. *punto*). Berceo even employs this expression when referring to the Blessed Virgin Mary in *Loores*, line 137a.

came there leading those good companions,
conducting themselves with matchless behavior.

274   Until the next morning, they guarded the bodies
of Vincent and his sisters Sabina and Cristeta;
they placed them in a solid and worthy tomb:
there was great rejoicing among those Castilians.

275   During the transfer[122] of that brother and his sisters,
many sick persons were healed of their pains,
some in their feet and others in their hands,
for which Christian men and women gave thanks to God.

276   Abbots and bishops and canons of Orders
all carried relics back from there to where they came from,
but the abbot of Silos and his closest associates
did not even venture to lay a finger on them.

277   The good and blessed abbot went to his monastery,
and was cordially welcomed by his companions;
he said in his most delightful voice, "Benedícite;"
in tones most perfect they replied, "Dominus."[123]

278   He told the community, "By God, may you hear me,
bishops and abbots send greetings to you;
and by God, may you do what they request:
may you include them in your prayers."

279   "Sir," they said, "since we have you back,
we are more joyful and give thanks to God;
we agree to do to everything else that you tell us,
but there is one little matter of concern to us.

280   Of the sacred relics[124] that you carried on your backs,
you gave some to all of those who requested them;
you never brought any of them back to your monastery;
in this we consider that you have been neglectful."

281   He spoke against those words with truthful lips;
his reply was eloquent, his response unequivocal:
"My friends," he said, "be not envious over this;
God will give you help in one way or another.

---

[122] It has been verified that the transfer took place in the year 1061. (See Dutton, 4:165, note 262ab, and Ruffinatto, 326, note 275a.)

[123] The Latin word *Benedicite* ('Blessed') is the first word of the blessing and the Latin word *Dominus* ('Lord') is the first word of the response to the blessing.

[124] The monks of Silos are referring to the relics of Sts. Vincent, Sabina, and Cristeta which were transferred to the monastery of San Pedro de Arlanza.

282   If you will be willing to be faithful to God,
        and you will be willing to keep His commandments,
        He will give you relics that you will be pleased with.[125]
        I know you will not possibly be wanting in that regard.

283   If our serious sins do not remove it from us,
        you shall have the sacred body that will please you;
        you shall be richly abounding in relics;
        you shall be envied by some of your neighbors."

284   The worthy St. Dominic, who said this to them,
        was prophesying what was to come about;
        although he foretold it, he did not understand
        that this prophecy had to do with himself.

285   Some of the monks who heard this from him
        gave no credence to this prediction;
        others of them, who were older and wiser,
        held that these words would not prove futile.

286   While he was alive they put all this aside,
        but after he died they witnessed the miracles;
        they remembered those words and then understood
        that what he had prophesied turned out to be true.

287   Gentlefolk, we must understand by this,
        that you can believe what we said before,
        for he was truly a prophet: God gave him great power
        and great inspiration in his words and his deeds.

288   Gentlefolk, thanks to God, we have told you
        whatever we can possibly discover of his holy life;
        henceforth, with the help of the God in Whom we believe,
        having finished this book, we will continue on another.

---

[125] Here I read *que avredes/auredes plazer* with Ruffinatto, 329, 282c and Orduna, 105, 282c rather than *que veredes plazer* with Dutton, 4:79, 282c.

Book II

289   We want to begin another little book,[126]
       and make known to you some of his miracles,
       those God willed to show through him while he lived;
       may He Whose minstrels we are deign to guide us.

290   A woman who came from Castro Cisneros,[127]
       who went by the name of María from birth,
       got dressed in her best, got ready her money,
       and went to go shopping with some companions.

291   She set out on the road indeed well and happy
       I do not know for sure if on foot or on horseback —
       when she suddenly was taken so violently ill
       that she became as stiff and as rigid as a board.

292   She could not move either one of her feet;
       she could not stretch the fingers of her hands;
       her sight was so blurred that she could not see;
       she had no power over any of her limbs.

293   Her speech was slurred because of her condition,
       and she uttered many words that were incoherent;
       she knew not where she was nor why she was there:
       those who were with her were sorely distressed.

294   As her eyes were glassy and her mouth twisted,
       and each of her arms like a crooked stick,
       she could not take a step from the hearth to the door:
       all who truly loved her would have rather seen her dead.

295   All those who knew her were troubled and grieved;
       her family and friends knew not what to do for her;
       it occurred to someone who pondered the matter
       that no mustard plaster would heal the lady.

---

[126] Berceo is following the usual plan of hagiographers which includes three separate sections or books about the saint: (1) the life of the saint, (2) the miracles that took place during his life, and (3) the miracles that took place after his death (Dutton, 4:166, note 289a, and Ruffinatto, 330, note 289 ac).

[127] According to Dutton, who refers to the Latin text of Grimaldo used by Berceo as his source, the town was actually called Castro Ceniza and not Castro Cisneros. Apparently Berceo confused it with Cisneros, 33 kilometers north of Palencia. The town of Castro Ceniza is about 11 kilometers north of Silos (Dutton, 4:166, note 290a).

296   He thought they should take her to the holy confessor
        who was native of Cañas and lived in Silos:
        he would take pity on her when he saw her;
        he would restore her health through the Lord our God.

297   Everyone thought this was a good piece of advice:
        they set out on the road bearing her on their shoulders;
        at times she turned green, at times she turned waxen,
        for her physical pains were varied in manner.

298   They carried the sick and suffering lady to Silos,
        and they laid her before the door of the confessor;
        she appeared to be more dead than alive;
        the people held out little hope for her life.

299   The worthy confessor whose deeds were abundant,
        swift and cheerful when it came to such matters,
        quickly went to them outside of the premises,
        and ordered them to come inside the house.

300   He ordered the hospitalers to look after the people:
        they ate what there was for lunch or for supper;
        he entered the church to pray to God,
        to obtain health for the paralyzed woman.

301   He gazed at the crucifix and said, "O Lord,
        You Who are the ruler of heaven and earth,
        You Who gave Eve to Adam for his wife,
        remove this suffering from this good woman.

302   Since she has arrived alive at this house,
        Lord, I beg Your mercy that she will get better;
        may this companion of theirs who suffers so greatly
        be freed from this hindrance on her return.

303   May these companions of hers who suffer so greatly,
        who are mournful and dejected and weary,
        acknowledge Your grace and be comforted by it,
        and praise Your name, joyful and content."

304   To comfort the people the wise gentleman
        cut short his prayer, not wanting to lengthen it;
        he quickly came out to them and gave them the meal,
        and uttered some very consoling words to them.

305   "My friends," he said, "let us all pray wholeheartedly
        to God for this lady who lies in such straits;
        may He restore her reason and her sight to her;
        may she be rid of this affliction and remain unscathed."

306 The prayer was devout and very powerful:
it was heard and granted by God Whom it pleased;
she opened her eyes and asked for a drink:
it pleased them more greatly than even great wealth.

307 The holy father ordered wine to be brought,
and he had some heated up in a vessel;
he himself blessed the cup into which it was poured,
and in His divine name, he gave her some to drink.

308 As soon as it had passed between her lips,
the pain diminished and the lady was healed;
she jumped quickly out of the bed and stood up straight,
saying, "Such a lovely day! May God be praised!"

309 She fell at the feet of the noble confessor:
"Worthy sir and father," she said, "lucky the moment you were born;
indeed I understand that you are beloved by God,
for He is greatly pleased by your services.

310 I believe and acknowledge I have been healed by you;
through you I recovered life, limb, and reason;
may you be thanked for this favor from God,
for I know it is through your grace that I left this bed."

311 The good father responded, wishing to correct her:
"My friend," he said, "you do not speak as you ought to;
it is only God Whom you must bless and praise,
because He deigned to free you from such great affliction.

312 His divine grace which deigned to heal you
is the only thing you must bless and praise;
you must not say such a thing to me:
I neither wish you to say it nor wish to hear it.

313 Daughter, go in blessing and return to your home:
you have time to go back to the shopping you set out for;
but with all your might, protect yourself from sinning,
and you must keep this suffering in mind forever."

314 The holy father stayed within his monastery,
doing service to God and to Holy Mary;
the lady went her way indeed well and happy,
and the neighbors with her were very joyful.

315 Gentlefolk, if you would bear with me a little,
I would rather not take my leave of you with that;
I would like to tell you another miracle
which you should hear, for love of the good father.

316   There was a young person whose name was Oria,[128]
        a mere child in years, according to the story;
        she gloried in doing service to God;
        she never had her mind on anything else.

317   This young person was in love with God,
        and she paid no mind to anything foolish;
        a mere child in years but mature in reason,
        she would rather have been blind than to be married.

318   She preferred to hear the hours[129] rather than ballads,[130]
        the words of priests more than those of any minstrels;
        if she were allowed she would stay close to the altars,
        or she would walk discalced[131] through holy places.

319   She felt great envy for the sister of Lazarus[132]
        who used to sit calmly at the feet of Christ,
        hearing the words that His precious lips uttered,
        while Martha her sister ran anxiously about.

320   When the young person saw that the time was ripe,
        she abandoned the home where she had been raised;
        the suffering young pilgrim went to the holy confessor:
        after she had arrived she fell at his feet.

321   She said, "I have come to you, worthy sir and father:
        I want with your help to adopt a form of life;
        I have indeed taken leave of the life of the world;
        if I return there again I believe I will be lost.

322   Sir, if God be willing, such is my desire:
        to take orders and the veil, and live in chastity,
        to lie in poverty in some remote corner,
        to exist for God on what Christians may give me."

323   "My friend," said the holy father, "may God be willing
        that you be able to endure such a harsh life as that;
        if indeed you do not succeed, you would be far better off
        to live in the same manner as your mother."

---

[128] For diverse opinions over whether this Oria is in fact the St. Oria of the *Vida de Santa Oria* by Berceo, see Dutton, 4:167, note 316a; Ruffinatto, 336, note 316a; and Orduna, 111, note 316a.

[129] The religious hours, that is, prayers said throughout certain hours of the day.

[130] Ballads sung by troubadours.

[131] 'Barefoot' like men and women in some religious orders.

[132] In quatrain 319, Berceo refers to the sisters of Lazarus, Mary and Martha. See Luke 10:38–42.

324   "Father," said the young person, "I beg you as a favor,
that my request to you be carried out at once;
for God's sake, prudent father, do not delay;
do not let this matter lie forgotten."

325   The confessor realized that she was inspired:
by his own hand he made her a black-veiled sister;[133]
in just a few days she was made an anchoress;[134]
she was very joyful when they shut her in.

326   She ended up living a good life of great abstinence,
humble and true and very patient,
prayerful and happy and pure in behavior;
she put every effort into serving God.

327   The deadly enemy, full of his tricks,
who sought his ill fate in the heavens above,
to fill the young woman with terror and dread,
made many evil shapes and vile faces before her.

328   The confirmed traitor took the form of a serpent,
and, raising his neck, placed himself before her;
now he was small and now he was huge,
at times very thin and at times very thick.

329   The one cursed by God waged fierce war against her;
to fill her with fear he did many filthy things;
the blessed young person, a friend of God's,
lived in great suffering: let no one tell you otherwise.

330   It is certainly a fact that in that same form
he attacked Eve who was Adam's companion,
when they both took a bite of the forbidden fruit;[135]
we, their descendants, still regret that desire.

331   The troubled anchoress knew not what else to do:
she sent to inform the good father about it;
he realized at once what it might be;
he set out on the road and came to see her.

---

[133] A Benedictine sister. The Benedictines wear the black habit.

[134] This kind of penitence and ascetic life was very common during the Middle Ages. The anchorite or anchoress usually lived in a small cell with the door walled up and just a small window through which bread and water could be passed. There they remained, spending their time in contemplation and in mortification of their flesh. (See Dutton, 4:167, note 325c, and Ruffinatto, 340, note 325c.)

[135] See Gen. 3:1–19.

332   When he got to her he heard her confession,
        and sprinkled holy water over her dwelling place;
        he himself said the Mass and gave her communion;
        the evil neighbor fled regretfully away.

333   The holy confessor returned to his church;
        the young servant of God remained in peace;
        the dragon of a traitor was taught a good lesson,
        and he never showed up around there again.

334   We have heard the same about the worthy San Millán.[136]
        I have clearly read that he performed such a miracle:
        from the house of Onorio he pursued a devil
        who engaged in conduct filthier than a dog's.

335   I should like to tell you yet another fine miracle
        worked by this confessor, and delightful to hear;
        although you may be weary you should endure:
        you will say it was one that was worthy of writing.

336   In the area of Silos, we do not know the place,
        there was a blind man whom we will tell you about;
        our text does not say how he was blinded:
        we will not state what has not been written.

337   His name was Juan, if you care to know;
        he lived in great sadness which you can imagine;
        and besides that affliction which you have heard of,
        his ears ached so badly he was climbing the walls.

338   Whether of noble ancestry, or whether a peasant,
        the text does not say, so I am not informed;
        but let us leave that aside and tell the best part,
        what pertains of value to the holy confessor.

339   This suffering blind man had himself brought
        to the house of the monk mentioned above,
        for he was firmly convinced and he had faith
        that through him he would be rid of that affliction.

340   When he got to the door of San Sebastián,[137]
        the unfortunate man would not ask for bread or wine,
        but said, "O father, by the worthy San Millán,
        may you take pity on this affliction of mine.

[136] Berceo refers briefly here to a miracle performed by San Millán. See *San Millán*, quatrains 181–198.
[137] See note 94 above.

341   Father, I have come to where you are to seek you:
either you come out or command me to come in;
sir, I could not possibly depart from this place
until you command me to stay or to return.

342   Father of the suffering, deign to visit me,
lay your hand on me and bless me with your thumb;[138]
if I could only just manage to kiss your hand,
I believe I would be healed of all this affliction."

343   The blessed father, right inside where he was,
heard the cries that this blind man uttered;
he came out and asked what it was that he wanted;
he replied that all he ardently desired was his eyesight.

344   The worthy St. Dominic, quick about such matters,
took him by the hand and guided him himself;
the perfect Christian put him inside the house,
and he was given what they gave to the others every day.

345   The holy confessor prayed all night long
to the King of Heaven, the exalted ruler,
that He should give this unhappy man his sight,
and remove from his ears the pain he was suffering.

346   In the morning he went in to celebrate the Mass,
and the blind man came with great pleasure to hear it;
the unfortunate man knew nothing else to ask for,
except that God should deign to open his eyes.

347   When he had completed his duties at Mass,
the abbot with his well-trained community of friars
had the blind man summoned, and after he had come,
he fell prostrate on the ground at their feet.

348   With the hyssop twig[139] he sprinkled holy water on him;
he blessed his eyes with the holy cross;
the pain and affliction were instantly diminished;
he completely recovered the sight he had lost.

349   You can imagine, gentlefolk and friends,
that he had many different types of illness:

---

[138] The symbolic gesture made by tracing the sign of the cross three times with the index finger or thumb of the right hand first on forehead, then on lips, then on chest. In this way, God was implored through the sign of the redemption of humanity, to free the person from his enemies, including illnesses. (See Ruffinatto, 344, note 342b.)

[139] Allusion to Ps. 51 (50):9, recited as an antiphon at the beginning of Mass.

one was blindness and another chronic pains,
but, healed of them all he gave praise to God.

350   "My friend," said the holy father, "go your way,
and thank God that you go relieved from suffering;
take care not to sin and do nothing foolish,
for you will be undone if you relapse into sin."

351   Many are the miracles we know about this father:
some we have heard and others we have read;
we pause in doubt about which one we will exclude,
but whichever it is, we will have to digress.

352   I want to skip the other ones from this period,
and tell one you will remember as long as you live,
about how he earned the grace that frees captives,
wherefore they send him votive bread[140] from distant lands.

353   The Moors at that time were living close by:[141]
men did not dare to go walking on the roads;
those wicked people staged sudden early morning raids,
cruelly taking the unlucky away bound with ropes.

354   One time when they launched a surprise attack,
those ungodly people made their way to Soto;[142]
in that raid on horseback they seized a young man:
his name was Domingo; I will not skip a thing.

355   They put him in irons and on a heavy chain;
they caused him dreadful anguish in suffering and hunger;
he was fed a rotten lunch and an even worse supper;
had they given him oat[143] bread he would have gladly eaten it.

356   He who falls in such hands is indeed unlucky,
and when he is a Christian he is at the mercy of dogs;
in word and in deed he is offended every day;
he is badly off in winter and no better in summer.

---

[140] Sacred bread offered as a vow.

[141] It should be remembered that until the conquest of Toledo on 6 May 1085, the lands south of the River Duero were in the hands of the Moors. Therefore the Christians who lived in that area or on the fringes of the border endured many trials and tribulations due mainly to incursions by the Moors who held the power there. (See Ruffinatto, 346, note 353a, and Dutton, 4:167, note 353a.)

[142] The town of Soto de San Esteban (Osma) six kilometers to the west of San Esteban de Gormaz (Dutton, 4:168, note 354b).

[143] At that time, oats were fed exclusively to animals.

357   The parents of the captive were sorely grieved:
                they were forced to arrange to pay ten thousand pieces;
                yet they got no help to enable them to pay,
                for they could not possibly earn the money.

358   With all they put together to cover the cost,
                they scarcely gathered half of the ransom;
                they were in a quandary and, pondering the matter,
                they figured he would have to remain in prison.

359   A thought occurred to them, sent by God,
                that they should go and ask the worthy confessor;
                no one who asked him was ever turned away;
                if he did not help them then all was lost.

360   Those of them who were brothers or cousins
                went to kiss the hands of the holy father;
                "O father of the sick and the well," they said,
                "hear our entreaty and give us some help.

361   A relative of ours is a captive of the Moors:
                he is lying in prison suffering terribly;
                we have determined the price of his ransom with the Moors,
                but what we have or were given falls short of the amount.

362   Good sir, we have come to ask your help,
                since we do not chance to know where to turn;
                you know what is involved in the ransoming of captives,
                and how God is grateful to him who can achieve it."

363   The compassionate father began to weep:
                "My friends," he said, "if I had money to give,
                I could not possibly use it on anything better
                than putting it towards the freeing of captives.

364   We have neither money, nor gold nor silver;[144]
                the only thing we have in our house is a horse;
                we will gladly give him as a gift to you:
                may the Almighty King make up what is lacking.

365   Take whatever we can give you for now;
                while you lead him along we will get you something else;
                we will send you whatever we can possibly obtain;
                as we trust in God we will recover the prisoner."

366   They went their way to arrange the business
                of selling the horse to get what they could;

---

[144] Cf. Acts 3:6.

the compassionate father went in to his altar
to pray to God as he was wont to do.

367   The night having passed, immediately at dawn
he celebrated holy Mass with his monks;
they raised their prayers and cries for the prisoner,
that God should deliver him from such captors.

368   The prayer of the father of great holiness
was carried to heaven by sacred charity;
it reached the ears of the King of Glory:
the captive escaped from his captivity.

369   The irons that bound him opened up;
the yard tightly locked did not hold him;
he returned to his parents laden with his irons;
he himself was filled with amazement at this.

370   The promise that the true father made to them,
he would not even take three days to fulfill;
he got rid of the Moor who was the jailer,
so the Moor never got a single cent out of him.

371   They discovered what time the captive had escaped:
they found it was the time when he celebrated Mass;
they realized it was planned by the holy father,
that this was the help he had promised to them.

372   The parents and friends and companions of the captive,
and all the other people together with them,
and all those around there were pondering the fact
that that confessor worked really priceless miracles.

373   The worthy St. Dominic, perfect in goodness,
for being so devout and filled with such charity,
for freeing captives from their captivity
received fine grace from God as his legacy.

374   Those merits earned him noble grace,
for he does a great deal of harm to the Moors;
he breaks open their jails, he casts them into sleep,
he frees captives from those ill-fated wretches.[145]

---

[145] I have read quatrain 374 with Ruffinatto, Orduna, and Logroño, thus omitting
line 374e *de guisa que non aven nin oro nin argientos* which Dutton includes in his edition.
See Dutton, 4:93, note 374e.

375   May that confessor, so holy and of such noble deeds,
        who did more good works than are told in writing,
        protect our souls and defend our bodies;
        may our lives be peaceful and free from strife.

376   On another occasion he did a great favor
        I would certainly tell you if you cared to hear it;
        in my view I would not be keeping you long:
        the lunch you will eat will not be colder for that.

377   The perfect gentleman had a fine garden:
        it was well provided with excellent leeks;
        thieves from the area, moved by the devil,
        came to steal them when the people were asleep.

378   All night long until break of day,
        they dug in the garden of the sacred monastery,
        but they failed to pull up a single leek or parsnip,
        for they ploughed nothing but untilled land.

379   At dawn, the gentleman summoned those who kept the keys:
        "Friars," he said, "you should know we have some laborers;
        be assured of this, they have been digging in the garden:
        make them some food and let them take their wages."

380   The holy confessor went to them in the garden:
        "My friends," he said, "you have done a good job;
        may the Lord our God thank you for it:
        come and you shall eat in our refectory."

381   At this, the laborers were dreadfully ashamed;
        they threw down their shovels and fell at his feet;
        "Mercy, sir," they said, "for God's sake forgive us:
        many are the reasons why we are terribly guilty."

382   "My friends," said the holy father, "do not fear:
        this time you shall be completely forgiven;
        for these your pains you shall have your wages,
        but do not make a habit of such nightly sprees."

383   They were given their fill and went back to where they came from;
        they never forgot how afraid they had been;
        all those who heard of it thought it was extraordinary,
        and said they had never seen a man of such kindness.

384   Who could possibly tell all of his miracles?
        We would never have time to reach the end of them;
        from those that we have told, you can just imagine
        what a noble and distinguished gentleman he was.

385   If you have a great desire to hear miracles,
       hasten to the monastery of the holy confessor;
       you will see with your own eyes, and you will know better,
       for he works them every day, thanks to God.

386   And there you will find many who know about them,
       whether they be young or whether they be old;
       they will tell you a thousand that are similar or better,
       and whoever wants copies should look for a scribe.[146]

387   Even with that I do not think I will withdraw:
       there are still a few miracles I want to tell;
       I do not want to miss out on[147] any graces by so little;
       I do not want to drown at the end of the river.

388   A count from Galicia who was a person of power,
       whose name was Pelayo, a man strong and sturdy,
       became hindered by the loss of his sight,
       for a man who cannot see ought not to have been born.

389   While going on one or another holy pilgrimage,
       persevering with doctors and buying their medicines,
       he spent a fortune on useless remedies,
       so much that he soon would have made himself poor.

390   He heard of that confessor who was so perfect,
       so beloved by God in all of his affairs;
       had he only got to know him long before,
       he was certain he could have been cured by him.

391   He arranged his affairs as best he could;
       he had himself brought to the house of the confessor;
       he began to entreat him ever so gently
       that he might be willing to pray for him to God.

392   If he prayed for him, he had great faith
       that the Almighty King would give him help;
       he began to weep with such persistence
       that he made all the people most pitifully weep.

393   The worthy confessor was grieved for the count,
       for he saw such a noble prince brought so low;

---

[146] At that time, it was a custom for anyone wanting copies of the miracles of a saint to go to the monks who knew how to write and ask them to make copies of the most interesting miracles performed by the saint of that place (Ruffinatto, 354, note 386d).

[147] Here I have read *menoscabar* with Ruffinatto, 355, 387c; Orduna, 124, 387c; and Logroño, 67, 387c rather than *acabdar* with Dutton, 4:96, 387c.

he turned with his usual customary zeal
to pray to Jesus Christ Who was crucified for us.

394   When he had finished his prayer and supplication,
he had water brought from his famous fountain;[148]
he blessed it himself with his sacred hand,
and sprinkled a handful on each of his eyes.

395   Heavenly grace made its way there at once:
the count recovered the sight he had lost;
the darkness was instantly removed from his countenance
which had never looked so lovely in all his life.

396   He made a fine offering, a significant gift,
giving thanks to God and to the holy prelate;
like one who has finished a good piece of business,
happy and pleased he returned to his shire.

397   That famous gentleman worked another miracle
on which he labored both long and hard,
enduring great fasting and praying daily,
while suffering severe bodily affliction.

398   There was a good man, a native of Gomiel[149]
named García Muñoz, who had a dreadful illness;
at times he was seized by an epileptic fit:
no one who saw it had ever seen the like of it.

399   That seizure usually affected his mind:
it took away his intelligence, his speech, and his sight;
he had no sense nor did he understand reason;
on his account all lived in great anguish.

400   He was seized in such a way by the cursed fits
that he lost every single one of his senses;
and what was worse for them were the faces he made,
for many people thought him possessed by the devil.

401   The wicked thing was of such an evil nature
that it made his features look terribly disturbed;
the good man made so many ugly grimaces
that all of his friends lived sorely distressed.

---

[148] Here Berceo is referring to the famous Fountain of the Saint, located in the southeast corner of the cloister at Silos (Dutton, 4:168, note 394b).

[149] This could be the town of Gomiel de Izán, 40 kilometers southeast of Silos, in the vicinity of Aranda de Duero (Dutton, 4:168, note 398ab, and Ruffinatto, 358, note 398a).

402   They all held out little hope for his health,
        they saw so many unseemly signs in him;
        if he should die they would not be more pained,
        for they all thought themselves dishonored by this.

403   Neither prayer nor fasting helped him at all,
        neither spells nor doctors nor candles nor offerings;
        they could not find any way at all to reach him;
        no one had ever seen such a terrible affliction.

404   The sick man himself would have rather been dead,
        for he found no comfort anywhere at all;
        if it were not that his soul would be done an injustice,
        he would just as soon have chosen to hang from a rope.

405   The perfect confessor, filled with charity,
        heard the reports about that illness;
        he was deeply sorry and his heart was grieved;
        he said, "O King of Glory,[150] have mercy on him."

406   He sent a written message sealed by him
        to the parents of the man who lived in suffering,
        that they should bring him directly to his house,
        and perhaps he might be healed when he returned.

407   His parents and friends and García himself
        were filled with joy at that fine message;
        they arranged their affairs to make their pilgrimage,
        to carry the sick man to the monastery of Silos.

408   The pilgrims had made their way to the monastery,
        and were cordially welcomed by the blessed father;
        they were given good lodgings and very fine service;
        they believed that in the end they would be well sent off.[151]

409   As was his wont, the holy confessor
        went into the church to pray to God,
        to remove that terrible affliction from that man
        who was totally drained of any blood or color.

410   The disease was one that was advanced and stubborn,
        very difficult to cure and violent in nature;

---

[150] Here I read *Rey de gloria* with Ruffinatto, 361, 405d; Orduna, 127, 405d; and Logroño, 69, 405d rather than *Sennor* with Dutton, 4:99, 405d.

[151] Meaning that when they left the monastery, they would be accompanied by a well man.

there was no doctor who could possibly cure it;
he said, "Help me, Christ, Son of the Glorious Lady."

411   The good man said with all his heart,
"Help me, King of Glory, One in three Persons:
I am in terrible trouble with such an illness,
if Your great mercy does not come to my aid.

412   But although we suffer, as we trust in You,
we will obtain from You the grace that we ask for;
Lord, we grant that in You lies everything,
in You we await the outcome of the matter."

413   The merciful father took great suffering on himself:
he kept vigil and he prayed and recited the psalter;
he had some help from friars in the monastery;
they were all devoted to this ministry.

414   He imposed great suffering upon his body,
tasteless food and freezing cold meals,
often engaging in prayer and supplication,
and at other times shedding many tears.

415   The father persevered in such pain and suffering,
and in such novenas[152] for García Muñoz;
he became as lean during those forty days
as a prisoner who lies a long time in chains.

416   Even though the seizure was stubborn to heal,
the perfect confessor managed to exorcise it,
for he refused to desert the field of battle
until it departed,[153] with great ill will.

417   García was healed, thanks to God;
the holy confessor was victorious;
everyone thought this was a major miracle
which seemed more noble than all the others.

418   Others were sent away healed in a day,
for he restored their sight and the use of their limbs;
in that healing, he put great effort with his good Christians
who certainly helped him like good brothers.

---

[152] The novena is a devotion of prayers or services on nine consecutive days, or on one particular day in nine consecutive months, as for example, on the first Friday of nine consecutive months.

[153] For parallel healings performed by Christ where he released demons from epileptics, see Matt. 8:28–32 and Mark 5:1–13.

419   Another man from Yécola[154] acquired a bad habit —
        he was also named García Muñoz;
        he had proven indeed to be a false neighbor,
        to such an extent that he deserved to be hanged.

420   At harvest time he robbed them of their grain:
        the dishonest man could not have picked a worse quarrel;
        if he were hapless enough to be caught by them,
        he could not escape for love nor money.

421   He abandoned the region for fear of being caught,
        and went over the mountains to gather the harvest;
        he refused to desist from his wicked work;
        they caught him while reaping: they wanted to hang him.

422   St. Dominic came to where they would harm him;
        he managed to get them to hand him over;
        he told him not to rob his neighbor of his bread,
        or else he would have to suffer dearly.

423   When the unlucky fool had escaped,
        the moment he was gone he forgot all about it;
        the hapless man returned to his foolish behavior,
        and the holy father was to be slandered.

424   So as to provide better proof of the matter,
        they brought the grain that he had harvested;
        they threw it before the patron of Silos,
        and he said, "This matter is most unjust."

425   He went into the church to pray to God;
        the sheaves[155] were laid before the altar:
        "Lord," he said, "You must judge this matter;
        Yours is the shame, look after avenging it."

426   Hardly could the prayer be brought to conclusion,
        when the fury of God fell upon the man;
        in no time at all he had lost his mind,
        and the strength of his body was completely spent.

427   He came to beg a favor of the holy father,
        that he should deign to pray to God for him;
        if He healed him this time he would not go on stealing:
        he would even swear an oath to the truth about that.

---

[154] Yecla, an old town that has disappeared but was two kilometers to the west of Si-
los and that is mentioned up to the fourteenth century in old documents of Silos (Dutton,
4:169, note 419ab; Ruffinatto, 362, note 419a; and Orduna, 129, note 419a).

[155] The sheaves of stolen wheat.

428   The father was most tactful and very wise
inasmuch as he refused to get involved in that;
he would not prolong the matter any further,
and quickly cut him short about what was to happen.

429   "García," he said, "you know that is what I feared;
that is why I said what I did to you,
that if you ever returned to such foolish behavior,
you would be in dire straits and fall dreadfully ill.

430   This suffering of yours was a judgment from heaven,
for you continued to behave with such lack of respect;
we got you out of a terrible predicament once,
and you had no desire to mend your ways.

431   You should understand it is all for your own good;
God has done this to prevent you from sinning:
if you did not suffer this you would not understand
what a great a sin it was to rob your neighbor's grain.

432   It is better for you to go to paradise disabled
than to fall into hell, well and healthy;
it is fitting you should bear this even though you suffer,
for you will have no hope if you return to what you were."

433   The worthy St. Dominic, inspiration of prelates,
had Moors in his church who were in shackles;[156]
they fled one night from where they were enclosed,
due to the carelessness of those who guarded them.

434   They deceived the guards, for they were clever;
they traveled all night until break of day;
early in the morning, for fear of some shepherds,
those terrible traitors hid themselves in a cave.

435   It was out of the way, so few people knew of it —
I believe that they had spied it well before;
they thought they would emerge when the people were asleep,
and arrive safe and sound where they had nothing to fear.

436   The good father was traveling outside of his deaconries,[157]
looking after his affairs for the good of his companions;
he heard this curious piece of news through God,
and discovered where they entered the cave and the mountains.

---

[156] Even up to the fourteenth century, there were Moors in the region of Silos who were slaves and who were used as artisans to repair churches and monasteries. (See Dutton, 4:169, note 433b, and Ruffinatto, 366, note 433b.)

[157] See note 47 above.

437   The night that they fled, the gifted gentleman
          had taken lodgings in the town of Cruña;[158]
          in the morning, as soon as silence[159] was over,
          he told his friars; he did not conceal it.

438   Some of the friars believed it to be true,
          others of them said it was foolishness;
          the message reached them from the community,
          and then they realized the whole thing was true.

439   Men were scattered and took to the highways;
          a generous reward of money was promised,
          but they could not get any accurate reports,
          for those cunning fellows were lying very low.

440   The holy confessor got hold of his men,
          and went into the mountains as he wished;
          he went straight to their lair like a fine hunter
          who indeed stays flawlessly right on the trail.

441   With his scapular[160] girded,[161] the perfect champion
          came home joyfully with those who had escaped;
          everyone called it a marvelous deed
          that should be put into writing for the glory of God.

442   The Moors never dared to flee again,
          for they knew of no way that they could escape;
          taught a good lesson, they took care to serve
          the glorious confessor, and to carry out his work.

443   A young man in the house, keeper of the grain,
          almost lost the use of his hand due to pain;
          the generous man said a Mass for him:
          he was instantly cured and had never been better.

444   Whether before or after or at that time,
          whenever it was, there is a story

---

[158] Here I read *Cruña* with Ruffinatto, 369, 437b; Orduna, 133, 437b; and Logroño (*Crunna*), 74, 437b rather than *Clunna* with Dutton. Also called Clunia or Crunia, today Coruña del Conde is about 23 kilometers south of Silos. (See Dutton, 4:169, note 437b; Ruffinatto, 368, note 437b; and Orduna, 133, note 437b.)

[159] See note 43 above.

[160] The scapular is the outer garment, usually sleeveless and without seams, that is part of some monastic habits.

[161] Berceo applies an epic formula to the divine here: scapular=sword (Dutton, 4:169–70, note 441a, and Ruffinatto, 368, note 441a).

that they fell into terrible want in that house:
the monks did not know where they would get their next mouthful.

445 The monks were sorely anguished,
for there was neither flour nor grain in the house,
nor enough bread for them for a single night;
the cloister, though spacious, did not contain them.

446 The cellarer came to his father abbot;
he said, "Sir, you do not know how poor we are;
you should certainly know there is no bread in the house:
if God does not help us we will be in utter misery."

447 The holy father went outside of the oratory;
he ordered all the monks to come to the parlor;[162]
"My friends," he said, "I see that you are grumbling,
because the refectory of ours is so empty.

448 Stand firm in Christ and do not lose your calm:
within a short while you shall indeed have help;
if you really trust in God you shall never suffer want;
you shall see everything I tell you turn out to be true."

449 The year was distressing and hard for all peoples:
there were shortages[163] and failures all over the land;
no loan of any bread or food could be found;
each house suffered want because of wicked sin.

450 The holy father went in to the altar at once,
and began to pray most earnestly to God,
that He should deign to send them some help,
for they were about to be destroyed from it.

451 "Lord," he said, "You Who are called the Bread of Life,
Who satisfied the multitude with just a few loaves,[164]
send us a reasonable amount of food,
that faith in this monastery may be upheld.

452 You rule the tamed and the untamed beasts,
You feed the birds both large and small,
You form the ears and make the grain grow,
You feed the worms that lie under the ground.

---

[162] The room where visiting and talking can be done in a monastery or convent which is cloistered..

[163] Berceo refers here to the shortages which affected all of Spain and France in the year 1043 (Ruffinatto, 370, note 449ab).

[164] See Matt. 15:32–39 and John 6:1–14.

453   Lord, You Who give food to every living creature,[165]
        send us Your help, for we are in desperate straits;
        You see how this community is grumbling;
        they all turn against me; I am in a predicament."

454   It was after midday, around the time of none,[166]
        the sexton rang the bell and they came to pray the hours;
        the community took plenty of time to recite them,
        though suffering from want, they did not like to hurry.

455   They came out of none to go in for supper:
        there was mighty little bread, not even a box full;
        had they had oats it would have tasted like wheat to them;[167]
        had they had only bread they would have had no suffering.

456   The prior had not yet even rung the bell
        when a messenger came to them from the king;
        he was cordially welcomed by the abbot and the friars:
        indeed they were grateful for the message he gave them.

457   "Gentlemen," he said, "the good king greets you:
        he heard you are wanting and is sending you help;
        he gives you sixty measures of sifted flour,
        provided it will not be exchanged or sold.

458   Abbot, send your mule drivers at once,
        be not blamed by your companions;
        monks who rise early at the crow of the cock
        cannot fast like those who rise at terce.[168]

459   Gentlemen, when you shall have eaten this,
        I have heard that the king will give you something else;
        as far as I know you shall never suffer want,
        nor shall you ever eat any food that is unseasoned."

460   They sent for it and it quickly arrived;
        the steward was kind and gave them good measure;
        they took it to the oven and baked it right away;
        as long as it lasted it was faithfully shared.

461   From that time on, because they shared it fairly,
        God kindly helped them and they never suffered want;

---

[165] Allusion to Ps. 145:15–16.

[166] About three o'clock in the afternoon, the time when the canonical hour of none is prayed by the monks.

[167] Cf. quatrain 355 above, with note 143.

[168] Terce is the third hour or nine o'clock in the morning.

those who doubted before repented thereafter,
for the words of the father turned out to be true.

462   May such a gifted father always be blessed:
he ought to be glorified by every human being;
kings behaved properly in paying him honor,
for whoever pleased him was indeed a wise person.

463   The worthy gentleman was in Monte Ruyo,[169]
sowing his blessings throughout the land;
he was giving a sermon to important people:
many fine phrases poured from his lips.

464   He was seeking the road to Paradise for them;
he told them to protect themselves from the deadly trap,
to faithfully pay their tithe in grain at the harvest,
and to give a fair portion of their animals to God.

465   They should not harbor hatred, for it is a mortal sin,
or look to omens, since God forbids it;
except for relations with the woman they married,
fornication was forbidden, else they would be damned.

466   Anyone who thought he was sinning in such ways
should undergo penance from an ordained priest;
anyone who robbed or stole from his neighbor
would not be forgiven until he made restitution.

467   "My friends, never forget the giving of alms:
you will always get back what you give to the poor;
if you are givers of alms you will receive alms:
whatever you sow, so shall you reap.[170]

468   Remember above all, your neighbors who are poor,
who stay in their houses in want and misery;
ashamed, they do not go about like pilgrims;
they are starved and bent over like hooks.

469   Shelter the wandering and discouraged pilgrim,
give of your clothing to those who go naked,
instruct your children not to be so brazen
as to pasture their animals on land sowed by others.

---

[169] Monterrubio, 35 kilometers northeast of Silos, in the province of Burgos, near the town of Salas de los Infantes, a tributary of the monastery of Silos (Dutton, 4:170, note 463a; Ruffinatto, 374, note 463a; and Orduna, 137, note 463a).

[170] See Gal. 6:7.

470   Teach the *Pater Noster*[171] to your children,
        instruct them to recite it when they go pasturing:
        it will serve them better than jokes or foolish talk,
        for such boys usually utter many coarse words.

471   The habits of the child at a very early age
        he retains thereafter as his legacy;
        if he has good habits early, then later goodness follows;
        the same goes for evil, and that is the plain truth.

472   Do not swear to a lie by everything you love,
        for you will be lost if you swear to a lie;
        do not get involved in any false witness:
        if you get involved you are breaking the law.

473   We command children to honor their parents:
        may they willingly keep them warm and well-fed;
        may they give them bread taken from their own mouths;
        this law has been given to every single believer.

474   Keep in mind something else that we witness daily:
        everything we acquire here will be left here by us;
        if we were born with little, little more will we take with us;
        may God guide us all that we may save our souls."

475   Having finished his sermon, the worthy confessor
        was approached by a sick man in very great suffering:
        a leper from the area and severely disfigured,
        ashamed, he had hardly the courage to appear.

476   He fell at his feet and began to entreat him,
        "I come to you, Father, to ask for healing;
        if you would only deign to say a Mass for me,
        I believe I would become healthy and well."

477   The merciful father was grieved for the poor man;
        he went to the church of the worthy St. Martin;[172]
        when he had completed the divine office,
        the leper had no need of any other advocate.

478   At the end of the Mass the good priest
        blessed salt and water with his sacred hand;
        he poured it on the sick man who was instantly so healed
        that not a trace of the leprosy appeared any longer.

---

[171] See note 7 above.

[172] A church in Monterrubio (Dutton, 4:170, note 477b, and Ruffinatto, 378, note 477b).

479   The worthy St. Dominic, patron of monks,
        was seated in his monastery among his companions;
        a company of naked pilgrims arrived:
        you have never heard tell of such crafty persons.

480   Those impudent devils had thought up a trick:
        they had left all their clothing in San Pedro;[173]
        they came to the good father loaded with requests;
        they asked him to give them some fresh clothing.

481   The blessed man found it hard not to laugh,
        for he was aware of all they had done;
        he told them he would be most willing to do it,
        for it fell within his duties to perform such things.

482   While they were eating he sent one of his men,
        to bring their clothing over from where it was;[174]
        they gave each one as many pieces as were due him:
        those who understood it could hardly keep from laughing.

483   They came out of the house and into the alley,
        each of them chattering with one another;
        one of them said, "That looks like my cloak";
        another one said, "I recognize my hood."

484   When all of them took a good look at each other,
        they saw they had acquired not a single new thing:
        they were taking away the same clothes they had brought;
        they never again tried to test the blessed father.

485   Who could possibly find such a witty person
        who could poke such fun at his fellow Christian?
        No healthy or sick person ever approached him
        who was not made joyful by his word or deed.

486   In this and all else we have many proofs
        that his cup was filled with heavenly grace;
        he prays for us all to the Heavenly[175] King
        to protect us from evil in life and in death.

487   I will move on to his death, leaving all else aside,
        otherwise we will spend all our time in this;

---

[173] San Pedro de Canónigos, a church in Silos (Ruffinatto, 378, note 480b).

[174] That is, from the Church of San Pedro where the clothing had been left by the pilgrims.

[175] Here I read *celestial* with Ruffinatto, 381, 486c rather than *spiritual* with Dutton.

we have even got left enough deeds beyond these
which would make a book complete in itself.

488   What the holy father desired ardently to see
— to depart from this wicked world and go to the good one,
and receive his reward for all his pains —
the appointed time was approaching for this to happen.

489   The appointed time was approaching for him to die,
when his soul was meant to leave his body,
and when he was meant to receive the three crowns
which you heard us previously tell you about.

490   As it is the nature of human beings
to feel mortal pangs in the presence of death,
the holy father was to feel such things,
which pleased him more than a good-sized trout.

491   He was losing his strength but not his faculties;
he was aware that it was time for his ultimate release,
for he received a message from the good King of Glory
that he should know he was close to victory.

492   The illness was greatly weighing him down;
the father took to his bed — God, such a bitter day!
Even though he experienced pleasure at dying,
the good father was grieving for his companions.

493   The man of great tact was indeed very wise:
he commanded his holy community to approach;
he gave them a fine sermon concerning their conduct,
from which all derived good sense and satisfaction.

494   He told them, "Friars, I am dying and have little time left:
consider that all my business is completed;
I entrust you to God, my beloved flock;
may He protect you from trouble and from falling into evil.

495   We looked after the house as best we could;
we put our heart into whatever was accomplished;
may God provide someone to succeed where we failed,
and may he be endowed with better sense than we were.

496   When I have passed on, bury me immediately,
name an abbot at once as the Rule commands;
have love and charity for one another,
and serve God with all your hearts.

497   Concerning the obedience you promised to God,
for to save souls you abandoned the world
and chose the better part of the two portions,[176]
see that you hold to it, else unlucky was your birth.

498   Remember what was done by our Redeemer
Who was raised on the cross in very great dishonor;
even though He was Lord, He refused to come down[177]
until the moment when He willed to give up his soul.

499   If you will take my advice,
and keep the promise that you made,
you shall never lack food for lunch or for dinner,
and this holy place will improve every day.

500   We found it like a vine in the state of ruination,
very run-down for having been neglected;
now it is a priceless[178] new bud on the vine,
and it is all set to go on improving.

501   I trust in Jesus Christ, the Father of mercy,
to invest this new bud with such good qualities,
from which the whole neighborhood will draw consolation,
and those from near and far will obtain from it charity.

502   And besides, if by any chance you have forgotten,
a very long time ago we said in your presence,
concerning some things that you were lacking,[179]
that God would give you help that would please you."

503   While the holy father was giving them his sermon,
the community was weeping very profusely,
for he was so dearly beloved by them all
that every single one of them was deeply grieving.

504   "My friends," said the good father, "do not weep:
in doing so you resemble women;
we will tell you more news not known by you;
get everything ready, for you will have guests.

---

[176] That is, the contemplative life vs. the active life of the world. The allusion is to Luke 10:42.

[177] Cf. Mark 15:30.

[178] Here I read *en buen precio tornada* with Ruffinatto, 383, 500c; Orduna, 143, 500c; and Logroño, 83, 500c rather than *en buen pelo tornada* with Dutton, 4:113, 500c.

[179] A reference to the relics dealt with in quatrains 279–283.

505   Within four days you will have important guests:
        the king and the queen splendidly escorted,
        and with them the bishop and some fine company;
        see to the matter of serving them properly."

506   They all were astonished at these words;
        where could such awesome guests come from?
        The king and the queen were very far away;[180]
        not in six days could they possibly get there.

507   They judged that the bishop might well be there,
        for he was in the area and near the place;
        but as for the king, that was more astonishing,
        for he was far away and could not possibly get there.

508   On the day they thought they would have the guests,
        for they had their food all prepared,
        the bishop arrived and was well taken care of,
        but they had no news or any message from the king.

509   Hence there was great confusion among the monks:
        some of them thought that he had gone crazy,
        because of some cold spoiled wine they had given him;[181]
        others said, "No," but that he was deceived,
        he managed to hear this even though it was whispered.

510   Even though he was suffering he questioned them all:
        he said, "What confusion have you stirred up?
        There is not a wise person among the lot of you,
        or else you would not think that I have lost my mind;
        search for the trail while you have your quarry.[182]

511   Today you keep the feast of the Virgin Mary,
        when her Lord and Messiah was placed inside of her;[183]

---

[180] While the monks understood him to mean Alfonso VI, King of León and Castile, and his wife Agnes, who were reigning in 1073 when the saint died, we will see further on in quatrains 510–512 that St. Dominic means the King and Queen of Heaven on the occasion of the feast of the Annunciation, celebrated 18 December according to Mozarabic tradition (Dutton, 4:170, note 506c, and Ruffinatto, 384, note 506c).

[181] Here I read *quel' dieran/quel dieran* respectively with Orduna, 145, 509c and Logroño, 85, 509c rather than *o'l dieron* with Dutton, 4:115, 509c.

[182] Note that in the opinion of Ruffinatto, 386, note 510c, this line was added at a later time (making a cinquain like the previous one).

[183] See note 180 above.

they have the advantage over any king and queen,
you should all know: indeed it is on their account I said it.

512   Since early dawn I have been speaking with them;
I am meant to follow them, for they have invited me;
I have arranged for them to give me a deferment
of just a few days to accept their hospitality."

513   The monks and the clergy and all who heard him,
all of them thought it was a curious thing;
they did not contradict the good father's words,
and all those who doubted before begged forgiveness.

514   Early next morning, on the feast of Holy Mary,
the bishop, who wished to depart, took his leave;
"Sir," said St. Dominic, "there is something I should like,
that you should remain here until the third day.

515   As you can understand, sir, I am pained
that you go away today and have to come back tomorrow;
you will get nothing else but twice the suffering;
if you will do this, sir, you will do me a great favor."

516   For some reason or other the bishop could not stay:
he departed from the monastery mounted on horseback,
but even before he could journey two days,
he received a message that he needed to return.

517   He returned to the monastery deeply anguished,
for he feared to witness something very painful;
he found the holy father in terrible distress,
the community weeping and expressing their sorrow.

518   They opened a path for him to reach the bed;
he realized the whole thing was already accomplished;
he said, "O father and shepherd most righteous,
I am sick at heart because you will depart.

519   Father, many were governed by your advice;
your common sense repaired bodies and souls;
anyone who came to you sad returned joyful;
anyone who took your advice was well-off."

520   The monks and the people were making loud lament,
saying, "What shall we do about our holy father?
We are all sorely grieved over his death;
we shall nevermore find as good a refuge for ourselves."

521   The holy confessor was closing his eyes;
        he compressed his lips tightly: he never looked better;
        he raised both his hands to the Lord our God;
        he gave his soul up to Him[184] with very great pleasure.

522   The angels nearby gathered it up
        and carried it to heaven in very great honor;
        they gave it three splendidly radiant crowns:
        we told you above how finely they were wrought.[185]

523   The holy patriarchs from the early times,
        and then the apostles, the messengers of Christ,
        and the hosts of martyrs accompanying Abel,
        were all of them joyful and pleased with him.

524   The confessors were giving glory to God
        that such a worthy friar was joining their party;
        the virgins replied to them, sweetly singing:
        they all paid him honor singing psalms and hymns.

525   The worthy St. Benedict with his clerics
        who had shunned the world for the cloistered life
        were all greatly pleased with this monk:
        they sang praises to God, polyphonic songs.

526   The Cogollan gentleman, a native of Berceo,
        San Millán, with whom he desired to dwell,
        took great pains to honor his disciple
        who for his sake had fought a dreadful joust.[186]

527   May his soul rest in God, joyful and honored,
        let us return to his body which we left dead;
        let us properly fulfill what is its due;
        let us give it a tomb where it will be guarded.

528   Grieved and weary, the monks of the house
        prepared the body as they were trained to do;
        they made the shroud from his very own clothing;
        the poor men uttered cries all around the premises.

529   When the glorious body was all prepared,
        it was borne to the church to be better honored;

---

[184] St. Dominic died 20 December 1073 (Dutton, 4:171, note 521d).
[185] See quatrains 233–234 above.
[186] The reference here is to quatrains 127–181 concerning what St. Dominic went through in order to protect the treasures and the lands of the monastery of San Millán against the avarice of King García.

many Masses were offered to God for him,
which he did not need but they were pleasing to God.

530   There was a great gathering of important people,
of abbots and priors and monks from their houses,
and plenty of large groups of other clergy,
and of rich and poor who could scarcely be counted.

531   They guarded the body and gave it burial:
earth covered earth according to nature;
they put a great treasure into very narrow straits,
a bright shining lamp into a dark lantern.

532   With the body laid to rest and the cries contained,
the bishop departed with his retinue;
abbots and priors went to their places,
people and clergy, vassals and lords.

Book III

533   Gentlefolk and friends, God be praised,
we have finished the second little book;
we are pleased and willing to begin another:
let the books be three and the text be one.

534   As the Persons are three and God is one,
let the books be three and one single truth:
let the books signify the Holy Trinity,
the one single subject, the one single Deity.

535   The Father and the Son and the Holy Spirit,
one God and three Persons, three melodies, one key,
single in nature and plural in perfection,
the beginning and the end of all things that exist.

536   In the Holy Name of Him Who is true God,
and of St. Dominic, a righteous confessor,
we wish to make known to you in the third book
the miracles of the dead man dwelling in heaven.

537   From the time that St. Dominic passed from this world,
it would be beyond belief how much God did through him;
so many sick came, they would have made a huge army:
we could not put the half of it down in writing.

538   There was a young man born in Aragón,
according to the text, his name was Pedro;

he fell so violently ill it was astonishing:
no man or woman could give him any help.

539   His illness was severe and very prolonged;
no doctor who saw him helped him in the least;
the people held out little hope for his life,
for he could not even eat a single bite of food.

540   From the dreadful affliction his limbs were weakened;
his hands and his feet were all out of joint;
his eyes were sunken, his arms without strength;
his parents were deeply grieved by his trouble.

541   The unhappy young man finally lost his sight:
this above all was his greatest impairment;
the other disability was more bearable;
without his sight he was inconsolable.

542   They reached a decision, with the help of God,
to bring that sick and suffering person
to the precious tomb of the worthy confessor;
if he did not help them, then all was lost.

543   They got the man ready as best they could;
they brought him there to the monastery of Silos;
they laid him on the floor before the tomb;[187]
they knelt down and recited their prayers.

544   They remained before the body three days and nights;
they made their offerings and uttered their prayers;
they shed many tears and made many supplications;
few were the days, but great was their suffering.

545   At the end of three days they were heard by God:
Pedro opened his eyes which he had closed;
those closest to him were joyful and healed;
they would not have missed coming there for anything.

546   When he had recovered the sight in his eyes,
he believed his case would indeed be resolved;

---

[187] It must be noted that the tomb of the saint is in the cloister near the door of San Miguel, where he rested until 5 January 1076 when the bishop of Burgos transferred the body to a new tomb under an altar dedicated to St. Dominic in the church of the monastery. When the Romanesque church of Silos was knocked down, the remains were transferred to a platinum and glass case on 19 April 1733. Thus it is impossible to know if the tomb was the original one in the cloister or the second one in the church (Dutton, 4:171, note 543c, and Ruffinatto, 394, note 543c).

    he stretched out his arms, his features undefiled;
    the pain in his legs had completely abated.

547   Thanks to Jesus Christ and the good confessor,
    the sick man was healed of all his suffering,
    but he was so weak that he did not have the strength,
    poor sinner that he was, to walk on his feet.

548   Together with the health granted him by God,
    Pedro indeed soon recovered his strength;
    he took leave of the monastery and its companions;
    he returned to his home most joyful and healthy.

549   There was a disabled man from Tabladiello:[188]
    according to the text his name was Ananías;
    he was severely afflicted with epilepsy;
    for a good four months he had been lying abed.

550   The unhappy man had his arms doubled up,
    stiffened and bent right up to his chest:
    he could not extend them or even raise them,
    or put in his mouth even one or two morsels.

551   As news usually spreads by word of mouth
    about healing the sick and restoring their health,
    from where he lay, the sick man came to know
    of how St. Dominic had such great power.

552   The sick and suffering man got himself prepared,
    and when he was ready they set out on the road;
    they came to the tomb of the worthy confessor —
    lucky for the Spaniards the moment he was born.

553   The sick man's parents and others who were helping
    bought plenty of wax and made tapered candles;
    they surrounded the tomb with a good many tapers,
    keeping up their vigils and common prayers.

554   The pleas that they made were heard by God;
    his arms that had been crippled were released;
    the pains that severely afflicted him were calmed;
    those who surrounded him were weeping profusely.

---

[188] In the old days, the valley of the Ura River (today Mataviejas) was called Val de Tabladillo (the Valley of Tabladillo). Near Santibañez del Val, five kilometers to the west of Silos, lay the town and the monastery of San Juan de Tabladillo which was destroyed by the Moors in 979 (Dutton, 4:171–72, note 549ab; Ruffinatto, 396, note 549a; and Orduna, 153–54, note 549a).

555   His limbs were all healed of their physical pains:
        Ananías raised both of his hands up to God;
        those good Christians sang to God their praises;
        the people who came with him now were content.

556   As the sick man was in a very weakened state,
        he could not depart until he had gained strength;
        when he dared to walk, congratulated by all,
        he returned to Tabladiello joyful and content.

557   A woman who came from the city of Palencia
        fell on dreadful misfortune because of her sins:
        she lost the power of hearing and speech,
        and her faculty of reason was sorely deficient.

558   Saturday evening when the bells rang for vespers,
        the people who were ready went to hear them,
        dressed in their best and with clean faces,
        the men in the lead and the women behind.

559   This woman refused to go to the church
        to hear vespers like all the other people;
        she preferred to knead her dough, to flatten and squeeze it,
        and take it to the oven, doing just as she pleased.

560   God would not suffer that great pride of hers:
        He took away both her speech and her hearing;
        and even with all that He would deal her more blows,
        that the people should know what it means to serve God.

561   The servants went around weeping for their mistress,
        and all who knew her sorely grieved for her;
        all of her friends and neighbors were mournful,
        but the worst stain of all fell on her parents.

562   While this lady was in such affliction,
        and receiving no help from any human being,
        they remembered the confessor who lay at Silos,
        and the many miracles God worked through him.

563   People from her area took the sick woman,
        those closest to her and her mother and father;
        they put her on a beast with many gold coins,
        and such people as were suitable went along with her.

564   They arrived at the tomb early Sunday morning;
        they laid the sick woman upon the flat ground;
        they remained there with her all that week,
        entreating the confessor to make her well.

565   When the eve of the following sabbath arrived,
        many people came to the tomb to keep vigil;
        all kept up their prayers with the best of intentions,
        so that God might make her hear and speak.

566   Once matins[189] were sung and prime[190] celebrated,
        they went in to the Mass, to the one said separately;[191]
        all the people settled down quietly to hear it;
        the church was filled with plenty of candles.

567   Once the reading from Wisdom[192] was finished,
        the priest read the Gradual[193] on the left side;
        after the reader had said the Sequence,[194]
        the woman from Palencia said, *Gloria tibi Domine.*[195]

568   The people were enormously pleased by the miracle:
        they could not contain their tears for pure joy;
        the monks began to ring the bells,
        and to mightily sing the *Te Deum laudamus.*[196]

569   When the *Ite missa*[197] was sung at the end,
        indeed she was healed and returned to the state of grace;
        she made her worthy offering at the tomb;
        she took leave of all and departed for her home.

570   From that time on, you can well imagine
        that she would not miss Saturday vespers;
        she had no dough to be baked at that hour;
        you can see for yourselves that refined gold glitters.[198]

571   On that same day that she was healed,
        a blind man from Espeja[199] recovered his sight there;

---

[189] Early morning prayers.

[190] One of the seven canonical hours recited after lauds.

[191] The Mass said separately for the intention of the sick person.

[192] Berceo probably refers here to the Mass of the Virgin where the Epistle is taken from the Book of Wisdom (Dutton, 4:172, note 567a; Ruffinatto, 400, note 567a; and Orduna, 157, note 567).

[193] The Gradual and the Alleluia: antiphons which come right after the reading of the Epistle and are read on the left side of the altar. (See Ruffinatto, 400, note 567b.)

[194] The Sequence is the prose or verse recited in certain Masses after the prayer of the Gradual.

[195] 'Glory to You, Lord (said before the Gospel).'

[196] The hymn "We praise You, God."

[197] 'Go, the Mass is ended.'

[198] See Zech. 13:9 and 1 Peter 1:7.

[199] For more information concerning the identification and location of this town, see Dutton, 4:172, note 571bc, and Ruffinatto, 400, note 571b.

Juan was his name, if another told the truth,
the one who wrote this story first.[200]

572   There was a poor blind woman from Asturias,
        a native of the town that is called Cornejana;[201]
        she saw as much in the morning as in early evening;
        for a good thirty months she had not been well.

573   According to the text, her name was Sancha;
        the unfortunate woman lived sorely distressed,
        for anyone who does not see is in dire straits:
        he does not even know where is Burgos or Extremadura.

574   She took the person who was her usual guide;
        she made great haste to set out on the road;
        she went to the holy body to ask for a favor;
        she was confident indeed that she could obtain it.

575   When the blind woman came before the holy body,
        she flung herself to the ground in terrible anguish;
        she said, "Worthy sir and father lying under this stone,
        turn your head towards this lamentation of mine.

576   Sir, you who have obtained such power from Christ,
        that you make the blind see and the dumb speak,
        obtain my sight for me and deign to heal me,
        that I may carry your praises throughout the world."

577   Her prayer completed, thank the good Lord,
        the sacred grace of the holy confessor worked;
        he gave sight to the poor woman: a great shout was raised,
        and she returned to Cornejana with no need of any guide.

578   In Agosín,[202] there lived another blind woman,
        María was her name: she lived in great affliction;
        she went to every possible shrine that she knew of,
        but she never got better, for it was not God's will.

---

[200] Berceo makes reference here to Grimaldo whose Latin version of the text he is following.

[201] According to Ruffinato, 402, note 572b, Cornellana in the province of Oviedo. For more information on the identification and location of this town, see also Dutton, 4:172, 572 ab.

[202] Ausin, or los Ausines, a town 20 kilometers south of Burgos and 35 kilometers north of Silos near the town of Lara (Dutton, 4:172, note 578ab; Ruffinatto, 402, note 578a; and Orduna, 159, note 578a).

579   She went to St. Dominic to ask him for a favor;
she held her triduum[203] before his altar;
weeping profusely, she persisted in praying;
indeed the community was ready to help her.

580   At the end of three days divine grace was forthcoming:
thanks to the good confessor the blind woman was healed;
she offered what she could, and having heard Mass,
she returned to her home and lived a healthy life.

581   We want to tell you of another paralytic
who had no power to command her limbs,
a native of Fuentoria[204] in my opinion,
and I think I am correct that her name was María.

582   She could not walk on her feet or grip with her hands,
even if she were put in charge of Moors and Christians;
because she lay in such agony a good many summers,
she had been severely weakened by her daily pains.

583   They thought there was no help for her in this life;
she was reduced to nothing but skin and bones;
she suffered alike on Sundays and weekdays;
all those around her were grieved by her affliction.

584   The unhappy woman heard all that news
of how many the worthy St. Dominic had healed;
uttering cries, she said to her parents,
"Take me to the tomb where they heal the disabled."

585   She was taken by those who were grieved by her illness;
she was loaded on a stretcher and fastened with a rope;
they went to the tomb of the famous confessor
whom God had invested with such perfect grace.

586   They carried the sick woman to the glorious tomb
from which so many precious miracles proceeded;
they placed her before the powerful father,
and she lay there howling like a mangy cat.

587   All that night they never slept a wink:
they were on their knees reciting prayers,

---

[203] Three days of unceasing prayer.
[204] Possibly Hontoria de Valdearados, 25 kilometers south of Silos, or Hontoria del Pilar, 25 kilometers southeast of Silos. For more information concerning the identification and location of this town, see Dutton, 4:172, note 581c and Ruffinatto, 404, note 581c.

burning a good many bunches of candles,
and promising offerings of sheep and lambs.

588   The night having passed, immediately at dawn
they celebrated Mass keeping up their prayers;
her pains were vanishing little by little;
the paralytic said, "I give praise to God."

589   The paralytic woman was healed of the illness,
but could not overcome the weakness so instantly;
yet Christ was quick to take pity on her,
and she returned to her neighborhood on her own feet.

590   Everyone said this was a perfect miracle,
that he healed so quickly a person so weakened;
for it was told so often as if she had died,
and that he had restored her from death to life.

591   There was a poor man with a dreadful illness:
he was called Cid by all, for such was his name;
for a good long time he had been unable to move;
he never even stirred from his bed to his yard.

592   For more than three years and almost four,
he had overwhelming pain in his feet from gout;
he heard that news about the good confessor,
of how he worked great and famous miracles.

593   He begged the good people from his neighborhood
to take him there for God and for charity;
being good people they were moved to pity,
and they had to take him to that holy place.

594   He lay for one week before the confessor;
the community kept praying daily for him;
on the eighth day at the high Mass,
Cid was healed and his pain had vanished.

595   When he felt that his feet had been healed,
he raised both his arms lying on the ground;
"Lord, " said he, "be praised and thanked
for not forgetting a request from your servants."

596   He recited many prayers to the holy body;
he bid three or four farewells to all;
he set out on the road to make his journey;
all the people were contented with the miracle.

597 There was another cripple who could not walk,
and he could not see an inch in front of his nose;
he lay quietly in everyone's way like a hindrance;
he could not get a thing but what he begged for.

598 Sancho was the name of this crippled man
who had kept to his bed for a good long time;
he saw nothing but what was under his roof:
whatever the reason, he was in a sorry state.

599 We can imagine that he lay in great misery,
for he had double the pain and double the suffering;
he told them to take him to the famous confessor:
he would only be happy once he arrived there.

600 There were some good people who took pity on him:
they took him to the tomb and laid him before it;
they cried mercy for him to God and the confessor;
they prayed wholeheartedly for Sancho to be healed.

601 Out of love for the confessor, God gave His help:
He healed the sick man of all his pains;
indeed his eyesight had never been better,
and he walked about on his feet just as he pleased.

602 He returned to his home joyful and healed,
spreading the news of the glorious confessor;
everyone said he was a marvelous saint
who had so much compassion for the afflicted.

603 Fruela from Coriel[205] and Muño from Villanueva[206]
were both crippled, according to the text;
they both lay bound like prisoners in a cave;
if they were made kings they would not go to Burueva.[207]

604 Both of them came, each from his region,
to the tomb of the father of precious life;
they held their vigils with perfect sincerity,
and their petition was heard by God.

---

[205] A town five kilometers north of Peñafiel in the province of Valladolid (Dutton, 4:173, note 603a, and Ruffinatto, 408, note 603a).

[206] Probably Villanueva de Carazo, eight kilometers west of Silos (Dutton, 4:173, note 603a, and Ruffinatto, 408, note 603a).

[207] La Bureba is a district to the northeast of Burgos. Berceo is using an expression here which he has extracted from a proverb (Dutton, 4:173, note 603c [sic], and Ruffinatto, 408, note 603d).

605   Thanks to the good confessor they soon recovered,
        they soon obtained what they asked from God;
        their feet were healed and they could walk again;
        joyful and content they returned to their homes.

606   There was a suffering woman who came from Nebreda:[208]
        she had a withered hand and she was mute;
        she could not use her hand or say a single word;
        she was chronically ill and had plenty of suffering.

607   She went to St. Dominic to beg him for a favor:
        she fell beseechingly before him but could not speak;
        but the Lord, who knows how to judge the will,
        understood what she sought and was willing to grant it.

608   He healed the withered hand that she had,
        and he loosened her tongue tied by evil;
        she gave thanks to the father and master of the house;
        she returned to Nebreda freed of her afflictions.

609   A blind man stopped there, wherever he was from —
        it is not explained very well in the manuscript,
        for the writing is poor and the Latin obscure:
        by the worthy St. Martin, I could not make it out.[209]

610   He was a good twelve days in vigil at the tomb;
        he was on his knees and weeping profusely,
        indeed very confidently awaiting the moment
        when he would feel the sight returning to his eyes.

611   The good confessor did as he was wont to:
        he sent the persistent blind man his sight;
        every trace of darkness fell from his eyes;
        he saw the floor and the ceiling of the church.

612   When the blind man had recovered his sight,
        he took leave of the body and went to his home;
        they immediately brought a demoniac in,
        a woman abused and afflicted by the devil.

613   If you care to know the name of the lady,
        then you should believe that her name was Orfresa;

[208] A town 19 kilometers west of Silos and between Silos and Lerma (Dutton, 4:173, note 606a; Ruffinatto, 410, 606a; and Orduna, 164, 606a).

[209] The name of the town seems to be Alcózar, near the Duero River, 22 kilometers west of Osma and 38 kilometers south of Silos (Dutton, 4:173, note 609d, and Ruffinatto, 410, note 609b).

we did not want to put the town down in writing,
for it does not have an attractive name.[210]

614   They placed the sick woman before the holy body
from which more graces flowed than I can recite;
the demon within was severely agitated:
it convulsed her body some ten times more than usual.

615   The monks in the monastery were grieved for the woman;
they were prepared to do what they could for her:
they applied themselves with the greatest good will
to imploring God to grant her health and healing.

616   Whether because of their many fervent prayers,
or because of the people's unwavering faith,
God removed the wicked scourge from the lady,
and evil had no further power over her.

617   Ximena of Tordómar[211] lost the use of one hand,
but which one it was I do not know for certain;
it resembled dry straw, and the good one fine grain,
the withered one winter, and the healthy one summer.

618   The lady Ximena came to entreat the holy body;
"Worthy sir and father," she said, "you see my suffering:
my hand is more useless than if it belonged to another;
it affords me no help and keeps me enchained.

619   Sir, do pray for this unfortunate sinner,
for the love of the good father who lies in Madriz;[212]
great is your grace told by your deeds:
sir, do pray for this unfortunate sinner."

---

[210] The name of the town which has since disappeared was Mamblas. The memory of it still remains in the Sierra de las Mamblas and in the town Mambrillas de Lara (Burgos) 16 kilometers north of Silos. Las Mamblas are two hills having precisely the form of a woman's breasts (Dutton, 4;173, note 613d; Ruffinatto, 412, note 613cd; and Orduna, 165, note 613d).

[211] A town on the shores of the Arlanza River 10 kilometers west of Lerma and 38 kilometers from Silos (Dutton, 4:173, note 617a; Ruffinatto, 412, note 617a; and Orduna, 166, note 617a).

[212] The "good father" is San Millán. The town of Madriz no longer exists, but it was the main town of the valley of San Millán de la Cogolla until the fourteenth century. In this way, Berceo may be alluding to the monastery of San Millán de Yuso, near Madriz, where the remains of the saint lay until 1053 (Dutton, 4:173, note 619b; Ruffinatto, 412, note 619b; and Orduna, 166, note 619b).

620   According to the proverb which tells the truth,
that the persistent pilgrim gets his morsel of food,
Ximena was helped by her steadfast prayer,
and by sticking stubbornly to her request.

621   The good confessor helped: he healed her hand;
her arm that was withered became well and healthy;
if clumsy before, after that it was quick:
Ximena, now healed, did her weaving in the sunshine.

622   In Agosín[213] there lived a suffering blind woman:
she was named María from when she was baptized;
her sight was destroyed by a severe illness;
were she lying in jail she would not be more confined.

623   She begged them to take her where others were cured,
where those who were blind recovered their sight;
she was taken by persons who took pity on her,
and laid at the foot of the glorious tomb.

624   The poor blind woman loudly cried out,
"Hear me, holy father, patron of Castile;
remove this dreadful blotch from my eyes,
so that I may return home with my sight."

625   The request of the blind woman was heard,
for love of the confessor to whom she prayed;
she was cured of the blindness that held her captive;
she returned to Agosín with the healing she had sought.

626   The blind woman healed and having gone her way,
a demoniac arrived who was from Celleruelo;[214]
Diago was his name and that is the truth:
that is how it was written in the early times.

627   He was often possessed by a cruel demon
who now made him deaf, now made him mute;
at times he made him utter a piercing cry;
the wicked guest caused him to be considered crazy.

628   If it were not for the fact that he was kept tied down,
he would have been up to some nasty tricks;
he would have gladly done harm to himself or another;
since he had no sense he was bold and brazen.

---

[213] See note 202 above.
[214] Probably Celleruelo de Arriba, 22 kilometers southwest of Silos (Dutton, 4:173, note 626bc, and Ruffinatto, 414, note 626b).

629   They lived thus troubled with him day and night:
        if they let him free he committed terrible folly;
        his aunts and uncles would have rather seen him dead,
        for he uttered words that were crazy and impious.

630   A thought occurred to them, sent by God,
        to take him to the tomb of the good cleric
        who was abbot of Silos and is adored there:
        by chance he might be freed from the devil.

631   They put into action the thought they had had:
        the sick man was taken to the tomb;
        they placed him in the hands of the worthy community;
        for fear of harm he was carried tied up.

632   The monks of the house, perfect in goodness,
        trained in great holiness by the good father,
        did everything humanly possible for him;
        they applied themselves to him with all their hearts.

633   The perfect Christians applied themselves to him:
        they unbound his hands as well as his feet;
        they kept up vigils and daily prayers:
        if they were his brothers they would not be more concerned.

634   Their prayers were heard by the Creator;
        their vigils did not fall into a void;
        the good confessor of perfect habits labored;
        he healed the sick man of his dreadful afflictions.

635   Indeed well and happy he returned to Celleruelo;
        those who used to grieve rejoiced greatly with him,
        it was said of the good father by young and old,
        that he certainly knew how to hook the devil.

636   I want to gather for you three miracles into one;
        as they are similar I want to link them together:
        three sick women, but not from one place,
        who all were healed before his altar.

637   One was from Olmillos,[215] Oveña was her name;
        another was from Yécola,[216] and she was called María;
        the third poor woman was named Eulalia:
        each one of those three was a demoniac.

---

[215] Possibly the town of Olmillos de Muño fairly near Silos, in the province of Burgos. For more on the identification of this town see Dutton, 4:173, note 637a; Ruffinatto, 418, note 637a; and Orduna, 169, note 637a.

[216] See note 154 above.

638   All of those women were possessed by the devil:
        they lived a life of great suffering and misery;
        the poor women were a nuisance to people,
        for they often fell to the ground in convulsions.

639   They bore great suffering in many ways,
        walking the highways with nothing to eat,
        and disgracing themselves by falling into flames;
        the poor women suffered from impaired vision.

640   There was no medicine that could heal them,
        no pact nor spell nor any other heresy,
        no vigils nor tears nor any long pilgrimage,
        except for St. Dominic, patron of monks.

641   They ended up having to come to his body:
        until they came there they could not be healed;
        they had to painfully depart from their homes;
        they went to ask the holy body for a favor.

642   The ordained men of the monastery of Silos
        grieved for those women: they undertook processions;
        they made supplications, and prayed before the tomb:
        the demons had no peace of mind at all.

643   The poor sick women ended up being cured,
        and once they were cured they felt like queens;
        with perfect sincerity they praised the confessor,
        and male and female neighbors rejoiced with them.

644   We want to tell you a precious miracle:
        you must open your ears in order to hear it;
        you should listen to it with steadfast will;
        you shall see the good father rise in great esteem.

645   In a place called Cozcorrita near the Tirón,[217]
        there was a worthy commoner, a native from there;
        Serván was his name, according to the text:
        he tried to harm the Moors and fell into their prison.

[217] Berceo identifies this town with Cozcorrita de Río Tirón, 10 kilometers west of Haro, but there is another Cozcorrita de Juaros 17 kilometers southeast of Burgos, and yet another one in Soria, 30 kilometers north of Medinaceli. Only the last was in the region threatened by the Moors in 1088, the year in which this miracle happened. For further details about the identification of this town, see Dutton, 4:173–74, note 645ac; Ruffinatto, 420, note 645a; and Orduna, 171, note 645a.

646   The strong and sturdy commoner fell into wicked hands;
he was taken to Medinaceli[218] in chains;
laden heavily with irons he was put into jail,
in a very narrow place completely walled in.

647   The ungodly Moors abused him in prison;
he was plagued by hunger and his heavy irons;
by day he suffered with the rest of the captives,
by night he lay imprisoned under wicked lock and key.

648   At times he was given a lashing with a whip,
but what grieved him most was to hear foul words,
for they called them dogs and scoundrels and heretics,
throwing insults at them and lines from filthy songs.

649   Serván, in terrible anguish, knew not where to turn,
except to Jesus Christ Whom he began to implore;
"Lord," he said, "You Who command the winds and the sea,[219]
take away my grief, deign to gaze on me.

650   Lord, I do not hope for any help from elsewhere,
except from You Who are the true Creator;
You are three Persons in one single God;
You alone without help created all things.

651   I am insulted by the enemies of the cross;
for keeping Your name I am maltreated by them;
Lord, You Who suffered martyrdom and death for me,
may You vanquish my sin by Your mercy."

652   When Serván had concluded his prayer,
midnight had passed and it was nearly dawn;
immeasurably tired, he fell asleep for a while,
in a desperate state for his life and salvation.

653   In the midst of the jail there fell a radiant light:[220]
he suddenly awoke, terrified by it;
he raised his head and invoked the Creator;
he blessed himself and said, "Help me, Lord!"

---

[218] According to Dutton, 4:174, note 646b, this town, 70 kilometers south of Soria, was in the hands of the Moors until 1125 except for a brief period from 1195 [sic] to 1104 when it was in the hands of King Alfonso VI. See also Ruffinatto, 420, note 646b, and Orduna, 171, note 646b.

[219] The allusion is to Matt. 8:27.

[220] Cf. Acts 12:7.

654   He seemed to see a man clothed in white,
        as if he were an ordained priest at Mass;
        the captive was seized with a dreadful fright;
        he turned his head away and fell on his face.

655   "Serván," said the vested man, "have no fear,
        know for certain that God has heard you;
        I am sent by God to get you out of here:
        stay close to God to free yourself from suffering."

656   "Sir," said the captive, "if that is what you are,
        tell me who you are, by God and the Glorious Lady;
        let me not be deceived by a ghost that is lying,
        for I believe in Jesus Christ and His precious death."

657   The holy messenger replied with these words:
        "I am Friar Dominic who was a cloistered monk;
        though I was not righteous, I was abbot of Silos,
        and I was buried there in a coffin made of wood."

658   "Sir," said the captive, "how can I leave,
        when I am unable to shake off these irons?
        If you are that doctor who comes to heal me,
        to manage that, you will have to bring help."

659   The worthy St. Dominic gave him a mallet:
        it was made all of wood, not of iron or steel;
        with that soft wood he crushed all the irons;
        he would not crush garlic in a mortar more quickly.

660   When he had crushed and dismantled his shackles,
        he was commanded to depart boldly and fearlessly;
        then he said that the walls were extremely high,
        and he had no steps or stairway to scale them.

661   The holy messenger, who was above,
        threw him a rope which he held in his hand;
        the prisoner below tied himself tightly,
        while the saint held the end of the rope.

662   The one above pulled him up along with his irons,
        just as easily as if he were pulling on a spindle;
        he placed him quickly at the door of the jail:
        at that time he was used to freeing captives.

663   "My friend," said the good confessor, "go your way:
        the doors are open and the Moors are sleeping;
        you will have no trouble, for you will have a good guide;
        you will be far, far away by break of day.

664 Do not hold back, but go as far as you can;
go to my monastery with those chains;
place them on the tomb where my body lies:[221]
believe me, indeed nothing will hinder you."

665 When he had instructed him in this way,
the man clothed in white vanished from his sight;
Serván moved immediately without being hindered:
not a single one of the gates was closed.

666 By break of day he was far, far away;
he did not lose his path or wander astray;
so well guided and not the least hindered,
he arrived at the monastery as he was commanded.

667 It happened by chance to be a very famous feast:
it was the day of the consecration[222] of the church;
important clerics had arrived for the feast,
and the laity could scarcely be counted.

668 A cardinal from Rome who had come as a legate,
whose name was Ricart,[223] was holding council then;
a host of bishops and abbots were there,
and many a good tonsured priest had come with them.

669 That captive entered laden down with his chains,
with his tattered clothing and his run-down shoes,
with his tangled hair and his shaggy beard;
he went and fell at the tomb of the worthy confessor.

670 "Worthy sir and father," he said, " I thank you:
due to you, I appear in the land of Christians;
I know I am out of jail and saved because of you;
as you commanded me, I offer you my irons."

671 The news spread throughout the whole city
that the holy confessor had done such a kindness;

---

[221] According to Dutton, 4:174, note 664c, in the church of Silos there is a huge pile of chains left there by prisoners freed by the saint.

[222] The consecration of the church of Silos, restored by the saint himself, took place on 29 September 1088 (Dutton, 4:174, note 667b; Ruffinatto, 424, note 667b; and Orduna, 175, note 667b).

[223] Cardinal Ricart was also abbot of St. Victor of Marseilles. In 1080 he presided over the Council of Burgos where the Mozarabic rite was abolished by decree. In 1088, after the Council of Husillos, Ricart presided over the consecration of the church of Silos. For further information, see Dutton, 4:174, note 668b, and Ruffinatto, 426, note 668ab.

there was not an abbot or a bishop in the town
who did not treat Serván with very great ceremony.

672   The legate himself, with so many good men,
sang "Tibi laus"[224] while in procession,
and then "Iste Sanctus"[225] after the prayer;
that day the people obtained great pardon.[226]

673   They saw the confessor highly exalted,
for he had worked such a great and marvelous miracle;
they said such a treasure and such a bright candle
should be placed in a more exquisite vault.

674   If he had been held in great esteem before,
from that time on he was much more revered;
Ricart the legate preached about him in Rome;
he was acknowledged by the pope to be a perfect saint.

675   Two women who were crippled, one in one hand,
the other in both, were healed by that good highlander;
happy the pomegranate tree that bore such a pomegranate,
happy the pomegranate fruit that produced such a fine seed.[227]

676   The one from Yécola[228] was called María:
her arms were just as thin as a board;
she could not grasp a thing or hold it with her hands;
any person who saw her would consider her unfortunate.

677   The text does not tell us where the other one was from,
but at Saturday vespers she did one thing and another:
she washed her hair and swept out her yard,
and guilty of that, she fell into such danger.

678   Both of those women who were so maimed
were healed by St. Dominic in just a few days;
with just a few vigils held for just a few nights,
thanks to God, they returned home healed.

679   There was a demoniac from Peña Alba[229]
who was suffering severely for her sins;

[224] 'Praise to You.'
[225] An antiphon from the Common of the Saints.
[226] Remission for their sins.
[227] Meaning 'Happy the monastery that produced such a saint and happy the saint who produced so many miracles.' The pomegranate was also a symbol of the Virgin Mary.
[228] See note 154 above.
[229] Probably Peñalva de Castro (Burgos) between Silos and Aranda de Duero, 20 kilometers south of Silos (Dutton, 4:174, note 679a, and Ruffinatto, 428, note 679a).

she was made mute by her grave illness,
and her faculties were greatly diminished.

680   She was often seized by the poisonous beast,
and she wandered astray like a crazy woman;
no help could be found anywhere to heal her;
her parents would rather have seen her dead.

681   One day where she was wandering astray like a lunatic,
she told this story with her very own lips:
a rather large figure placed himself before her;
he was clothed in a dalmatic[230] whiter than a veil.

682   She was sorely afraid and halted in terror;
the image said to her, "Fear not, daughter:
God has been grieved that you suffer so greatly.
He is sending you help whereby you shall be freed.

683   I will tell you, daughter, just so you will know,
what my name is so you will not be afraid;
I am St. Michael:[231] I bear God's standard;
I am sent to you by the Lord our God.

684   If you want to be cured of this illness of yours,
go to the monastery of St. Dominic of Silos;
there you will be pleased with the help you will find:
never spend a penny on any other remedy."

685   When the good archangel had instructed her,
the figure in white vanished from her sight;
even though she was disturbed, she understood him well;
she believed she was nearing the end of her trouble.

686   The devil heard those words that were uttered,
and he seized and abused her more than ever before;
he was highly annoyed and deeply upset,
for he counted on her being away from her home.

687   Between her lips he placed a fragment
that looked like a lump of very black glue;
it was tantamount for her to a heavy mallet blow,
or a thrashing with a stick from a very strong hand.

688   Although she was injured, she set out on the road,
for there was no way she could remove it from herself;
she went to St. Dominic as a truly suffering pilgrim,
confident indeed that she would get better.

---

[230] See note 107 above.
[231] St. Michael, the Archangel of God, called 'standard-bearer' in the liturgy.

689   For one whole week she lay before the tomb,
        eating oat bread and dressed in wool clothing;[232]
        on Sunday morning of the following week,
        a holy seed popped from the holy pomegranate.[233]

690   While she was at Mass the devil seized her;
        he hurled her to the ground and dragged her painfully around,
        twisting her mouth which was spewing foam,
        while making ugly faces and speaking vile language.

691   One of the monks who always used to do so, began
        to read the holy words of exorcism over her;
        the devil understood what was to come about,
        that he was to lose the place where he dwelt.

692   When he saw that he was to be dislodged,
        he spit out the wicked blemish[234] from her lips;
        that young woman's features were undefiled,
        and her lips were purified of the blemish.

693   That wicked snake cast his glance at the reader,
        and said, "Do not press me, Friar, so help you God;
        others better than you are urging me to leave:
        they are right close by you, so do not worry."

694   The reader said, "By Christ, I implore you
        to assure me and tell me what you see;
        or else I promise you indeed and I truly swear
        to cause you trouble, for I will not withdraw easily."

695   "I will not deny," said the devil to him,
        that I see St. Martin[235] standing close to me,
        and with him St. Dominic, patron of this place;
        rest assured, they both come to wage war with me.

696   Due to them, rest assured, I reluctantly depart;
        there is no way I can protect myself from them:
        that is why I want to beg of you and ask you as a favor,
        not to put such an effort into chasing me away."

697   The exorcist was very much pleased with those words;
        he applied himself with much greater fervor to exorcise him;

---

[232] Something like sackcloth or penitential clothing.
[233] A direct reference to lines 675cd above.
[234] Here I read *manziella/ mançiella* with Ruffinatto, 433, 692b; Orduna, 179, 692b; and Logroño, 111, 692b rather than *postiella* with Dutton, 4:142, 692b.
[235] See note 112 above.

the devil was weakened and lost all his might;
if they had given him permission he would have been out already.

698   When forced to come out of the mute woman's body,
he uttered an appallingly dreadful shriek;
the filthy evil thing came out stinking worse than hemlock,
and with God and his help, he never returned to her.

699   The sick woman was healed and freed from the devil:
she completely recovered her speech that was impaired;
she returned to the state of good health she had been robbed of;
she was over her illness and went back to Peña Alba.

700   There was a knight, a native of Hlantada,[236]
a highly prestigious and worthy knight;
he departed with his lord by whom he was paid
to engage in a raid and wage war on the Moors.

701   Pedro was the name of that knight:
the text says he was neither minstrel nor zitherer;[237]
they did damage to Alarcos[238] in their first attack,
but they were not guided by a wise soothsayer.

702   They thought to take captives and they were captured;
they thought to make gains and they were deceived;
they were all taken captive by the ungodly Moors;
the number that escaped were hardly worth counting.

703   When the Moors had arrived to a safe haven,
they divided the captives that they had won;
they scattered them all throughout Moorish lands:
they were never again seen together in this world.

704   Pedro of Hllantada was taken to Murcia —
his lord indeed found a way to arrange it;
he was not kept in jail but was well guarded,
laden heavily with irons at the back of a cave.

705   His mother and father prayed for him to God
and to St. Dominic, the worthy confessor,
that they should take pity on the sinful captive,
that he be freed from the oppression of the treacherous Moor.

---

[236] A town in the province of Palencia. (For more details about the identification of this town, see Dutton, 4:175, note 700a; Ruffinatto, 434, note 700a; and Orduna, 181, note 700a.)

[237] A player of the zither, or one who accompanied minstrels singing their lays.

[238] An old town and fortress six kilometers west of Ciudad Real. (See Dutton, 4:175, note 701c; Ruffinatto, 434, note 701c; and Orduna, 181, note 701c.)

706   And he himself prayed with all his heart
       for God to remove him from such a dark prison,
       for if He did not help him within a short while,
       he would be blind or dead or severely injured.

707   It was on Wednesday evening when the stars were out,
       but the people had not yet gone to sleep;
       such news made its way to the captive
       as good and delightful as ever he had heard.

708   A great and marvelous radiance entered
       into the midst of the dark and gloomy cave;
       the prisoner was terrified by such a strange thing:
       he said, "Help me, Christ and the Glorious Virgin!"

709   He saw the figure of a man in the middle of the doorway
       who certainly resembled a monk in all his ways;
       he was holding a walking stick like a traveler;
       he waited to see if he would say something to him.

710   He called him by his name and told him good news:
       he said, "Pedro, take heart and forget the past;
       God has granted you what you asked of Him;
       you will soon be over this trouble of yours."

711   The prisoner was fearful of being hindered
       by the actions of his master who kept him imprisoned,
       for if he rose up he would be severely punished,
       or[239] he would be beheaded as a lesson to others.

712   The sinful prisoner meekly replied;
       he said: "If the Lord our God does not rescue me,
       or if he who holds me will not do me a favor,
       I am afraid I will be unable to get out of here."

713   The bearer of the news gave him this reply:
       "Pedro," he said, "you are proving to be very foolish;
       no jail or cave can protect itself from God;
       be not moved to doubt that He is doing you a favor."

714   "Sir," said the prisoner, "I ask you this favor:
       if you are from God, then make me believe it;
       if you are something else, then do not confuse me,
       whereby I may be maltreated by my master.

---

[239] Here I read *o* with Orduna, 183, 711d and Logroño, 114, 711d rather than omitting this word with Dutton, 4:145, 711d.

715   If you are here to save me or you want me to believe you,
       then reveal who you are so that I may be sure;
       for if I stir easily I fear there will be a struggle,
       and I know that my body will get a whipping."

716   The messenger revealed the entire secret:
       he said, "Listen, my friend, and you will know for sure:
       I am Friar Dominic, truly a sinner;
       I was named abbot of the monastery of Silos.

717   God showed me great mercy in His compassion,
       for He assigned me as a guardian over Christians,
       to release from captivity those prisoners
       who cry out to Him with all their hearts.

718   Your prayers have been favorably heard by God.
       I offered them to Him, unworthy priest that I am;
       the prayers that your grieving folks have uttered
       have not fallen into a void, do believe me.

719   I have come here to pay you a visit:
       you should be comforted by such a visitation;
       you must quickly escape from this prison,
       and I will tell you how it is to be done.

720   This coming Friday, the day after tomorrow,
       is a day of great rejoicing for the Moors;
       they eat the best of food as on a feast day;
       anyone important will be part of the company.

721   For his own glory, the man who holds you
       wants to take you out of the cave that day;
       he wants to send you and two other captives
       to go and do some digging while they are dining.

722   You will be invited by one of the others
       to take a little rest, and you should gladly do so;
       he will lay his head upon your side,
       and when he has done so he will fall asleep.

723   Watch for this, and escape from him quietly,
       and put something underneath his fat neck;
       if you look on the ground you will see the iron ring
       lying with its links detached from your ankle.

724   Be quick to escape right away without delay;
       be careful to go wherever God guides you;
       fear not to stray, you will be well guided;
       you may be sure that you have to go through this."

725   When he had instructed him in this way,
           the happily-encountered one vanished from his sight;
           there was never a Friday in this world more longed for;
           he thought that Thursday would never be over.

726   When Friday came he could hardly stay still:
           rest assured that they did not need to call him twice;
           before he was told, "Pedro, go and do some digging,"
           he had already started to get his shovel.

727   That is what Pedro went through and how he was freed,
           just as the blessed monk had told him;
           the one in priestly vestments who had spoken to him
           gave him guidance and food for his journey.

728   Walking through wild and deserted lands,
           with only God as his companion to guide him,
           in tattered clothing and totally weakened,
           on the twelfth day he arrived in Toledo.

729   He told of his suffering to those Toledans,
           how he had escaped from prison from the infidels,
           how all in one piece his irons fell off him;[240]
           they all nearly went and kissed his hands.

730   Through all Allend-Sierra[241] and Extremadura,
           and through all Castile this story was spread;
           they ardently gave thanks to the good confessor,
           and the entire border was considered much safer.

731   Anyone at all, man or woman, who says
           that the patron of Silos does not rescue nobles,
           should repent of his words, for they are not true:
           he insults the confessor and shall be poorly rewarded.

732   Even if he realizes that his words are not true,
           I want to add another deed similar to that one,
           of yet another knight who never paid taxes,[242]
           who was rescued by St. Dominic from terrible straits.

733   Fita[243] is a strong and powerful fortress,

---

[240] Again cf. Acts 12:7.

[241] In ancient times the region of Castilla la Nueva was called Allend-Sierra (Dutton, 4:175, note 730a, and Ruffinatto, 440, note 730a).

[242] Noblemen were not obliged to pay any taxes to the king.

[243] Hita, located 24 kilometers to the north, northeast of Guadalajara. The region was reconquered by Alfonso VI in 1085. (See Dutton, 4:175, note 733a; Ruffinatto, 442, note 733a; and Orduna, 187, note 733a.)

> solid and alert, well-peopled in its lowlands;
> it was under the command of good King Alfonso,
> who won Toledo, if I remember correctly.

734 On the shore of Henar,[244] a short day away,
     lies Guadalajara, a most intemperate town;
     then it belonged to the Moors, but was very secure,
     for it was taken over by King Alfonso.[245]

735 He was served by the town and all its villages:
     they kissed his hand and were under his orders;
     he threatened that he would put them in chains,
     if they tried to stir up any trouble with Christians.

736 The noblemen of Fita, in their ignorance,
     neither feared the king nor paid him any homage;
     they conducted an attack on Guadalajara
     which some of them would end up greatly regretting.

737 They carried out a raid on Guadalajara,
     ambushing its people before break of day;
     they were secure and afraid of nothing;
     great harm was done them in that incursion.

738 When they went out to their morning labors,
     they were suddenly attacked by those horsemen;
     many of the peasants were killed and captured;
     among all those found, no noblemen were left.

739 The king was immensely grieved and angered;
     he was very displeased with the council of Fita:
     he said they had done him a terrible disservice,
     for they had destroyed and plundered his people.

740 He placed his hand on the cross and swore to God
     that they would get the same as they had done or worse;
     a subject who transgresses the commands of his lord
     no guarantor should help when he is in trouble.

741 The king, with great anger and great displeasure
     (which in truth he had plenty of reason to feel),
     slapped a heavy tax on the council of Fita,[246]
     so that they should hand him those who did that deed.

---

[244] The Henares River flowing to the north and southeast of Madrid.

[245] Berceo refers here to the years immediately before the conquest of Toledo when the Moors of Toledo were pacified by Alfonso and he was protecting them.

[246] A tribute meant to guarantee that the council of Hita would hand over the wrongdoers.

742   He ordered them to hand him all the wrongdoers,
       or else he would consider all of them responsible;
       all would be touched by the evil misfortune;
       both just and sinners would be under one ruling.

743   When what he had written was read in council,
       the beards of many bold fellows trembled;[247]
       they would have given anything to maintain peace;
       indeed they would have given a quarter of their wealth.

744   The solid and very tough council of Fita
       dared not transgress the order of the king;
       the proclamation was issued for them to go to council,
       and in no time at all they were all in the marketplace.[248]

745   Young and old came to an agreement,
       fathers and sons, subjects and lords;
       they took the raiders into custody,
       obtaining good surety and guarantors for them.

746   Shortly thereafter the king sent to them
       to hand him the men and not to say no;
       the council handed them to him and he put them in prison;
       all the people thought it was unlikely they would be pardoned.

747   One among the others was more distinguished:
       all followed his orders and were guided by him;
       he had been severely threatened by the king;
       he was terribly afraid that he would be condemned.

748   Juan was the name of the aforementioned knight;
       apart from other habits he served his parents well,
       and was therefore held to be a righteous man;
       the above transgression was the only one known.

749   They all prayed for him to the Lord our God,
       and to St. Dominic, such a noble confessor,
       that they should show pity and compassion for him
       beyond anything they had ever shown for any other sinner.

750   In jail he himself did the very same thing:
       his tongue never rested although he lay in prison;

---

[247] For the irony used by Berceo in this line and also in lines 744ab, see Dutton, 4:176, note 743b; Ruffinatto, 444, note 743b; and Orduna, 189, note 743b.

[248] The market or main square was the place where the council met usually on Sundays after Mass, convoked by the ringing of the bells or by the town crier (Ruffinatto, 444, note 744d).

> he prayed to God and the confessor, and said
> that if they freed him from this he would nevermore be wicked.

751   Just how he got freed I could not say,
for it was missing in the book where I learned it;
a folio was lost, but not through my fault;
to chance to write it would be a great folly.

752   If the book had endured we would still endure;
we would never tire of telling about the good saint;
we would tell all about how the prisoner escaped;
if the text had endured we would not say "Tu autem."[249]

753   But that St. Dominic rescued the gentleman,
there is no doubt about it, of that I am certain;
but the final judgment on the other prisoners
I never really heard or even dreamt of it.

754   Gentlefolk, let us praise God in Whom we believe,
from Whom we receive every goodness that we have;
we have come to the end of the deeds of the confessor;
we have written whatever we could possibly discover.

755   But you certainly should believe, just as we do,
that we have not got even a tenth of his miracles,
for we see them grow daily with our very own eyes,
and they will be growing every day after we are dead.

756   We ought to serve and revere such a Lord
Who knows in such a way how to honor His servants;
no human being could even think or imagine
what reward is obtained by doing service to God.

757   I who am called Gonzalo de Berceo,
disciple of San Millán and in his favor,
was immensely eager to do this work,
and now that I have done it I give thanks to God.

758   Indeed I do believe that the worthy St. Dominic,
for this small service that I have done him,
will entreat the Lord Jesus on my behalf
to save my soul when I die.

---

[249] The Latin formula used to end the reading of the text at Matins, or in the refectory or the choir (Dutton, 4:176; note 752d; Ruffinatto, 446, note 752d; and Orduna, 191, note 752d).

759   Gentlefolk, I cannot leave you in this way:
        I wish to take something from you for my service;
        but I would not like to burden you greatly,
        for then you would call me a bothersome minstrel.

760   In grace I ask that you do this for God:
        that each of you help me with a few *Pater Nosters*;[250]
        I will feel satisfied and well rewarded;
        in charity I beg you to say them right away.

761   Worthy St. Dominic, perfect confessor,
        feared by the Moors, beloved of Christians,
        protect me, sir, from the sin of the devil;
        may I be not wounded by his arrow.

762   Worthy father to many, servant of the Creator,
        you who were a loyal subject of our Lord and God,
        be an intercessor to Him for all of us,
        that He may save our souls and give us His love.

763   Father, you who free captives from prisons,
        and you whom all peoples greatly bless,
        do help us, sir, so that we may be people
        who will not be overcome by evil temptations.

764   Father full of grace, who in order to serve God
        left the town and went to live in the wilderness,
        deign to hear those who acclaim you,
        and deign to ask God to have mercy on them.

765   So that you could live a life of even greater hardship,
        and not be so bold as to speak without permission,
        you became a cloistered monk and practiced obedience,
        and your service to God was pleasing to Him.

766   Father, do help us to save our souls,
        that the devil may snatch nothing from us;
        sir, since you knew how to protect yours,
        we beg you to deign to look after ours.

767   Father who shunned your body for your soul,
        when you placed your will in the hands of others,
        and you who refused to ever look backwards,
        pray for us to God Whom you served so greatly.

768   Father, you understand and know very well

---

[250] Here Berceo is asking his audience to say a few "Our Fathers" for him as a reward for his services.

what a subtle disturber the devil is;
you experienced it all but you were the victor:
protect us from him, for he is a treacherous dog.

769   Father, we know indeed that he tried to bite you,
but lacked the power to sink his teeth into you;
his only occupation is to keep on pursuing us;
sir, deign to protect us from his wicked snare.

770   Father, our sins and our wickedness,
in word and in deed and in our hearts,
we confess to you, patron of abbots,
and we beg your mercy and your compassion.

771   Father, deign to receive this confession of ours,
and place in our hearts perfect contrition;
obtain for us some remission from Christ,
and guide us to make worthy reparation.

772   Worthy sir and father, beg God to give us peace,
and true charity, which pleases you greatly,
health and clement weather, enough bread and wine,
and may He give us in the end His face to see.

773   Pray for the sick and obtain health for them;
look after captives and obtain their freedom;
obtain safety for pilgrim travelers,
and may Christians righteously observe their faith.

774   Implore God to protect the Church,
to extinguish its error and kindle its charity:
may He always keep it in His sacred care;
may it carry out its office and be free from strife.

775   Father, for myself I want to beg your mercy,
for I have been most willing to be your minstrel;
deign to accept this small service,
and deign to pray for Gonzalo to God.

776   Father, leave me not unprotected amongst others,
for they say that you usually look after your minstrels;
if you will pray for me, God will grant me a fine death;
I will be saved by the prayer from your lips.

777   We must give thanks to the Holy Spirit
Who gave us such excellent and perfect help:
through His sacred merit God protect us from harm,
and take our souls to His heavenly kingdom.
Amen.

Bibliography

Primary Sources

Editions of Berceo's Works: See Abbreviations List.

Other Works and Sources of Reference

Andrés Castellanos, María S. de, ed. *La Vida de Santa María Egipciaca*. Madrid: Aguirre Torre, 1964.

Baró, José. *Glosario completo de los "Milagros de Nuestra Señora" de Gonzalo de Berceo*. Boulder: Society of Spanish and Spanish-American Studies, 1987.

Bartha, Jeannie K. "Four Lexical Notes on Berceo's *Milagros de Nuestra Señora*." *Romance Philology* 37 (1983): 56–62.

———. *Vocabulario de los "Milagros de Nuestra Señora" de Gonzalo de Berceo*. Normal, IL: Applied Literature Press, 1980.

Blecua, J. M., ed. *El conde Lucanor*. Madrid: Castalia, 1969.

Cejador y Frauca, J. *Vocabulario medieval castellano*. Orig. 1929; repr. New York: Las Américas, 1968.

Corominas, Joan, ed. *Libro de Buen Amor*. Madrid: Gredos, 1967.

———. and José A. Pascual. *Diccionario crítico etimológico castellano e hispánico*. 6 vols. Madrid: Gredos, 1980–1991.

Covarrubias Orozco, Sebastián de. *Tesoro de la lengua castellana o española*. Orig. 1611; repr. Madrid: Turner, 1977.

Dutton, Brian. "A Chronology of the Works of Gonzalo de Berceo." In *Medieval Hispanic Studies Presented to Rita Hamilton*, ed. A. D. Deyermond, 67–76. London, Tamesis; 1975.

———. *A New Berceo Manuscript, Biblioteca Nacional Ms. 13149. Description, Study and Partial Edition*. Exeter Hispanic Texts 32. Exeter: University of Exeter Press, 1982.

———. ed. Gonzalo de Berceo, *Obras Completas*. 5 vols. London: Tamesis, 1967–1984.

Goicoechea, Cesáreo. *Vocabulario riojano*. Madrid: S. Aguirre Torre, 1961.

Gulsoy, J. "The -i Words in the Poems of Gonzalo de Berceo." *Romance Philology* 23 (1969–1970): 172–87.

Honnorat, S. J. *Dictionnaire Provençal-Français*. 3 vols. Orig. 1848; repr. Marseille: Laffitte Reprints, 1971.

Keller, John Esten. *Gonzalo de Berceo*. Twayne World Authors Series 187. New York: Twayne, 1972.

———. *Pious Brief Narrative in Medieval Castilian and Galician Verse: From Berceo to Alfonso X*. Lexington: University Press of Kentucky, 1978.

Koberstein, G., ed. *Gonzalo de Berceo, "Estoria de San Millán": Textkritische Edition*. Münster, Aschendorff, 1964.

Kulp-Hill, Kathleen, trans. *Songs of Holy Mary by Alfonso X, The Wise: A Translation of the* Cantigas de Santa María. MRTS 173. Tempe: Arizona Center for Medieval and Renaissance Studies, 2000.

Labarta de Chaves, Teresa, ed. *Vida de Santo Domingo de Silos*. Madrid: Clásicos Castalia, 1973.

Lacarra Ducay, Ma. Jesús. "La maestría de Gonzalo de Berceo en la *Vida de Santo Domingo de Silos*." *Dicenda* 6 (1987): 165–76.

Lanchetas, Rufino. *Gramática y vocabulario de las obras de Gonzalo de Berceo*. Madrid: Sucesores de Rivadeneyra, 1900.

Lappin, Anthony. *Berceo's Vida de Santa Oria: Text, Translation and Commentary*. Oxford: Legenda, 2000.

Latham, R. E. *Revised Medieval Latin Word-List*. London: Oxford University Press, 1965.

Lazar, Moshé, ed. *La Fazienda de Ultramar*. Salamanca: Cervantes, 1965.

Levy, Emil. *Petit Dictionnaire Provençal-Français*. Orig. 1909; 5th ed. Heidelberg: Carl Winter, 1973.

Marden, C. Carroll, ed. *Libro de Apolonio*. Orig. 1922; repr. Millwood: Kraus Reprint Co., 1976.

Menéndez Pidal, Ramón, ed. *Cantar de Mío Cid. Texto, gramática y vocabulario*. 4th ed. Madrid: Espasa-Calpe, 1969.

Montgomery, Thomas, ed. *El Evangelio de San Mateo: Texto, gramática, vocabulario*. Madrid: Aguirre Torre, 1962.

Mount, T., and Annette G. Cash, trans. Gonzalo de Berceo, *Miracles of Our Lady*. Lexington: University Press of Kentucky, 1997.

Nebrija, Antonio de. *Vocabulario de Romance en Latín* (1516), transcr. Gerald J. MacDonald. Philadelphia: Temple University Press, 1973.

Ramoneda, Arturo M., ed. Gonzalo de Berceo, *Signos que aparecerán antes del Juicio Final, Duelo de la Virgen, Martirio de San Lorenzo*. Madrid: Castalia, 1980.

Real Academia Española. *Diccionario de la lengua española*. 19th ed. Madrid: Espasa-Calpe, 1970.

Ruffinatto, Aldo. *La Lingua di Berceo: osservazioni sulla lingua dei manoscritti della "Vida de Santo Domingo de Silos."* Istituto di Letteratura Spagnola e Ispano-Americana, Collana de Studi 27. Pisa: Università, 1974.

Solalinde, A. G., ed. *Milagros de Nuestra Señora.* 8th ed. Madrid: Espasa-Calpe, 1972.

Walsh, John K., ed. *El Libro de los Doze Sabios o Tractado de la Nobleza y Lealtad.* Madrid: Aguirre, 1975.

Willis, Raymond S., ed. *El libro de Alexandre.* Orig. 1934; repr. Millwood: Kraus Reprint Co., 1976.

———. *Libro de Buen Amor.* Princeton: Princeton University Press, 1972.

INTRODUCTION TO *LA VIDA DE SAN MILLÁN*
DE LA COGOLLA[1]

TRANSLATED BY ANNETTE GRANT CASH

La Vida de San Millán de la Cogolla (Life of St. Aemilianus of La Cogolla) is possibly the first attempt Berceo made to write in the area of saints' lives. He must have felt particularly at home, even so, for as he penned the 1900-odd verses or 489 quatrains, he could gaze from the window of his cell or from the casement of the monastery library at the very scenes which had been familiar to St. Aemilianus,[2] who died in 574, and ranked among the notable ecclesiastics of the late Visigothic era in Spain. He flourished just before the cultural awakening set in motion by St. Isidore of Seville (570?–636) and was considered important enough to merit a biography written by no less a personage than St. Isidore's disciple, St. Braulius, bishop of Saragossa. It was understandable, then, that Berceo felt a deep personal pride in the saint who had founded the very monastery which meant so much to him. By the mid-thirteenth century when Berceo was writing, and even from long before, the life and miracles of Aemilianus had had time to assume all the attributes of tradition, legend, and local folklore. After all, some 600-odd years had passed, and the memory of the saint had become a familiar part of the fabric of life in La Rioja. Berceo, no doubt, knew the legends and the folk beliefs, and most certainly he had perused the documents which set down the life and miracles of Aemilianus. His first saint's life was based upon a manuscript of the *Vita Beati Aemiliani (Life of Blessed Aemilianus)* which Braulius had composed in Latin prose so long before, and this document verified in Berceo's mind the belief that Aemilianus himself had founded the monastery which later bore his name. Quite probably the saint was, indeed, the actual founder of the monastery, although this cannot be proven, since no monastic document earlier than 924 is extant,

---

[1] This introduction is adapted from John Esten Keller, *Gonzalo de Berceo* (New York: Twayne Publishers, 1972), 67–71.

[2] Brian Dutton, *La "Vida de San Millán de la Cogolla" de Gonzalo de Berceo* (London: Tamesis, 1967), 164–66, is a definitive study of this *vida*. See PL 80: 699-714.

and this document states only that King Garci Sánchez of Nájera granted the parish church of Santa María de Cañas to the monastery.[3] No mention is made of any previously established monastic house in the village of Berceo.

A long tradition about San Millán, then, had developed by Berceo's time, and the poet quite obviously had steeped himself in it. He knew the region's history and the great events his monastery had seen, from the time it stood on its original site in the mountains and then from a later period when it was reestablished on the plain near Berceo. Heroes, like Fernán González, had donated to it, as had certain of the kings of Navarre. Moorish armies led by Almanzor, caliph of Cordova, had in the year 1002 sacked and burned the monastery. Monarchs of Navarre, however, had, during the eleventh century, restored and embellished it.[4] After all, San Millán had become a patron of Navarrese and Castilian peoples. Indeed, in Berceo's own time someone had written an epic poem in *cuaderna vía*, the *Poema de Fernán González*, in which San Millán appeared in battle against the Moslems.

In 1030 the remains of the saint had been exhumed from the tomb in the cave where he had sequestered himself while he lived, and had been given honored entombment under the altar in the monastery church. Berceo knew, also, as would have any inhabitant of so sacred a place, that in 1053 a king of Navarre had begun a new church and a new monastic house on the plain near the village of Berceo and had carried it to conclusion by 1067. For a while, Berceo knew, both the old monastery and the new had functioned, almost within sight of one another, the old one called "San Millán de Suso" (Upper San Millán) and the new "San Millán de Yuso" (Lower San Millán).

Berceo surely assessed the situation of his beloved monastery, and must have realized, as did all the clergy concerned, that the age-old prosperity of San Millán was waning. Pilgrims still appeared, but their numbers grew smaller. Many preferred the more recent and probably more popular centers of pilgrimage wherein accommodations may have been better. The situation of San Millán was critical, and clearly something had to be done. Brian Dutton has established with considerable certainty that something was done, and that quite probably Berceo, among others, worked hard to improve the monastery's situation and to reinstate it as an effective shrine. Dutton points to numerous false documents written to enrich the monastery.[5] Some of these documents sought to convince patrons and

---

[3] Dutton, La "Vida", xi.

[4] Dutton, La "Vida", xii–xiii.

[5] Dutton, La "Vida", with a detailed account in a section entitled "Los Documentos" which appears in his book's Primera Parte, 1–9. Américo Castro, in The Structure of Spanish History (Princeton: Princeton University Press, 1954), 353–54, touches also upon the practicality of Berceo and upon his sophistication which some scholars refuse to see hidden behind a façade of simplicity.

others who had promised donations, or who might be led to subscribe, that San Millán himself was ever ready to reward the generous or punish the stingy. Other documents attempted, apparently with great success, to prevent various bishops from claiming tithes and levies from the monastery's coffers. Pope Innocent IV himself in 1245 was asked to arbitrate and, deceived by false documents, his appointed judges were led to rule in favor of the monastery and against those who made claims against it.

The most startling falsification, and the one which brought most honor and wealth to San Millán, was the copy of the vows of donation to the saint, vows which sought to force all the towns of Castile and in parts of Aragon and Navarre to pay an annual quota to the monastery. The documents alleged that Fernán González, the local region's great epic hero, had founded the monastery in 934. It was like proving today that George Washington or Abraham Lincoln had founded a church in America. The results were most gratifying to the monks, since great prosperity came to San Millán thereafter.

Dutton believes that Berceo, who lived through the period of falsification of documents, may actually have been the notary of Abbot Juan Sánchez of San Millán, and that quite possibly Berceo engaged actively in such falsifications. A kinder view might be that the simple Berceo, if he were as simple as such scholars as Menéndez y Pelayo and Valbuena Prat believe him to have been,[6] merely copied what the abbot handed him, or wrote down what the abbot told him to write, accepting it for truth. This is difficult to accept, however, when one considers Berceo's familiarity with monastic holdings at San Millán and the knowledge he must have had about the case. But even if the poet falsified willingly, or allowed himself to be used by the falsifiers, he might well have considered that the end justified the means. Those who are interested in such matters may read a complete and convincing account of them in the Primera Parte of Dutton's *La "Vida"*. The entire matter is pertinent, of course, to those who read Berceo, because it poses a new and practical reason for the writing of one of Berceo's most famous saints' lives, *La Vida de San Millán de la Cogolla*. This contradicts, of course, the hitherto accepted reasons attributed to Berceo's commendable and pious desire to honor the patron saint of his own monastery and to glorify the Holy Trinity and the Blessed Virgin, who stood behind the saintly Aemilianus. Dutton points to page and line in *La Vida de San Millán* to support his supposition.

The donations to San Millán certainly are alluded to in the fourth line of the first quatrain; and surely the last line in the second quatrain refers to small

---

[6] M. Menéndez y Pelayo, *Antología de poetas líricos castellanos*, vol. 2 (Madrid: Casa editorial Hernando, 1940); Ángel Valbuena Prat, *Historia de la literatura española* (Barcelona: G. Gili, 1946), 1: 75–76.

donations: donations to the monastery and not to some troubadour, which latter supposition was strongly supported by Menéndez Pidal.[7]

It can be seen, then, that Berceo may have composed his *Vida de San Millán* for more than one reason: out of piety and a desire to honor the local saint and the monastery he was believed to have founded, thereby attracting pilgrims to his shrine; or because Berceo believed that such writing could lead people to pay the donations they had agreed to pay. Whatever his reason, he produced an interesting document based upon a five-hundred-year-old Latin text.

Berceo's Spanish rendition of the *Vita Beati Aemiliani* differed as greatly from the Latin prose account set down by St. Braulius as had his *Milagros de Nuestra Señora* from its Latin original. The same embellishment of the simple Latin, the same use of local color, proverbial phrases, the quaint and rustic vocabulary of La Rioja, and Berceo's own particular handling of Castilian syntax are to be found. And, of course, the same poetic demands of the *mester de clerecía* regulated the poem's presentation.

Berceo as a priest knew his parishioners well, and no doubt realized how valuable close and intimate affinity with his people could be. Therefore, in his works, particularly in the *Vida de San Millán de la Cogolla*, he wrote in a manner designed to identify himself as a member of a simple religious community.

Berceo structured all of his saints' lives in a tripartite pattern[8] and according to a conscious plan, although variations occur from *vida* to *vida*. In so doing he was not demonstrating originality, for age-old custom in the compositions of hagiographical writing dictated such structuring. The typical *vita sancti* (saint's life) in those times was divided into three parts: the saint's background, parentage, and so on, together with a miraculous announcement of his future greatness; his childhood and youth, his deeds as a man, his virtues and the miracles he wrought while alive; the veneration given him and the miracles after his death.[9]

As would be expected, from what has been said above, a third section or part concludes the *vida*. Berceo ends his second part and uses what today would be called in writers' terminology a "narrative hook," readying the reader for the dénouement and arousing his interest.

---

[7] R. Menéndez Pidal, *Poesía juglaresca y juglares* (Madrid: Espasa Calpe, 1945), 275, n. 3.

[8] Of great assistance to those interested in poetic structure is Valbuena Prat, *Historia*, 1:73; see also T. Anthony Perry, *Art and Meaning in Berceo's "Vida de Santa Oria"* (New Haven and London: Yale University Press, 1968), 8–13, for a general discussion of tripartite structure in Berceo with special emphasis on such structure in *Santa Oria*, 14–17; see also Frida Weber de Kurlat, "Cronología de las 'Vidas' de Berceo," *Nueva Revista de Filología Hispánica*, 15 (1961), 113.

[9] Hippolyte Delehaye, *Les Légendes Hagiographiques* (Brussels: Société des Bollandistes, 1906), 110–11.

Berceo was well aware of the symbolic justification for the tripartite division of his *vida,* knowing that his audience would quickly make the necessary association with the Holy Trinity. He did not, however, actually make the parallels apparent in the *Vida de San Millán,* perhaps because he knew that the comparison was implicit, or perhaps because he simply overlooked the opportunity to state the parallels. In his second *vida,* however, the *Vida de Santo Domingo de Silos,* Berceo is more explicit, stating plainly that his tripartite division is symbolic of the Trinity.

THE LIFE OF SAINT AEMILIANUS

Here begins the history of San Millán turned into Romance from Latin, composed by Master Gonzalo de Berceo.

1   Whosoever would like to know about the life of San Millán
and be sure of his story,
pay attention to what I want to read aloud
and you will see where the people send their tribute.

2   According to my belief and in spite of the Devil,
as soon as the treatise is read,
you will be pleased about what you will learn
and giving your little bit will not grieve you.

3   Near Cogolla on the eastern side,
two leagues from Nágera,[1] at the foot of San Lorenzo,[2]
lies the district of Berceo near Madriz:[3]
there indeed was San Millán born.

4   As soon as he was born, those who engendered him
carried him to the church wrapped in swaddling clothes.
They asked for baptism, as the law demands.
The clerics gave it to him and anointed him with oil.

5   As soon as he was grown, when he could walk,
his father sent him to tend the sheep.
His son obeyed and went to guard them immediately.
He dressed in the clothes that shepherds are accustomed to wear.

6   He kept his flock well, like an expert shepherd;
his staff in hand, like shepherds do.
He frightened away wolves and evil rustlers.
The sheep enjoyed being in his care.

---

[1] Nágera is 15 kilometers from Berceo and was the site of the court of the kings of Navarre in the 11th century.

[2] San Lorenzo is the highest peak of the sierra, some 15 kilometers south of San Millán.

[3] Madriz is the head of the valley of San Millán.

7   The shepherd about whom I am speaking had another habit.
         He always carried a zither with him
         to stave off sleep so that the evil enemy
         could not steal either lamb or goat from him.

8   The celestial Shepherd gave him an unusual gift.
         Neither wolf nor other wild animal could harm him.
         He returned his flock safely to the corral.
         He did his filial duty to his parents.

9   But the King of Glory, who is very wise,
         wished to change this ministry in a different way.
         He wanted to raise him from the dust and give him a greater inheritance,
         which He arranges quickly when He so wishes.

10   While going through the mountains, leaning on his staff,
         fulfilling his duty, guiding his sheep,
         he was struck by an oppressive sleep.
         He bent his head and went nodding off.

11   He slept a sweet and easy sleep, as long as God wished.
         While he lay sleeping, he was inspired by God.
         When he opened his eyes, he awoke instructed.
         In order to part from this world, he left his sheep behind.

12   He understood that the world was full of deceit.
         He wanted to leave it and become a hermit.
         He did not think of taking food or bread.
         The day seemed longer than a whole year to him.

13   He thought of a good plan; God worked it all out.
         But to undertake such a life, he needed instruction.
         He knew that Saint Felices[4] was dwelling in Bilibio.[5]
         He could not wait for the moment when he could see him.

14   He did not put it off, nor did he wish to delay it.
         He left the sierra and began to descend
         through Valpierre,[6] a dry place,
         until he had arrived at Bilibio.

---

    [4] Saint Felices was San Millán's teacher.
    [5] Billivio is a large rock that together with another called Buradón forms the mouth of the River Ebro where it comes out on the plain of La Rioja. See Dutton, *Obra completa* 128, v. 13c.
    [6] Valpierre is a rocky plain between Haro and San Millán. This is an addition by Berceo to the text of San Braulio. See Dutton, *Obra completa*, 130, v. 14c.

15   He entered the castle. He found the chatelaine,
            the Benedictine man, the happy gentleman,
            the hermit, praying on the top of the hill,
            more humbly than a cloistered monk.

16   He fell at his feet as soon as he had risen.
            He said to him, "Mercy I ask of you, willingly I beg you for it.
            I have sworn an oath to leave this world
            and I want you for my teacher; it is for this that I have come.

17   I want to change this life for the other,
            to live in solitude, to save my soul.
            I want to leave the vices of this world.
            For this reason I have come to ask your advice.

18   I know nothing of reading: you are going to teach me.
            I do not understand the root of the holy doctrine.
            Father, lying at your feet, I beg you for mercy
            to help me in this travail.

19   If you wish to know from whence I come,
            I was born in Berceo; it is nearby Madriz.
            My good nurse gave me the name of Millán.
            I have made my life as a shepherd until now."

20   Saint Felices was very happy at this.
            He gave thanks to God and Saint Mary.
            He understood that this was not done by trickery,
            but that God had prescribed it from his pharmacy.

21   He received him gladly; he gave him strength.
            He taught him the psalms with which to say his prayers.
            With ardent enthusiasm, he gave him such instruction
            that he understood the form of the perfection.

22   In a short time the shepherd knew the Psalter,
            the hymns, and the canticles all by heart.
            He completely mastered all the doctrine.
            The teacher was truly astounded.

23   The more he absorbed the science,
            the more he was illuminated in the belief.
            He already wanted to be out of the castle,
            to return to the mountains, to live in hiding.

24   When he had achieved all he had sought
            and was assured of all he had doubted,
            the boy asked his teacher for permission to leave,
            because he wanted to return to the sierra very much.

25   The teacher, in grief and great sadness,
granted him license; he could not deny it.
He gave him his blessing as he should,
as a good teacher does to his good student.

26   The teacher remained where he was accustomed to dwell.
The student had to return to the mountains.
Never again do we read nor can we find
that they both met anywhere while alive.

27   Near Berceo, there where he was born,
he finds la Cogolla, an ancient valley.
It was at this time a thick wildwood;
serpents and snakes made their home there.

28   There were great rocks in the middle of the ravine.
Under the rocks there were very desolate caves.
A great company of evil beasts inhabited them.
It was a harsh place at the hour of sext.

29   The blessed man, in order to be hidden,
rendered to God the vow he had promised.
With God's strength, our Spiritual Guide,
he went into the caves about which you heard.

30   The wild beasts were very disturbed by him.
They all flee from him, their heads lowered.
Whether they liked it or not, they changed their lairs.
The angry beasts abandoned the caves.

31   They tell something else, but they did not write it.
They show there the holes that the serpents made.
They burrowed in rocks when they could not stay there,
but they could not make the good man afraid.

32   The good man remained in the caves alone,
serving his Lord like a good knight.
He tormented his flesh like a loyal worker.
He wanted to deserve the gain in every way.

33   He said his hours well, all the psalms,
the hymns and the canticles, all the litany.
He chanted his Psalter every day as is the custom.
He had great joy from all this suffering.

34   He loved being freed from this world.
He was very bored with the temporal life.
He very much wished that his life would be over,
so to leave this exile of worldly evil.

35   He had forgotten relatives and neighbors.
      He did not remember whether they were alive or dead,
      because all of his memory and all his cares
      were of the other world where the weary rest.

36   To the blessed man, although he was so exhausted,
      his long studying seemed little to him.
      He spent his time well; he studied hard.
      The teaching that he had did not diminish.

37   He made a good sowing; he planted good seeds.
      The land was good; he hoped for good fruit.
      The left hand did not know what the right was giving.[7]
      He followed the Gospel as God guided him.

38   The good man said numerous prayers
      for God to give peace to the erring souls;
      for Him to keep the good ones, save the afflicted,
      so that they be not deceived by the evil enemy.

39   The perfect Christian of consummate goodness,
      old in knowledge, young in age,
      was living this life in such great holiness
      that we could not tell half of his goodness.

40   Although he wanted to hide and go far away,
      his good fame had to go out to the world,
      because the Creator would not allow
      such a great luminary to hide himself thus.

41   His good fame was sounded among the Riojans;
      the news of the wilderness came to the plains.
      The sick and the healthy were moved by his fame
      to see the holy man and kiss his hands.

42   The mountain was dense, the place frightening.
      It was in many ways wild and dangerous.
      No one thought that it was delightful,
      except for the little shepherd who was determined.

43   The holy man understood that he was betrayed.
      The one who had betrayed him, he thanked him very little.
      He would have lived, if they had let him, without so much fuss;
      he had gotten used to chanting his Psalter.

---

[7] Matt. 6:3.

44   The friar was bothered by the noise.
        He was very tired of these processions.
        Because he had ordered his life in another way,
        he cared little for the honors of this world.

45   He gladly preferred to live with the serpents,
        although they are bothersome and have bitter teeth,
        than to see so many people around the caves,
        since for that reason he had left behind his relatives.

46   He saw that he could not free himself from all the fuss.
        If he wanted to live in that place,
        he had to move from the caves.
        He did not wish to break his vows willingly.

47   For that reason he had to move from the caves,
        so that no one could know about him.
        He went into the mountains to hide himself better.
        He would have his life with the beasts of the mountains.

48   The man, strengthened in his holy belief,
        had his loyalty to God alone.
        He led a hard life; he was very abstinent.
        He held great ill will toward worldly vices.

49   He went through the mountains, through the hard places,
        along the steep hills and through the brambles.
        Still today the altars are seen,
        those that he made with his holy fingers.

50   Neither snow, nor ice, nor deadly winter,
        nor weariness, nor hunger, nor bad storms,
        nor cold, nor heat, nor other such things
        could take him from among the thickets.

51   Never did the resolute man turn his face away;
        never did he lose an iota of all he had gained.
        He even improved; he was always bolder.
        The Devil was greatly scorned because of this.

52   The cursed beast made many attempts
        to disturb the life of the saintly hermit,
        but God's holy and blessed virtue
        guarded him as one protects the pupil of his eye.

53   He [the devil] made war on him in many ways.
        Wherever he went, he kept him at bay.
        He assaulted him on the road,
        but it was less valuable to him than three reeds.

54   Christ's good servant, bearing such sufferings,
        tormenting his flesh among the barren mountains,
        went to Cogolla, ever climbing,
        and the more he climbed, the more he improved.

55   Who could tell you about his holy life?
        No one could reckon or conceive it.
        No one could perceive it,
        except he himself, who suffered it.

56   The lone hermit, going through the sierra,
        climbed la Cogolla to the summit of the hill.
        There the holy man suffered a great war
        of strong storms and the living devil.

57   Here he is today; still he is not defeated.
        They say that he had built a chapel,
        and there he gave God the right to his flesh,
        tormenting it in the extreme and giving it a bad bed.

58   He wanted, if the celestial King so wished,
        since he had climbed to such a high peak,
        to take away the burden of his mortal flesh,
        which God had put off for a later day.

59   The good Christian said when he was praying,
        "Lord, King of Glory, hear my plea.
        Take me out of this suffering, this terrible passion.
        I desire your face and no other thing.

60   Since you brought me to so high a place
        from which all land is viewed to the sea,
        if you wish to concede to me your grace,
        Lord, here I would gladly wish to die.

61   If you deign to allow and grant this,
        I would not wish to return from the hill to the valley,
        but if you wish something else, and order me to stay,
        although I suffer, I await your mercy."

62   Then the good man, born at a propitious moment,
        because he would be discovered by men,
        moved from the peak; he looked for another hill,
        since he was not weary of serving God.

63   He lived forty years alone in the mountain.
        He never had the comfort or company of any person,
        nor food, nor clothes which is the greater feat.
        Never did Spain have such an excellent confessor.

64   Blessed are the mountains where the saint walked.
        Blessed are the valleys where he was hidden.
        Blessed the trees under which he stayed,
        because he was an angelic thing, full of blessing.

65   He was a holy creature, much loved by God,
        who without any sermon was inspired by God.
        He suffered such great affliction for a prolonged time.
        It is indeed clear that he was guided by God.

66   It seems a very great thing that he was guided by God.
        If not, he would not suffer such fierce cold,
        nor so many bad days, nor so much fright,
        but God was his celestial help in all this.

67   He went on fleeing from mankind as much as he could,
        eating herbs, drinking cold water,
        until he came to Moncayo,[8] having bad nights,
        always climbing well, walking and then resting.

68   We could not tell you all his sleepless nights,
        nor all the places where he stayed.
        We want to spare his harsh steps,
        to take him out of the wilderness to the populated lands.

69   The King of Heaven Who never forgets,
        Who knows everything before men think it,
        did not wish the fame of His servant's exemplary life
        to be hidden in the mountain.

70   He did not miss anything of the forty years
        in which he had such a difficult and painful life.
        God cast him into a good trap.
        It was necessary that he be caught.

71   They call it Taraçona;[9] it is a righteous city.
        It lies among three kingdoms on all their borders:
        Aragon and Castile and the third one Navarre.
        Whoever knew it would say, "This is the truth."

---

[8] Moncayo is part of the Iberian Mountains, situated between the provinces of Soria and Zaragoza. It is the eastern limit of the travels of San Millán. See Dutton, *Obra completa*, 142, v. 67c.

[9] Taraçona is a bishopric 85 kilometers from Zaragoza where the borders of Castile, Navarre, and Aragon met in the thirteenth century. Berceo adds these details. See Dutton, *Obra completa*, 144, v. 71a.

72   It would be tedious to speak to you
        of all the other nobilities of the city.
        It is our will to turn to the bishop,
        who was a wise man and lover of goodness.

73   His name was Dimio, so says the writing,
        a well-taught man, a man of discretion.
        I tell you sincerely, without any exaggeration.
        He looked for every good fortune for us all.

74   The loyal cleric, bishop of the city,
        had a certain report; he knew the secret.
        He sent him his letters, requests of friendship,
        that he make himself visible for God's sake and charity.

75   The holy confessor was in prayer,
        praying and sending prayers to the Creator.
        The order of the bishop, his lord, came to him.
        The good man had little pleasure from this.

76   The holy man began to weep constantly,
        because he was very grieved about that direction.
        The great obligation moved him, because he feared to sin
        if he disdained to be obedient.

77   With what clothing he had, he thought to move.
        I don't know how to tell you where it came from.
        He descended from the mountains where he was staying.
        He began to take the road to the city.

78   He entered the city with his head lowered,
        his beard very long, his hair shaggy.
        Everyone said, each to himself,
        such wildness was never heard of before.

79   The holy hermit was superbly received.
        The bishop considered himself very fortunate when he saw him.
        He knew very well that he was a man of good sense,
        and that he came so submissive due to obedience.

80   "Brother," said the bishop, "I thank you
        because you obeyed my command so well;
        but still I do not consider that I am well-informed,
        if I am not assured of more of your affairs.

81   For charity's sake, I beg you and I ask you as a favor,
        that you tell me your name and what you have suffered,
        where you are from, how were you converted,
        for your merit is not to be hidden."

82   Millán was disturbed by the supplications.
        He did not think to find himself in such a predicament.
        He could not rebel against such a commandment.
        He answered the bishop very completely.

83   He told him about his parents, the town they were from,
        how Saint Felices schooled him,
        the years and the time he had been in the forest,
        during that time what food had maintained him.

84   The bishop said, "Thanks be to the Celestial King
        Who revealed such a precious sign to the world.
        This is not a treasure that has a price.
        From Whom we see this, we will see even more."

85   "Brother," he said, "you have given me a very good account of your life.
        I am very well pleased by it.
        We see that you merit a good reward in heaven,
        because you have borne great penitence in this world.

86   But if you wish to bring your suffering to a good end,
        and you wish to gain greater grace from the Creator,
        I want to give you advice you ought to take.
        You should take priestly orders for God.

87   If you take priestly orders and say mass,
        you will fulfill your office in God's holy Church.
        You will save many souls, men and women.
        If you deign to believe me, you will not postpone this advice.

88   You ought to listen and believe the Gospel.
        You ought not risk capital without benefits.
        You must risk your soul for your fellow men.
        If not, God could have a complaint against you.

89   Some with advice, others with prayer,
        others with good works, some with sermons,
        you will free many souls from prison
        and for this, you will receive God's good reward."

90   The holy man replied; he was obedient.
        "Lord," he said, "I will do it gladly.
        The Omnipotent King guides our matters,
        as He guided the three kings in the East."

91   He was then shorn thoroughly.
        They shaved his beard and clothed him better.
        They gave four minor orders to the holy confessor
        and then the other orders of greater dignity.

92   When the excellent confessor was ordained,
he asked the good and holy bishop for permission,
as he would like to go, if he would grant it,
to the district of Berceo where he had been reared.

93   When he had the bishop's permission,
he left Taraçona, having received the blessing.
The honored person began his journey.
He came to Berceo, to his own birthplace.

94   When the penitent man came to Berceo,
his contemporaries did not recognize him.
Some were pleased; others were not,
but the clergy conceded a prebend to him.

95   He entered Santa Eulalia Church[10] as a prebendary.
The town council was worth more because of the good companion.
The just pastor guided his people well,
not like a mercenary nor a hireling.

96   He spread a sound doctrine among the clergy,
because he thought that some of them were doing unwise things.
He suffered every day with laymen and clerics,
and struggled to bring them to a better state.

97   He fulfilled his office well, just as the order demanded.
Even though he was a novice, he seemed a master.
Millán never tired doing God's service,
but he strove especially for alms over other things.

98   He divided among the poor as much as God gave him.
The perfect Christian did not remember tomorrow.[11]
Whomever he counseled about a complaint
returned pleased after leaving him.

99   If it pleased Christ, His divine power,
that the wheel [of Fortune] turn as it had begun,
the village of Berceo would have been very happy,
but in a short time things changed.

100   The holy man strove to please God.
He converted the wayward and fed the poor,
but among the clergy was born
the very envy that made Lucifer fall.

[10] This is the parochial church of Berceo.
[11] Matt. 6:34.

101   Some of them were touched by envy;
        the bad were corrupted by an evil poison.
        The stupid traitors accused him of crimes
        which he had never done nor ever considered.

102   They accused him of being a swindler,
        that he spent the community's money.
        The holy confessor read their hearts,
        and he was sorely grieved, because they had erred so badly.

103   He said to himself, "Alas, glorious Father,
        do what You will as a powerful king.
        I always wanted to flee this ill-fated world,
        because I knew that it was bad and dangerous.

104   Lord, I could not win this from You.
        I had to return to it for my sins.
        Instead of serving You, I brought You great grief,
        when because of me men have to sin.

105   Lord, if You wish, and I very much desire,
        to live alone, as I was accustomed to live.
        I would gladly return to the hermitage,
        because I am a great annoyance to this clergy."

106   The blessed priest and just priest
        left Santa Eulalia, where he was almsgiver.
        He left in secret, all alone and solitary.
        He returned to the caves where he had first dwelt.

107   To fulfil his office, he made his chapel there.
        Near the chapel, he constructed his cell.
        Although his house was narrow and very small,
        it was very full of valuable treasure.

108   Gentlemen, thanks be to God, we have told you
        as much as we know of his holy suffering
        and of his wanderings, as we have read them.
        For now, if you please, it is time that we rest.

Book II

The living miracles and death of St. Millán

109   Gentlemen, if you still would listen to me,
       the second little book is to be recited.
       I would tell you some few miracles
       that God deigned to show to the world through him.

110   Many and countless they are, but if God gives us life,
       we will tell you a goodly number of them.
       Those that happened after he left (Berceo)
       and before his soul parted from his flesh.

111   Beelzebub, he who deceived Adam,
       considered himself insulted by this great man
       because he had attacked him many times,
       but he always left with his plan routed.

112   The cursed beast, full of trickery,
       took on the form and flesh of a human being.
       He stopped in front of him in a narrow path
       telling him strong and frightening words.

113   "Millán," said the demon, "you have a bad habit.
       You are very mercurial; you are not firm.
       In all your words you seem to be very mild,
       but your deeds embitter more than strong black soot.

114   When you first came to this place,
       you did not like it and wanted to leave.
       You entered the woods to make war on me.
       You said you never wanted to return to town.

115   Finally, when you were near death,
       you had a strong desire to go back to town.
       You returned to Berceo, but you stayed a short time.
       You pleased the convent very little with your reputation.

116   You left Santa Eulalia due to a great fickleness.
       You did not thank them on leaving and
       yet now you want to inhabit another place.
       I would consider myself an imbecile if I agreed to this.

117   I will tell you something, since I have thought about it:
       let us both fight for who will have this house.
       The loser leaves it, as is just, and
       let the other be at peace, the war thus decided."

118   As soon as the contaminated beast said this,
       he tried to lay a malignant hand on the holy man.
       He grappled him to trip him up,
       but it did not avail him at all.

119   The excellent confessor said his prayer,
       "Lord, Who for Your servants deigned to suffer the passion,
       defend me today from this very strong beast.
       Let him be conquered and me left unharmed."

120   As soon as San Millán had finished his prayer,
       the devil lost all his strength.
       His great pride had fallen in the dust
       so that he had gained nothing from his coming.

121   He raised great dust, a fierce whirlwind.
       He fled badly broken, saying, "Ay, wretched me!
       I have always heard it said, and it happened to me,
       that a bad day dawned for him who has a bad neighbor."

122   He fled and exiled himself to a foreign land.
       The excellent confessor remained on his mountain.
       While the world lives and Spain endures,
       this good deed will always be told.

123   The good champion, in spite of his victory,
       did not give way to any pride in himself.
       He maintained his course and remembered well
       so that the transitory life might not deceive him.

124   He served the Creator with the twenty nails
       of his hands and his feet,[12] with his mouth and his ears.
       He kept himself from the devil, giving him no access,
       since because of that one, the sheep left the Father.

125   This struggle could not be so hidden
       that it was not quickly discovered by the people.
       The people were completely amazed
       that the good man did such a singular thing.

---

[12] This is an expression meaning how hard San Millán worked. Cf. "Milagros", quatrain 331.

126   There was in that land a very unfortunate monk.
       He lay a long time and was very afflicted.
       He had his stomach so swollen by his humors[13]
       that they thought he would soon be dead.

127   They called the sick man Armentero.
       The doctors did not help him one iota.
       A messenger told him news about this holy man
       and that he would cure him as he had been before.

128   The sick man's relatives took him,
       because they were upset by his long affliction.
       They brought him to the priest about whom they were speaking so much,
       because they understood that his suffering would end there.

129   The blessed man, full of holiness,
       when he saw this man so gravely ill,
       had pity on him since he was merciful,
       and prayed to God for him with all his will.

130   After the perfect Christian made the sign of the cross
       with his holy hand over the swelling,
       the sickness fled from the body immediately.
       The sick man returned home completely cured.

131   When Armentero was cured in this way,
       the wonderful news went throughout the land.
       Everyone blessed God, Lord and perfect King,
       because He gave them such a father of such noble feeling.

132   Among his miracles is the third one.
       We want to tell you about a paralytic.
       She was all crippled and had no control.
       She lay prostrate on her bed because she could not walk.

133   The people recounted his good reputation,
       and her relatives brought the sick lady there.
       They brought her to the priest of excellent manners,
       the one who threw out the devil and conquered the serpents.

134   The sick, suffering lady was placed at the door.
       She was very exhausted from sickness and suffering.
       The poor woman lay prostrate on the ground,
       because she could not stand up at all.

---

[13] The four humors of the body: blood, yellow bile, phlegm, and black bile in the right proportions were necessary to maintain good health according to medieval medicine.

135   The blessed man came out of his dwelling.
        He saw this sick woman, despairing of life.
        "Creator," he said, "help the poor suffering lady.
        Take away this trouble by which she is hobbled."

136   As soon as he had prayed to God with great devotion,
        he extended his holy hand and gave her his blessing.
        The sick lady was freed from her affliction.
        She returned home cured without any lesions.

137   According to what we have read in his holy life,
        this cured woman was called Barbara.
        They say she was born in the region of Amaya;[14]
        Braulio, who wrote the truth, recounts this.

138   In that same land of that *peña real*,
        there was a native of the place who was crippled.
        Since her childhood, she did not control her feet.
        She could not go from her bed to the corral for a thousand marks.

139   This sick lady heard the sweet news,
        how this monk had cured so many.
        The wretched one shouted loudly,
        saying that she wanted to touch his clothes.

140   She said that if she could touch his clothes,
        according to her belief, she would be immediately cured.[15]
        She begged that they put her at his feet,
        since she would not need help on her return.

141   The men then took the young woman,
        who was placed and carefully arranged in a small wagon.
        They went with her; they crossed Castile
        and came to the door of the cell of so much merit.

142   As luck would have it, they found the door locked,
        but the sick, suffering lady shouted very loudly,
        demanding the father, lord of the dwelling
        in whom God had put so much gifted virtue.

143   The holy confessor had a habit,
        that all Lent, the most important one,
        not to talk to anyone or go out to work
        until the end of holy Easter.

---

[14] A town in the district of Villadiego (Burgos), some 60 kilometers northwest of the capital.
[15] Matt. 9:21, 14:36; Mark 5:28, 6:56; Luke 8:44.

144   In addition, at this time, the good immured one
was living like a recluse in his closed-up cave.
A minister served him who had been sacredly indoctrinated,
giving him food through a small hole.

145   The sick lady was brought at this very time.
She shed many tears, lying at the door,
because she saw the holy devout man in his struggle
eating bread and water, not eel and trout.

146   The wretched one had come to this hole.
"Sir," she said, "and father, who are locked up,
save this wretched one, this anguished body,
a body which is dispossessed of its feet.

147   If you do not wish to come out, or you cannot do so,
send me the staff that you usually carry.
If I could look at or touch it,
I am certain to be immediately cured."

148   The good man was moved by her pain and his pity.
He prayed to God for her with all his might.
He sent her the staff, it was of great holiness,
on which he had leaned with great weariness.

149   When the poor, sick lady saw the staff,
she considered herself richer than a queen.
She said, "Now I see clearly the medicine
which will cure me with divine grace."

150   She immediately seized the staff; she began to kiss it,
not one time but many; she was not to blame.
Although they asked her for it, she did not want to release it.
Her eyes did not stop crying for a minute.

151   The holy prayer that San Millán said
and the holy belief that was surging in her
pierced the sky where the Lord,
in Whose hands all remedy lies, was.

152   For the love of the good servant, who He loved very much,
God granted the lady what she requested.
He took away the trouble that imprisoned her.
Blessed be the vessel from whence such virtue flowed.

153   Afterward the young woman was happy and pleased.
She took leave of the doctor who had cured her
and returned to her land, having received the blessing,
blessing God and his sacred virtue.

154   Sicorio, a good man, rich and worthy,
         had a servant who did his bidding.
         She lost her vision, for which he was troubled,
         because he felt the lack of her good service.

155   He sent her to the doctor who cured others,
         since his belief was such that he could cure her.
         The blind girl was led; she could not see.
         She came to the sanctuary where she hoped for light.

156   When San Millán saw her, he was grieved.
         He prayed to the Creator that He give her sight.
         When the holy confessor had prayed,
         her vision was clearer than ever before.

157   Scarcely had San Millán achieved this,
         when they brought a cleric possessed by the devil.
         He was a deacon ordained by the bishop.
         He was humiliated by his companions.

158   The devil made him say crazy things:
         besides the words, he did other dirty things.
         The sickness had many bad characteristics,
         whence the sick one made many faces.

159   The holy man saw a very fierce devil.
         He turned to God and said, "Oh, glorious King,
         have pity on this cleric, since You are merciful,
         so that he not dwell with such an angry host."

160   The devil could not suffer the prayer.
         In total confusion he left the deacon.
         Having received the blessing, the cleric
         returned to his church all safe and sound.

161   Tüencio was the name of a famous man,
         a man of good manners who had good sense.
         He had a very bad problem, since one of his beloved slaves
         was powerfully oppressed by the devil.

162   This sick man was carried to the servant of God.
         Tüencio sent him provided with all necessities.
         When San Millán saw him, he received him willingly.
         He had great compassion for him, since he had suffered so.

163   He prayed to God for him as was his custom.
         The demons complained in a strange way,
         because the holy prayer made with a sincere purpose
         made them burn hotter than a huge bonfire.

164   He turned and asked them how many they were,
        because he wanted to know their names and the details;
        however, only one of them was to respond to him.
        He told the whole truth, which was not to his liking.

165   He said to him, "There are five of us who live here.
        We have these names; we serve this master.
        We have been together here a long time,
        but we fear that you are to move us."

166   The good man said, "It is a very unjust thing
        to have such bad guests in such a good dwelling.
        This is a house of God, anointed with holy oil.
        It is bad that it has been violated for so long."

167   He put his gifted hand on the sick man;
        he made the sign of the cross on his forehead in the smoothest place.
        The evil group came forth all confounded
        and Tüencio's slave was cured.

168   He told him how to live and not to seek folly.
        He gave him his blessing and he went on his way.
        The good man remained in his hermitage,
        serving Him who was born of the Virgin Mary.

169   Later they brought him another man possessed,
        a slave of Eugenio, a worthy man.
        He fell at the feet of the honored confessor,
        begging for advice, because he was battered.

170   Millán prayed to the spiritual Father for him.
        He made the holy sign of the cross on his forehead.
        The sick man was cured, purged of the evil,
        and praising God he returned cured to his home.

171   A lady, Proseria, was possessed.
        She was very harassed by two strong demons.
        She was married in the church to a good husband.
        Alas, this good man had this grievous defect.

172   The good man's name was Nepocïano.
        He had a twofold demon and therefore was not healthy.
        They assaulted both of them daily and so
        they lived in great suffering all year round.

173   All these demons had certain mannerisms.
        They acted like brothers, making certain gestures.
        They each did the same thing, taking turns,
        and were companions in all their behavior.

174   They went to the confessor, a native of Berceo,
       the one who conquered Beelzebub in the tourney.
       He understood at once that they were agitated
       and saw that they were living in hopes of being cured.

175   He understood how the demons were double
       and how they appeared to be contaminated filth.
       He prayed to the King of Heaven to pardon their sins
       which helped these people who were so battered.

176   As soon as the man from Cogolla completed his prayer,
       the cure was immediately granted by God.
       Proseria was healed; Nepocïano cured.
       God give us the grace of this mass-singer.

177   Another possessed woman was Colomba,
       the daughter of Máximo; this is a proven truth.
       She endured great suffering and lived a grievous life.
       If death would come to her, she would consider herself fortunate.

178   The lady was carried to the holy monastery and
       she told her suffering to the esteemed confessor.
       She begged him to chant the Psalter for her
       so as to rid her of this terrible mortification.

179   The good man put on his clerical robes,
       as the law requires for saying mass.
       He said the holy mass to gain her cure,
       because he so wished to send her away healed.

180   When San Millán had finished the mass,
       the evil enemy left the body.
       He gave her his blessing with his holy hand
       and sent her away all cured of the evil.

181   There was a noble senator from Parpalinas;[16]
       he was called Onorio, a man of great worth.
       He suffered a great irritation: you never saw a greater one.
       Only mentioning it to you gives my mouth a bad taste.

182   In the house of this potentate was living
       a malignant demon, full of malice.
       He caused disgusting filth in the dwelling;
       he considered it as his own property.

---

[16] According to Dutton this is really an unidentified village: *Obra completa*, 172, v. 181a.

183   When Onorio wanted to carve his roast
        or eat any type of food,
        the cursed beast, full of deviltry,
        threw defecation and atrocities on it.

184   When he wanted to drink water or wine,
        the traitorous neighbor poured it out.
        He made the house stink worse than a bad poison.
        He gave them more grief than bailiffs or judges (constables).

185   He [Onorio] could not find a way or any advice
        so that he could throw him out of his house.
        They lived in this distress, which you have heard me tell,
        and they were just about to be ruined.

186   The good man, don Onorio, thought of a good plan,
        to go on pilgrimage to the holy oratory
        and to pray to the holy man, patron of the territory,
        in whom all found health and audience.

187   He came to the holy father, completing his pilgrimage, and
        entered the hermitage on his knees.
        He told him his concerns and in what tribulation he was living,
        begging him to help him for God's sake and Saint Mary's.

188   The holy man understood the problem and how to solve it.
        Leaning on his staff, he started the journey.
        He did not want to ride on an animal, even though he was thin,
        since he had in such matters a ready will.

189   The excellent man entered Parpalinas, and,
        as soon as he arrived, he gave them his sermon.
        He ordered all those of that house
        to keep a three-day fast with great affliction.

190   The holy commandment was strictly observed.
        Everyone ate bread and water and wore hairshirts.
        The demon understood that all this activity
        was because of his afflictions and evil coming.

191   When the three days were past and the fast completed,
        the honored confessor sang mass.
        The office sung, he blessed the salt and the water
        and the devil was very grieved at these doings.

192   He thought about hiding in some attic
        and not making anyone angry at lunch or at dinner.
        Millán would go on his way to observe Lent and
        then he would take control and double their affliction.

193   San Millán, dressed in his sacred robes and
        sprinkling the water with his holy hands,
        went to all the rooms of the house, and the upper level,
        praying and saying the litany and psalms.

194   The traitorous guest, in spite of lying hidden,
        came out of his hiding place unwillingly.
        The proven traitor stood there very stubbornly
        saying that such tricks did not worry him.

195   The strong man, who knew him well,
        said that his stubbornness would not help him.
        He began to afflict him as much as he could
        because he was sure that God would not fail him.

196   The filthy traitor, when he saw himself so harassed,
        began to throw stones at the excellent confessor.
        The false perjurer thought he could scare him,
        but the servant of Christ worried not.

197   He harassed him with psalms and the litany.
        The bad neighbor came out; he had to go on his way.
        He did a great villainy at his exit.
        I cannot tell you what it was because it would shame me so.

198   Onorio's house, that had been scorned
        by all that filth, was completely recovered.
        The blessed priest of excellent life
        returned to his church having won the battle.

199   I want to speak to you about his salvation
        and how God wished to defend and protect him,
        so that you will always know how to tell and recount
        how much good faith can help mankind.

200   Many sick people with grave illnesses came
        to the blessed holy house of the father.
        He willingly held novenas for them and
        God did them mercy and charity for this.

201   The good man lay with the possessed,
        those who had rabid and irate demons.
        He slept with both eyes shut; he was as free from fear
        as if guarded by a thousand men.

202   Many times the evil ones tried to scorn him.
        They made bad faces to frighten him,
        but their efforts to dispute or plot against him
        did him not a straw's worth of harm.

203   The perfidious devils went to hold a council
       concerning these matters, the evil creatures,
       to set up a meeting and constitution
       to destroy this saint with some speeches.

204   When they were together, they discussed their order,
       how to reorganize the vices that they had forgotten:
       those of deceiving the souls of good Christians and of
       laymen and clerics, those yet to marry and the married ones.

205   Although they mentioned many other matters,
       they were offended by this sole matter.
       They said that this watchman had dishonored them
       and they considered themselves dead and beheaded.

206   They were so upset about this that they began to shout
       that in another time he had conquered them in Cogolla.
       If by such a vile man they remained scorned,
       it would have been better that they had not been born.

207   The one who had fought with him in San Pelayo[17] said,
       "Listen to me, if you don't faint,
       see in what condition I have my shoulders and ribs;
       never had we had such a bad trial."

208   The five that he had taken out of Tüencio's slave
       had to break the silence with their misfortune.
       They said, "Companions, your suffering
       in comparison with ours has no worth nor merit."

209   Onorio's guest, who was badly persecuted,
       with his hand on his cheek was complaining of his bad fate.
       He said that he would not go out because of his shame,
       if the pride of Millán was not avenged.

210   They had to deal with this calumny so much
       that they could not deal with any other problem.
       But they did not draw up a judgment or opinion,
       because they could not control the bitter conflict.

211   One of the plaintiffs stood up in their midst.
       He made bad signs and traitorous gestures.
       "Listen to me, council," he said; "we are all disgraced;
       if it were not for such a vile man, we would not be so tearful.

---

[17] A hermitage no longer in existence where San Millán had fought with the devil.
See Dutton, *Obra completa*, 178, v. 207a.

212   But I have a plan: I think it makes good sense.
         At dusk let us all join together,
         let us take burning torches in hand
         and set fire to the bed where he lies asleep.

213   If we attacked him when he was awake,
         when he heard us, he would get reinforcements.
         Believe me, council, do what I command
         because we will never avenge ourselves by crying."

214   This seemed to all a very good plan.
         The filthy council was then dispersed.
         They all spread out through the valley
         to look for dried sheaves or old bushes.

215   When the good man had his eyes well shut,
         the false believers followed their plan
         and then with burning torches they came,
         all prepared to burn the holy man.

216   Before they applied the burning wood to the bed,
         the flames turned backward like needles
         that burned their beards and their chins.
         All their plans turned awry.

217   The play of the flames reached their teeth;
         each one accused the other.
         They each believed that the other was burning them
         and each one cursed the other.

218   This belief was held by as many as came there.
         They fell into great discord;
         devoid of goodness and full of disbelief,
         they behaved badly each to the other.

219   They began to hit each other with zeal;
         neither pardoned the other.
         There was great dissension among the wretched.
         In Babylon there had not been greater confusion.[18]

220   They wounded each other in the face with great blows from fiery brands.
         Their eyebrows were bloody and burned
         and their foreheads badly beaten, their beards singed.
         You never saw drunks so badly tousled.

---

[18] That is, the Tower of Babel.

221   After they had thrown the fiery brands,
        they pulled out each other's hair by the headful
        giving each other spur prods and strong spikes.
        They set their minds to do all sorts of evilness.

222   The excellent confessor, servant of the Creator,
        raised his head; he looked all around.
        He saw the revolt; he understood the fervor.
        He almost laughed out loud from such delight.

223   He gave thanks to the Son of the Glorious Virgin,
        who was born of His wife[19] to save the world.
        Because he understood that such a thing came about through Him
        and that he alone could not harm such a host.

224   The good man continued in his custom,
        healing the sick as he was accustomed to do.
        The demons fled; they left the place.
        They could never more avenge their indignation.

225   Every day the holy man's expenses increased.
        The poor people followed him to ask for rations.
        He wanted to build a granary for this purpose,
        for the benefit of the wretched ones, not for any other reason.

226   He searched for good wood that he needed.
        He asked for the workers; he set the daily pay.
        They measured the beams as they had to be
        so that they could not make a mistake.

227   They aligned the beams; they thought about the rough-hewing.
        What was extra long, they cut off.
        Then they cemented the joints and sealed the seated stones.
        They received a good salary and justified it well.

228   When they had rough-hewn all the wood,
        one beam came out one full cubit short.
        The workmen stopped, very disconcerted,
        because they understood that they had been very mistaken.

---

[19] There must be a corruption of the text here because all the versions I have seen say, "Rendió gracias al Fijo de la Virgen Gloriosa, / qe por salvar el mundo nació de su esposa." A modernized Spanish edition, Amancio Bolaño e Isla, *Milagros de Nuestra Señora, Vida de Santo Domingo de Silos, Vida de San Millán de la Cogolla, Vida de Santa Oria, Martirio de San Lorenzo* (México: Editorial Porrúa, 1988), 368, gives the following translation of the Old Spanish:, "Dio gracias a Cristo nuestro Señor, que, por / salvar al mundo, nació de la Virgen María," (He gave thanks to Christ, our Lord, who, to save the world was born of the Virgin Mary), which makes perfect sense.

229   While all the carpenters were contemplating this,
        the excellent confessor came out of his chapel.
        He saw them so disconcerted, their skin pale.
        He understood that there was some problem.

230   They told him the worry they had,
        that one of the beams had come out short.
        He said, "Be strong, do not bemoan this.
        God will help us with His wondrous power.

231   Friends, go to eat; it is time for lunch.
        We will go to the church to chant our hours
        to the King of Heaven, Who deigned to create us;
        He alone can quickly send us help."

232   The whole company went to eat lunch right then
        and the excellent confessor began to pray.
        We cannot know what he said or did not say,
        but just at the right time he resolved the problem.

233   He and they, after they had eaten, came out of the church.
        It was little satisfying since they were so worried.
        They did not know what remedy they could find,
        except to go to the woods to find another beam.

234   One of the workmen went to measure the beam,
        to see how much was lacking, what was needed to complete it.
        He found it was more than the right measure,
        indeed a full palm longer; I am not lying to you.

235   They had to be certain of this;
        then they could not have been happier.
        They said that the holy man was very powerful,
        because God wished to help them so quickly.

236   The good man said to them, "Don't say a word;
        for love of yourselves, do not repeat it.
        The words that you said, forget them completely,
        since you recovered what was lost."

237   The extra palm's length was cut off the beam.
        It was kept as a relic in a enclosed place, and
        many very good miracles happened due to this wood
        that cured very twisted bodies and very possessed souls.

238   The carpenters completed the granary with God's help.
        The excellent confessor paid them their money, and
        the workers went on their way to their homes.
        He remained with the poor and with his companions.

239   One day, by chance, many poor people came
hungry and all very much in need of clothing.
They asked the good man for clothes with much insistence,
but he had nothing to give them and was greatly anguished by this.

240   Since he had nothing else, he took the cape that he wore
over the sleeves of the tunic in which he was dressed.
He gave this to the poor, since he had nothing else.
If he had had personal funds, he would not have hidden them.

241   There was among them a very impertinent person;
he tried to flee with the cape; he did so unjustly.
But it would have been better for him if he had stayed,
because there justice ruled and he paid for the loan.

242   When the other companions learned this,
they struck him with their shepherd's staffs.
They punished him justly for the evil thing he did to them.
I consider that they did not do him any injustice.

243   It was very clear that God loved him
when He gave him such justice against the evil man.
In addition, the good example is like that of Saint Martin,
who shared the cape he wore with the poor man.

244   A short time later, a great many people came,
a very numerous group of both sick and healthy,
to see the holy man for whom the Cogollan woods
were famous, and to kiss his hands.

245   Afterwards, they were troubled, because it was so hot,
and they drank a great deal of wine from very mature grapes.
The vassal of Christ was in a tight spot,
because he had very little wine, just a small measure.

246   The father of the poor, the strong man,
steadfast in the face of misfortunes, beloved by God,
ordered that the people be seated in the meadow,
and be given the wine he had left over.

247   The people sat down; they brought the wine
which easily filled a small cooking pot.
The good man ordered his steward
not to bypass either rich or poor.

248   He blessed the glasses with his holy hand,
and the good cupbearer gave them the wine.
There was not large or small or sick or healthy
who did not have plenty of wine.

249   Everyone was happy and pleased,
        and they all marveled at the abundance.
        They saw that it was virtue that had fed them,
        for if not, not even thirty would have been satisfied.

250   The perfect charity that was in San Millán
        and the holy belief that is its companion:
        these things made the wine increase in this way.
        Where these things are joined, food is never lacking.

251   O holy mother Charity, how excellent you are!
        Your name is so sweet, your grace so elegant.
        You never close your door, nor do you cast aside any thing.
        Never do you grimace, even if the undertaking is costly.

252   So noble this virtue, so great this grace that
        he, with so little wine, satisfied so many.
        It came from the woods, it echoed through the countryside,
        all saying that never before was such a man born in Spain.

253   The poor people came, each from his place.
        They went to dwell with the good man
        and took sound advice to avoid hard labor,
        because they believed that he could maintain them without funds.

254   One day it happened that he had nothing to give them.
        He could not have greater grief in this world.
        He asked the key-keeper to be absolutely sure,
        but he did not offer any worthwhile help.

255   San Millán scolded him because he saw that he had erred.
        He told him that he was dimwitted and lacking in faith,
        because He who in the Virgin was made incarnate for us,
        He would give us counsel, since He is a father who succors.

256   Having said this, a short time later,
        a great quantity of food came to the excellent man.
        His friend Onorio, whom he had freed from great tribulation,
        gave it to him as a gift.

257   He received the food and gave thanks to God.
        He gave food to the people who were insistent.
        The holy man received many such gifts,
        but he shared them immediately so that they would not become rancid.

258   Onorio's gift was so very generous
        that a long time passed before it was used up.
        The steward himself was amazed,
        and he knew that he had erred when he had doubted.

259   If we paid attention, both these miracles
       seem very similar; they were very convenient.
       A little wine abundantly served many people,
       and now the food increased among the eaters.

260   The good man was gravely weakened;
       with old age he had become weak.
       Some holy women of perfect understanding
       served him in his needs like a beloved father.

261   They sat as his feet, hearing his wisdom.
       They willingly shared their food with the poor.
       All had placed their hearts firmly in God,
       for which the devil had sharp pains and stomach cramps.

262   The good man sat together with them,
       speaking and telling them many good deeds.
       The mortal enemy full of evil tricks
       pondered how to seek a way to avenge his anger.

263   The cursed beast climbed on his back.
       He gave the good man a crazy response:
       "Millán," he said, "no one has ever done
       anything so contemptible as you.

264   Your whole life's work is turned into something else.
       You sport with the ladies day and night.
       Although I said nothing, I understood very well
       that your hypocrisy would end up like this.

265   Since now I see what I wanted to see,
       I would not give a jot for all your fasts.
       The merit of gentility lies in esteem
       that you have turned into pure knavery."

266   The blessed man of miserable life
       knew indeed who it was and did not give it a thought.
       He answered him so strongly and so irately
       that it was as if he had given him a drubbing:

267   "You lie, false traitor, you do not speak the truth.
       You say falsehoods, as is your custom.
       You and your cohorts ought to know me
       and not bring false crimes against me.

268   You gained very little when you fought with me.
       My friend Onorio scorned you greatly.
       When you tried to burn me, you did not like the result,
       and you will carry the shame with you as long as you live.

269   The One who has given me justice from you so many times,
Who made you give yourselves thrusts with burning brands,
He will be the custodian of this wretched flesh.
Your malicious words cannot harm me."

270   The demon was confounded at these words.
He never thought he would fall into such a predicament.
He left the good man, having lost his strength,
and no longer wanted to attack him for anything.

271   The excellent confessor, who was very generous,
had a mule as a beast of burden.
Turibio and Simpronio had a bad time,
and, due to their evil, they moved it from the Varga pasture.

272   The good man did not have it to ride,
but rather to carry wood for the poor.
The stupid men were blinded by greed and
at an unlucky moment they went to steal the mule.

273   They were hardly away from the monastery,
when they were confounded for their grave sins.
Each of them had one eye put out,
so that a nut would fit in the hole.

274   They returned to the good man in spite of their shame.
Very embarrassed, they returned the animal to him
and begged him for mercy on bended knee.
He gave them back their eyes that had been damaged.

275   The holy man spoke to them harshly:
"Friends, you acted with pride and insanity.
The Creator was angered by your deed
and wanted to punish your insolence.

276   I hope that you understand how lucky you were to have escaped,
because you deserved to be hanged.
But it is better to save you from your sins with one eye
than to see yourselves condemned to hell with both eyes.[20]

277   Go to your homes, do your penitence, and
take care not to ever fall into such sin again.
Since God gave you such a just sentence,
you should, friends, suffer in patience."

---

[20] Matt. 5:29, 18:9; Mark 9:47.

278   They went on their way, each to his house.
        Millán sold the beast, because he no longer wanted to have it.
        He immediately used the money for the poor,
        the lame, and the crippled, who had need of it.

279   The perfect man whom God loved so much
        was old in days: in years he was approaching one hundred.
        He heard the news that God sent to him and understood
        that all his suffering would end in one year.

280   The good man was pleased with this good news.
        Never had he heard a better message in this world.
        He returned to his devotion, even though he was tired, and
        led as strenuous a life as when he was middle-aged.

281   Martyring his body, maintaining a rigorous life,
        he understood that Cantabria[21] had failed God, and
        if it did not improve, it would be destroyed
        because God was angry; He hated it.

282   He left the monastery and went to preach to them.
        His suffering did not ail him when he saved souls.
        They refused to believe and to listen, and
        in the end they had to pay for this dearly.

283   In council he told them a mighty prophecy,
        that if they refused to stop their madness,
        the day was approaching when they would all be destroyed,
        because they were drunk with heresy.

284   A stupid knight, abandoned by God,
        named Abundancio, spoke very badly.
        He said to him, "Crazy, forgetful old man,
        you have returned to the understanding of a child."

285   He was villainous and proud, badly behaved.
        He said ugly, ill-seeming words to him.
        His great error grieved the good man, who
        turned to him and gave him a strong judgment.

286   "Know, knight, this will be true.
        I want to reveal an important secret to you.
        Foreign armies are coming to besiege this city,
        and they will give me justice for your maliciousness.

---

[21] See Dutton, *Obra completa*, 2nd ed., Chap. IX, 2 (26), 225–26. The vestiges of Cantabria can still be seen on a hill of the same name that separates La Rioja from Navarra.

287   On going out to the tournament, you will be in the front lines, and
        no matter how many go there, you will be the first to die.
        They will destroy the town; the heights will be worthless:
        neither infantrymen nor knight will remain in it."

288   Having spoken the prophecy, the good preacher
        returned to his church to serve the Creator.
        Cantabria remained in its bad error, but
        if they had believed Millán, they would have done much better.

289   A few days hence, due to their heinous sins,
        Leovigildo[22] came with his mighty army
        and challenged Cantabria and all its inhabitants.
        He attacked them with his mail-coated soldiers.

290   He began to fight with bravery,
        breaking down the doors to get to the people.
        He gave them a bad gift not a tasty present,
        which is what such a disobedient people deserved.

291   Those of the town came out to fight them,
        Abundancio the first in order to have the first blows,
        but he could not guard himself from the bad charge,
        and he was the first of all to die.

292   Then all the others were thwarted,
        the town destroyed, and the walls brought down.
        Never again were they rebuilt or restored,
        although three large towers still stand there.

293   They had to see that they could not escape
        the prophecy that San Millán had given.
        Indeed, they had a bad life, because they died a bad death.
        The arrogant reply had cost them dearly.

294   The blessed body, martyred willingly,
        true prophet, God's loyal worker,
        was indeed certain that he would end his suffering,
        because in that month he was near his last days.

295   Waiting for the time when the orders would come,
        his side began to pain him a little.
        His whole body was very infirm, and
        he understood that the course of his life had ended.

---

[22] Leovigildo (568–586) was the last Arian Visigothic king to rule Spain.

296   He called his companions together when he saw himself ailing:
Anselmo, a good man with whom he had been reared,
other holy disciples not of little worth,
and in a short time a great council had gathered.

297   Everyone saw that he wanted to pass from this life.
They were very grieved; they mourned his death, and
due to their sorrow they could not read or pray,
because they were losing this counsel that they could never again find.

298   The excellent confessor, always very reasonable,
did not lose his judgment in spite of his pains.
He instructed his disciples, an honored company,
how to maintain themselves when he had departed.

299   He told them the hour when his soul would leave:
"Friends, you do see that I want to die;
the hour has come: I want to say good-bye to you
gracefully and leave this world."

300   Then he raised his gifted hand
and blessed them all with his blessed mouth.
He commended them to God, to the Glorious Virgin,
to keep them safe from danger.

301   He crossed himself to fulfill his duty.
He extended both his palms, joining them prudently.
He closed his eyes without any trouble and
rendered his soul to God, having completed his passage.

302   Close at hand were the angels, who received his soul at once.
Singing great praises, they carried it on high and
offered it to God in great processions, and
with him all the saints said the solemn liturgy.

303   All the confessors were very joyous
to have such a man among them.
They said that their brotherhood was better
and wished that three like him would come every day.

304   The holy patriarchs, venerable men,
and all the prophets of mysterious words,
were very joyous, singing holy songs.
All did him honor with great processions.

305   All twelve apostles, perfect princes,
who were advocates of Christ's law,
considered that they were very honored to have such a noble guest.
They sang sweet and modulated chants and liturgies.

306   The chorus of martyrs who died for Christ,
        who to save their souls despised their flesh,
        made a procession in their white amices.
        The honors given to him could not be calculated.

307   The joy of the virgins, who could estimate it?
        They came to visit him with their golden crowns and
        could not be more joyous nor show it.
        They concentrated all their devotion on honoring him greatly.

308   The King of Heaven and His glorious Mother
        gave him a rich throne and a beautiful crown,
        in heaven and on earth, a marvelous honor
        for which he is held in the highest renown.

309   May his soul remain with God: let us turn to his body.
        Let us not abandon such wonderful relics.
        Let us give him burial and let us relate his miracles
        that were shown there as we read.

310   His holy disciples whom he had nurtured,
        men of holy life, sane and very retentive,
        were very sorrowful near the saintly body,
        pouring forth tears and heaving sighs.

311   Although they were so grieved and so very sad,
        they saw another endeavor from which they had great joy.
        They knew that it was something of such great authority
        and that it would be the luminary of the whole province.

312   Anselm, his servant, excellent colleague,
        with many good and very religious men
        prepared the body of the worthy man
        to give him burial and make a procession for him.

313   The stone was cut to the length of the body,
        in width and length measured to the right size,
        but, as we believe, it had been wrought earlier,
        as he himself, while alive, had prepared it.

314   The body was bathed and dressed in its robes,
        enclosed in the timbers, nailed carefully shut.
        It was put in the tomb with great reverence,
        having been loyally served with all the mystery.

315   The King of Heaven, blessed Lord,
        to honor the good body of His good confessor,
        showed many miracles at this work. .
        I could not tell them much better.

316   Many possessed were cured at the sepulcher.
Those who were deprived of their eyes saw.
The lame and crippled returned cured, and
all the sick found marvelous help.

317   Gentlemen and friends, as many as we are here,
we must adore the excellent confessor.
What we had promised you, we have fulfilled,
because the second book is here ended.

318   We have told you of his excellent life,
until his soul was parted from his flesh;
but still the whole story is not complete,
because afterward his memory was even brighter.

319   Thereafter the honored confessor accomplished virtues
for which he acquired great fame, more than he had already won.
His monastery was richly endowed, and
there God is served and San Millán renowned.

BOOK III

San Millán's Posthumous Miracles and Vows

320   Gentlemen, I still want to treat this matter.
With him still guiding me, I want to talk to you about him.
The material is notable about this worthy man
and it would be a great discredit [to him] to shorten it.

321   The third little book that we must tell
is of precious miracles, delightful to hear.
If it please you and you will permit me,
I would prefer not to take leave of you so quickly.

322   It was rapidly told throughout the land
that the holy man had passed from this world;
that he was proven a most perfect saint
and that he had cured many sick people since his death.

323   In a village there were two very unfortunate blind men.
They were living in great misery, lacking everything.
They heard this news, these good announcements,
and had great faith that they would be restored to sight.

324   Both left their homes with their guides.
        They went on their way leaning on their canes.
        The two unfortunate men came to the tomb
        but they were happy in their hearts.

325   They shouted, as this was their nature:
        "Lord," they said, "help us, hear our complaint.
        Understand our need, our grave misfortune,
        how we forever live in dark twilight.

326   Sir, who help so much, for whom God did so much,
        you who are both health and protection in all places,
        pray to the holy Father for these sinners,
        that He deign to end our long lament.

327   Sir, if you do not cure us, we will never leave here.
        Here we will remain, if we are to go as we came.
        Father, if you wish it, we truly believe
        that we will return successful in our petition."

328   The voices of the blind men were heard by the Creator.
        Their sight returned to them at once.
        Due to the holy virtue, the darkness fled
        and the deformed returned to perfect form.

329   When their sight returned, they were so unaccustomed to seeing
        that they were suddenly afraid.
        The whole day they were stunned
        and could not regain consciousness at all.

330   They came to after the entire day had passed.
        They saw that their petition had ended favorably
        and gave thanks to God and to the honored man.
        They returned to their homes, not needing their guides.

331   In front of the excellent body whom God loved very much
        was hung a lamp which was always lit.
        It was never without oil day or night
        except when the sacristan changed the wick.

332   One time it happened on one evening —
        it was the vigil of Saint John —
        that those of the convent had no oil;
        they did not have even the smallest drop to burn.

333   The sacristan had gravely erred.
        He was very upset, because he was without any oil.
        He could not buy or borrow any, and
        it grieved him that the tomb was not lit.

334   The King of Heaven, of perfect power,
who had eternal affection for His servants,
saw this need, because He is merciful,
and sent them very generous help.

335   When night came, the hour to rest,
the sacristan entered to look at the tomb.
He saw the lamp burning before the altar
full of the best oil which he did not usually buy.

336   The good man was astonished
seeing the light so clear, the oil so pure.
He understood that it was not bought from peddlers
but that God had sent it from Heaven.

337   They tolled the bells; they made a great sound.
The clerics sang lauds to the Creator and
made reverence to the holy confessor
who had been so well received by God, our Lord.

338   The next day they had a better plan.
They put in another oil; the other oil was carefully kept,
as it was a holy thing and so full of grace
that it cured many sick afflicted people.

339   However many came, at any time and of whatever malady,
and these were many each and every day,
they anointed them with this oil and they improved.
They never needed to look for another medicine.

340   There was, among the many, an unfortunate woman
who had a twofold sickness in her body.
Her feet were numb, her vision clouded;
the wretched woman lay badly imprisoned.

341   They anointed her with the oil where she had pain,
her eyes and her feet causing her to moan.
She was immediately cured, thanks to the Creator
and the holy virtue of the holy confessor.

342   There were two good people in the town of Prado,[23]
a husband and wife, who had a harmonious marriage.
They had a daughter whom God had given them and
they loved her more than anything else that they had.

---

[23] Dutton notes that he only found a town called Pradilla in the area of San Millán and that the only Prado he found was a town of Mena (Burgos): *Obra completa*, 2nd ed., 147.

343   The little girl was going on three.
       Her parents always had her well dressed.
       The unfortunate little girl became very sick,
       so sick that her soul was about to leave her.

344   For this reason her parents were very upset:
       they would not be more afflicted at their own death.
       They went through the streets shouting, as if they were drugged by
            poison,
       as their eyes were anguished because of her.

345   Both parents decided that they had
       to fix their attention on their daughter
       and carry her to the tomb, from where everyone
       left happy in spite of coming in pain.

346   They prepared their daughter and began their journey,
       carrying a beautiful offering of oil and wax.
       But before they had completed the first day,
       their daughter, for whom all this effort was made, had died.

347   The parents were wild with grief,
       tearing out their hair and ripping their clothes.
       Those who accompanied them
       were very sorrowful and surrounded the body.

348   Nevertheless, with all the consternation that they suffered,
       they had to calm down.
       They thought of a plan that was provided by God,
       since the end result shows that it was completely perfect.

349   They decided to bring her, even though she was dead,
       to the holy confessor to whom she was commended.
       If she could not see his dwelling while she lived,
       then in death she would be buried near him.

350   They prepared her body and with great mourning
       they had to bring her before the holy body.
       They put her on the ground covered with a mantle,
       because when they saw her they were so very brokenhearted.

351   The brothers of the house, very wise men,
       saw the people so sadly brokenhearted
       that they judged that they had not eaten,
       since they knew that in such grief, food is bitter.

352   They begged them to eat a little
       to ease their trouble and temper their suffering.
       They left the body near the altar
       and went to the refectory to have some food.

353   But as they were so heartbroken from their grief
       and so weary from their journey and their tears,
       each one slept a little after they had supped.
       However, they got up quickly due to their pain.

354   While they were resting, the excellent confessor
       prayed to the glorious Lord for the dead child.
       The King of Heaven, holy and powerful,
       received the prayer, as He is very merciful.

355   The grieved company came out after a short time,
       hitting their heads with their closed fists.
       In front of the group came the father and mother,
       who had their hearts the most wounded.

356   They went to the church to see their dead daughter;
       some came to accompany them and others to weep,
       and others to keep the vigil and for the funeral rites.
       But God wanted things to happen in another way.

357   As soon as they came near the altar,
       they saw their dead daughter standing up,
       alive and cured, laughing and playing,
       as if she had been reared in that place.

358   The parents doubted when they saw this.
       All the other people were very frightened.
       The whole day they just did not believe it,
       because they never thought to see such a thing.

359   But finally they were certain of it.
       His glorious virtue had helped them.
       They gave thanks to God and sang the liturgy,
       the *Te Deum laudamus*, which is a beautiful laud.

360   The parents cried from such great joy, and
       the whole town was delighted as well as the clergy.
       Everyone said that the day was blessed
       when such a man was born with such power.

361   They held a vigil with large tapers, and
       they heard matins and the morning mass.
       They made their offerings generous and to all, and
       with great joy they returned home.

362   Gentlemen, the story of the honored confessor
       cannot be told either in Romance or in Latin.
       I want to shorten it for you and go to the most important part
       when he won the vows and how he had fought.

363   The year was 612
       when San Millán died; this is certain.
       But it was 972[24]
       when he won the very rich prize.

364   According to this that we have told you,
       360 years had passed
       since San Millán had died and was buried,
       when he won the vows, a great and honorable tribute.

365   But it indeed seems right and just to me
       to reveal the reason and how it was done,
       because when you understand why it was ordered,
       you will say that whoever does not pay them commits a great sin.

366   Due to the fault of the Christians who were sinners,
       many among them bad and evil-doers,
       who did not want to amend their bad errors,
       these had suffered misfortunes for a long time.

367   God abandoned them because He was angry with them.
       They had to fall into the power of the Devil.
       Every day they insisted on doing injustices
       like a people abandoned by God.

368   Because there was such an enormous evil in them,
       God gave great power to the pagan people
       who put them under such a great and severe obligation
       that a similar one had never before been heard of.

369   King Abderrahman,[25] lord of the pagans,
       a mortal enemy of all Christians,
       had put fear in the mountains and in the plains,
       and they had no plan to escape from his grip.

370   He ordered the Christians, may he go to hell,
       to give him sixty women each year as tribute,
       half noble and half of humbler origin.
       May he go to hell who demands such an offering.

371   All of Spain lay in servitude,
       giving this tribute each year as was the custom.
       It made anniversaries a very dirty business,
       but they had no way to get out of it.

372   All this affliction, this mortal shame,
       was more pressing in Castile and Leon,

[24] See note to quatrain 378.
[25] This is Abd-ur-Rahman III (891–961), caliph of Córdoba.

but all Christendom was afflicted,
because for all it was a grievous wound.

373 There was never such strong affliction among Christians
due to putting their fellow Christians in such an outrage.
It would be a great thing to get out of such an agreement,
to wheedle out of this astutely.

374 Many a worthy lady of noble lineage
was offended, suffering great scorn.
It was a very bad example, a worse deed
for Christians to give their ladies to Moors in such tribute.

375 The sorrow and weeping, the general grief,
such terrible perdition, such a mortal sin,
grieved the celestial King to His very depths,
the One Who, whenever He wishes, can prevent evil.

376 He showed strong signs that He was angry at them,
that He was very displeased with their behavior,
from which all the people were terribly frightened,
because without a doubt they thought they would be destroyed.

377 But it seems just, even though we delay,
to tell you the signs as we read them,
for when you know them, we surely believe
that you will be frightened by what we tell you.

378 To begin it says, in the middle of July,[26]
fourteen days before August,
the sun lost its light: it was impeded;
it was totally deprived of its role.

379 It was Friday when this happened.
From prime to tierce the sun did not appear.
A more frightening day never dawned
except Good Friday when Christ died.

380 Afterwards in September, right at the beginning,
at noon on Wednesday, it died again.
It turned yellower than strained beeswax.
A long time passed before it reappeared.

381 All the people were extremely frightened,
as if they were certain to be destroyed.

---

[26] Our author has the year wrong: the correct year for this eclipse was 939 (Friday 19 July: D. J. Schove, *Chronology of Eclipses and Comets A.D. 1–1000* [Woodbridge: Boydell Press, 1984], 226–28).

The wretched people were sad and helpless,
crying profusely and blaming their sins.

382   A short time hence, with a dark night
and all Christendom being in this bitterness,
a great opening appeared in the sky
and immensely huge flames came out through it.

383   While the people were looking at this sign,
the stars were moving through the sky.
They flew through the air, striking each other
like men who fought returning and fleeing.

384   From midnight on until it was day
this revolt, this controversy lasted.
How great the fear was I could not say,
because all else, compared with this, were just stories.

385   Everyone thought and firmly believed
that the end of the world could have come.
They could not begin to measure this worry;
if it lasted, they would be lost due to their fear.

386   The bad surprise of the powerful scare
had the people oppressed even though it had passed,
but before they had even forgotten it,
another even stronger and more grievous one happened to them.

387   An African wind came up, a very hot wind,
together with a hot and raging fire.
It came from the west, pushed by the Devil, and
did great harm before it was quenched.

388   It did mortal damage throughout Extremadura,
burning towns, scorching villages.
It charred the burgs and principal cities
and did great harm in barren and populated places.

389   It came to Sahagún;[27] it burned one part;
nearly one-half of Carrión[28] was scorched.
Almost all of Frómesta[29] was consumed, and
Castro,[30] among others, did not remain unharmed.

---

[27] City in Leon.

[28] This is Carrión de los Condes in Palencia.

[29] This is Frómista, some 18 kilometers south east of Carrión. See Dutton, *Obra completa*, 224, v. 389c.

[30] Castro is Castrogeriz, some 36 kilometers west of Burgos. See Dutton, *Obra completa*, 224, v. 389d.

390 Hornillos del Camino was badly singed.
Tardajos,[31] which lay in a corner,
it spared Burgos that lay spread out,
because it was not at that time in a populated place.

391 It burned a great deal in the front part of Monasterio,
and in Pancorbo[32] it did not pardon even ten houses.
Many other places that I do not mention
did the fire scorn and greatly mock.

392 All Christendom had fallen into consternation,
having no strength because it had lost everything.
They understood that they had failed God
and that still He had suffered them a long time.

393 They knew their failing; they had gone astray.
They saw that because of their guilt they were so reproached,
and they said, "Alas, wretched, abandoned people,
will we ever see ourselves freed of this evil?"

394 The King of Heaven, of perfect goodness,
in Whom the fountain of mercy never dries up,
did not want to focus on their evil ways:
He wanted to return to them and do charity for them.

395 In the meantime, He gave them a venturesome lord,
the leader Ferrán Gonçalvez, a very powerful count.
(Since the sins were so great, there were no more kings and so
the reign of Castile had turned into a countship.)

396 He was the leader of the kingdom of Castile.
King don Ramiro was over Leon.
Both were Catholics, as the book tells, so therefore
we must pray for them every day.

397 They saw that this was not right and
that this adversity came to them for that reason.
They decided to rebel, to make every effort, for
it would be better to be dead than to give such tribute.

398 They sent messages to the renegade people
not ever to come again to ask for this tribute,
because the kingdoms had made a pact against them, so
if they intended to do something else, they would be affronted.

---

[31] Hornillos del Camino and Tardajos, both towns in Burgos.

[32] Monasterio de Rodilla, Brivesca (Burgos), and Pancorbo, a town of Miranda de Ebro. See Dutton, *Obra completa*, 224, v. 391a and b.

399   But in the midst of this feud, there were preparations,
        organizing the castles, closing the towns,
        because they were few and the others very many.
        They knew that they could not meet them in the field.

400   King Abderrahman and the other pagans
        heard this message that the Christians said.
        In scorn they almost bit their elbows,
        uttering great mockery; many exaggerated remarks.

401   The older men who were wise,
        those who were important advisors of the court, said,
        "Hear us, if you will, friends and lords:
        we will tell you our opinion, even though we are your subjects.

402   We say it seriously and with all good sense:
        if you knew how to understand your good fortune,
        you would give thanks to God and to His magnificent grace
        who wants to give Spain to your lineage.

403   Know certainly and have no doubt about this:
        all these signs which you have seen
        are for their detriment; you will yet prove it, because
        if you just wish for it, it will be in your power.

404   We heard the oldest men say
        that the moon is ours, the sun is the Christians';
        when it is disturbed, we are not healthy, and
        when the sun dies, the kites are glad.

405   The fires and the winds terrified us;
        all the other signs ran against them.
        Know that the fates wanted to exempt you,
        but since they did not destroy them, they did us a great favor.

406   You were indeed right and you are better:
        they sought war, but you did not seek it, and
        they rebelled against you with your surety and
        took the tribute from you that you valued highly.

407   If it seems right to you, our opinion is this:
        Go against the Leonese to begin with and
        break Ramiro, take him out of the way, and
        then the others will not be even worth a pear."

408   The badly mannered and ill-natured people
        considered this good sense and called it wise.
        They guided themselves by the advisors, to their misfortune;
        if they had not listened to them, they would not have done this madness.

409 They believed these words, these prophecies.
     The letters and messages went
     with this news and in a few days
     the people and the knights were together.

410 When the renegade people had arrived,
     there were so many that they could hardly be counted.
     They were lodged in a huge encampment;
     it was two leagues long from one end to the other.

411 As a first step, as they had planned,
     they moved the armies to Leon.
     Although the Leonese are firm and strong,
     they were terribly frightened by this news.

412 King don Ramiro, a noble knight,
     whom neither Roland nor Oliver conquered by force,
     when he heard this news, the exact message,
     he was very frightened on that first day.

413 He saw an enormous obstacle, a tremendous power.
     He saw many Moors and few Christians, and
     he told his problem to the Castilians.
     They answered that they would help him with it.

414 He sent the same message to the Alavese,
     to don Garcia, king of Navarre.
     They responded very courteously
     that they would join him in two months.

415 Meanwhile the Moors did not lose time.
     They had their hosts enter the kingdom, and
     they laid waste to the land and whatever they found,
     because they had no plans to protect themselves against them.

416 Count Ferrán Gonçalvez, who commanded Castile,
     did not delay, because it grieved him to his very soul.
     He joined together the Castilians whom he most valued,
     and he, who arrived later, considered himself a failure.

417 They were all happy with this arrangement and
     gladly wanted to go on this pilgrimage.
     Everyone agreed; they began their march and
     entered into battle with the Muslim forces.

418 King don Ramiro, even though he was frightened,
     returned quickly with a stout heart.
     He assembled all the power of his kingdom
     because he was always fortified by God.

419   Everyone was arriving at the agreed time,
           for the moment of confrontation had come:
           which of the two would fall into the trap,
           which could tan the other's hide.

420   King don Ramiro, of good fortune,
           thought out a good plan of great worth and wisdom:
           to award Santiago in some measure
           and turn him to his favor in this so difficult battle.

421   He spoke with his men and with the ordained forces,
           with bishops and abbots who were there:
           "Listen to me," he said, "everyone, layman and cleric:
           our grave sins have attacked us ferociously.

422   However, I have decided on something,
           if it seems a just plan to you,
           to promise the apostle a reasonable tribute,
           the one who lies in Galicia, primate of Spain.

423   If it please all of you, I intend
           to give him three small coins' worth from each household
           forever and every year on a given day:
           if we did this, we would see great happiness.

424   We could win his protection for all times.
           He would always be disposed to us in our difficulties and
           God would give us help for our prayers.
           Our three coins would take care of all this."

425   The Leonese thought that he said something very reasonable.
           They considered that it was a good piece of advice.
           It was immediately authorized by laymen and clerics and
           was later confirmed with good prerogatives.

426   Count Ferrán Gonçálvez with all of his army
           came to the battle; all were well equipped.
           They heard this message, the plans that were made, and
           they considered them as well thought out.

427   All the Castilians held council
           with their lord the count, a man of action.
           "Hear me," said the count, "friends and brothers.
           The Leonese did as good Christians should.

428   The wise men took good advice.
           They left a good example for future generations.
           Such rich armor was not found in this world.
           Count on the fact that the Moors are conquered without fail.

429   But I want to open my whole heart to you.
        I want us to make another vow:
        that we send to San Millán such a tribute
        as the king of Leon sent to the apostle.

430   He is an excellent confessor, much loved by God.
        He was always full of virtue in life and in death, and
        whoever asked him for mercy was never refused.
        In this dispute he would be a good advocate.

431   He is the first person of the reign, an honored body,
        patron saint of Spaniards, excepting the apostle [Santiago].
        Let us honor him, men; let us give him this gift."
        All responded, "Lord, very willingly."

432   Then the count said, "This will be done,
        if God helps us, if He were pleased with us.
        The battle over, may it be affirmed,
        placed in writing, and the prerogatives given."

433   The armies moved: they took to the road
        to help the king, who was in difficulty.
        But when the vanguard arrived,
        the kings were already treading on the soil of the field.

434   Now both parties were in the field.
        Both kings had struck the first blows, and
        the army of Moors was already confused,
        because Christ's anger had confounded them.

435   Gentlemen and friends, all of you here,
        if you will listen, you can understand
        what help the vow that you know of brought
        and how God did mercy unto them for it.

436   When the kings were in the field with their armies in formation,
        they struck the first blows with their lances lowered.
        The Christians feared the other troops,
        because they were few and the others very many.

437   While the good people were in this doubt,
        they were looking up, paying attention to the sky.
        They saw two beautiful and shining people,
        who were whiter than new-fallen snow.

438   They came on two horses whiter than crystal
        with arms that no mortal had every seen.
        One had a staff and a pontifical miter;
        the other a cross; no one had ever seen such.

439   They had angelic faces and celestial figures, and
        they descended through the air at great speed, while
        looking at the Moors with a fierce look,
        swords in hand, a sign to fear.

440   The Christians were greatly strengthened by them.
        They bent their knees and knelt on the ground and
        struck their chests with clenched fists,
        promising atonement to God for their sins.

441   When the knights were close to land,
        they went against the Moors, striking fierce blows.
        They did such damage in the front ranks
        that fear reached the last of the host.

442   Both having returned to the sky from whence they came,
        the Christians took heart and began to strike.
        The Moors swore by the faith they held
        that never in their life had they had such a hard time.

443   The heathen Moors fell very quickly.
        Some lost their memory; others were frightened.
        They were very sorry that they had come there,
        because they understood that things were to turn out badly for them.

444   Something happened that they never would have dreamed of:
        the very same arrows that the Moors shot
        turned against them and pierced them.[33]
        The dishonor that they did they paid for dearly.

445   Now they freed the ladies that they used to require.
        They would return those carried off, if they gave them the opportunity.
        God knows how to prepare and fulfill such things, and
        such a Lord is good to serve and pray to.

446   The people and the princes, everyone understood
        that the two knights who descended from heaven
        were the two men to whom they had given tribute, and
        that before they had earned it, they had received it.

447   The one with the miter and crook in his hand
        was the apostle, Saint John's brother.
        The one with the cross and the cape on his back
        was San Millán, the man from Cogolla.

---

[33] See H. Goldberg, *Motif-Index of Medieval Spanish Folk Narratives*, MRTS 162 (Tempe: ACMRS, 1998), 25 (nos. D2091.11, .17).

448   They did not want to take the tribute in vain.
        First they wanted to earn it and sweat for it.
        Such lords are to be served and honored,
        who know how to come quickly when there is trouble.

449   King Abderrahman, who commanded the Moors,
        when he saw that the dispute was turning out badly,
        abandoned the battle, the dispute in which he was,
        because the other side was attacking fiercely.

450   All his army abandoned the field,
        many noble men and many of good lineage.
        He paid for his stay with bad money, and
        he did not want to send another with the message.

451   As soon as they understood that he had left,
        his large army was at once in disarray.
        They lost all their strength and all their sense and
        fell into disorder like a conquered people.

452   They fell into disarray; their memory became clouded.
        They did not dare to flee, nor could they turn back, and
        in spite of the mocking of the Moors,
        the battle was won with God and the saints.

453   But those who wanted to fulfill their duty
        were in the field fighting to the death.
        As for the others, who intended to escape and flee,
        there were very few who could save themselves.

454   We do not know if the king escaped or not,
        but all his forces were lost.
        They never again came to ask for the tribute, and so
        the Christians were freed from a great adversity.

455   They lost two Muslim wonders in the defeat
        for which their generation was forever distressed.
        They lost their bishop, a very honored person, and
        the book in which their faith is written.

456   Whoever wants to know it, understand this well,
        because we read it as such and the text says it is so.
        In Campo de Toro[34] this event took place,
        and Christians took this compensation from the Moors.

---

[34] This is Campo de Toro, the fertile plain around Toro (Zamora). See Dutton, *Obra completa*, 240, v. 456c.

457   The battle won, the Moors were pursued.
        The honored men returned to their tents and
        took off their armor because they were very tired.
        They rested at ease, happy and pleased.

458   The next morning, after hearing mass,
        the royal troops held council.
        They divided the booty, which was very great, and
        the holy churches received a good portion.

459   As soon as they had divided the booty,
        they offered thanks to God and the saints.
        They confirmed the tribute they had promised
        to those who struck the first blows.

460   King don Ramiro, may he be in paradise,
        bequeathed to the apostle as he had promised.
        He confirmed the tribute like a prudent man.
        In the whole kingdom there was not a household that did not contribute.

461   Count Ferrán Gonçálvez and all his men,
        bishops and abbots, mayors and bailiffs,
        swore and promised to give in all seasons
        these small tributes to the monastery of San Millán.

462   As the river flows which runs through Palencia
        (it is called Carrión, as I recall),
        to the Arga River, all this land lies under tribute
        and each household must give this recognition.

463   It passes Extremadura and the sierras of Segovia,
        and goes to the other sierra called Araboya,[35]
        and then to the sea that lies beyond Vitoria.[36]
        All are subject to give this legacy.

464   The large and small towns gave it;
        those not heavily populated, as well as those that were.
        The vows were confirmed by the pope in Rome,
        and those that did not give were excommunicated.

---

[35] This is the Altos of Barahona, to the west of Somosierra, Guadarrama which corresponds to the eastern border of the Tribute to San Millán. See Dutton, *Obra completa*, 242, v. 463, a & c.

[36] The sea that lies beyond Vitoria is the Bay of Biscay.

465   They put a great deal of temperance in this
        to avoid inconvenience and oppression.
        They allowed that something else in abundance
        be given at the correctly appraised value.

466   Some lands gave wine, some money,
        some grain, and others goats.
        They brought iron from Álaba and dies of steel.
        Throughout the region of Camberos,[37] they gave cheese as an offering.

467   Each land and what it owes as it was so ordered,
        the privilege tells from where this was taken.
        But I do not know how, because everything is changed.
        For whatever reason the sin is very great.

468   Frómista del Camino,[38] which is near Fitero,
        Herrera with all its towns, Avia, the one on the hill.
        Eight households must send one goat
        as they did in earlier times.

469   In Amaya with all its lands and the same for Ibia,
        each house must send a cubit of sackcloth.
        In the lands of Valdivielso on both sides of the valley,
        each household must send a cubit of canvas.

470   Ubierna and Úrbel River with all its surrounding lands,
        In Castrogeriz and Villadiego and Trivinio
        eight households must send one goat for this holy service
        by judgment of the council.

471   In both villages called Fitero,
        a third Hinojosa, a fourth Villodre,
        and a fifth Villalaco, as it first was,
        each contributor owes a cubit of sackcloth.

472   It was set down and sworn that in Melgar and Astudillo
        each household would give a demijohn of wine.
        In Santa María del Pelayo, as it is called,
        from each house a cubit of sackcloth per year.

473   Valdesaz, Valdeolmillas, Reinoso, and Quintana,
        Villambistia, the surrounding lands of Torquemada,

---

[37] Camberos (Cameros) is the region between Logroño and Soria.

[38] All of these towns paid tribute to San Millán, but, as Berceo tells us in quatrains 475 and 476, he cannot name them all since it would be difficult to rhyme them and some of the towns are no longer inhabited.

from Tariego down to where the plains lie,
Monzón and Baltanás, each house
with all the lands around owes silver money as payment.

474   The contributors of Cevico de la Torre and Cevico Nabero[39]
owe three measures of wax.
In Valbuena, Palençuela, Agosín, Escuderos,
and Muñó which is very rich in vineyards and plowed fields,
every sixteen households must send two goats.

475   The names are listed and difficult to make rhyme.
We cannot mention them all in verse.
I want to tell you about this more plainly
rather than make a long work and damage the style.

476   Although we have told you of many towns,
we have omitted many others of this land,
because, while some were omitted,
others were not inhabited at this time.

477   Great and small, inhabited and not,
all were obliged to give this tribute.
Those which did not give the tribute are indeed assured
of being cursed: you can believe it without a doubt.

478   We have heard it said and recounted many times
that those who refused to pay the tribute
were to see themselves in difficulty for it,
so much so that they had to pay twofold.

479   If these tributes were loyally sent,
these excellent saints would be pleased.
We would have bread and wine, temperate weather,
and we would not be grieved with sadness.

480   Friends and gentlemen, you can understand
that you are in debt to these two saints.
Be sure of this, you will be very comfortable,
if you send them what you owe them.

481   They earned it wonderfully and they deserve it indeed,
because the difficulty was very great when they helped us.

---

[39] Stanzas 474 and 475 are quintains, which occur occasionally in Berceo's works. Cf. "Milagros" quatrains 219 and 911.

> May God give us their grace because they were born at a propitious
>   moment.
> They did very good things in life and even better things after they died.

482   I want to return to the theme of San Millán,
        to continue our story and keep on course,
        to close our work with a few verses
        saying the "Tu autem Domine",[40] and finish the lesson.

483   The King of Heaven gave a great privilege,
        a special gift to His loyal servant.
        When there was a great drought, he redirected the storm.
        Everyone comes to his door to obtain rain.

484   When they devoutly go to his oratory
        and carry his body from where it first lay,
        then God gives us rain and temperate weather.
        I saw this with my own eyes and I am certain of it.

485   Two small bells hang over his altar
        on the rope from which the crown usually hangs.
        They cannot be bigger than two eggs, so that
        if you did not look closely, you could miss them.

486   They have a great and marvelous power:
        when some extraordinary event is about to happen,
        like the death of a great man or a dangerous critical moment,
        they ring by themselves in a miraculous way.

487   Thus the glory of God can be seen,
        since I heard them ring with my own ears.
        There could be many witnesses for this event,
        clerics who are to be believed.

488   Many other noble things of great value
        happened in the monastery of the holy confessor.
        God through His grace gave us His love, and
        this book is finished, thanks be to the Creator.

489   Gonzalo was the name of the author of this work.
        He was reared as a youth in San Millán.
        He was a native of Berceo where San Millán was born.
        May God guard his soul from the power of the Devil.
        Amen.

---

[40] Beginning of the antiphon that signals the end of reading the lesson, in monastic usage. Cf. "Miracles", quatrain 429.

Bibliography

Primary Sources

Editions

Dutton, Brian, ed. *Gonzalo de Berceo. Obra completa, La Vida de San Millan de la Cogolla*, with Isabel Uría. Madrid: Espasa-Calpe, 1992.
———. *La "Vida de San Millán de la Cogolla" de Gonzalo de Berceo*. London: Tamesis, 1967.

Other Works

Baños Vallejo, Fernando. "Hagiografía en verso para la catequesis y la propaganda." In *Saints and Their Authors: Studies in Medieval Hispanic Hagiography in Honor of John K. Walsh*, ed. Jane E. Connolly, Alan Deyermond, and Brian Dutton, 1–11. Madison: Hispanic Seminary of Medieval Studies, 1990.
Baró, José. *Glosario completo de los Milagros de Nuestra Señora de Gonzalo de Berceo*. Boulder: Society of Spanish and Spanish-American Studies, 1987.
Bower, Robin M. "Prescriptions for Reading: The Medicinal Prologues of Gonzalo de Berceo's Saints' Lives." *Modern Language Notes* 118 (2003): 275–97.
Capuano, Thomas M. "The Season Laborer: Audience and Actor in the Works of Gonzalo de Berceo." *La Corónica* 14 (1985): 15–22.
Corominas, Joan, and Jose A Pascual. *Diccionario crítico etimológico castellano e hispánico*. 6 vols. Madrid: Gredos, 1980–1981.
Diccionario de la lengua española. 19th ed. Madrid: Real Academia Española 1970.
Grande Quejigo, Francisco Javier. "Orígenes del castellano literario: Testimonios formulares de la composición y difusión en Gonzalo de Berceo." In *Actas de IV Congreso Internacional de Historia de la Lengua Española*, ed. Claudio García Turza, Fabián González Bachiller, and Javier Mangado Martínez, 485–95. Logroño: Universidad de la Rioja, 1998.

————. *Hagiografía y difusión en la vida de San Millán de la Cogolla* de Gonzalo de Berceo. Gobierno de Rioja: Instituto de Estudios Riojanos, 2000.

————. *El formulismo expresivo en Gonzalo de Berceo: calas críticas en la Vida de San Millán.* Cáceres: Universidad de Extremadura, 2001.

Keller, John Esten. *Gonzalo de Berceo.* New York: Twayne Publishers, 1972.

Lanchetas, Rufino. *Gramática y vocabulario de las obras de Gonzalo de Berceo.* Madrid: Sucesores de Rivadeneyra, 1900.

Levy, Emil. *Petit Dictionnaire Provençal-Français.* 4th ed. Heidelberg: Carl Winter, 1966.

Introduction to *The Life of Saint Oria*

TRANSLATED BY RICHARD TERRY MOUNT

Berceo's *The Life of Saint Oria* is based on a Latin *vita* written by the anchoress's confessor, a certain Munno or Munnio, shortly after her death in 1069. This was some two hundred years before Berceo, in his old age, undertook to versify this Latin account. Unfortunately, the Latin original is lost and its contents survive only in two later versions: Berceo's account in verse and another account in prose by Fray Prudencio de Sandoval, which was published in 1601. It is likely that Sandoval had access only to Berceo's work. If such is the case, then this is not only the oldest but also the most authoritative account of the life of the little-known Spanish saint, whose feast day is March 11.

The poem is structured according to the tripartite division seen in Berceo's other saints' Lives. In this work, however, rather than an organization based on a series of miracles recounted one after the other, Berceo creates a more pleasing and balanced structure around three of Oria's visions, which he contextualizes, placing them after a prologue and an introductory synopsis of her childhood and adolescence. In the first vision, which occurs when Oria is approximately eighteen years old, she visits Heaven where she sees the hierarchy of the blessed as well as a sumptuous throne that represents her place in Heaven and the reward awaiting her after her death. The second vision is set in Oria's own cell and comprises a glorious appearance by the Virgin Mary, who foretells Oria's death and eventual entry into the Heavenly Kingdom. In her final vision, Oria is transported to another spiritual garden setting, the Mount of Olives. This vision comes just prior to her death, and she is able to recount it to her confessor Munno before she dies.

In his conceptualization of the universe, Berceo in general follows the tradition of a division into physical and spiritual realms, earth and Heaven. In *The Miracles of Our Lady*, for example, the earthly life is metaphorically a pilgrimage which has Heaven as its goal. In each of the three visions in *The Life of Saint Oria*, the audience witnesses in some way interaction between the two realms as either an earthly creature (Oria) moves to or through Heaven, or heavenly beings (the three virgin martyrs, the Virgin Mary, the "company" of "preciosos varones") appear in specific locales on earth. Oria's first and most elaborate vision serves to show her the reward that awaits her in Heaven. She is led upward by the aforementioned three virgin martyrs. They have been sent by Christ to invite her to Heaven so that she may glimpse and receive the promise of reward for her ascetic life of humility, service, and sacrifice (embodied in her *saya de lana*). This "trip" is specifically characterized as a pilgrimage (*romería*) in quatrain 60. Led by the saints, Oria rises via a column and ladder, or stairway, to arrive in a garden paradise reminiscent of the allegorical meadow of Berceo's *Miracles*, which was also discovered, so to speak, by a person (the narrator) while on a pilgrimage. The arrival of Oria and the three virgins here does not, however, complete the journey, for they have only reached what might be called the threshold of Heaven. They continue to ascend through three of the seven levels of Heaven proper, and Oria sees the martyrs at the fourth level, the hermits at the fifth, and the apostles and the evangelists at the sixth, in what can be described as a dazzling series of processions.

Oria's mother Amunna has two visions, the second of which occurs after her daughter's death. In it, Oria appears to her mother and tells her of the life of bliss which is hers in Heaven among the Holy Innocents, the male children martyred at the hands of Herod (Matthew 2:16).

The Life of Saint Oria

1   In the name of the Father who created us,
and of Jesus Christ who came to save us,
and of the Holy Spirit, Comforting Light,
I wish to sing the life of a holy virgin.

2   Though tired, I would like in my old age
to set into romance this holy virgin's story;
may God, through her petition, be pleased with me
and not take retribution for my sins.

3   In the beginning and at the outset
I beg her for mercy and ask her to guide me;
may she pray to the Glorious One, Holy Mother Mary,
to be our guide by night and day.

*9[1]   We should tell you now at the beginning
what name she was given when she was baptized;
since she was more precious than any precious stone,
she was given a golden name: she was called Oria.[2]

4   That precious virgin of whom we speak
was from Villavelayo, according to what we read;
we have it written that her mother's name was Amunna,
and her father's name García.

5   Munno was the name of the learned man
who knew her deeds well and wrote her story;
it had been told to him well by her mother,
who would not lie even for a wealthy county.

6   We named her above — as you will remember;

---

[1] The extant manuscript is defective and some of the quatrains are out of order. Scholars have proposed various reorderings; the one presented by Dutton in his Támesis edition is the ordering followed in this translation. The asterisk here and elsewhere in the translation calls attention to the reordering.

[2] The name Oria/Aurea is derived from *oro/aurum* (gold).

she was an anchoress, within walls,
who led an understandably harsh life
and, if you read her life, you will find it so.

7 Holy and just no doubt were the parents
who were worthy of producing[3] such a daughter;
from infancy she did very good deeds
at which all the people marveled.

8 As the lesson says of St. Paul the Apostle,
this holy virgin was a vessel of prayer,[4]
for God blessed her fully
and she saw in Heaven many great visions.

*10 Too long have we tarried in the prologue
and now it behooves us to continue the story.
The days are not long, night will fall soon,
and it is a burdensome task to write in twilight.

11 Amunna was a native of Villavelayo,
and so was her saintly husband García;
they always strove for the good, avoided evil,
and coveted the grace of the Heavenly King.

12 They were Christians who lived righteous lives
and gave due tribute to each of their lords.
The Devil, who constantly stalks the good,
could find no fault in them.

13 They never wished to indulge in worldly pleasures,
but strove with all their might to serve God;
this they considered a great feast[5] and a great delight
and put God first in all their undertakings.

14 They always prayed to God with firm hearts
that He might give them a child
who would be dedicated to His service and to no other

---

[3] *Engendrar*: to produce, in the sense of beget.

[4] Reference to the lesson for 30 June in the Roman Breviary: "Tu es vas electionis, sancte Paule Apostole" (You are a chosen vessel, St. Paul the Apostle). The phrase is based on Acts 9:15 where the Lord, speaking to Ananias of Saul (Paul), says "Go thy way: for he is a chosen vessel unto me, to bear my name before the Gentiles . . .".

[5] The term *pascua* implies a great feast day of the Church such as Easter or Christmas. The term also implies the delight of eating meat (*carne*) after the observation of Lent. Since *carne*, in another sense (flesh), is used in 13a, "feast," in its various joyous connotations, seems appropriate as a translation.

and that this devotion might grow ever stronger.

15   The text does not tell us if He gave them other children,
        but He did give them a daughter of spiritual works
        who struggled mightily with her flesh.
        She never slackened the reins in order to indulge her body.

16   She learned the ways of her good parents
        and took their admonitions to heart;
        she held her little lips tight against her teeth
        so that no unbecoming words might come from her mouth.

17   Her mother wished to lead a harsher life
        and so, dressed in sackcloth, she cloistered herself;
        she martyred her flesh to the utmost degree
        so that her soul might not be conquered by the Devil.

18   If she had been good before, she was even better afterwards
        and the Lord Our God was pleased with her service;
        the people of the land paid her great honor
        and her high praises spread to faraway lands.

19   Let us leave the mother to turn to the daughter;
        let us praise the one whose feast we celebrate;[6]
        if we are to sing her praises (for which we have great material),
        we will need to exercise all our talents.

20   A few years after she lost her baby teeth,
        she became unhappy with her worldly garb;
        she donned other clothing that was just like the monks';
        her shoes could have been worth only a very few coins.

21   Oria, wearing the black habit, abandoned the world,
        cloistering herself in a small narrow cell;
        she suffered much abstinence and lived a harsh life,
        which, in the end, earned her a rich reward from God.

22   This recluse was a vessel of charity,
        a temple of patience and of humility;
        she did not like to hear words of vanity
        and was a light and comfort to her community.

23   Although her cell was small,

---

[6] *Essas laudes tengamos cuyas bodas comemos*: "bodas" is a reference to food given to the poor in the name of a saint; thus Berceo is saying "Let us praise the one in whose name we have been given food to eat." The concepts of feast/nourishment and feast day overlap here, and my translation attempts to encompass both.

her good heart took it to be quite large;
she constantly recited psalms and prayers
and her devotion pierced Heaven.

24   So pleased was God with her prayers
        that He showed her great visions in Heaven
        which should change the hearts of men;
        neither words nor sermons[7] could relate them.

25   It was the third night after Christmas,
        the feast day of St. Eugenia;[8]
        she saw an infinite number of visions
        which indicated that she was full of holiness.

26   After matins, after she heard
        the lesson read with great devotion,
        Oria wished to sleep a little, to take consolation,[9]
        and in a short time she saw a great vision.

27   She saw three holy virgins of high rank;
        all three were martyred at a very young age:
        Agatha in Catania,[10] that rich city,
        Eulalia, a child of great beauty, in Mérida;[11]

28   Cecilia[12] was the third, a precious martyr
        who wished to be Christ's bride
        and wanted no other mother-in-law than the Glorious One,
        more beautiful by far than lily or rose.

---

[7] Dutton gives the Latin phrase *loquele nec sermones* citing the other occurrence of this Latin expression in Berceo: "Non dizrien el adobo, *loquele, nec sermones*"(SD 232d) which echoes Psalms 18:4: *Non sunt loquele neque sermones quorum non audientur voces eorum* (KJV Psalms 19:3): "There is no speech nor language, where their voice is not heard"). See also SM 362b. Manuscript F (*Oria*) reads "palabras ni sermones," which I have translated here. [The abbreviations SD and SM refer to Berceo's *Vida de Santo Domingo de Silos* and *Vida de San Millán de la Cogolla*, respectively.]

[8] In the Mozarabic calendar, St. Eugenia's day was celebrated on 27 December, although in the Roman calendar it falls on 25 December. Eugenia was a Roman virgin martyred under the emperor Valerian in the third century.

[9] "Consolation" in the sense of "rest" or "relief."

[10] St. Agatha was martyred in Catania (Sicily) in the third century. Her feast day is 5 February.

[11] St. Eulalia was martyred at the beginning of the fourth century in Mérida (Spain). Her feast day is 10 December.

[12] St. Cecilia's feast day is 22 November. She was martyred in Rome in the second or third century.

29   All three of these virgins, about whom you have heard,
were alike and dressed in the same color.
They appeared to have been born on the same day
and were so beautiful that they shone like stars.

30   Each of these three holy virgins, crowned in Heaven,
held in her uplifted hand a dove
which was whiter than the untrodden snow
and appeared not to have been raised in a dovecote.

31   This child who was closed up within walls
was very disturbed by the vision,
but she was promptly comforted by the Holy Spirit;
so she asked the three virgins who they were and was very much
           heartened.

32   The three virgins, Agatha, Eulalia, and Cecilia,
spoke to her in a lovely manner:
"Oria, it is because of you that we make this great journey;
know that you may consider yourself our companion.

33   We come to invite you as our sister;
Christ from whom all blessings flow sends us
so that you may go up to Heaven to see what is gained
through your service and your woolen habit.

34   You take great delight in our passions,[13]
and gladly and lovingly you read the stories of our lives;
in the visions we want you to see
the rewards and the glory which we have received."

35   The recluse named Oria responded,
"I would not be worthy of seeing such glory,
but if you will just keep me in your memory,
my entire life will be completely fulfilled."

36   "Daughter," said Eulalia, "do not say such a thing,
for you have friends in Heaven;
you discipline and chastise your flesh in such a way
that you have proved yourself worthy of ascending into Heaven.

37   Take this advice, my beloved daughter:
keep your eye on this dove and forget all else:
go where it goes, do not be deceived;
and be guided by us, daughter, for Christ bids you come."

---

[13] Probably a reference to the reading of the passion books or passionals on the saints' feast days. The passionals contained accounts of the saints' lives (of their acts or martyrdom).

38   Hearing this advice that Eulalia gave her,
        Oria lifted her gaze upward toward the dove;
        she saw a column rising up to Heaven,
        so high that she could scarcely see it.

39   There were stairs and steps on the column
        like those we often see built onto towers.
        I have climbed similar ones many times.
        That is the way the souls of the blessed ascend.

40   The dove moved, began to fly,
        and upwards toward Heaven it rose;
        Oria watched to see where it would alight;
        not for anything could she get it out of her mind..

41   The martyred virgins began to climb
        and the lady recluse began to follow them.
        When Oria looked, God willed it done;
        to tell you the truth, she was raised to the top.

42   Remember Jacob who, while beside a road,
        saw angels climbing such a ladder
        which gleamed, for it was the work of God;
        later he lost his leg in that arduous battle.[14]

43   The virgins had now arrived, thanks be to God,
        and had reached the flat top of the column;
        they saw a fine tree, with a perfectly balanced crown
        that was exuberant with flowers of diverse kinds.

44   Green were its branches, heavy with leaves;
        it made a delightful shade and a very pleasant place;[15]
        surrounding its trunk was a marvelous meadow,
        which in itself was worth more than a rich kingdom.

45   These four maidens, who were lighter than the wind,
        were pleased and delighted with this tree;
        they all climbed it with great eagerness
        and found in it comfort and great fulfillment.

46   Up in the tree, these storied women,
        pleased and happy with their doves in their hands,

---

[14] Reference to two episodes in the life of Jacob: Jacob's Ladder and Jacob's Struggle with the Angel (Genesis 28:10–22 and 32:24–32). In the second, the Angel touches Jacob's thigh which becomes withered, hence Berceo's reference to the lost leg.

[15] The meadow here is presented as a *locus amoenus*, not unlike the one in the Introduction to Berceo's *Miracles*.

saw windows opened in Heaven's vault
through which lights, difficult to describe, issued forth.

47   Three persons came out through those openings,
angelic beings clad in white garments;
each held a staff of lovely colors,
and approached them in human form.

48   These holy men lifted the virgins
with those staffs as if they were feathers;
they placed them higher up, in other regions,
where they saw many noble processions.

49   Oria the Recluse, who was greatly beloved of God,
watched the dove quite prudently
as Eulalia had earlier instructed her to do,
and rose behind the others to that great dwelling place.

50   She rose to the Heavens with no help whatsover
and with neither the sun nor the moon having presented an obstacle;
she had to have pleased God in some way,
for otherwise the daughter of Amunna would not have risen so high.

51   They entered into the Heaven which was open,
and the court that dwelt there was happy with them.
It was pleased with the fourth one who accompanied the three,
and did not feel degraded by the presence of that mountain girl.

52   There immediately appeared before them a very large company,
dressed in white garments and marvelously beautiful;
to Oria it was a wondrous thing,
for she had never seen anything like it.

53   The girl from Villavelayo asked the others,
"Tell me, for God's sake and San Pelayo's,[16] what is this?
My heart holds great apprehension;
this sight is lovelier than the flowers of May!"

54   The others said to her, "Listen, dear daughter:
these were canons, men of holy lives,
who subdued their flesh in the world,
and now they are in glory, in perfect bliss."

---

[16] St. Pelagius (San Pelayo). Spanish martyr, born in Zaragoza, who lived c. 912–925. Though just a boy, as a hostage of the Moors in Córdoba he refused to denounce Christianity and embrace Islam. He was tortured to death.

55   There the daughter met four good men
        whom she had never before seen:
        Bartolomeo, who was skilled in writing passions;[17]
        don Gómez de Massiella, who was generous in giving alms.

56   Don Xemeno was the third, a loyal neighbor
        and native of Velayo;
        Galindo, his servant, was another just like him
        and knew much of good and little of evil.

57   Onward they went in that pilgrimage,
        the martyrs leading, the anchoress following them;
        there appeared before them another very large company,
        superior by far to that of the canons.

58   All wore chasubles[18] of lovely colors
        and carried staffs[19] in their left hands, like preachers,
        and chalices more precious than gold in their right;
        they looked like ministers of important lords.

59   The mountain girl asked what they were:
        "What procession is this, so grand and so lovely?"
        The martyrs gave her a very pleasing reply:
        "These were bishops, servants of the Glorious One.

60   Because they gave the people the drink of good doctrine,[20]
        each one of them is carrying a chalice;
        with their staffs they held at bay the mortal enemy,
        the one who deceived Eve with a nefarious fig."[21]

61   The recluse recognized in that procession
        the bishop don Sancho,[22] who was a worthy man,
        and with him don García,[23] his loyal companion,

---

[17] The identity of Bartolomeo, Gómez, Xemeno, and Galindo has not been established. See footnote for strophe 34a for the explanation of passions.

[18] The outer garment that covers the others worn by the celebrant during mass. The color of the chasuble worn depends on the season of the church year or on the feast day that is being observed.

[19] The bishop's crozier, symbol of the pastoral office.

[20] The drink of good doctrine, i.e., the wine of Holy Communion.

[21] For the sake of the rhyme in *–igo*, Berceo names the forbidden fruit the fig (*figo*). In *Vida de Santo Domingo de Silos* he identifies it as the pear (*pera*): "Acometió a Eva de Adam compannera, / Quando mordieron ambos la devedada pera" (*SD*, 330bc)

[22] Abbot of the Monastery of San Millán from ca. 1028 to 1036. He also served as bishop of Nájera (1028–1046).

[23] Succeeded don Sancho as abbot of San Millán (1036–1037), named bishop of Álava in 1037, died in 1056.

who served Christ with a steadfast heart.

62   Said the martyrs to Oria the mountain girl,
        "The bishop don Gómez[24] is not here, sister.
        Though he wore the mitre, he was a very unworthy thing,
        like the tree that flowers but bears no fruit."

63   Having seen this assembly, this holy company,
        the anchoress was taken to another region;
        the choir of virgins, such a noble procession,
        came out most pleased to receive her.

64   They came out to receive her singing *discantus*[25]
        and to embrace her with uplifted arms;
        their hearts were well pleased with this bride;
        they had not celebrated so joyfully for years.

65   Oria was bewildered by such a reception,
        for she felt that she was not worthy of it;
        she was flustered and quite confused,
        but nothing had ever given her such satisfaction.

66   If the King of Glory had granted it to her,
        she would willingly have remained with the virgins;
        however, the time had not yet arrived
        for her to receive the reward for sufferings endured.

67   The choir of virgins, in a beautiful line,
        one by one gave the anchoress the kiss of peace.
        They said to her, "Oria, in you we are well pleased;
        you are indeed worthy to be in this company.

68   Not by our own merit did we earn this;
        we did not deserve to be here where we are,
        but our Spouse to whom we pledged our troth
        granted us this blessing because we loved Him so."

69   Oria, who had been very timid before,
        after these kind words became more bold;
        she asked the virgins, that holy company,
        about the teacher who had educated her.

---

[24] Abbot of the Monastery of San Millán from 1037 to 1046, named bishop of Nájera and Calahorra in 1046, died in that office in 1067. He removed St. Dominic of Silos from his position as prior of the monastery in order to pacify King García, after St. Dominic had stood up to him and refused to turn the treasures of the monastery over to him.

[25] Also termed *responsos doblados*, responses sung in two parts, one an octave higher than the other.

70   She had a teacher who led a holy life.
        This very good woman was named Urraca
        and she lived in the cloister for a long time.
        Oria was loved dearly by this teacher.

71   The anchoress asked about Urraca,[26] as you will now hear:
        "Tell me, my ladies, for the sake of God whom you serve,
        if Urraca is here among you.
        You will do me a great favor if you tell me this.

72   The one about whom I am inquiring was my teacher in the world;
        much did she suffer with me and teach me;
        I hope she is here in your company,
        for, sleeping and awake, I consider myself in her debt."

73   The virgins gave her very good news:
        "The nun Urraca, about whom you ask,
        is a companion of ours and dwells among us
        with Justa her disciple, servant of the Creator."

74   "I beg you," said Oria, "to call her for God's sake:
        if you let me see her, you will do me a great favor.
        It was because of her teaching that I cloistered myself;
        I will gain much from seeing her and you will lose nothing."

75   The other companions called her by name
        and Urraca responded to their first calls.
        Oria recognized her voice, for she knew its characteristics,
        but she could not see Urraca at all.

76   The long line was blocking her view
        and she could not see Urraca, for she was at its end;
        the voice that was guiding Oria led her onward,[27]
        but she never forgot her teacher.

77   At the end of the line of virgins, once she had passed them all,[28]
        Oria found a very rich throne wrought of gold
        and all set with very precious stones,
        but it was vacant and very well sealed.

---

[26] The exact identity of Oria's mentor Urraca (and her disciple Justa) is not known.

[27] Lappin maintains that this is the voice of Urraca, since no other disembodied voice has been mentioned so far. Thus Urraca continues her role as spiritual guide to Oria in this celestial realm of virgins. See A. Lappin, *Berceo's Vida de Santa Oria: Text, Translation and Commentary* (Oxford: Legenda, 2000), 150 (note to strophe 76).

[28] An apparent contradiction presents itself here. If Oria had passed the entire procession of virgins, why had she not seen Urraca?

78   She saw covering the throne a very rich tapestry;
nothing in this world could have been so bright.
Only God, who protects His servants, could make such a thing,
and the whole land of Lara could not buy it.[29]

79   A beautiful young lady, a damsel
whose name was Voxmea,[30] was watching over this throne.
The king of Castile would give his realm for such a thing,
and such a trade would be the subject of legend.

80   Oria lifted her eyes toward the north
and beheld a great throng of beautiful persons,
all of whom seemed to be dressed in vermilion.
She asked the others, "And these? Who are they?"

81   The virgins who were serving as her guides said,
"These are all martyrs, noble persons.
They allowed themselves to be killed by arrows,
for which Jesus Christ gave them rich crowns.[31]

82   There is St. Stephen, who was stoned to death,
and St. Lawrence, the one whom Caesar had roasted,
and St. Vincent the Virtuous, servant of Valerius,
and many other good people, both lay and ordained."[32]

83   Further on, in a place apart, she saw
a lovely gathering of saintly hermits,
who suffered many bitter adversities for Christ's sake
in order to win their souls' salvation and eternal life.

---

[29] Dating from the ninth century, Lara was the most important and largest of the political districts, called *alfoces*, in Castile. As such it enjoyed immense wealth.

[30] *Voxmea* means "my voice" in Latin; therefore, this woman is the spokesperson for God, or perhaps God's (or Christ's) voice personified. Cf. Proverbs 8:4, "... et vox mea ad filios hominum" (and my voice is to the sons of men).

[31] Red is the color of blood and symbolizes martyrdom, hence the red (vermilion) garments observed by Oria. The mention of arrows evokes the symbolism of St. Sebastian (fourth century), one of the most famous of Christian martyrs, who was ordered shot through with arrows by the emperor Diocletian. Since he did not die from the arrow wounds, Diocletian later had him beaten to death.

[32] St. Stephen (died ca. 35), first deacon of the Church and first Christian martyr, was stoned to death. St. Lawrence (died 238), a Spanish deacon and Church treasurer under Pope Sixtus II, was martyred by being roasted on a grill over burning coals (the central figure in Berceo's *Martyrdom of Saint Lawrence*). St. Vincent (died 304), Spanish deacon under St. Valerius, was martyred at Valencia; he is associated in legend (and in Berceo's *Martyrdom*) with St. Lawrence.

84   She recognized among them all an ordained monk
        whose name was Monio, according to the book,
        and another, a disciple of his, called Munno,
        who was a consecrated abbot of Valvanera.[33]

85   She saw Galindo there in that group;
        he was killed by thieves in the hermitage.
        There she saw her father whose name was García,
        he who always rejected folly.

86   She saw the apostles in a place higher still,
        each on his throne where he sat in judgment;[34]
        There she saw the Evangelists
        whose brightness no one could describe.

87   These are our fathers, our general leaders,[35]
        princes of the peoples; they are important men;
        Jesus Christ was Pope and these were His cardinals,
        who freed the world of the deadly serpents.

88   As Oria was mulling this over in her mind,
        she heard Christ speak among that good congregation,
        but she could not see Him as she would have liked,
        for apparently she was not deserving of such.

89   Let us leave all the rest and return to the throne.
        This is a lofty subject and I do fear we will sin,
        but we should not be reproached in this,
        for we write down nothing other than what we read.[36]

90   The written word tells us and we have already said
        that Voxmea was the name of the one who watched over the throne
        which gleamed like the rays of the sun.
        Blessed was the soul for which it was intended.

91   This young woman was wearing a precious garment,
        more precious than gold, more precious than pure silk;

---

[33] Monio was prior of the monastery of Cañas, which was affiliated with the one at Valvanera. Munno, Monio's contemporary, was prior at Valvanera.

[34] Luke 22:30: "That ye may eat and drink at my table in my kingdom, and sit on thrones judging the twelve tribes of Israel."

[35] This strophe is an elaboration of the importance of the apostles and the evangelists introduced in the previous quatrain (86).

[36] Berceo fears being accused of misrepresenting the facts and thus reaffirms that he is following his source text.

it was all covered with fine writing —
no living person ever wore such fine clothing.[37]

92 Upon it were the names of great men
who served Christ with all their heart,
but the majority of them were the names of recluses
who subdued their flesh to the highest degree.

93 The names of the just, the ones of greater holiness,
seemed more legible and of greater brightness;
the others of less importance, the less worthy ones,
were darker and of extreme obscurity.

94 The anchoress could not tear herself away from the throne;
she told Voxmea that she wanted to know
to whom such a finely worked article could belong,
since in no way could it be purchased.

95 Voxmea answered her and told her good news:
"Friend, you have done well and well have you asked;
all this that you see is granted to you,
because the Creator is pleased with your service.

96 All this craftsmanship is intended for you —
the place as well as the throne, God be praised —
if it is not taken from you by the counsel of the Devil,
who led Eve to eat the bad morsel."

97 "If, as you say," Saint Oria replied,
"such great glory is promised me,
I would like to be the bride in this nuptial bed now,
for I do not wish to leave the gold for the dross."

[37] Voxmea's garment serves various symbolic functions. Since she is the voice of God or Christ, she represents the Church, which guarantees the salvation of the just. The names of the just upon her garment echo biblical listings such as the Book of Life (Revelation 20:12) and Aaron's garments (including the Breastplate of Judgment engraved with the names of the children of Israel) (Exodus 28). In addition, the fabric of Voxmea's robe evokes the inscribed textiles highly valued by Iberian Muslims and Christians during the Middle Ages. Arabic *tiraz* tunics had inscriptions embroidered or woven into the fabric of the *tiraz*. Such clothing was used not only on ceremonial occasions, including processions, but also was worn to identify and to show the important status of its wearer. The burial tunic of Archbishop Ximenez de Rada, who was contemporary with Berceo, is an example of an inscribed garment from the Arabic tradition being used by eminent ecclesiatics.

98   The other one, in a well-reasoned manner, replied,
        "That cannot be, Oria, not this time;
        you must return to your body and remain cloistered,
        until your entire life is over."

99   The three holy martyrs who came with her
        at no time left her side;
        they were always with her, they walked with her,
        until they had led her right back to her house.[38]

100   She fervently besought these saints
        to pray on her behalf to the King of Majesty,
        that through His mercy He might allow her
        to remain with Voxmea in that promised place.

101   They prayed to God as best they could,
        but they were unable to secure what she requested;
        from Heaven, God spoke to them and they heard His voice clearly,
        yet His great Majesty they did not behold.

102   He said to them, "Have Oria plan to return to her place;
        the time to dwell here has not yet come.
        Her body must suffer a little longer still;
        after that will come her time to claim the throne."

103   "Lord," she said, "and Father, although I do not see You,
        I always was desirous of winning Your grace;
        if ever I leave this place where I am,
        I will never return to it, or so do I believe.

104   The Heavens are very high and I am a lowly sinner.
        If ever I return to my mortal body
        I will not find in the world either mistress or godmother[39]
        through whom I might sooner or later claim this place."

105   The voice of the Creator said to her yet again,
        "Oria, have no fear of being of little merit:
        with what you have suffered, you have earned My love
        and no enchanter can take it from you.

106   What you so fear, and I know that you are afraid,
        is that the Heavens are high and the climb is steep;

---

[38] The use of "house" (*casa*) here allows for the double interpretation "cell" and "physical body." Oria was returned to her cell and her spirit was returned to its earthly body.
[39] "Mistress or godmother" (*sennora nin madrina*), in the sense of "superior" and "sponsor." Oria is afraid that she will be unable to place herself under the patronage of an abbess who will sponsor her before God.

I will make them flat for you, My beloved daughter,
and you will have no trouble on your journey.

107 By what you so fear you will not be hindered;
you will have no difficulties, so be not afraid.
My daughter, go blessed and signed with the cross;
return to your cubicle and pray your morning prayer."

108 The martyrs who guided her earlier led her
down the same stair by which they had ascended.
In a very short while, they returned her soul to her body,
and she awoke as soon as they left her.

109 She opened her eyes and looked all around,
but she did not see the martyrs and was very displeased.
She saw herself far removed from such great sweetness;
she felt very great affliction and extreme sorrow.

110 She thought she would not see the hour nor the day
when she would be able to rejoin that company;
she grieved for the throne that was empty,
the one that God had made with such great skill.

111 Doña Oria, the recluse, because of these visions,
did not allow into her being any vainglory at all;
out of love for her soul, in order not to lose such a victory,
she showed her flesh no mercy.

112 She martyred her flesh, giving it much punishment;
night and day she carried out all her duties,
fastings and vigils, and praying the Psalter;
in all ways she wanted to follow the Gospel.

113 The King of Kings, Lord of Lords,
whose hand holds the righteous and the sinful,
wanted to remove Oria from these sufferings
and make her a member of better congregations.

114 At least[40] eleven months must have passed
since she saw the things that we have related,
of male and female saints and very honorable assemblies,
but Oria still had not forgotten them.

---

[40] "Onze meses senneros podrié aver passados." While the verse alone would translate "Just eleven months could have passed," the expression *mas . . . encara* ("but . . . still") in 117d points to a different reading.

115   In that eleventh month, she saw a great vision,
        as great as the others which are written down;
        God did not leave her at any time,
        for she always kept her heart on Him.

116   The third night before the martyr Saturninus's Day,[41]
        which falls in November near St. Andrew's,[42]
        a great boon came to her; never did a better come,
        sweeter and more pleasing than bread or wine.

117   Half the night must have passed;
        Oria had kept late vigil and she was tired.
        She lay down for a while, weak and very worn;
        the bed was not of softened down.

118   She saw three virgins come, all with the same appearance;
        all came dressed in white cloth.
        Never had she seen chemise or wimple so white;
        nor had Genoa or Pisa ever had such a thing.[43]

*126   They were all equal, of one quality,
        of one aspect, and of one age;
        not one surpassed the others in goodness;
        rather, in all things all three were equal.

127   These three virgins brought a noble bed,
        with luxurious adornments, not poor nor lowly;
        they spoke to Oria, God's good friend:
        "Daughter, listen a little while, and thus may God bless you.

128   Get up from the cold, hard ground
        and climb into this bed where you will lie more comfortably.
        Listen, of this you can be sure: if the Queen
        finds you on the ground, She will be displeased with you."

129   "Ladies," said Oria, "this is not right,
        for this bed is for an old, frail person.
        I am a strong young girl who can bear anything;
        if I were to lie down there, God would take offense.

[41] Saturninus (third century), after serving as a missionary in the Pamplona region of Navarre (Spain), became the first bishop of Toulouse. He was martyred during the persecution of the emperor Valerian. His feast day is 29 November.

[42] St. Andrew's feast day is celebrated 30 November.

[43] Genoa and Pisa were wealthy commercial centers and ports during the thirteenth century and were emerging as important textile producers, especially in the wool and silk industries. The implication that neither of the two cities could produce or afford such a thing points to the pricelessness of the white fabric.

130 I want a rough bed of prickly cloth;
  my flesh does not deserve to lie in such luxury.
  For God's sake, do not insist in this matter;
  such lovely things are for very great men."

131 The virgins took her, reproaching her greatly,
  and threw her onto those rich linens;
  Oria, with great displeasure, let out strange moans,
  for she was not accustomed to lying in such luxury.

132 As soon as the anchoress was thrown onto the bed,
  her cell was illuminated by very bright light;
  in a short while it was filled with many virgins,
  all having come to honor the cloistered one.

*119 Then in a short while came Holy Mary,
  and the virgins were overcome by happiness and joy;
  since with such a lady everyone would have a good day,
  the entire gathering there was blessed.

120 They said to Oria, "You who lie sleepily,
  arise, receive the Glorious Virgin,
  who is Mother of Christ, and Daughter and Spouse;
  you will be foolish if you do otherwise."

121 The anchoress answered them with great humility,
  "If it should please her, by her grace,
  that I should approach her majesty,
  I would fall at her feet willingly."

122 Hardly had Oria completed the statement
  when the Glorious One arrived — God, what a wonderful encounter!
  The entire place shone with doubled light;
  anyone who might have such a guest would be fortunate!

123 The Blessed Mother, Mistress of Heaven,
  more beautiful by far than the dawn,
  did not hesitate for a moment;
  she went straightway to embrace Oria the anchoress.

124 Oria was very happy with that compliment
  and asked her if she was Holy Mary.
  "Doubt it not, my dear daughter," she said to her,
  "I am the one to whom you pray both night and day.

125 I am Holy Mary, whom you love so much,
  who freed all women from disgrace.
  Daughter, God is with you, if you remain steadfast,
  and you will go to great riches, daughter, when you die."

*133   "Mother," said Oria, "if you are Mary,
        the one of whom Isaiah spoke so much,[44]
        I would like a sign in order to be certain,
        in order to be sure that I will be saved."

134   The Glorious One said to her, "Oria, my suffering one,
        you have been for such a long time cloistered;
        I will give you a sign, a good, sure signal;
        when you see the signal you will be pleased.

135   Take this as a sign, as a certain signal:
        within a few days you will become very sick.
        You will be overcome by a fatal illness
        which you never had before; you shall take it as such.[45]

136   You will see yourself in great suffering and by death you will be cut off;
        within a few days, you will have passed from this world.
        You will go where you wish to go, to the honored throne,
        that Voxmea holds for you so well."

        [16 stanzas are missing]

137   Oria was lying in distress inside her cubicle,
        while outside the cell there was a great gathering
        praying the Psalter, all in their chairs,
        and not one had a dry cheek.[46]

138   The sick one, lying in such tribulation,
        nevertheless murmured her prayers;
        she wanted to beat her breast but was unable to do so,
        though she did try to move her hand to that end.

139   She slept a little because she was exhausted.
        She was transported to the Mount of Olives in a vision,
        where she saw things that filled her with joy.
        If they had not awakened her, she would have considered herself at rest.

*141   She saw around the mount a beautiful plain,
        and on it a thick grove of olive trees,
        loaded with olives in extreme abundance;
        a man could live under them in great comfort.

---

[44] Isaiah 7:14, "Behold, a virgin shall conceive, and bear a son . . .".

[45] "Take it [the illness] as the promised sign."

[46] Cheek (maxiella). See Milagros 364b and 508b where Berceo uses maxiella (masiella, massiella) in the sense of "cheek" rather than "jaw."

144   She saw many people coming through that shade.
        All came joyfully to receive Oria,
        all well groomed, well dressed, and well shod.
        They wanted, if it was time, to take her up to Heaven.

143   These companies were made up of worthy men,
        all dressed in white tunics.[47]
        All their adornments were like those of angels;
        at times she had seen[48] similar ones.

144   Among the others she saw an old man,
        a gentleman from Mansilla whom they called don Sancho.
        Never had she seen him or touched him with her hand;
        however, the mountain girl recognized the mountain man.[49]

*140   The mother in her distress could not rest,
        for everyone thought that Oria was going to die.
        Entering the cell to see for herself,
        she began to shake Oria, and Oria awoke.

145   With this the sick one became very distressed.
        At that time, she did not want to wake up;
        for she was in great glory, in a delightful place,
        and feared she would never be able to return there.

146   She was not at all pleased with those who roused her,
        neither with her mother nor with the nuns,
        for she was in great glory, among good people,
        and did not feel a bit of all the pain.

147   She murmured in a weak voice,
        "Oh, Monte Oliveti,"[50] and she said nothing else;
        no one in the place could understand her,
        because her speech was not intelligible.

---

[47] *Ciclatones: cyclas,* luxurious medieval tunics of brocaded silk. The allusion is to Revelation 6:11, 7:13–14.

[48] The MS reads *vidieran* which the editions by Dutton and Uria Maqua, following Maria Rosa Lída de Malkiel, "Notas para el texto de la *Vida de Santa Oria*," *Romance Philology* 10 (1956–1957): 19–25, correct to *vidiera.*

[49] *Serrano/a:* person from the *sierra* (mountains), in this case the Sierra de la Demanda where lie Villavelayo and Mansilla, the hometowns of Oria and don Sancho respectively.

[50] Mount of Olives. In the MS Oria says "Monte Olivete, Monte Olivete," but for reasons of versification (syllable count) Dutton corrects to "O Monte Oliveti."

148   Other good women who were near her
        saw that she was murmuring, but they did not understand her;
        they took this as a marvelous thing;
        they were in great doubt as to whether it was good or bad.

149   The woman's mother called for me[51]
        and had me go into the daughter's cell,
        that I might urge Oria to speak if she could,
        for she was trying to say something that they could not understand.

150   They said to her when I went in,
        "Oria, open your eyes, and you will hear good news;
        receive don Munno, your honored mentor,
        who comes to take leave of your good company."

151   As soon as Oria heard this news,
        she opened her eyes, recovered her senses,
        and said, "Oh, wretched me, I was in great glory!
        I am greatly distressed because they awakened me.

152   If only they had let me be for a little longer,
        they would have shown me great love and I would be finished;
        for I had arrived among such people
        that compared to their blessings the world is nothing."

153   Munno took great pleasure from these words.
        "Friend," he said, "let us understand something
        that we do not understand well and would like to know;
        you should do this that we ask of you!"

154   "Friend," said she, "I will in no way lie to you,
        for I am obligated to grant your request.
        I was taken to the Mount of Olives in a vision
        and saw there things that pleased me very much.

155   I saw there a good place, an excellent grove,
        where the fruit of the trees would be beyond price.
        There were a great expanse of fields and a great crop of flowers,
        the fragrance of which would cure a sick man.

156   I saw there many people, distinguished persons,
        who were all well dressed and well shod.
        All received me with well-sung lauds
        and were of one mind and in harmony.

---

[51] The voice of Munno, Oria's confessor, is evident as he moves to first-person narration. This seems to be the first time that the narrator becomes a participant in the action.

157 Such was the company, such was the place,
and a person who lived there would never see sorrow.
If I had stayed there a little longer,
I could have returned with many blessings."

158 Said Munno to Oria, "Do you desire to go there?"
Said Oria to Munno, "Indeed I do, more than to live,
and you would lose nothing by coming with me."
Said Munno to her, "Would that God might consent to that!"

159 Pleased by the vision, she tried to get up,
like someone who wishes to set out on a journey.
Munno said to her, "Oria, rest in your cell;
it is not yet time to embark."

160 I do not wish to dwell on this matter;
if you think it fitting, I wish to cut it short.
I wish to move on to the lady's demise,
take her to her throne, and then go take my rest.

161 It was the month of March, the second week,
the feast day of St. Gregory, partner[52] to St. Leander's day;
at the hour when people take their midday rest,
the woman who always wore wool was suffering.

165 The woman's mother, beloved of God,
was very afflicted because of her daughter's suffering.
She had not slept during the night; she was exhausted,
and what she ate amounted to almost nothing.

163 I, Munno, and don Gómez, the cellarer[53] of the place,
strongly urged Amunna
to go to her bed to rest a short while,
for we would attend to Oria if she reached death's door.

---

[52] *Cormana*: *cohermana*: cousin. St. Leander's day fell right after St. Gregory's, so Berceo refers to them as "sister feast days." St. Gregory died on 12 March 604; St. Leander died on 13 March 600 or 601. Their feast days, previously celebrated on 12 and 13 March respectively, are now celebrated on 12 March and 27 February. St. Leander was from Spain, the brother of St. Isidore of Seville. He and St. Gregory met in Constantinople and became great friends.

[53] Officer of a monastery entrusted with the general provisioning of the community. The Rule of St. Benedict (Chapter 31) says that the cellarer should be "as a father to the monastery," and if he is unable to give what is asked for, to answer gently, because "a good word is above the best gift."

164   As soon as Amunna lay down, she went right to sleep
           and she had a vision that quickly ended.
           She saw her husband, a man of holy life,
           father of the recluse who lay gravely ill.

165   She saw don García, who had been her husband,
           was Oria's father, and had long before died.
           She well understood that he had come for his daughter,
           and that her course, without a doubt, was completed.

166   Amunna said to him, "Tell me, don García,
           why you have come, for I would like to know.
           For Christ's sake and Holy Mary's,
           tell me about our daughter and if she will see the morrow!"

167   "Know," said García, "I assure you
           that Oria is near the end of her journey.
           Count her as dead, for the hour awaits;
           this is the last of her days."

168   She saw that three people were with don García,
           so white that no one would be able to believe it.
           All were of one age and of one aspect,
           But they said nothing and made no gestures.

169   Her vision over, Amunna awoke.
           If before she had been troubled, now she was troubled more,
           for she knew that her daughter would soon pass on
           and that she herself would remain, sad and forlorn.

170   The woman did not forget this dream
           nor what Garcia, her husband, had told her.
           She related it all to her beloved Munno,
           who, as a man of much wisdom, committed it to memory.

171   He memorized it well, like everything else.
           She related it to him well and he did not learn it badly.
           He made a great book of her life,
           and I took this from that missal of his.[54]

172   Amunna begged her daughter Oria,
           "Daughter, God take you to His holy glory,
           if you saw a vision or some manifestation,
           tell it to me while you still remember it."

---

[54] Dutton (130) suggests that Munno wrote Oria's life on the blank leaves of a manuscript or missal that he wrote, hence the reference to the *missal* as the source.

173   "Mother," said her daughter, "why do you press me so?
Leave me be, may God the good Holy Father help you;
I have enough pain and misery
and my tongue feels like it weighs more than a heavy stone.

174   You want me to talk to you, but I cannot talk;
you see that I cannot form my words.
Mother, if you insist on pressing me so,
I may expire before my time.

175   Mother, if God should will that I might live,
I would have many things to tell you,
but when the Creator does not will it,
all that He does will must be endured."

176   Oria's last hour was approaching
and she was suffering more as night began to fall;
she raised her right hand in a lovely way,
signed the Cross on her forehead, and blessed her crown.[55]

177   She lifted both her hands and placed them together
as one who gives thanks to the Spiritual King.
The loyal recluse closed her eyes and her mouth;
she yielded her soul to God and never again felt pain.

178   She was well accompanied in that passing:
the good abbot don Pedro,[56] a prudent person,
monks and hermits, the entire community,
all paid honor and full respect.

179   This holy body was well attended,
and in the order's habit richly dressed.
They prayed the Psalter many times
and did not leave her body until it was buried.

180   If you wish to know with all certainty
where this lady of such great holiness is buried,
I tell you true, it is in San Millán de Suso.
May God, through her, grant us mercy and charity.

181   Near the church lies her grave,
just a few steps away, in a narrow place,
inside a cave and under a hard stone.
It is not of the fine quality that she deserved.

---

[55] *Mollera*: the topmost part (crown) of the head.
[56] Don Pedro: last abbot of the monastery of San Millán de Suso (1062–1072).

182   The daughter and the mother, both of holy lives,
        as they always shared great and perfect love,
        have nothing separate, even in death,
        for Amunna lies buried near Oria.

183   Their bodies are worthy of veneration,
        for they suffered very great mortifications for Christ.
        May they make multifold entreaties to God
        that He save our souls and pardon our sins.

*185   I do not yet want, sirs, to bid you farewell,
        as there still remain a few things to tell you.
        I wish to complete well the work begun,
        so that no one will have reason to scorn me.

186   After the daughter, the holy cloistered one, died,
        her mother went about grieving for her.
        If only she could dream of Oria once,
        she would count herself cured and very comforted.

187   God understood her heart well;
        He showed Amunna a great vision,
        by which she learned what had and had not become of her daughter.
        We have that part of the whole story yet to tell.

188   It was a great feast day, a special day,
        the day of Pentecost which is in the middle of May.
        This lady dreamed a wished-for dream,
        for which she had prayed to God many times.

189   After matins had been sung and permission granted
        for all who so wished to go to their cells to rest,
        Amunna, quite tired, lay down for a while
        and then dreamed of her beloved daughter.

190   They embraced one another as they did in life.
        "Daughter," said the mother, "you have comforted me.
        I want you to tell me why you have come
        and if you are in purgatory or if you have left there."

191   "Mother," said the daughter, "today is a general feast day,
        like Resurrection Sunday or like Christmas;
        today all Christians take spiritual nourishment,
        the body of Christ, my natural Lord.

192   It is a feast in which Christians must take Communion,[57]
receive *Corpus Domini*[58] consecrated at the altar.
I want to receive and take that, Mother,
and be on my way; I want to go there.

193   Mother, if you love me and seek what is best for me,
have the priests come and give me Communion,
for then I would gladly return,
and I would not want to tarry, neither a lot nor a little."

194   "Daughter," said the mother, "where do you want to go?"
"Mother," said the daughter, "up to Heaven."
"I want to tell you that you treat me unjustly,
by wishing to part from me so soon.

195   But, daughter, I want to ask you one thing.
At your passing, did you receive punishment?
Or did they give you a place in Heaven at once?
Or did they make you wait outside the gate?"

196   "Mother," said the daughter, "on the first night
I did not enter the mansion; I do not know why.
The next morning, the doorwoman opened for me
and all received me, Mother, as their companion."

197   "Daughter, on that night when you could not enter,
who kept you company while you were outside?"
"The holy virgins, Mother, whom you heard about previously,
and I was in bliss, the like of which you have never heard.

198   May the Glorious Virgin be praised,
for she did for me what she had promised.
In my passing she did not leave my side
and she placed in me much of her holy grace."

199   "One more thing, my daughter, I wish to ask you.
What company are you in? Let me know that."
"Mother," said the daughter, "I am in a good place,
which I could never attain through my own merit.

---

[57] Pentecost was one of the three Holy Days of Obligation (on which the faithful were obliged to take Communion) from the year 507 (Council of Agde) until 1215 (the Fourth Lateran Council).

[58] The body of the Lord, i.e., the Eucharist.

200   I have inherited, Mother, a place among the Innocents,[59]
         those whom Herod put to the sword in order to get Christ.
         I did not deserve to be so honored,
         but such a thing pleased Christ's sacred virtue."

201   Having said these words and many others like them,
         Oria, the blessed one of spiritual deeds,
         fled from the eyes of her mother's heart.
         The mother awoke then and she began to cry.[60]

202   In addition to these, she saw other great visions,
         about which one could write very good stories,
         but I have other matters to take care of.
         I want to leave those until another time.

203   Whoever thinks that what we are setting down
         is not exactly as we relate it
         will sin gravely against God whom we adore,
         for we found everything that we say written down.

204   The one who first wrote it would not tell a falsehood,
         for he was a good man of very great holiness.
         He knew Oria well, he knew her inmost thoughts;
         in everything that he said, he told the truth.

205   He learned some of it from Oria and the rest from her mother;
         to them both he was a very loyal confessor.
         May God the Good Spiritual King grant us His grace,
         so that neither here nor there may we ever see evil.
         Amen.

*184   Gonzalo was the name of the versifier
         who wrote this work on his portico.

---

[59] The Holy Innocents, the male children in and around Bethlehem murdered at the order of Herod (Matthew 2:1–18) in his attempt to get rid of the infant Jesus. Venerated as martyrs, their feast day is 28 December.

[60] The eyes of the heart (*ojos corales*), or of the spirit, are placed in opposition to the eyes of the body (the tear-producing eyes, *ojos lagremales*) to emphasize the fact that what Amunna has just seen is spiritual rather than corporeal. When she awakens, her corporeal eyes fill with tears. A more literal translation of the last line of this strophe ("despertó luego ella, mojó los lagremales") would be: "the latter awoke then and wet her tear-producing ones [eyes]."

> May God Our Lord grant him grace,
> that he may see His glory in the Greater Kingdom.
> *Hic liber est scriptus: qui scripsit sit benedictus.*[61]

The lines written below are the ones that are inscribed on the stone where lies St. Aurea, Virgin.

> *Hunc quem cernis lapidem scultum: sacra tegit menbra*
> *beata. simul Auria virgo cum matre Amunna quiescunt*
> *femina. Et quia pro Christo artham duxerunt vitam.*
> *symul cum eo. meruerunt coronari. in Gloria.*[62]

> Beneath this stone that you see lies the body of St. Oria
> and that of her mother Amunna, a woman of much worth.
> They observed great abstinence in this transitory life
> for which reason their souls are with the angels in Glory.[63]

---

[61] Latin: "This book is written. May the one who wrote it be blessed" (a leonine hexameter line).

[62] The Latin inscription is presented as it appears in the extant manuscript and in Dutton's edition.

[63] The English is not a direct translation from the Latin shown; rather, it is a translation of the Spanish translation given in the manuscript and in Dutton's edition. A closer, direct translation of the Latin would be: "Beneath this carved stone that you see lies the holy body of St. Oria the virgin and that of her mother Amunna. For Christ's sake they observed great abstinence in this life for which reason they deserved to be crowned with Him."

Bibliography

Artiles, Joaquín. *Los recursos literarios de Berceo.* 2a ed. Madrid: Gredos, 1968.

Baro, José. *Glosario completo de los "Milagros de Nuestra Señora" de Gonzalo de Berceo.* Boulder: Society of Spanish and Spanish-American Studies, 1987.

Burke, James F. "The Four 'Comings' of Christ in Gonzalo de Berceo's *Vida de Santa Oria." Speculum* 48 (1973): 294-312.

Dutton, Brian, ed. Gonzalo de Berceo, *Obras completas V: El Sacrifiçio de la Misa. La Vida de Santa Oria. El Martirio de San Lorenzo.* London: Támesis, 1982.

Lappin, Anthony. *Berceo's "Vida de Santa Oria": Text, Translation and Commentary.* Oxford: Legenda, 2000.

Lída de Malkiel, María Rosa. "Notas para el texto de la *Vida de Santa Oria." Romance Philology* 10 (1956-1957): 19-33.

Mount, Richard Terry. "Levels of Meaning: Grains, Bread, and Bread Making as Informative Images in Berceo." *Hispania* 76 (1993): 49-54.

———. "Light Imagery in the Works of Gonzalo de Berceo." In *Studies in Language and Literature, Proceedings of the 23rd Mountain Interstate Foreign Language Conference,* ed. Charles Nelson, 425-30. Richmond: Department of Foreign Languages, Eastern Kentucky University, 1976.

———. "Oria's Second Vision and María Rosa Lída's Emendations." *Crítica Hispánica* 3 (1981): 159-64.

Perry, T. Anthony. *Art and Meaning in Berceo's "Vida de Santa Oria."* New Haven: Yale University Press, 1968.

Uría Maqua, Isabel, ed. Gonzalo de Berceo, *Poema de Santa Oria.* Madrid: Castalia, 1981.

———, ed. Gonzalo de Berceo, *Poema de Santa Oria.* In *Obra Completa,* ed. Dutton et al., 491-551. Madrid: Espasa-Calpe, 1992.

———. "El *Poema de Santa Oria.* Cuestiones referentes a su estructura y género." *Berceo* 94-95 (1978): 43-55.

Walsh, John K. "The Missing Segment in Berceo's *Vida de Santa Oria." La Corónica* 5 (1976): 30-34.

———. "The Other World in Berceo's *Vida de Santa Oria."* In *Hispanic Studies in Honor of Alan D. Deyermond: A North American Tribute,* ed. John S. Miletich, 291-307. Madison: Hispanic Seminary of Medieval Studies, 1986.

INTRODUCTION TO *THE MARTYRDOM OF SAINT LAWRENCE*

TRANSLATED BY JEANNIE K. BARTHA

The martyrdom suffered by St. Lawrence was a well-known subject in the Middle Ages ever since St. Ambrose wrote about it in the fourth century. Ambrose was one of the greatest of the Church Fathers, and his works had been copied, recopied, and handed down across the centuries. Berceo appears to have followed Ambrose's account, though he was also influenced by the Spaniard Prudentius who recounted the martyrdom of St. Lawrence in his *Peristephanon* (ca. 400). Since Prudentius himself relied on St. Ambrose's account, the Ambrosian origins are both directly and indirectly reflected in Berceo's works.

The Martyrdom of Saint Lawrence is poetically presented by Berceo. The poem falls in the category of *passiones* of saints that draws on two varieties of religious literature. The first finds its origins ultimately in the *passio* (the Passion of Jesus Christ on the cross and its imitation in the saint's suffering) while the second derives from the *vita sancti* (hagiography and especially martyrdom). Berceo's work is a skillful blend of the two — *passio* and *vita sancti*.

The originality in Berceo's version of this ancient story lies in the manner of presentation. For the first time, the circumstances of the famous martyrdom were rendered into Spanish verse; hence they were made accessible to the public at large. The poet uses, as was his custom for narrative verse, the *cuaderna vía*. The story is presented in all of its dramatic and horrifying details that both draw on and contribute to the medieval imagery of saintly martyrdom. Berceo recalls the story of Saint Lawrence, a talented and much sought-after member of the papal court, who tries to use his cunning in protecting the Church and the faithful against a vicious Roman emperor. When he fails, Lawrence is not only prepared but even eager to sacrifice himself. He becomes a martyr by enduring the horrible suffering of being thrown on a grill and roasted alive. The poem ends *in medias res*, as it were, though probably not by Berceo's design, as the concluding quatrains appear to have been lost.

In *The Martyrdom of St. Lawrence* we have Berceo's single effort in the area of the *passio*. As in his other works, Berceo's poetic language was put to the service of his didactic objective: to attract and hold the attention of the audience and thus to inspire greater faith in the people.

Abbreviations

Dutton   Dutton, Brian, ed. *El Martirio de San Lorenzo*. In Gonzalo de
                Berceo, *Obras Completas*, 5: 146–80. London: Támesis, 1981.
Ramoneda   Ramoneda, Arturo M., ed. *Martirio de San Lorenzo*. In Gon-
                zalo de Berceo, *Signos que aparecerán antes del Juicio Final,
                Duelo de la Virgen, Martirio de San Lorenzo*, 229–62. Madrid:
                Castalia, 1980.
Tesauro   Tesauro, Pompilio, ed. *Martirio de San Lorenzo*. In Gonzalo
                de Berceo, *Obra completa*, with Isabel Uría, 455–89. Madrid:
                Espasa-Calpe, 1992.

THE MARTYRDOM OF SAINT LAWRENCE

1   In the precious name of the Almighty King
        Who makes the sun and moon to rise in the East,
        I want to compose the Passion of St. Lawrence
        in Romance[1] so that all may come to know it.

2   Vincent[2] and Lawrence, men without fault,
        were both from Huesca, according to the text;[3]
        both were Catholics, both extremely wise,
        pupils of Valerius,[4] descendants of his family.

3   At the time that Valerius held the bishopric,
        the illustrious canonship and see of Huesca,
        he nourished those pupils and showed them the way
        they should love the Son of the Virgin Mary.

4   They wisely obtained good sense from him,
        as if they had been taught by St. Paul himself;
        they kept their archdeaconships strictly in order,
        and did not conceal profits made from their loans.

5   They spared no effort to carry out their duties:
        they converted sinners with their preaching;
        they arrived at correctly reasoned judgments,
        and were abundantly blessed by Jesus Christ.

6   The papacy was held in Rome at that time
        by a holy pope whose name was Sixtus:[5]

---

[1] The vernacular or common language of the people.

[2] Martyred in the year 204, Vincent was the best-known Spanish martyr during the persecution of Diocletian. He may have been a relative of St. Lawrence. (See Tesauro, 462, note 2a.)

[3] The Latin text used by Berceo as his source.

[4] St. Valerius was bishop of Zaragoza, and exiled to France in 304 where he died in 315. (Dutton, 5:159, note 2d.)

[5] St. Sixtus, Sixtus II, pope from 31 August 257 to 6 August 258. (Dutton, 5:160, note 6b.)

it is certain he was born and raised on Greek soil;
he was first a philosopher[6] and then elected pope.

7   To put in order those matters in his trust
       that were not demanded of his soul by God,
       he sent sealed letters throughout the lands
       to order the clergy to gather together.[7]

8   The bishop Valerius, in all things agreeable,
       came to Rome, his two pupils with him;
       Sixtus was as pleased as with bread of finest wheat,
       and he told St. Valerius, "I am delighted with you."

9   He was heartily pleased with those companions,
       for they were just as innocent as cloistered monks;
       the words they uttered were prudent and decisive,
       and they were good spokesmen in any discussion.

10   Sixtus declared his will to Valerius:
       "I entreat you, my friend, for God and for charity,
       to accept my request, and to be so kind
       as to give me these scholars for this city.

11   I will thank you with all my heart,
       and I will forever be obliged to you;
       Friar, think rightly and do not say 'no',
       for you would act wrongly and against the law."

12   "Sir," said Valerius, "Father of Christendom,
       by the order you hold and by your mercy,
       understand my weakness and my need,
       otherwise my city and I are both lost.

13   You do understand, for you are well informed, Father,
       that one is my tongue[8] and the other my confidant;
       without them I would consider myself poor and diminished;
       I would sooner you removed, sir, my bishopric from me."

14   The pope replied that he did a great wrong
       if he did not obey him who was his pope;
       whoever might hear of it would see it as an insult,
       and another person might chance to do the same.

15   "Sir," said Valerius, "let us have an agreement

---

   [6] See Dutton, 5:160, note 6d for what may have been a mistaken identity of Pope
Sixtus II with a Greek Pythagorean philosopher also called Sixtus.
   [7] Meaning 'to convoke a general council in Rome'.
   [8] St. Valerius suffered from a speech defect and consequently St Vincent had to
preach for him. (See Dutton, 5:160, note 13b.)

not to allow our dispute to be mentioned;
take whichever one you want, you make the choice;
I will live with the other one, but not without regret."
The pontiff said, "I grant the decision."

16 Valerius and St. Sixtus stuck to the agreement,
each with his own deacon perfect in charity,
although regretfully, Lawrence with St. Sixtus,
sadly and dejectedly, Vincent with Valerius.

17 There would be plenty of material to speak about them both:
it would make a great story, but you might find it tedious;
let us return to the Passion of St. Lawrence;
let us prepare to go back to what we promised.

18 Sixtus was immensely delighted with St. Lawrence:
he saw that through him he received great advantage;
he was famed throughout the entire Roman world,
and all were enormously pleased and happy.

19 Except for the apostles who rank higher,
never was the council more pleased with anyone;
everyone said he had been sent by God,
for which He should be both thanked and praised.

20 The Holy Church was edified by him:
those in distress saw him as their father;
he held no old rancor hidden in his breast,
and no improper word issued from his lips.

21 He served Sixtus at the holy altar,
and became outstanding in reading and singing;
indeed he knew how to be a faithful servant,
and how to see that fair judgments were rendered.

22 A very faithful counselor when it came to advising,
he was very apt at distributing the alms God gave him;
he was no gossiper and kept a secret well,
and had no use for any who were flatterers.

23 He was a man who was perfectly discreet,
a good listener and discerning of those with troubles;
he pitied those souls on the road to perdition;
he was dying to suffer martyrdom and the Passion for God.

24 Matters stood well with a temperate wind blowing;
the stepson was not seizing the son from his house;[9]

---

[9] Berceo refers to the situation between the Christians and the Romans (pagans) at the time of St. Lawrence. (See Tesauro, 468, note 24.)

but the wheel[10] turned and the axle was upset,
and summer was changed completely into winter.

25   The Romans brought to power an evil emperor:
if Nero was so base, this one was no better;
he fostered such a hatred against Jesus Christ
that just to hear His name caused him displeasure.

26   He challenged the world and Christianity:
he began to perpetrate much cruelty on the clergy;
showing no mercy he caused them harsh suffering,
and with all his will, he committed evil deeds.

27   It came to the attention of Sixtus, who was pope,
how harshly and angrily Decius[11] was acting;
he realized that his case was completely lost,
that without any question he was to be martyred.

28   Within his heart he experienced great joy;
he gathered his council and all his clergy;
"My friends," he said, "may Holy Mother Mary help us,
for we are in deep trouble and in terrible straits.

29   The emperor is waging war against the faith:
he wants to make Christians deny Christ,
to go and make offering and pray to the idols,
and he wants to martyr those who will not do so.

30   My friends, let us not greatly value this life:
let us forget the world and think of our souls;
everything we leave here we will recover;
unhampered by fear, let us trust God alone.

31   God, to save and redeem His Holy Church,
gave His body to suffering and willed to die on a cross;
the apostles died to follow Christ,
to build up the Church and suppress evil faith.

32   It is fitting that we who live now should die:
by dying, let us follow those who came before us;
for the Church let us give the bodies that we feed;
for a little suffering let us not lose our souls."

---

[10] Meaning "the wheel of fortune."
[11] Concerning a possible confusion of identity of the Roman emperors Decius and Valerian, see Dutton, 5: 161, note 27b. Decius did indeed carry out a persecution in the third century.

33   While St. Sixtus was giving that sermon,
      and comforting his priests like a holy person,
      a message came for him shortly thereafter
      to appear before Decius to defend his case.

34   He saw that he could not escape from martyrdom,
      and was just as pleased and willing as ever;
      he called his deacon and worthy pupil,
      and made him keeper of all his treasures.

35   The holy bishop went before the emperor,
      and contended with the wolf like a faithful shepherd:
      "Decius," he said, "kindly tell me what you wish,
      and indeed we will answer you, thanks to God."

36   Said Decius to Sixtus, "I would like for you
      to give me the treasures of your bishopric;
      if you will do exactly that, you will have my thanks;
      if not, both you and your clergy will suffer."

37   Said Sixtus to Decius, "You speak with impiety:
      you seem a wise man but you utter foolish words;
      it would not be right for the treasures of the Church
      to be given for use in vile or evil traffic.

38   The Church's property must belong to God,
      or if there be need, given to the poor;
      those who worship idols must not have it,
      for anyone who gave it should fall into hell."

39   Said Decius to Sixtus, "Your words are rash:
      you speak with haste and you will quickly stumble;
      you may stir a man to unseemly action;
      if you get injured you will never be avenged."

40   Said Sixtus to Decius: "Listen here, Emperor,
      give me time to speak for our Lord and God;
      you are a great man: God is much greater;
      I do not care a tuppence for your threats.

41   The treasures you request are safely deposited;
      he who received them has them carefully guarded;
      neither you nor your followers can possibly get them,
      for then I would consider they were put to ill use."

42   "Sixtus," said Decius, "you seem crazy:
      you are off the track and hopelessly confused;
      sacrifice with us and alter your path,
      or else you are in for a terrible time."

43   "Decius," said Sixtus, "your words are empty,
      and utterly lacking in kindness or compassion;
      you aim to destroy all of Christianity,
      but it is you who will prove to be destroyed.

44   I will sacrifice to the Lord Jesus Christ
      Who made a Host of Himself in order to save souls;
      I will not adore or pay service to your idols
      who make no sense and have no power."

45   Decius became enraged against Sixtus:
      he ordered him taken out to the arena,
      so that he should be nothing less than beheaded;
      Sixtus said, "May the beloved Almighty God forgive you."

46   While Sixtus was engaged in a struggle with Decius,
      Lawrence, who had been entrusted with the treasures,
      gave them all to the poor, as it is written in Scripture:
      Dispersit, dedit pauperibus,[12] and he did a fine deed.

47   Lawrence was a man extremely holy,
      and immensely charitable to the poor,
      he removed every illness from the sick,
      and gave to the blind sight and health.

48   If he laid his hands upon the infirm,
      those who were afflicted were instantly healed;
      those who before could hardly walk on level ground
      were afterwards out playing ball in the sun.

49   Much good flowed from his sacred hands:
      they healed the sick, they fed the poor,
      they gave sight to the blind, they clothed the naked;
      all those who believed in him were greatly favored.

50   The blessed gentleman, free of wicked guile,
      while distributing the treasures like a faithful vicar,
      walking through the town, stumbled on a district,
      and found there a widow most saintly and gracious.

51   There was in that area a suffering widow
      without a husband for thirty-two years;
      she concealed many Christians in her home,
      performing for them an extremely great service.

---

[12] 'He scattered, He gave to the poor.' See Ps. 112: 9 and 2 Cor. 9:9.

52   She suffered daily from so many headaches
          that she was always more ill than she was well;
          she said, "Worthy sir and father, from whom such good flows,
          lay your sacred hands upon this Christian woman."

53   Of all who were there, Christian men and women,
          he washed their feet with his sacred hands;
          he uttered certain words praying over the widow,
          and she instantly lost all her daily pains.

54   He took leave of all and gave them his blessing;
          he gave each one his portion of the treasures;
          he went on to do further works for the poor,
          to wash their feet and give them consolation.

55   At the home of Narcissus, a famous senator,
          he found many needy who were servants of God,
          believers in Christ, the Lord and Savior of the world,
          yet they were in fear of the evil emperor.

56   Although they were poor in material goods,
          for through wicked judgment they had been disinherited,
          they were enriched and comforted by the good man;
          they believed he had freed them from great affliction.

57   He washed and then dried their feet with his towel,
          and performed this bath on all who were there;[13]
          he divided the treasures openly among them,
          heaping no scorn or rebuke on anyone.

58   When he had served and pleased them all,
          he said, "My friends, may you be entrusted to God;
          I will perform my office, I will seek out the poor,
          for very soon we will be summoned by Decius."

59   Among those companions in the home of Narcissus,
          there was a good man who had lost his sight;
          he said, "I beg you, may you thus see paradise!
          Lay your hands on me and save me from ridicule."

60   He laid his hands on him and uttered his prayer:
          "Christ, through Whom Your mother was left unharmed,
          You Who gave sight to the man born blind,[14]
          bestow Your compassion on this man."

---

[13] Cf. John 13:4–14.
[14] Cf. John 9:1–38.

61   When Lawrence had completed his prayer,
        his whole blindness was healed by faith;
        the good man immediately took his departure,
        for he already wished that his time had come.

62   Having already put the whole treasure to good use,
        the servant went swiftly in search of his bishop;
        he found him whom they wanted to take from the city
        to carry out the sentence of his martyrdom.

63   When St. Lawrence saw his bishop being taken away,
        the tears began to fall heavily from his eyes;
        he began to cry at the top of his voice,
        "Sir, why do you wish to forsake me like this?

64   Father, with all my heart I beg you the favor,
        not to forsake me, for God and for charity;
        if you do not take me away with you, Father,
        I will remain like an orphan in utter poverty.

65   Whenever you wanted to sacrifice to God,
        and wished to say holy Mass at the altar,
        you used to take me along to serve you:
        you ought not to forsake me now, Father.

66   If in any way, Father, I caused you sorrow,
        in this situation you ought to forgive me;
        you should not conceal such anger from your servant;
        for that, your soul can only suffer.

67   You will be thought, holy Father, to have greatly erred,
        if you go in to such a supper while I stay famished;
        I beg you this favor, sir, take me there:
        I would like to go first to answer this call.

68   The treasures that you left entrusted to me,
        by the grace of Christ, lie safely guarded;
        Decius will not find them, for they are well hidden;
        we will not lose them for we gave them on loan.

69   They lie safely hidden where indeed we will find them;
        we will not be denied them, we will get them back doubled;[15]
        Father, do not disdain me: we will suffer together;
        as master and servant we will manage very well."

---

[15] In quatrains 68 and 69 there is a clear allusion to the doctrine of divine grace, to the good or evil use made of it by human beings who have free will. See the example of the parable of the talents in Matt. 25: 14–30 (Ramoneda, 246 note 68–69).

70   Said the sacred bishop to his holy Levite,
"Son, you have said enough, do not be so insistent;
of far greater worth will be your mantle[16]
than ours will be, I predict that to you.

71   As we are old and diminished in strength,
we are very slack in approaching the deed,
but you young men with greater strength
will be able to fight and earn greater riches.

72   Before five days are gone, I predict to you
that you will be in desperate trouble and dire competition,
but be assured that you will hold the field:
you will earn a great crown of finest pure gold.[17]

73   When you have drunk the cup they will give you,
you will come straight to us wearing a fine mantle;
you will be cordially welcomed in the heavenly court,
and you will see how God honors His servants."

74   "Father, if indeed you would[18] see justice done,
you ought to send your servant ahead of you:
you ought to take this example from the patriarch
who wished to sacrifice his son to God."[19]

75   "Son," said the father, "if they granted us more time,
indeed we could say some words to the contrary:
Elijah when he was to depart from this world
left behind in his place his holy servant."[20]

76   The pagans who were taking him prisoner were worried,
and they said, "We are stupid and act without sense;
if he tries to rebel let us carry him bodily;
if not, Decius will give us bitter garlic and cheese."[21]

---

[16] The special mantle the martyrs receive in heaven (Dutton, 5:162, note 70d).

[17] Cf. Ps. 21:4.

[18] Here I read *quissieses/quisieses* with Tesauro, 481, 74a; Logroño, 249, 74a; and Ramoneda, 247, 74a rather than *quisieres* with Dutton, 5:155, 74a.

[19] The patriarch Abraham who was going to sacrifice his son Isaac to God. See Gen. 22:1–18.

[20] See 2 Kings 2 regarding Elijah and Elisha.

[21] The Spanish here for *bitter garlic and cheese* is *amargos ajos queso*. According to Dutton, 5:162, note 76d, no satisfactory answer to the meaning of this expression has been found. He mentions, however, a Catalan soup, *almadroc*, made from garlic and cheese. Ramoneda, 266 under *ajo-queso* has 'guiso o salsa en que entran el ajo y el queso' and gives documentation under this entry. In context, the meaning here is: 'Decius will give us a stiff punishment.'

77   The faithless men performed a faithless act:
        Sixtus had to undergo the harsh sentence;
        his sacred body expired with great patience,
        in exemplary manner, with two of his servants.

78   While Lawrence was saying these things,
        the wicked men had their minds on him;
        very soon then they hastened to take him into custody,
        which greatly pleased Decius when he heard it.

79   Decius' henchmen, those greedy dogs,
        put him in jail with some other companions,
        for Decius would pay them plenty for him,
        or draw up a letter to exempt them from taxes.

80   Among those companions lying in prison,
        there was a knight whose eyes were blind;
        he entreated that holy man, St. Lawrence,
        to say some prayers for his benefit.

81   St. Lawrence told him, "If you will believe in Christ,
        and will receive baptism in His holy name,
        you shall have all your sight — but if you will not do so,
        you shall never regain the sight that you desire."

82   Lucillus[22] replied to him with great prudence:
        "I would have been most willing to do so,
        for I wanted and I wish to keep your command;
        from head to toe I am entirely in your hands."

83   As he was very quick about such matters,
        first of all he made Lucillus a Christian;
        after he baptized him with his sacred hand,
        he recovered his whole sight and was joyful and well.

84   The story spread throughout the whole land,
        of how Lucillus had recovered his sight,
        and many people came, each from their homes,
        to see this man of such grace and holiness.

85   All who came showed him their afflictions:
        if they came sick they indeed returned healed;
        those who were needy took from him alms;
        countless were the many who were cured by him.

---

[22] The name *Lucillo* might be a play on words in Spanish, the diminutive form of *luz* meaning 'little light.'

86   The Emperor Decius sent for Lawrence;
      he that had imprisoned him stood before him:
      "Produce the treasures, I tell you, my fine Christian,
      or else you shall pay for it today before you dine."

87   St. Lawrence told him, "All your threats
      taste better to me than finest gooseberries;
      all your henchmen and you who abuse me
      frighten me no more than gentle doves."

88   This aggravated Decius who wanted to get angry,
      but in his greed to obtain the treasure,
      he said he would give him one day's grace,
      so he went with Valerian[23] to rest the night.

89   Valerian was afraid to take him with him,
      for he was not his friend and he cared little for him;
      he passed him to Hippolytus[24] saying, "Let him go with you,
      for he is a deadly enemy of our entire law."

90   Hippolytus was pleased to be in his company,
      for he judged him to be of benefit for all;
      he healed the sick of every illness,
      and worked miracles on blind people every day.

91   God inspired him through his kindness:
      it entered his mind to turn Christian;
      he requested baptism, the law of Christianity;
      the deacon of great holiness conferred it upon him.

92   Early next morning, the duke Valerian
      said, "Go and get Lawrence who heals the sick:
      we will see what good are his empty words,
      for I fear we will end up with scarcely any profit."

93   As soon as he had come, Valerian said,
      "Lawrence, you seem more cracked than sound.
      Show the treasures, hand them to us,
      or else you may die like a common peasant."

---

[23] Valerian was leader of the Senate under Decius (249–251) and afterwards emperor (253–258). His complete name was Publius Licinius Valerianus (Decius' was Gaius Messius Quintus Traianus Decius). Berceo calls him "duke Valerianus" in 92a (Dutton, 5:163, note 88d).

[24] 'Valerianus dedit eum (*San Lorenzo*) cuidam vicario nomine Yppolito' *Passio Polycronii* 19. Hippolytus became a Christian and suffered martyrdom. In many martyrologies, Sixtus, Lawrence and Hippolytus are mentioned together – See Carmen García Rodríguez, *El culto de los santos...*, 178–181" (Dutton, 5:163, note 89c).

94   Said Lawrence, "Give me three days' grace:
        I will take counsel with my brotherhood;
        I will show you the treasures, but I cannot today."
        Valerian said, "That is what I would like from you."

95   The duke Valerian believed those words:
        he thought he had everything in his grasp;
        he boasted to Decius, a hasty thing to do,
        for he promised it all down to the very last item.

96   When the three days' grace had come and gone,
        he gathered together all the poor he could find;
        he brought them with him and began to preach:
        "These are the most beloved treasures of God.[25]

97   These are the treasures that never grow old:
        the more they are scattered the greater they always grow;
        those who love them and offer for them
        will gain the Kingdom where souls are saved."

98   Valerian saw that he had been deceived;
        the matter did not turn out as he had expected;
        he went to the emperor enraged and furious:
        he told him how the matter had suffered a reverse.

99   They could do nothing else but return to Lawrence.
        They said, "You either sacrifice or suffer the Passion.
        There is no way that you can escape this."
        "I desire," he said, "to embrace the Passion."

100   To give him a more painful and horrible death,
        they made him a bed that was exceptionally hard;
        it had no bedclothes or a single bit of wood:
        everything to do with it was made of iron.

101   The slats on the bed were made of iron
        with space for the fire to penetrate between them;
        they had him bound both hand and foot,
        and ordered him thrown at once on the bed.

102   They gave him a bath[26] such as you shall hear tell of:
        the wicked servants began stoking up the blaze;

---

[25] A topos in hagiography, told of several saints.

[26] Berceo uses the word *bath* figuratively here symbolizing contentment or pleasure (Dutton, 2:73, note 152b). Compare several instances in the *Miracles* above, and M.R. Lída, "Estar en (un) baño, estar en un lecho de rosas," *Revista de Filología Española* 3 (1941): 263–70.

they stirred up the fire taking no rest,
causing Lawrence more pleasure than pain.

103　　The flames were immeasurably lively and scorching:
they burned the holy body with enormous heat;
the entrails were bubbling from the roasting—
let no one fail to imagine the pain!

104　　"Take care," said Lawrence, "to turn me over,
season me good, for I am roasted enough;
get ready to eat, for you have suffered —
God forgive you, my sons, for your grievous sin.

105　　A fine meal you gave me, a fine bed you made me,
and I do rightly to thank you very much;
I will not wish you worse for this deed of yours,
I will hold neither anger nor malice against you."

Bibliography

Primary Sources

Editions of Berceo's Works (in addition to those given in the Abbreviations)

Gonzalo de Berceo, *Martyrio de Sant Laurençio*. In idem, *Obra completa*, intro. Rufino Briones. Logroño: Instituto de Estudios Riojanos, 1971.

Other Works and Sources of Reference

Andrés Castellanos, María S. de, ed. *La Vida de Santa María Egipciaca*. Madrid: Aguirre Torre, 1964.

Baró, José. *Glosario completo de los "Milagros de Nuesta Señora" de Gonzalo de Berceo*. Boulder: Society of Spanish and Spanish-American Studies, 1987.

Bartha, Jeannie K. "Four Lexical Notes on Berceo's *Milagros de Nuestra Señora*." *Romance Philology* 37 (1983): 56–62.

———. *Vocabulario de los "Milagros de Nuestra Señora" de Gonzalo de Berceo*. Normal, IL: Applied Literature Press, 1980.

Beresford, Andrew M. "The Figure of the Martyr in Gonzalo de Berceo's *Martirio de San Lorenzo*." In *Proceedings of the English Colloquium*, ed. A. M. Beresford and A. Deyermond, 107–18. Papers of the Medieval Hispanic Research Seminar 5. London: Dept. of Hispanic Studies, Queen Mary and Westfield College, 1997.

Blecua, J. M. ed. *El Conde Lucanor*. Madrid: Castalia, 1969.

Cejador y Frauca, J. *Vocabulario medieval castellano*. Orig. 1929; repr. New York: Las Américas, 1968.

Corominas, Joan, ed. *Libro de Buen Amor*. Madrid: Gredos, 1967.

———, and José A. Pascual. *Diccionario crítico etimológico castellano e hispánico*. 6 vols. Madrid: Gredos, 1980–1991.

Covarrubias Orozco, Sebastián de. *Tesoro de la lengua castellana o española*. Orig. 1611; repr. Madrid: Turner, 1977.

Dutton, Brian. "A Chronology of the Works of Gonzalo de Berceo." In *Medieval Hispanic Studies Presented to Rita Hamilton*, ed. A. D. Deyermond, 67–76. London: Tamesis, 1975.

———. *A New Berceo Manuscript, Biblioteca Nacional Ms. 13149. Description, Study and Partial Edition.* Exeter Hispanic Texts 32. Exeter: University of Exeter Press, 1982.

———, ed. Gonzalo de Berceo, *Obras Completas.* 5 vols. London: Tamesis, 1967–1984.

Goicoechea, Cesáreo. *Vocabulario riojano.* Madrid: Aguirre Torre, 1961.

Gulsoy, J. "The -i Words in the Poems of Gonzalo de Berceo." *Romance Philology* 23 (1969–1970): 172–87.

Honnorat, S. J. *Dictionnaire Provençal-Français.* 3 vols. Orig. 1848; repr. Marseille: Laffitte Reprints, 1971.

Keller, John Esten. *Gonzalo de Berceo.* Twayne World Authors Series 187. New York: Twayne, 1972.

———. *Pious Brief Narrative in Medieval Castilian and Galician Verse: From Berceo to Alfonso X.* Lexington: University Press of Kentucky, 1978.

Koberstein, G., ed. *Gonzalo de Berceo, "Estoria de San Millán": Textkritische Edition.* Münster: Aschendorff, 1964.

Kulp-Hill, Kathleen, trans. *Songs of Holy Mary by Alfonso X, The Wise: A Translation of the* Cantigas de Santa María. MRTS 173. Tempe: Arizona Center for Medieval and Renaissance Studies, 2000.

Lanchetas, Rufino. *Gramática y vocabulario de las obras de Gonzalo de Berceo.* Madrid: Sucesores de Rivadeneyra, 1900.

Lappin, Anthony. *Berceo's Vida de Santa Oria: Text, Translation and Commentary.* Oxford: Legenda, 2000.

Latham, R. E. *Revised Medieval Latin Word-List.* London: Oxford University Press, 1965.

Lazar, Moshé, ed. *La Fazienda de Ultramar.* Salamanca: Cervantes, 1965.

Levy, Emil. *Petit Dictionnaire Provençal-Français.* Orig. 1909; 5th ed. Heidelberg: Carl Winter, 1973.

Marden, C. Carroll, ed. *Libro de Apolonio.* Orig. 1922; repr. Millwood: Kraus Reprint Co., 1976.

Menéndez Pidal, Ramón, ed. *Cantar de Mío Cid. Texto, gramática y vocabulario.* 4th ed. Madrid: Espasa-Calpe, 1969.

Montgomery, Thomas, ed. *El Evangelio de San Mateo. Texto, gramática, vocabulario.* Madrid: Aguirre Torre, 1962.

Mount T., and Annette G. Cash, trans. Gonzalo de Berceo, *Miracles of Our Lady.* Lexington: University Press of Kentucky, 1997.

Nebrija, Antonio de. *Vocabulario de Romance en Latín.* Orig. 1516; transcr. Gerald J. MacDonald. Philadelphia: Temple University Press, 1973.

Real Academia Española. *Diccionario de la lengua española.* 19th ed. Madrid: Espasa-Calpe, 1970.

Solalinde, A. G., ed. *Milagros de Nuestra Señora.* 8th ed. Madrid: Espasa-Calpe, 1972.

Walsh, John K., ed. *El Libro de los Doze Sabios o Tractado de la Nobleza y Lealtad.* Madrid: Aguirre, 1975.

Willis, Raymond S., ed. *El libro de Alexandre.* Orig. 1934; repr. Millwood: Kraus Reprint Co., 1976.

———. *Libro de Buen Amor.* Princeton: Princeton University Press, 1972.

III. The Doctrinal Poems

The Sacrifice of the Mass, The Signs Which Will Appear Before Judgment Day, and The Hymns

INTRODUCTION TO *THE SACRIFICE OF THE MASS*

TRANSLATED BY JEANNIE K. BARTHA

The Sacrifice of the Mass is a doctrinal work; it contains no novelesque sequence of events as is the case with Berceo's Lives and the *Martyrdom*, and no series of brief narratives in the form of miracles and visions as in his *Miracles* and Lives. It is actually a pious tract in vernacular verse — an allegorical interpretation of the Latin liturgy of the Mass, probably the first of its kind in a Western vernacular, as suggested by Teresa Clare Goode.

Cognizant of the fact that the vast majority of parishioners, and even some members of the clergy, did not know what each element of the ritual of the Mass signified, Berceo developed in 297 quatrains in the *mester de clerecía* a remarkable explanation and interpretation of the Mass with references to its origins in the Old Testament. He couched this in verse, making it a unique and appealing piece of instructional and yet wholly devotional writing.

As an ordained priest, Berceo had first-hand knowledge of the often shallow and poor quality of clerical education of his time. In fact, the comic or pathetic motif of the uneducated, ignorant, and even half-illiterate monk, nun, or priest is widespread in the Latin and vernacular literatures of the Middle Ages. Berceo himself wrote of this in his *Miracles* (number 3: "The Cleric and the Flower", and number 9: "The Simple Cleric"). Therefore, it is to his fellow clergy as much as to the faithful in general that Berceo's *Sacrifice* was addressed.

The underlying goal of this treatise is threefold: a description of ritual and doctrine during the period when God instructed Moses about how to build the Tabernacle and how to offer sacrifice; an explanation of the outcome of Old Testament ritual as it changed in the New Testament; and a painstaking, virtually line-by-line interpretation of the details of the Latin Mass, and their origin in Scripture. With a fine eye for graphic details, Berceo gives a visually compelling and liturgically accurate description of the Mass as it was celebrated in his day. The wealth of historical information makes this work not just an example of medieval didactic poetry, but also a valuable reference source for the modern reader and especially for clergy and those in the field of theology and medieval studies.

Abbreviations

Dutton   Dutton, Brian, ed. *El Sacrificio de la Misa*. In Gonzalo de
Berceo, *Obras Completas,* 5: 3–80. London: Tamesis, 1981.

Cátedra   Cátedra, Pedro M., ed. *Del Sacrificio de la Misa*. In Gonzalo
de Berceo, *Obra completa,* with Isabel Uría, 933–1033. Madrid: Espasa-Calpe, 1992.

The Sacrifice of the Mass

1   In the name of the King Who rightfully reigns,
Who is the beginning and the end of all creation,
if I might be guided by His holy discretion,
I would like to compose a poem in His honor.

2   I will speak first of the Old Testament,
of how they sacrificed and what altar they used;
then turn with sure steps from there to the New,
in order to harmonize and bring them together.

3   When the Law was given and received by Moses,
and written down by God's own finger,
on an earthen altar, not carved from stone,
the Hebrew people made their sacrifices.

4   When for the lords who commanded the people
they wanted a sacrifice, they offered a bullock;
for the common people they sacrificed he-goats,
and a sheep for the high priest[1] and his attendants.

5   But from out of the he-goats which they separated,
two, as commanded, were brought to the temple;
in fulfillment of their Law they slit one's throat,
and sent the other to the winds of the wilderness.[2]

6   The chamber that the priests had to watch over,
where those animals were usually sacrificed,
was divided by a veil that used to hang there,
between the greater room and the holy altar.

7   The chamber before the veil was where they chanted,
and there they offered he-goat, sheep and bullock,
turtledoves and pigeons, breads, silver and gold,
and behind the veil lay another treasure.

---

[1] Berceo makes frequent and indiscriminate use of the term *bispo/obispo* 'bishop' when referring to high-ranking clergy in the context of both the Old and the New Testaments. The translation uses whatever term is deemed appropriate.

[2] See Lev. 16:7–10.

8   In the first chamber stood a candelabrum[3]
         made of nothing whatsoever but solid, pure gold;
         a candleholder stood on all its seven branches,
         six on the sides and one in the middle.

9   There stood a table wrought beautifully in copper,
         and on it twelve loaves made of unbleached flour;
         no one else ever ate a single bite of them,
         except for the priests and the ordained people.

10   The loaves never lasted for more than a week,
         and the following week they were replaced by others;
         those loaves were considered to be holy by the priests
         who were quick to remove them at the end of each week.

11   Behind the veil in the second chamber
         is where the truly great relics were found;
         an exquisite ark made of precious wood,
         and inside it were relics of priceless value.

12   The ark was entirely covered in gold,
         and finely wrought by an expert hand;
         it was closed, not open, with a tablet above it,
         a marvelous tablet and beautifully worked.

13   Upon the tablet angels tumbled about,
         and covered the whole ark with wings unfurled;
         only two of them were standing very straight,
         each with his face turned towards the other.[4]

14   That aforementioned ark was a reliquary
         all filled with the utmost holy of relics;
         in it were the tablets on which the Law was written,
         and the staff of Aaron,[5] a priceless item.

15   A vessel worked in gold and not of earthenware,
         filled with holy manna that was sent from heaven,
         which God used to give to the Jews for food,
         was kept safely concealed in that holy ark.[6]

16   That holy chamber behind the veil,
         no one ever entered through door or tunnel,
         excepting for their high priest once a year
         with the blood of a calf, else he would be in trouble.

---

[3] The Jewish menorah. See Exod. 25:31–33.
[4] See Exod. 25:18–19.
[5] See Num. 17:16–26.
[6] Cf. also Heb. 9:4 for this and the preceding quatrain.

17   Of the two sanctuaries we have mentioned,
the first of those they used to call *sancta*,[7]
and the *sancta sanctorum*[8] the separate area
that lay behind the veil that was hanging.

18   All those offerings, the birds and the animals,
had their meaning in obscure commandments;
they were all fulfilled there in Jesus Christ
Who offered His body for our sins.

19   The he-goat that the priests used to slay
represented Him, His mortal body;
the one that stayed alive and came to no harm,
His divine nature and His spiritual root.

20   The innocent lamb that does no evil
signified Christ, for such was He;
the bullock that strikes with a mortal blow
was Christ Who destroyed the prince of darkness.

21   The dove is the symbol of His innocence,
the turtle, the sign of His chastity;
the loaves prefigured that He was the truth,
the way, the peace, and the life in bread of charity.

22   All the sacrifices of the Old Law,
all signified the true and authentic Host;
this was Jesus Christ Who opened the way
that enabled our return to the seat of glory.

23   Our own priest when he celebrates Mass,
and performs the sacrifice on the holy table,
the Host that he breaks is in remembrance of all that;
there all is appeased and brought to completion.

24   Whether sacrifices or whether prophecies,
the words of Daniel and those of Isaiah,
and those of Habakkuk and those of Jeremiah,
all was brought to conclusion on the cross of the Messiah.

25   The Messiah's coming put all that to rest;
the prophets were silent and the veil withdrawn;
there was rejoicing of he-goats and animals;
He put an end to all things of the past.

26   All those of old were yearning for Him,
and every sacrifice foretold His coming;

[7] 'Holy.'
[8] The 'Holy of Holies.'

when He appeared they stopped all killing:
from the moment He said "Fiat"[9] they dared not appear.

27   The legitimate priest who never leads astray,
      Son of the exalted King and Queen,
      came down from high heaven to this miserable light;
      He sacrificed His body and He tore the veil.[10]

28   From the moment Christ suffered the prophesied Passion,
      He brought to completion the Old Law sacrifices;
      He raised the New Law and placated the Old,
      and the Old Law lies veiled under the New.

29   On returning to heaven from where He came,
      He left a community of excellent apostles;
      they ordained churches where God would be served,
      like perfect human beings with perfect sense.

30   They ordained bishops and other minor priests
      to serve at the altars and absolve sinners,
      to recite before dawn the early morning prayers,
      and sing the offices in honor of the dead.

31   The pure vestments worn by the prelates,
      and even the clothing of the ordained priests
      represent those used in days gone by,
      and the body of Christ untainted by sin.

32   When the holy priest appears in his vestments,
      and emerges from the hidden place of the sacristy,
      he represents Christ Who was not understood,
      for otherwise the traitor would never have sold Him.

33   When he strikes his breast he proclaims himself guilty;
      then he kills the birds and slays the animals;
      when he does penance as he is commanded,
      he is behind the hanging veil in the *Sancta Sanctorum*.[11]

34   The office which then they begin to sing
      denotes the sighs, the glory and the praises,
      the *kyries*,[12] the prayers and the loud cries
      that the ancients raised for the Lord Jesus Christ.

---

[9] 'Let it be done.'
[10] Cf. Matt. 27:51, Mark 15:38, and Luke 23:45.
[11] See note 8 above.
[12] *Kyrie eleison*, the only Greek words used in the Mass, meaning 'Lord have mercy.'

*38[13]   The *Gloria in excelsis*[14] raised by the priest
            right at the beginning when he celebrates Mass
            represents the hymn and all the glory
            experienced by them at His holy birth.[15]

35   When that holy vicar says "Oremus,"[16]
            then he commemorates the famous incensory
            that was used to incense the entire sanctuary,
            which emitted smoke sweeter than a sweet electuary.[17]

36   We have that custom written in Scripture:
            fine prayer is called incense;[18]
            the lips of the famous David[19] confirm it,
            he who gave the Philistine a terrible stoning.[20]

37   While the priest is reading that holy text,
            he prays for the living as well as the dead;
            and all should offer their heartfelt prayers
            that God will hear him and his petition.

*39   When he celebrates Mass at the holy altar,
            whether with readings or whether with signs,
            it all comes back to Christ Who wishes to see it,
            for He ordered it all to be done in His memory.[21]

40   Once the prayer is finished the Epistle[22] is read,
            and it is read aloud to be sure that it is heard;
            the people are seated until the end of the reading,
            and until the deacon requests the blessing.

41   All that reading and that sacred speech
            signify the words that were preached
            by the apostles in the early times,
            when Christ sent them forth to spread the blessing.

42   As soon as the reader of the Epistle has finished,
            the choir replies to him shortly thereafter;

---

[13] See Dutton, 5:19, note 38 for his altering of the order of the quatrains here.
[14] 'Glory [to God] in the highest.'
[15] See Luke 2:14.
[16] 'Let us pray.'
[17] E.g. Lev. 16:12–13.
[18] Rev. 15:8.
[19] Ps. 141:2.
[20] See 1 Sam. 17:49.
[21] See Luke 22:19, and 1 Cor. 11:24–25.
[22] The New Testament Letters, primarily those attributed to St. Paul.

the response to him is: "You are a good counselor,
and I am very pleased to follow your advice."

43   The Laude[23] gives occasion to shout for joy:
       it is the hymn that causes the soul to rejoice;
       that is why it is said by the clergy then,
       because of the courtly words of the Epistle.

44   The Sequence[24] renders thanks to the Lord our God,
       to the Son of Mary, the Savior of the world,
       for through Him we are healed and saved from the affliction
       that we inherited from Adam and his spouse.

45   After the response, the Laude, and the prose
       comes the Gospel, sweet and delightful,
       the words of our Lord, Son of the Glorious Lady,
       Who saved us all with His precious blood.

46   All of the people rise from their places
       baring their heads, the better to hear;
       they trace with thumb the cross on forehead,
       lips, and breast, for it must be traced on all three.

47   Every Christian must make those signs,
       and while he makes them he must say the words:
       "Jesus of Nazareth, You Who are powerful and worthy,
       King of the Jews, save Your servants."

48   Those who are confused should certainly ask
       why the priest so swiftly changes place;
       he goes from right to left at the holy altar,
       and ends up by having to return to where he was.

49   The Jews are represented by the side on the right,
       to where the priest goes when he first comes out;
       they understood imperfectly the Law that they had,
       through which they were justified, not through good living.

50   The side on the left signifies the pagans
       who had from God neither law nor sign;
       that is why He especially instructed His disciples
       not to approach them for lodgings.[25]

---

[23] The Alleluia.
[24] The Sequence is the prose or verse that is recited in certain Masses after the prayer
of the Gradual (Cátedra, 962, note 44a).
[25] See Matt. 10:5, and Luke 10:10–12.

51   When those on the right refused to welcome him,
        He went and converted those on the left;
        they heard the Gospel unfamiliar to their ears,
        and obtained the whole Mass and even the Eucharist.

52   The Jewish people, unlucky the hour they were born,
        rejected Christ through their grievous sins;
        the pagans welcomed Him and they were fortunate:
        they became His sons, the others His stepsons.

53   What returning to the right side at Mass achieves
        is to show that, when the world comes to an end,
        the Jews will understand their improper behavior,
        and will believe in Christ Who came to save them.

54   Once the words of the holy Gospel are read,
        all those there make the sign of the cross;
        they raise their hands and give praise to God,
        that He may be blessed forever and ever.

55   What they do next makes truly good sense:
        they sing a fine hymn all about their faith,
        like people saying: "Christ, we have heard Your Word,
        and indeed we do firmly believe it."

56   This is clearly the appropriate thing,
        to listen first to the sacred reading,
        and show by words that their faith is perfect,
        then complete the job by offering their oblation.

57   When the Law was given in the early times,
        when they used to sacrifice, they did not offer money,
        rather bullock or bird or he-goat or sheep,
        but all was brought to conclusion in a lamb.

58   Christ was the lamb, Son of such a ewe
        whose equal there never was before or after;
        He brought the Old Law to its conclusion,
        and ordained the New Law steadfast and true.

59   While those ordained sing the offertory,
        the priest vested in his sacred garments
        offers at the altar the entrusted gifts,
        the chalice and the Host instead of animals.

60   Let no one think that he does without purpose
        the pouring of the water into the wine,
        for this is a gesture that carries great meaning;
        he who does not do it thus, indeed does wrong.

61   The wine signifies the Lord our God,
        the water signifies sinful humanity;
        as those two properties are blended together,
        likewise humanity blends lovingly with God.

62   He who will not mix the water with the wine
        divides man from God and leaves him poor and wretched;
        he commits a grave sin and grieves the Divine King
        Who through the Glorious Lady came for us sinners.

63   Besides, when He hung, arms outstretched, on the cross,
        from His right side there flowed both blood and water;[26]
        he who wished to separate them would do wrong,
        and such a deed would not please the Lord Jesus Christ.

64   When Abraham our ancestor, whose memory we honor,
        returned victorious from the business that engaged him,
        Melchizedek[27] offered him, according to the story,
        bread and wine, which greatly pleased the King of Glory.

65   The offering of bread and wine at the holy altar
        is an authentic offering, it could not be better;
        when Christ desired to sup with his disciples,
        He wished their Communion[28] to be only bread and wine.

66   He who lays out the Host for the sacrifice
        should be sure to place it on his left-hand side,
        the chalice on his right, to better remind him
        it was from the right side that the water issued forth.

67   Once the chalice is offered and the Host laid out,
        it is the custom of those gathered there to offer
        whatever they wish, votive offering or oblation,
        or a very fine offering of a candle made of wax.

68   When Solomon had the temple consecrated,
        many great people came to celebrate the feast;
        they made great offerings beyond all telling,
        thereby setting an example of offering at the altar.

69   The priest vested in his sacred garments
        returns to the altar and prays to himself;[29]

---

[26] See John 19:34.

[27] Gen. 14:17–20.

[28] Holy Communion, the partaking of the consecrated bread or wine.

[29] The Secret prayer is said inaudibly because here the priest acts as a mediator speaking directly to God on behalf of man.

the people hear nothing of what he is saying,
and they are waiting for him to turn around.

70   I would like to tell you the meaning of this:
you will have to listen to a story,
so in case they ask you will know the answer,
you will be able to ruffle many a good priest.

71   Once the Supper was finished that Thursday,
the false traitor went to prepare the betrayal;
the Lord Jesus Christ withdrew from His disciples,
and went to pray, a stone's throw away.[30]

72   He uttered His just and perfect prayer;
He returned to His disciples and found them sleeping;
He told them to keep watch and to be on the alert,
so as not to be attacked by evil temptation.

73   To fulfill the Law, three times he went to pray,[31]
for the Law commanded to offer three animals,
a bullock, a he-goat, and a peaceful lamb,
and that is the meaning of the triple prayer.

74   The good Lord, exempt from all evil, prayed
for Himself, His people, and those in high places;
He wanted to pay the tithe for them all,
for every stream flowed from that river.

75   He returned to his disciples who were in distress;
He consoled them and He told them, "Sleep on in peace;
the hour is at hand when the evil companions
will perpetrate a huge and enormous outrage."

76   The prayer that the priest recites to himself
signifies the one that was prayed by their Leader;
He eliminated the lamb, the he-goat and bullock,
and closed the door on the whole ancient Law.

77   When he says, "Per omnia"[32] in an audible voice,

---

[30] See Luke 22:41.

[31] See Matt. 26:39–44, and Mark 14:35–42.

[32] After the Secret prayer of the Mass and just preceding the Preface, the exact words the priest says in Latin are: *Per omnia saecula saeculorum* ('Forever and ever'), *Dominus vobiscum* ('God be with you'), *Sursum corda* ('Lift up your hearts'), *Gratias agamus Domino Deo nostro* ('Let us give thanks to the Lord our God'). The exact words the people reply in Latin are: *Amen* ('Amen'), *Et cum spiritu tuo* ('And with your spirit'), *Habemus ad Dominum* ('We have [lifted them up] to the Lord'), *Dignum et justum est* ('It is right and just').

he represents Christ when He returned,
and found St. Peter sleeping after the Supper,
and Judas was kneading the evil leavened dough.

78   This audible voice signifies something else:
the high priest who emerged from behind that curtain
that separated the chamber, the bran from the flour,
and who sprinkled healing blood everywhere around.[33]

79   He gives them a fine blessing as he is commanded,
saying, "Dominus vobiscum, and may [God] be pleased with you,"
then "Sursum corda," that they may reply to him;
what response do they give him that may be free from sin?

80   The choir responds: "Here is our reply:
we have lifted the hearts that you have mentioned";
he says, "*Rendamus gratias* to God in Whom we believe,"
and the choir says, "We hold it to be truly right and just."

81   Then the priest prays to the heavenly court,
the angels and archangels, and to Christ Almighty,
that our cries may be equal in value to theirs,
that such voices may please the eternal King.

82   Then they sing the *Sanctus*,[34] the sign of joy
which the angels sing every day before God;
those praises come down to us from Isaiah,
from the fine book of prophecy written by him.[35]

83   If you are pleased with this story of ours,
have it for lunch and just wait for supper;
now we will really get down to the matter,
to where we need to take the reins firmly in hand.

84   Now the priest is getting right down to the core:
the days grow longer, the sun grows stronger;
the more I think of it, the more I am amazed;
may God save us all and be on our side.

---

[33] E.g.Lev. 1:5 (and many other instances).

[34] Just after the Preface and before the start of the Canon of the Mass, the bells are rung and the congregation recites the *Sanctus* in the Latin words: *Sanctus, Sanctus, Sanctus, Dominus Deus Sabaoth. Pleni sunt caeli et terra gloria tua. Hosanna in excelsis. Benedictus qui venit in nomine Domini. Hosanna in excelsis* ('Holy, Holy, Holy, Lord God of Hosts. Heaven and earth are full of Thy glory. Hosanna in the highest. Blessed is He Who comes in the Name of the Lord. Hosanna in the highest'). It is preceded by "With angels and archangels, and with the whole company of heaven ..."

[35] See Isa. 6:3.

85   Above, you will recall that you heard it said,
when he wanted to enter the hidden area,
how the lawful priest went suitably clothed
on the established day once every year.

86   When he had to celebrate that annual feast,
he crammed the incensory full with live embers;
he put in so much incense ground in mortar
that the entire sanctuary was filled with smoke.

87   The blood of the animal slain outside
he brought in with him when he went inside;
he sprinkled everything with hyssop twigs,[36]
ark and candelabrum and whatever was there.

88   So much smoke poured forth from the vessel
that no one could possibly see the priest;
he performed his ministry according to the Law,
then, emerging from the veil, he offered them, "Pax vobis."[37]

89   That first chamber which was on the outside
signifies the Church of the Christian people;
the other small area at some little distance
represents heaven and the upper regions.

90   The priest clothed in such exquisite garments
signifies Christ, Son of the Glorious Lady,
for He was clothed in flesh, pure and unblemished;
St. Paul tells us so:[38] this is no false tale.

91   The priest who had to perform that ministry
could not enter that hidden place without blood;
he always had to visit it with blood,
both inside and outside; he had to do so.

92   What was done by the priest, greater than all others,
was done as well by Christ our Lord and Savior;
the good Lord died only once for us,
and returned to the heavens with signal honor.[39]

93   In another time, when the Old Law operated,
and even now when there are those baptized,
never was redemption achieved without blood,
and not even nowadays, if we think clearly.

---

[36] Cf. Exod. 12:22.
[37] 'Peace be with you.'
[38] See 1 Tim. 3:16.
[39] See Heb. 9:25-28.

94   In our times it is thus commanded,
          if the ordained priest wants to celebrate Mass,
          that he recall the blood that flowed from the side
          of the One Who died on the cross for our sins.

95   We of the New Law hold this belief,
          for daily we drink His holy blood;
          and he who does not drink it, we read in Scripture,
          cannot be saved, according to our faith.[40]

*98[41]   Redemption from sins never came without blood;
          blood washes souls from all evil poison;
          the path to heaven is paved with blood;
          where blood does not touch, Beelzebub is near.

*99   We have the figure of Christ before us,
          we see with our eyes how He looked on the cross;
          we must never fail to remember His blood,
          for if we forget it we will wreak our own havoc.

*96   Let us speak of the mystery with which we began;
          we are greatly prolonging this winding tale;
          if God does not help us we will be in such straits
          that we will need both our hands and feet to get out.

*97   In the first chapter[42] our ordained priest
          with his right hand traces the cross three times:
          it signifies the three things[43] from ancient times:
          the he-goat, the sheep, and the young bullock.

*100   Once his sacred hand has traced the crosses
          over the Host and the chalice with the wine,
          he prays to God for the Church He has purchased,
          that it may not be abused by the devil.

101   He recites a well-known prayer for the pope,

---

[40] Cf. John 6:53-58.

[41] See Dutton, 5:28, note 98 for his altering the order of the quatrains here.

[42] Meaning here the beginning of the Canon of the Mass, which starts with the Latin words: *Te igitur clementissime Pater...supplices rogamus...*('Therefore, most Merciful Father...we humbly beseech Thee...'). The first prayer of the Canon is the prayer for the Church.

[43] During the first prayer of the Canon, the priest makes the sign of the cross three times over the chalice with the wine and over the Host, while addressing to the Lord the Latin words: ... *supplices rogamus, ac petimus, uti accepta habeas, et benedicas, haec dona, haec munera, haec sancta sacrificia illibata*... ('... we humbly pray and beseech [Thee] to accept and to bless these gifts, these presents, these holy unspotted Sacrifices...').

and also for the bishop, nor forgets the king,
for himself and the people and for the redeemed,
that God may keep them all from falling into evil.

102   He prays to God to protect the Church,
to keep it peaceful and free from any strife:
may it be kindled by His holy love,
and may He be pleased with all its deeds.

103   In the next chapter[44] the ordained priest
prays for his friends and those entrusted to him,
for those nearby and seated around him
who firmly believe in the crucified Christ.

104   He prays for the people who make offering at the altar,
for those freed[45] by the Mass from evil entrapment,
for anyone contributing income to the Church:
may God help them all and protect them from evil.

105   He prays for the sick and for the disabled
who are either in danger or diminished in health,
and for those who lie in the state of sin:
may God help them all and loosen their bonds.

106   Everything required by the Law and the bloodshed,
as it is well known, Christ requested it all;[46]
that is what the priest does, forgetting nothing,
the New Law being more perfect than the Old.

107   The third chapter,[47] yet to be recited,
carries good material that should be heard;
if you will linger with me for your own good,
you will hear stories that will give you pleasure.

108   In the time of the Old Law, the native priest,[48]
when he wanted to exercise the highest office,

---

[44] Meaning here the second prayer of the Canon which begins with the Latin words: *Memento Domine, famulorum famularumque tuarum…* ('Be mindful, O Lord, of Thy servants and handmaids …'). This second prayer is the prayer for the living.

[45] Here I read *suelta* (manuscripts I and B) with Cátedra, 983, 104b rather than *sueltan* with Dutton, 5:29, 104b. (See Dutton, 5:29, note 104b and 59, note 104b as well as Cátedra, 982, note 104b.)

[46] See Matt. 5:17–18; cf. Luke 16:17.

[47] Meaning here the third prayer of the Canon which starts with the Latin words: *Comunicantes, et memoriam venerantes…* ('In communion with, and honoring the memory…'). The third prayer of the Canon is the Invocation of the Saints.

[48] Meaning here the 'high priest', native, because from the tribe of Levi.

if he entered the *Sancta Sanctorum*[49] from the portico,
he carried on his person many rich symbols.

109   He carried on his rich and liturgical vestments[50]
the names of the ancestors and principal prophets,
and of those who were the legitimate patriarchs;
he entered well adorned with precious things.

110   He carried them written on an ample pallium[51]
which the high priest wore over everything else:
half of them on the front where the pectoral is worn,
and the rest on his back on the humeral veil.

111   This officiating high priest took another adornment:
when he wanted to enter the larger sanctuary,
he carried in his hand the famous incensory
which was always kept stored in the cupboard.

112   In it he put the splintered live embers,
and generous handfuls of the ground incense;
it emitted such terribly thick clouds of smoke
that they saw neither priest nor sacred vestments.

113   He also carried with him the blood of the animal
that had already been slain in the larger chamber;
he shed it everywhere as he was commanded;
the Creator was pleased with his service.

114   Our own priests, celebrants at the altar,
when beginning to recite the words of this chapter,
renew by their words and deeds all of that
which in those times they were accustomed to sacrificing.

115   The names of the ancestors of times gone by
he carried fastened to the pallium on his person;
in remembrance of this, the ordained priests
mention here again the apostles and the martyrs.

116   That is why those holy people are named,
to remember the deeds done in those times,
and also for us to keep them in our hearts,
to imitate their customs and their ways.

---

[49] See note 8 above.

[50] In the manuscript alleged to be the probable source of Berceo's *Sacrificio*, we read the Latin words: *Quia pontifex quando intrabat in Sancta Sanctorum nomina patriarcharum portabat scripta in pectore suo* ('... the high priest, when he entered into the Holy of Holies, wore written on his chest the names of the patriarchs ...') (Dutton, 5:70).

[51] A breastpiece forming part of the priestly vestments. See Exod. 28: 15–30.

117   The blood of the calf as well as the he-goat
which the high priest from those times used to shed,
prefigured the blood of our redemption
which the Lord Jesus Christ shed during the Passion.[52]

118   If the celebrant of the Mass wants to celebrate it well,
he should keep that blood firmly in mind;
if he remembers it well it can help us more,
we are bound to believe, than that other blood did.

119   The real live embers of the holy incensory
which that holy worker[53] placed in the chamber,
prefigured the fire and the passionate fervor
which the priest on duty should always have.

120   The fact that the ground incense burned so much
that the vested priest was not visible through the smoke,
shows that the office of the Mass is so perfect
that no human being can possibly fathom it.

121   All that could be seen of the high priest then
was as much as any human being could fathom or imagine;
the full value of Divine Grace obtained from the Mass
God never gave to any human being to understand.

122   No he-goat or sheep or ox is worth more;
no pigeon or turtledove or any such thing
could stand up against this spiritual mystery:
it would be like the value of hay compared to wheat.

123   When the minister of old who was serving God
emerged from the platform where the ark was kept,
he visited the people who were praying outside,
and sprinkled them with blood as the Law commanded.[54]

124   All the mystery of those solemn proceedings,
He brought to fulfillment before His Passion;
He left His disciples and went to pray,
and they could not see Him during that time.

125   Then He returned to them and ordered them to pray;
they saw Him with their eyes and they heard Him speak;
that is what the old blood was intended to mean,
which the Law commanded to be sprinkled on the people.

---

[52] Cf. Heb. 10:4.

[53] Meaning here the high priest. (See Cátedra, 986, note 119b.)

[54] Again, cf. Lev. 1:5, 11; Heb. 9:21.

126   That is why He said, if you care to know,
           "Modicum tempus erit and you will not see me;
           iterum adhuc modicum[55] and you will see me;
           and the truth of this you will see for yourselves."

127   In the fourth chapter,[56] according to the story,
           the vicar of Christ makes remembrance of that;
           with arms outstretched he begs the King of Glory
           that there be nothing base in any part of the service.

128   The priest, who alone offers the Host,
           includes all his people to participate in it;
           he offers the true King for the benefit of all,
           for that is what Christ the supreme Judge did.

129   When Christ offered His precious body,
           and He died for us all in such a dreadful act,
           that one single Host which was so generous
           released us all from dangerous captivity.

130   So that slight little wafer offered by the priest
           saves and protects many, many people;
           it provides the Divine Grace that flows from Christ,
           and not from the priest, for he is unworthy.

131   The priest is the vicar of the spiritual Lord:
           the Host that he offers is offered for all;
           the word that he utters is uttered for all;
           since he offers for all, it benefits all.

132   Then at the entrance, the words are read
           that the Host is offered by the whole family;
           even though it is thin, it helps both living and dead;
           the seed is small, but the harvest is great.

133   He prays for us all that God in His mercy
           will order our days in peace and charity,
           and protect our souls from the darkness,
           where no ray of light shall ever enter.

---

[55] The Latin words *Modicum tempus erit* and *iterum adhuc modicum* mean respectively: 'in a little while' and 'again a little while'. See John 16: 16–19.

[56] Meaning here the fourth prayer of the Canon which begins with the Latin words: *Hanc igitur oblationem servitutis nostrae, sed et cunctae familiae tuae, quaesumus, Domine, ut placatus accipias* ... ('O Lord, we beseech Thee graciously to accept this oblation of our service and that of Thy whole household'). During this fourth prayer, the priest extends his hands over the oblation.

134   This prayer of his so earnestly uttered,
that God should not abandon his people,
recalls the mystery of times gone by,
when they used to offer the blood of the animal.

135   We have already told you not just once,
but I think, indeed this is the third time,
how the high priest of the Old Law would go
once a year down this holy path.

136   Of what he did inside I will not say anything,
and I want to skip over what he did outside;
otherwise we would find the workday too long;
we would tire in the middle and lose our day's wages.

137   When the priest had finished everything inside,
adorned in the same way as when he entered,
exquisitely vested, he came out to the people
who listened intently to the good things he read them.

138   He said, "Asperges me,"[57] O how remarkable!
and he sprinkled that sacred blood over them all;
then he withdrew far from the sanctuary,
and would not return until dusk to the temple.

139   He betook himself far from the place,
and returned to the people only at sundown;
he stayed there alone like one who is exiled;
he dared not do otherwise, for indeed it was forbidden.

140   In the reading of the fifth prayer of the Canon,[58]
we make mention of such a withdrawal,
when we beg our Lord to bestow His blessing
upon that family and upon its offering.

141   He prays for the family claimed by Christ,
that it be not cast from the book of life;[59]

---

[57] 'Sprinkle me:' Ps. 51 (50):9.

[58] The words of the fifth Canon prayer are: *Quam oblationem tu, Deus, in omnibus, quaesumus, benedictam, adscriptam, ratam, rationabilem, acceptabilemque facere digneris: ut nobis Corpus, et Sanguis fiat dilectissimi Filii tui Domini nostri Jesu Christi* ('Humbly we pray Thee, O God, be pleased to make this offering wholly blessed, to consecrate it and approve it, making it reasonable, that it may become for us the body and blood of Thy dearly beloved Son, our Lord Jesus Christ').

[59] In the fifth prayer of the Canon, the Latin words that apply to this line are: *atque ab aeterna damnatione nos eripi, et in electorum tuorum jubeas grege numerari* ('that we be rescued from eternal damnation and numbered in the flock of Thine elect'). Cf. Rev. 3:5.

he prays for the wine and for the wafer,
that His Divine Grace may transform it into *melius*.[60]

142   That the bread may become the body in which He died,
that the wine may become the blood that redeemed us,
that what was born human may become angelic substance,
that we may be returned to Heaven whence Lucifer fell.

143   Gentlefolk and friends, vessels of the Creator,
you who drink the blood of the true Savior,
be devout here and temperate in desire,
for herein lies the essence of our work.

144   To better harmonize and bring things together,
we have to go further back in the story,
to scratch beneath the surface down to the root,
and establish the work on solid foundation.

145   If God would help me to accomplish His will,
I would like to speak of the paschal lamb
that must not be forgotten or concealed,
for it led to the figure of the other One to come.

146   In the Old Law God had commanded
that the children of that great tribe of Israel,
when they were to keep the famous Passover,
they should slaughter a male lamb and not a ewe.

147   In Egypt was where this first took place,
when the people had been oppressed by the Pharaoh,
and the angel inflicted that terrible punishment
of slaying every firstborn male and animal.[61]

148   Moses, who was a messenger, commanded them
that in the first month when the moon was full,
every household should slaughter a lamb,
and carefully keep its blood stored away.

149   The people of Israel should celebrate their Passover,
and should eat the paschal lamb roasted, not boiled;
they should paint with its blood the letter T,[62]

---

[60] 'Something better.' The Latin words of the fifth Canon prayer here referring to the offering of the bread and the wine are: *ut nobis Corpus, et Sanguis fiat dilectissimi Filii tui Domini nostri Jesu Christi* ('so that it may become for us the body and blood of Thy dearly beloved Son, our Lord Jesus Christ') (as above).

[61] Exod. 12:29–30.

[62] The word *tau* ('T') was the last letter in the Hebrew alphabet, the nineteenth letter in the Greek alphabet, corresponding to the Latin *t* (Dutton, 5:60, note 149c).

so the cruel angel would pass over that door.

150   The door which was left unpainted with the blood
boded ill for those who dwelt in that house;
every oldest and firstborn male
was immediately pierced by the sword of the angel.

151   The T is a stick which in every way
would be a cross if the top were not missing;
that T, even though diminished, still saved them,
and we through the cross regain true life.

152   It was blood that saved them from temporal death,
and we through blood regained spiritual life;
through the blood of the lamb all evil ended,
and nowadays that sign helps us greatly.

153   It is patently obvious that Jesus was that lamb:
St. John the Baptist pointed Him out;[63]
that victory was achieved by His precious blood;
the king who played the harp had an inkling of this.[64]

154   The second lamb was from a finer ewe
of much finer flesh and much finer bone;
both of them had scarlet red blood,
but the Divine Grace was neither similar nor equal.

155   The body of the first one was roasted in fire,
the body of the second one martyred on the cross;
by the blood of the former, Egypt was subdued;
the blood of the latter struck hell a terrible blow.[65]

156   Divine Grace, from the blood that came last,
was what sanctified the blood that came first;
the one was a lady, the other a servant,
the one was the grain, the other the stubble.

157   I would think, gentlefolk, if you are all willing,
that the old lamb should be laid to rest;
let us please ourselves by turning to the new,
for our every advantage lies in Him.

158   This lamb was the Son of the Heavenly King,
the equal of His Father in every way;

---

[63] See John 1:29.

[64] Reference to King David who played the harp and to his psalms such as Ps. 2: 6–8.

[65] Reference here to what occurred when Christ descended to hell after his death.

He appeared in this world as a human being
to help the people who were lying in great evil.

159   That innocent lamb in all His simplicity
vanquished the evil wolf full of falsehood,
the one that cast Eve into such disgrace,
and brought upon Cain such awful enmity.

160   On the beautiful paschal day of Easter,
which is the Resurrection of our Savior,
we eat His body that tastes of bread,
and, thanks be to God, we drink His blood!

161   The bread which the abbot consecrates on the altar
turns into His body, and that is the truth;
the wine turns to blood, the salvation of Christians:
the taste does not correspond to the substance.

162   The bread tastes like bread and the wine like wine,
yet they are not bread and wine but something much better:
they are the body of our Lord and Savior Jesus Christ,
and he who does not believe that would be in great error.

163   When the sixth chapter[66] is about to begin
(with the words *Qui pridie*, if you want to recite it),
we are on the threshold of the sacred words
that transform the bread into the body of Christ.

164   When the priest comes to that part of the Mass,
he takes in both hands what is before him,
and utters those words that he knows by heart,
while his right hand appropriately traces the cross.

165   Once the words are said and the cross is traced,
everything instantly changes its nature,
the wine into blood and the wafer into flesh,
and humbly kneeling the faithful adore them.

---

[66] Meaning here the sixth prayer of the Canon with the Latin words: *Qui pridie quam pateretur, accepit panem in sanctas ac venerabiles manus suas, et elevatis oculis in caelum ad te Deum, Patrem suum omnipotentem, tibi gratias agens, benedixit, fregit, deditque discipulis suis, dicens: Accipite, et manducate ex hoc omnes: HOC EST ENIM CORPUS MEUM* ('Who, the day before He suffered, took bread into his venerable hands, and having lifted up His eyes to heaven, to Thee, God, His Almighty Father, giving thanks to Thee, blessed it, broke it, and gave it to His disciples, saying: Take and eat ye all of this: FOR THIS IS MY BODY').

166 That magnificent, priceless grace and blessing
 is bestowed by God upon the oblation,
 from which Christianity takes consolation
 as its means to obtain the remission of sins.

167 Neither human nor angel nor any other creature,
 save God Who does that through His generosity,
 could possibly understand that good fortune,
 for it is all through nothing whatsoever but grace.

168 Once the Supper was over, our Lord Jesus Christ
 distributed such food to His faithful followers;
 He commanded that this should not be forgotten,
 but should be repeated in remembrance of Him.[67]

169 If the vicar of Christ who celebrates the Mass,
 when he raises the *Corpus Domini*[68] above him,
 does not have Christ's Passion deeply rooted in his heart,
 he profanes the words the moment he says them.

170 He must always recall that He died for our sake,
 but especially there, there at that place,
 for indeed He commanded us to do so;
 otherwise then we could grievously sin.

171 What I said of the bread, I say of the wine:
 it is all *Corpus Domini*, all going one path;
 it is all salvation for poor human beings
 who in this world are guests and pilgrims.

172 I will tell you still more about *Corpus Domini*:
 the bread it is made of must come from wheat;
 it must not be mixed with anything else;
 I witness to this and I firmly believe it.

173 If any other grain is mixed with it,
 such bread will stay just as it was;
 only wheat becomes the true flesh
 that places souls on the right path.

174 I want to go back to the subject of the Host with you,
 and to all the things we should ponder about it;
 there are six items we ought to consider:
 anything lacking in them should be altered.

---

[67] Cf. note on quatrain *39 above.
[68] 'The body of Christ.'

175   This is the very first item to consider,
        that it be from pure wheat and no other grain,
        white and very small and round in shape,
        unsalted and unleavened and with true writing.[69]

176   The entire consecration now brought to completion,
        the vicar of Christ stands with arms extended,
        and indeed wide open, his face wet with tears,
        for he remembers Christ and how He was martyred.

177   When he stands that way with outstretched arms,
        it signifies those angels with their wings unfurled
        whom we mentioned above, that covered the ark,
        but something tells me you have already forgotten.

178   And there is something else about this figure:
        it shows how Christ suffered the Passion;
        that is how they nailed Him to the cross to redeem us,
        when the famous Longinus[70] struck Him the blow.

179   The blessed priest standing that way,
        with arms outstretched, gazing at the cross,
        weeping tears while remembering Christ,
        mentions three things that I will tell you.

180   He recalls three things of utmost importance:
        the first is the way in which Christ died,
        and following that, how He came back to life,
        and thirdly, how He ascended to heaven.

181   If we would like to walk the straight path,
        we must do in deed what we say in word,
        for if our actions do not accord with our words,
        they are flowers without fruit, unfulfilled promises.

182   Then we praise the death of the Lord Jesus Christ,
        when we mortify the evil that lies within us;
        we certainly do not revere His Resurrection,
        if we are not really eager to do good works.

---

[69] The letters *IHS*, originally from the Greek *iota* and *sigma* but popularly interpreted *IHESUS* or *IHESUS HOMINUM SALVATOR* or *IN HOC SIGNO* (See Dutton, 5:60, note 175d), are customarily incised on the eucharistic wafer.

[70] Longinus is believed traditionally to be the name of the centurion who thrust his lance into the side of Christ at the Crucifixion. See John 19:34.

183   If we want to fly with Christ to the heavens,
we must be borne on wings of divine virtue;
if we do not act in the way that we speak,
we are not authentic vicars of the altar.

184   Having said those words that I have explained,
the vicar of Christ with his sacred hands
traces three crosses over the sacrifice,
while uttering three words all extremely important.

185   He says, "Pure, holy and unblemished Host,"[71]
for such was Jesus Christ, in every way perfect:
He was proven to be sinless, pure and holy
with never a blemish or stain found upon Him.

186   Its primary nature is totally changed:
it is nothing like it was, neither bread nor wine;
it is fully the body of God, a substance deified,
a blessing that is given entirely through Christ.

187   After tracing three crosses, all in general,
then he traces two more and those are specific,
first over the bread and the altar linen,[72]
then over the wine made from deep purple grapes.

188   And here is another matter that comes to our attention,
something very essential, filled with blessing:
since the whole offering is already consecrated,
why does the priest bless it again?

189   We know that the Host was consecrated before,
and the wine as well needs nothing more;
why does the priest bless something consecrated?
There seems to be no apparent reason.

190   It is right to examine a matter like that one;
we should certainly seek a legitimate answer;
He Who ordained the Mass surely thought of it;
the King Who guided him did not let him err.

---

[71] The Latin words at the end of the eighth Canon prayer are: *offerimus praeclarae majestati tuae de tuis donis ac datis, hostiam puram, hostiam sanctam, hostiam immaculatam, Panem sanctum vitae aeternae, et Calicem salutis perpetuae* ('[we] do offer unto Thy most sovereign Majesty out of the gifts Thou hast bestowed upon us, a Victim which is pure, a Victim which is holy, a Victim which is spotless, the holy Bread of life eternal, and the Chalice of everlasting Salvation').

[72] The linen piece on the altar upon which are placed the Host and the chalice.

191   The signs traced by the good man at Mass,
        by the right hand of this vicar of Christ,
        are not for one reason, of this I am certain,
        for two noble ears issue forth from this grain.

192   Those signs that he traces at the consecration,
        consecrate the Host while giving the blessing;
        the others represent the trial of the Passion,
        the evil Christ suffered for our redemption.

193   My friends, those crosses we have just mentioned
        were five in number, we remember them well;
        about the Host we have nothing to add,
        but we do recall the wounds of Christ.

194   Without any doubt the wounds were five,
        four from the nails and a fifth from the lance;
        the crosses make us remember those five;
        Longinus offered Him one as a favor.

195   In the next chapter[73] the ordained priest
        begs the good Creator and Almighty King
        that this sacrifice should please Him just as much
        as the one offered Him by the good, slain Abel.[74]

196   He begs that this offering may please Him as much
        as the one presented Him by holy Melchizedek,[75]
        as well as the one He was offered by Abraham,[76]
        when he was willing to slay his son with the sword.

197   These three patriarchs that we have named
        were pious and beloved men of God;
        the deeds they performed were put down in writing,
        for they were servants highly esteemed by God.

198   We know for certain what happened to Abel,

---

[73] Meaning here the ninth prayer of the Canon with the Latin words: *Supra quae propitio ac sereno vultu respicere digneris: et accepta habere, sicuti accepta habere dignatus es munera pueri tui justi Abel, et sacrificium Patriarchae nostri Abrahae: et quod tibi obtulit summus sacerdos tuus Melchisedech, sanctum sacrificium, immaculatam hostiam* ('Deign to look upon them with a favorable and gracious countenance, and to accept them as Thou didst accept the offerings of Thy just servant Abel, and the sacrifice of our Patriarch Abraham, and that which Thy high priest Melchisedech offered up to Thee, a holy Sacrifice, an immaculate Victim').

[74] See Gen. 4:4–8.
[75] See note 27 above.
[76] See Gen. 22:1–13.

how the gift that he offered was welcomed;
God Who heard him graciously thanked him;
his soul is with God, as he justly deserved.

199   As a very small child he loved the Creator,
and knew very well how to do Him service;
Cain his brother, who was older than he,
killed him most treacherously out of envy.

200   The saintly Melchizedek was from the early days,
at the time when Abraham became the true father;[77]
he offered neither he-goat nor sheep to God,
but presented in sacrifice only bread and wine.

201   The holy sacrifice of that good gentleman
has a connection with that of Jesus Christ;
the former was the cement, the latter the finish;
David spoke of that in his preaching.[78]

202   Abraham performed a truly splendid deed —
except for Jesus Christ, we know of nothing similar,
for he led his little son up a high mountain
to offer him in sacrifice, something exceptional.

203   He had already gathered a heap of firewood,
and prepared the fire to burn his son,
his knife at the ready, grasped in his hand,
when God said, "Do not! For I am highly pleased with you."

204   These three patriarchs, perfect gentlemen,
all of saintly lives and illustrious deeds,
most certainly deserve to be mentioned in the Mass,
for they were very zealous in their love of God.

205   In the tenth chapter[79] the ordained priest
who is entrusted to celebrate the Mass

---

[77] Meaning the father of the Jewish nation.

[78] Ps. 110:4.

[79] Meaning here the tenth prayer of the Canon with the Latin words: *Supplices te rogamus, omnipotens Deus: jube haec perferri per manus sancti Angeli tui in sublime altare tuum, in conspectu divinae majestatis tuae: ut quotquot ex hac altaris participatione sacrosanctum Filii tui, Corpus, et Sanguinem sumpserimus, omni benedictione caelesti et gratia repleamur, Per eundem Christum Dominum nostrum. Amen* ('Humbly we beseech Thee, almighty God, to command that these our offerings be carried by the hands of Thy holy Angel to Thine Altar on high, in the sight of Thy divine Majesty, so that those of us who shall receive the most sacred body and blood of Thy Son by partaking thereof from this Altar may be filled with every grace and heavenly blessing: Through the same Christ our Lord. Amen').

bows his head before the sacred body,
and prays silently as he is commanded.

206   He crosses both arms over his chest,
as a sign that he forgets every ill will;
he forgives bad words and all evil deeds,
for he will take no hand in demanding justice.

207   From deep in his heart he entreats the true Father
to command His angel, who is His messenger,
to carry that sacrifice to the true altar,
into His presence, and may it please Him.

208   After praying for a time he kisses the altar;
he uncrosses his arms, and with sleeves tucked up,
he traces the cross over the Host and sacred chalice,
then blesses himself as he is commanded.

209   The kissing of the altar signifies the kiss
that the misguided Judas gave the Lord Jesus Christ;
no one in this world committed greater folly:
he thought to snare another and entrapped himself.

210   The deceitful unbeliever made an evil noose,
and the devil helped him to get his reward;
he hanged himself and his entrails gushed forth:[80]
he were far better off if he had never been born.

211   The three crosses that holy man traces
signify the three prayers that were uttered
by the Lord Jesus Christ before the Passion,
when He withdrew apart from His disciples.[81]

212   He traces the cross first over the Host,
then over the chalice and thirdly on himself;
then extends his arms while keeping to his course
by reading the word that is sacred and true.

213   The fact that the priest crosses his arms
when he genuflects before his King,
it is well to discover if such a secret act
has any meaning or whether it is foolish.

214   The question is a good and fair one to ask;

---

[80] See Matt. 27:5 and Acts 1:18; cf. Matt. 26:24 and Mark 14:21.
[81] Matt. 26:39–44.

God grant that we give it a proper reply,
for any human being is sincerely pleased
by obtaining a serious answer to his question.

215   The Jews signify the very right hand,[82]
for they unswervingly kept the Law;
they gave to God both tribute and sacrifice;
the land of Egypt was reproached through them.

216   Our Savior was accustomed to calling them His sons,
and like a loyal shepherd He searched for that flock;
He showed them grace, mercy, and great honor
that they returned with kicks and dreadful evil.

217   The left hand[83] which is badly handicapped
is meant for us, the people who are pagans,
for that foolish community went around sinning
by worshipping idols and man-made things.

218   When the Lord Jesus Christ, the earthly shepherd,
came to free the world from original sin,
His own flock refused to eat His salt,
but sought to do Him every possible evil.

219   The pagan people showed Him obedience;
they eagerly gave Him a very warm welcome:
if through their grave error they were His left hand first,
they ended up by becoming the almighty King's right hand.

220   The Jews who were the right hand of God,
for they kept His Law and languished in His love,
refused to believe and did the worst thing:
they fell to the left through their grave error.

221   Those who were counted as right-hand sons,
the wheel upset and they became stepsons;
those who were sinners and were the stepsons
moved to the right hand and became adopted.

222   The fact that he crosses his arms signifies
the demise of the sons and the rise of the stepsons;
those on the inside were cast outside,
and those outside were welcomed inside.

---

[82] See quatrains 49–53 where Berceo explains the movements of the celebrant to the right and left sides of the altar during the Mass.

[83] See previous note.

223   In the next chapter[84] the subject changes:
       the celebrant of the Mass presents his petition;
       with all his heart, he entreats the King of glory
       for the faithful souls who are missing amongst us.

224   He entreats the King of glory with all his heart
       for the faithful souls suffering in purgatory,
       that He may show some compassion on them,
       and may move them into the kingdom of His light.

225   The priest who is celebrating Mass entreats God
       to extract them from such suffering and affliction,
       and give them a place more refreshing and peaceful,
       where the believers in the holy Gospel are resting.

226   When the priest commences this chapter,
       he should have his mind focused on his friends,
       that God in His mercy may remove them from suffering,
       and place them in the glory of His light.

227   In the following chapter, the one that is last,[85]
       for twelve is of greatest importance and value,[86]
       he stands directly in front of the crucifix,
       and beats his breast as if striking a table.

228   When the Holy Savior was on the cross,
       women passing by took pity on the Lord,[87]

---

[84] Meaning here the eleventh prayer of the Canon, the prayer for the dead, with the Latin words: *Memento etiam, Domine, famulorum famularumque tuarum N…et N…qui nos praecesserunt cum signo fidei, et dormiunt in somno pacis. Ipsis, Domine, et omnibus in Christo quiescentibus, locum refrigerii, lucis et pacis, ut indulgeas, deprecamur. Per eundem Christum Dominum nostrum. Amen* ('Be mindful, also, O Lord, of Thy servants and handmaids N…and N…who are gone before us with the sign of faith and who sleep the sleep of peace. To these, O Lord, and to all who rest in Christ, grant, we beseech Thee, a place of refreshment, light and peace. Through the same Christ our Lord. Amen').

[85] Meaning here the twelfth and final prayer of the Canon with the Latin words: *Nobis quoque peccatoribus famulis tuis, de multitudine miserationum tuarum sperantibus, partem aliquam et societatem donare digneris, cum tuis sanctis Apostolis et Martyribus: cum Joanne, Stephano…et omnibus Sanctis tuis: intra quorum nos consortium, non aestimator meriti, sed veniae, quaesumus, largitor admitte. Per Christum Dominum nostrum* ('To us also Thy sinful servants, who put our trust in the multitude of Thy mercies, vouchsafe to grant some part and fellowship with Thy holy apostles and Martyrs: with John, Stephen…and all Thy Saints. Into their company we beseech Thee admit us, not considering our merits, but freely pardoning our offenses. Through Christ our Lord').

[86] The number 12, a multiple of 3, was especially significant during the Middle Ages. (See Cátedra, 1014, note 227b.)

[87] See Matt. 27:55, Mark 15:40, and Luke 23:27; cf. Luke 23:49.

and beat their breasts in sorrowful grief,
for the righteous One was dying and the traitor living.

229   That is what our priest represents,
when he beats his breast with his right hand,
and he moans deeply and heaves a great sigh,
acknowledging his guilt to the sovereign Father.

230   Then he petitions the Heavenly Father
for himself and for those here on earth,
that they may trust in no source of mercy but His,
that He may grant them a place in His spiritual court.

231   That He may grant them a place among the company
of the holy apostles for their compassion,
and of the holy martyrs, firm of purpose,
who suffered passion and death for the truth.

232   To open the pathway to that community,
he mentions some famous and powerful saints,
some apostles and martyrs among the company
who served Christ the Lord with all their hearts.

233   If we will recall what was said above,
the previous words and earlier phrases,
we might understand and feel more satisfied
as to why the saints are mentioned in two places.

234   Gentlefolk and friends, we heard above
about the high priest of ancient times,
when he was dressed in his holy vestments,
how he bore such witnesses on the pallium.

235   On the cloth he wore over front and back,
the names of the fathers from ancient times
that celebrant priest carried on his person,
and any acolyte could easily read them.

236   Our own priests, servants of the altar,
when they silently pray the words of the Canon,
the reason they mention the saints in two places[88]
is that some were on the front and others on the back.

237   Those they wore in front signify the first,
those they wore on their backs denote the last;
the old and the new were truly righteous,
upright and true in word and in deed.

---

[88] In the third and twelfth prayers of the Canon.

238   They would not be mentioned at daily Mass,
       were they not the dearly beloved of God;
       but they loved Him and were praised by Him,
       and at holy Mass they are invoked as witnesses.

239   After he has recited the list of the saints
       over the sacred blood and over the wafer,
       his venerable hand traces three crosses,
       while he utters three very secret words.

240   Once the celebrant has traced these three crosses,
       he removes the linen[89] over the sacred chalice;
       he traces three more with the Host that he raises,
       and two on the rim make the number required.

241   It is fitting that we ponder this sacred mystery:
       it is no mean task to subject it to scrutiny;
       but He Who was David's guide in the psalms
       will lend us His help concerning this desire.

242   The gospels say, and we are bound to believe them,
       that on the Friday that Christ willed to suffer the Passion,
       the tongues of the Jews, who should have perished,
       requested three times to have Him hanged.

243   Three times they shouted for Him to be crucified,
       never considering His cleverness with *vierba*;[90]
       they stopped at nothing in their words and deeds,
       for Caesar would be grieved if they did not kill Him.[91]

244   The three crosses traced by the ordained priest
       over the sacred Host and consecrated wine
       represent the requests[92] of the reckless people
       who wanted to harm Him with all their will.

245   The next three crosses tell another story,
       the three hours between terce and sext,[93]
       when the sinless person was placed on the cross,
       wherefore a solemn feast is kept by men and angels.

---

[89] The linen piece covering the chalice.

[90] 'Words' or 'speech.' See John 18:33–38 and 19:9–12.

[91] See John 19:12.

[92] Instead of reading *pueblos* here, I read *ruegos*. See Dutton, 5:62, note 244c, and Cátedra, 1020, note 244 c.

[93] The numbers terce and sext are the third hour and the sixth hour, that is, nine o'clock in the morning and twelve o'clock noon. See Mark 15:25 and 15:33. Also see Cátedra, 1020, note 245 b.

246   The two final crosses traced by the priest
        on the rim of the chalice with the sacred Host
        represent the blood and the unalloyed water
        that flowed from the lance blow suffered by Christ.[94]

247   Once the priest has finished this part of the Mass,
        he turns to his people in a very loud voice;
        the choir answers him in perfect accord,
        and all reply "Amen" with contented hearts.

248   Then he exhorts them to prepare to pray
        that the devil may be unable to tempt them,
        to say the *Pater Noster*[95] and be sure to beg God
        for a good death and a good place in heaven.

249   When the vested priest raises the voice
        that awakens the people who are drowsing,
        it is my understanding that it signifies the women
        seeking the place where Christ had been laid.[96]

250   The *Pater Noster* prayer is holy and divine:
        it is the sacred medicine of both living and dead;
        we should not be so quick to pass it by,
        for beneath this grain lies beneficial flour.

251   All we need ask for in this poor life,
        and even for the next, so entirely perfect,
        lies in this text as if sewn in a sack
        that is filled to the brim with finest flour.

252   Jesus Christ was asked by His good disciples,
        St. Peter and the other innocent companions,
        "Lord and holy Father, free from all error,
        tell us how to pray a very special prayer."[97]

253   The glorious Lord and perfect Master
        was pleased when He saw the sense of their words;
        He taught them the *Pater Noster*, a brief sermon
        composed and uttered by His holy lips.

254   Every single prayer, great and small,
        Greek and Latin, are included here;
        the words are few but loaded with sense,
        wise was the Master by Whom they were spoken.

---

[94] John 19:34.
[95] The prayer the "Our Father".
[96] See John 20:1–2.
[97] See Luke 11:1–4.

255   Seven petitions we make in this prayer:
         the first three of these will last forever;
         the final four are another matter:
         they will finish at the end of the world.

256   The first one blesses the spiritual Father,
         for His name is holy and everlasting;
         the second one pleads that the kingdom of heaven
         will last forever as a precious sign.

257   In the third one, we make the petition
         that His will that is full of blessing,
         just as in heaven where no thief enters,[98]
         may be done on earth, may there be such union.

258   Those three petitions that we have read
         will never be fulfilled in this world of ours,
         but will all come to pass in the world to come,
         where there never was heard any news of discord.

259   The fourth petition that we make to God
         is for the life of the body that we need for living:
         we mean all food when we say bread;
         when we mention bread we include all the rest.

260   The fifth petition is one we must keep,
         or else it is there we might grievously err;
         if we wish to obtain God's perfect pardon,
         then we should first forgive all others.

261   For this is what we say when we address God,
         "Lord, forgive us as we forgive one another;"
         but we labor blundering and miserably in vain
         if we ask for forgiveness and withhold it from each other.

262   If we beg Him for forgiveness and we do not forgive,
         we are sadly misguided and truly accursed;
         we are counterproductive to our own interests;
         we fall into the pit that we dug for ourselves.[99]

263   If we want to obtain pardon for our sins,
         let us pardon first, and go to confession;
         and then we can go away safe and secure
         that He will see[100] us freed from the evil we did.

---

[98] See Matt. 6:20.
[99] See Ps. 7:16; Prov. 26:27, 28:10; Eccles. 10:8.
[100] Here I read *verános* with Cátedra, 1025, 263d rather than *avrános* with Dutton, 5:51, 263d. (See Cátedra, 1024, note 263d and Dutton, 5:51, note 263d.)

264 When we present Him the sixth petition,
we should entreat Him with all our hearts
to protect us from falling into temptation,
which loosens the cart from the horse's harness.

265 There is still one last and final petition,
encircling the others like a fine key ring;
the words are few but extremely holy:
it is a tiny little ear chock-full of grain.

266 Finally we entreat the Heavenly Father
through His holy grace to deliver us from evil,
from the mortal enemy and the fires of hell
that never for a moment cease to burn.

267 Once the *Pater Noster* has been fully recited,
the ordained priest and vicar of Christ
says a quiet "Amen" and a few good words
to free us from evil and bless us again.

268 Then the vicar, the ordained priest,
unveils the paten that was covered;[101]
he says "Amen" in a low tone of voice,
and traces the cross on its spotless surface.[102]

269 He entreats God for himself and those entrusted to him,
that He may absolve them from all their sins,
from those of the present as well as the past,
and that we may not be tempted by those in the future.

270 The chalice which holds the consecrated wine
signifies the tomb in which Christ was laid;
the paten that covers the mouth of the chalice,
signifies the stone, according to the text.

271 When the three Marys, or maybe there were two,[103]
came to the tomb to embalm Christ's body,
they thought they could not possibly remove the stone,
and made loud lament, for they were deeply grieving.

272 They suffered great anguish concerning this matter,
for they were consumed with sorrow over Christ;
they had scarcely even approached the tomb,
when they saw that things were not as they had heard.

---

[101] A piece of altar linen is covering the paten upon which the Host is placed.
[102] See Cátedra, 1026, note 268d for an interpretation of this problematical line.
[103] See Matt. 28:1, Mark 16:1, and Luke 24:10.

273   They saw the stone withdrawn from the tomb,
        the sepulchre open and the shroud folded up;
        they thought that deceitful band of Jews
        had stolen the body of the Lord Jesus Christ.

274   The priest of Christ Who ordains the matter,
        when performing the office and kissing the paten,
        represents thereby the grief and the anguish
        that St. Magdalene suffered for Christ the Lord.

275   Then the holy priest who is celebrating Mass,
        while sighing deeply, takes the sacred Host;
        he breaks it in two, then he raises it up,
        after making three fragments of what he has broken.[104]

276   With the portion that he holds in his right hand,
        the priest traces the cross over the chalice:
        he does that for those Christians who are living,
        that God may free their souls from the furious kite.[105]

277   Of the two he has left, one is in memory
        of the souls that are purged and are with God in heaven;
        according to the text, with the third fragment
        he prays for the souls that are suffering in purgatory.

278   When the holy priest does that work
        of breaking the Host, the body of God,
        he reenacts the Supper of our Lord and Savior
        Who shared the broken bread with those around Him.

279   The broken fragments have yet another meaning;
        in the Old Law, they carried this image:
        when a fine white flour, semolina, was offered,
        a great deal was made from a very small quantity.[106]

---

[104] The priest first breaks the sacred Host into two halves over the chalice, then places the right half on the paten, and taking the other half, breaks that again. Taking a fragment of this second piece, he raises it as well as the chalice while saying in Latin: *Per eundem Dominum nostrum Jesum Christum Filium tuum, Que tecum vivit et regnat in unitate Spiritus Sancti Deus, Per omnia saecula saeculorum* ('Through the same Jesus Christ, Thy Son our Lord, Who liveth and reigneth with Thee in the unity of the Holy Ghost, God, World without end').

[105] A bird of prey.

[106] For a better understanding of this verse, the Latin words of the probable source used by Berceo read: *In veteri lege quando sacerdos offerebat similagines frangebat eas et aliter non sacrificabat nisi fractas. Similiter noster redemptor in sua cena aliter non distribuit discipulis panem nisi fractum* (Dutton, 5:74); cf. Lev. 2:1.

280   Then the *Agnus*[107] is sung in a different key;
it is sung and resung three times in all;
there is a reason for that: it is not done in vain,
for the Church would never do something improper.

281   We people of this world sin in three ways:
by will, by word, and by the deeds that we do;
we pray three times to the Lamb of God
to shield us from the blow whereby we lose our souls.

282   That is why we sing the *Agnus* three times,
because in three great ways we are guilty;
we double our prayers to the Lord Jesus Christ,
that our vanities may not count against us.

283   Then the deacon who is serving at the altar
receives *Osculum pacis*,[108] a sign of charity;
all those present receive Communion,
and the choir most solemnly sings the *laude*.[109]

284   Concerning this general Communion and peace,
that it is good and not evil that all take Communion;
there is a perfect answer to why that is so,
which should please us all, for we all stand to gain.

285   In the early times, we heard it said
that all who attended Mass in the church
had to receive the body of Christ,
and they had to consume it every day.

286   Men of good sense were bound to think
that daily Communion was a very grave danger,
for human beings cannot always be pure,
so they had to make some modifications.

287   They designated Sundays as very special days
for all who confessed, to receive Communion;
on that day all would be more sober,
and all were pleased with this matter.

---

[107] The *Agnus Dei* prayer during the Mass: *Agnus Dei, qui tollis peccata mundi: miserere nobis. Agnus Dei, qui tollis peccata mundi: miserere nobis. Agnus Dei, qui tollis peccata mundi: dona nobis pacem* ('Lamb of God, Who takest away the sins of the world, have mercy on us. Lamb of God, Who takest away the sins of the world, have mercy on us. Lamb of God, Who takest away the sins of the world, grant us peace').

[108] The 'kiss of peace'.

[109] See note 23 above. The fact that the entire congregation receives Communion indicates that Berceo is taking as his model the high Mass celebrated at Easter during which season every Christian has the annual obligation to receive Communion.

288   For a good long while this custom was kept;
       the people were good and God was feared;
       but sometime later it was removed and changed,
       and Communion on major holy days was then established.[110]

289   Then it was established that instead of Communion
       all who came daily would receive the peace;[111]
       and since they could not take Communion every Sunday,
       the consecrated Host was kept in its place.[112]

290   Those who wish to take peace or the consecrated Host
       should come with piety and great devotion;
       they should harbor no hatred within their hearts,
       no more than if they wished to receive Communion.

291   Those who go to take peace or the consecrated Host
       should certainly be free from mortal sin;
       may their hearts and minds be firmly fixed on Communion,
       otherwise they will utter many evil cries in hell.

292   After the peace and the Communion are over,
       the vested priest turns to his people;
       he says, "God be with you, my beloved people;
       let us all pray to God Who is perfect Lord."

293   He says these words to conclude the Mass:
       he turns and invites them all to prepare to pray;
       here he wants to symbolize Christ the Lord,
       what He did when He wanted to return to heaven.

294   He ate with His disciples keeping them company;
       He rebuked them greatly for their hardness of heart;
       He ordered all people to go and preach peace,
       for therein lies all the well-being of this world.[113]

295   He grants each one of them permission to go home;
       he tells them that the Host offered in sacrifice
       is carried to God by the hands of the angels;
       they all tell him loudly, "*Deo gratias*".[114]

---

[110] For more on this subject, see Cátedra, 1030, note 288d.

[111] A ceremony during the Mass whereby the people were given a statue or relic to kiss.

[112] The consecrated Host not distributed at Communion during the Mass is safely kept inside the ciborium which is placed within the tabernacle.

[113] Cf. Matt. 28:19, Mark 16:15, and Luke 24:47.

[114] 'Thanks be to God.'

296 Thanks be to God Who was pleased to guide us,
  Who guides the pilgrims that go to the Holy Land;
  the poem is finished and safely stored away;
  we have suffered for days and we want to go and rest.

297 Gentlefolk and friends and all who are here,
  I ask you all a favor, by the Law that you keep:
  may each of you help me with a *Pater Noster*:
  you will benefit me and lose nothing yourselves.

Bibliography

Primary Sources

Editions of Berceo's Works (in addition to Dutton and Cátedra)

Gonzalo de Berceo. *Del Sacrifiçio de la Missa*. In idem *Obras completas*, intro. Rufino Briones. Logroño: Instituto de Estudios Riojanos, 1971.

Other Works and Sources of Reference

Andrés Castellanos, María S de, ed. *La Vida de Santa María Egipciaca*. Madrid: Aguirre Torre, 1964.

Baró, José. *Glosario completo de los "Milagros de Nuestra Señora" de Gonzalo de Berceo*. Boulder: Society of Spanish and Spanish-American Studies, 1987.

Bartha, Jeannie K. "Four Lexical Notes on Berceo's *Milagros de Nuestra Señora*." *Romance Philology* 37 (1983): 56–62.

———. *Vocabulario de los "Milagros de Nuestra Señora" de Gonzalo de Berceo*. Normal, IL: Applied Literature Press, 1980.

Blecua, J. M. ed. *El Conde Lucanor*. Madrid: Castalia, 1969.

Capuano, Thomas M. "A Literal Interpretation of Berceo's *Sacrificio* 218c." *Hispania* 71 (1988): 711–12.

Cejador y Frauca, J. *Vocabulario medieval castellano*. Orig. 1929; repr. New York: Las Américas, 1968.

Corominas, Joan, ed. *Libro de Buen Amor*. Madrid: Gredos, 1967.

———, and José A Pascual. *Diccionario crítico etimológico castellano e hispánico*. 6 vols. Madrid: Gredos, 1980–1991.

Covarrubias Orozco, Sebastián de. *Tesoro de la lengua castellana o española*. Orig. 1611; repr. Madrid: Turner, 1977.

Dutton, Brian. "A Chronology of the Works of Gonzalo de Berceo." In *Medieval Hispanic Studies Presented to Rita Hamilton*, ed. A. D. Deyermond, 67–76. London: Tamesis, 1975.

———. *A New Berceo Manuscript, Biblioteca Nacional Ms. 13149. Description, Study and Partial Edition*. Exeter Hispanic Texts 32. Exeter: University of Exeter Press, 1982.

————. Gonzalo de Berceo, *Obras Completas*. 5 vols. London: Tamesis, 1967–1984.

Goode, Teresa Clare. *Gonzalo de Berceo's El Sacrificio de la Misa*. Studies in Romance Languages and Literatures 7. New York: AMS Press, 1970.

Goicoechea, Cesáreo. *Vocabulario riojano*. Madrid: Aguirre Torre, 1961.

Gulsoy, J. "The -i Words in the Poems of Gonzalo de Berceo." *Romance Philology* 23 (1969–1970): 172–87.

Honnorat, S. J. *Dictionnaire Provençal-Français*. 3 vols. Orig. 1848; repr. Marseille: Laffitte Reprints, 1971.

Keller, John Esten. *Gonzalo de Berceo*. Twayne World Authors Series 187. New York: Twayne, 1972.

Koberstein, G., ed. *Gonzalo de Berceo. "Estoria de San Millán": Textkritische Edition*. Münster: Aschendorff, 1964.

Kulp-Hill, Kathleen, trans.. *Songs of Holy Mary by Alfonso X, The Wise: A Translation of the* Cantigas de Santa María. MRTS 173. Tempe: Arizona Center for Medieval and Renaissance Studies, 2000.

Lanchetas, Rufino. *Gramática y vocabulario de las obras de Gonzalo de Berceo*. Madrid: Sucesores de Rivadeneyra, 1900.

Lappin, Anthony. *Berceo's Vida de Santa Oria: Text, Translation and Commentary*. Oxford: Legenda, 2000.

Latham, R. E. *Revised Medieval Latin Word-List*. London: Oxford University Press, 1965.

Lazar, Moshé, ed. *La Fazienda de Ultramar*. Salamanca: Cervantes, 1965.

Levy, Emil. *Petit Dictionnaire Provençal-Français*. Orig. 1909; 5th ed. Heidelberg: Carl Winter, 1973.

Marchand, James W., and Spurgeon Baldwin. "Two Notes on Berceo's *Sacrificio de la Misa*." *Modern Language Notes* 89 (1974): 260–65.

Marden, C. Carroll, ed. *Libro de Apolonio*. Orig. 1922; repr. Millwood: Kraus Reprint Co., 1976.

Menéndez Pidal, Ramón, ed. *Cantar de Mío Cid. Texto, gramática y vocabulario*. 4th ed. Madrid: Espasa-Calpe, 1969.

Montgomery, Thomas, ed. *El Evangelio de San Mateo. Texto, gramática, vocabulario*. Madrid: Aguirre Torre, 1962.

Mount T., and Annette G. Cash. trans. Gonzalo de Berceo, *Miracles of Our Lady*. Lexington: University Press of Kentucky, 1997.

Nebrija, Antonio de. *Vocabulario de Romance en Latín*. Orig. 1516; transcr. Gerald J. MacDonald. Philadelphia: Temple University Press, 1973.

Ramoneda, Arturo M., ed. Gonzalo de Berceo, *Signos que aparecerán antes del Juicio Final, Duelo de la Virgen, Martirio de San Lorenzo*. Madrid: Castalia, 1980.

Real Academia Española. *Diccionario de la lengua española.* 19th ed. Madrid: Espasa-Calpe 1970.

Solalinde, A.G., ed. *Milagros de Nuestra Señora.* 8th ed. Madrid: Espasa-Calpe, 1972.

Walsh, John K., ed. *El Libro de los Doze Sabios o Tractado de la Nobleza y Lealtad.* Madrid: Aguirre, 1975.

Willis, Raymond S., ed. *El libro de Alexandre.* Orig. 1934; repr. Millwood: Kraus Reprint Co., 1976.

———. *Libro de Buen Amor.* Princeton: Princeton University Press, 1972.

INTRODUCTION TO *THE SIGNS WHICH WILL APPEAR BEFORE JUDGMENT DAY*

TRANSLATED BY JEANNIE K. BARTHA

Berceo attached great significance to Judgment Day. He deals with this subject in 77 quatrains, again employing the symbolic numeral seven, significant in religious myths from ancient times. In his treatment, Judgment Day as the day of dread becomes concrete, almost tangible, visible and audible — a vision of reality for Spaniards. Prior to Berceo, only those who could read Latin, almost exclusively members of the clergy, could peruse St. Jerome's, or Pseudo-Jerome's, writings about Judgment Day. Berceo, as he puts it in the first quatrain, expressed in Spanish the narrative taken from a "little holy book" supposedly written by St. Jerome on the basis of what the saint had learned from Hebrew documents.[1]

Day by day, the portents are described as they will appear. Terrible events and signs will be manifest for fourteen days and nights. After that comes the summons to the Day of Judgment. The hordes of the risen dead embody all ages and classes of people. The poet waxes almost macabre as he discusses the details of this resurrection and dwells on the various categories of sinners sent to eternal damnation. In addition to the usual categories, and probably to the great delight of his contemporary audience, Berceo has a special place in hell for wicked clergy. By adapting Ps.-Jerome's work, ideology, and imagery, Berceo creates a kind of *Inferno* in Spanish not unlike that of Dante a century later and like the Latin author centuries before. He dwells upon their punishments, and with detailed descriptions of their torments he paints a hideous picture well calculated to instill dread in his audience and frighten the sinner back to the path of righteousness.

---

[1] For the pseudepigraphon *De XV signis* see J. Machielsen, *Clavis Patristica Pseudepigraphorum Medii Aevi* 2A (Turnhout: Brepols, 1994), 265–66 (nos. 926–927a). (Also cf. PL 145:840–842 and 198: 1611 AB; also 94: 633–638.) Berceo was probably working from De Voragine's version that combined material taken from Peter Comestor and Peter Damian. See W.W. Heist, *The Fifteen Signs Before Doomsday* (East Lansing: Michigan State College Press, 1952).

But then, like a ray of sunlight in the gloom, the poet depicts for the blessed the brilliant pageantry and pomp of Jesus' entry into the high court of God. Berceo writes with purpose and perhaps even with a certain relish about the punishment of the wicked. Yet he writes with even greater apparent pleasure of the rewards for the good. These come with the pomp and ceremony, colorful processions, marching hosts, choirs of singers, and spectacles that were dear to medieval man. The poem draws to a close with the reiteration of the fearfulness of Judgment Day when all, saint and sinner alike, will tremble before their fates are determined.

Abbreviations

Dutton   Dutton, Brian, ed. *Los Signos del Juicio Final.* In Gonzalo de
             Berceo, *Obras Completas*, 3: 121–44. London, Tamesis, 1975.
García   García, Michel, ed. *Los Signos del Juicio Final.* In Gonzalo de
             Berceo, *Obra completa*, with Isabel Uría, 1035–61. Madrid:
             Espasa-Calpe, 1992.
Ramoneda   Ramoneda, Arturo M., ed. *Signos que aparecerán antes del
             Juicio Final.* In Gonzalo de Berceo, *Signos que aparecerán antes
             del Juicio Final, Duelo de la Virgen, Martirio de San Lorenzo*,
             127–49. Madrid: Castalia, 1980.

THE SIGNS WHICH WILL APPEAR
BEFORE JUDGMENT DAY

1   Gentlefolk, if you would pay a little attention,
for just a short while I would like to tell you
a narrative taken from a little holy book,
written by St. Jerome,[1] a worthy leader.

2   Our father Jerome, our shield and shepherd,
among those writings which he read in Hebrew,
came across some strange and remarkable matters;
may he who lends an ear believe he eats a fine lunch.

3   Among other things, the good man discovered
that before that momentous Day of Judgment,
there will be a dreadful period with very great signs,
and the world will find itself in deadly straits.

4   That is why the gentleman prudently wrote
that those gone astray should be fearful;
they should please God by mending their ways,
so as not to be abandoned by Christ at that time.

5   One of the dreaded signs will be this:
the sea will rise as high as the sky,
higher than the mountains and higher than the hills,
so high that the fish will be left on dry land.

6   But in its straightness it will be very calm,
unable to flow as if it were frozen,
like a wall erected or a sturdy rampart:
anyone who sees it will be terribly frightened.

---

[1] St. Jerome, learned doctor of the Church (342?–420). He is supposedly the author of the *Signa Iudicii* (Dutton, 3:133, note 1d). However, it seems that this work was already erroneously attributed to St. Jerome in the source used by Berceo, which also attributes it to Hebrew origin ("Perlegens Jeronimus libros Hebreorum") (García, 1042, note 1c). See note to the Introduction.

7   On the second day it will appear sunken,
        as far beneath the earth as it rose above it;
        no one will even think of glancing at it,
        but soon it will return to its strength.

8   It is fitting for us to speak of the third sign
        which will cause great terror and dreadful sorrow:
        all the fish will be walking on top of the sea,
        shrieking aloud and unable to stay quiet.

9   The birds as well, both large and small,
        will all be screaming and horribly frightened;
        tamed and wild animals will do the same,
        unable at night to return to their lairs.

10   The sign after this should be greatly feared:
        rivers and seas will burn with great might;
        men will fall in confusion and go to perdition,
        wishing that they could sink through the earth.[2]

11   The fifth sign will be positively terrifying:
        from grass and trees and everything green
        pure blood will flow, so says St. Jerome;
        those who will not see it will be fortunate indeed.

12   The sixth day will be black and sooty:
        not a single concrete work will remain,
        no castle or tower or any other building,
        or any foundation will escape destruction.

13   On the seventh day there will be deadly trouble:
        all the stones will oppose each other in pitched battle;
        they will fight like men trying to injure each other;
        they will all be pulverized like tiny grains of salt.

14   Men in affliction and in those straits,
        at the appearance of such dreadful signs,
        in their distress will be seeking where to go;
        they will say, "Mountains, cover us,[3] for we are in trouble."

15   On the eighth day will come further disaster:
        a ghastly trembling of the entire earth;
        no man alive[4] who is standing on his feet

---

[2] Cf. also 2 Pet. 3:10.

[3] Cf. Luke 23:30, quoting Hos. 10:8; also Rev. 6:16.

[4] Here I have read García, 1047, 15c *calavera* rather than Dutton, 3:123, 15c *cannavera*.

will be agile enough not to fall to the ground.

16   On the ninth day more omens will come:
all the slopes and the mountains will be flattened,
and the valleys made level with the hills,
the highways and byways all made equal.[5]

17   On the day which will come after the ninth,
each and every man will come forth from his hollow;
people will be all confused and greatly bewildered,
but no one will even think of uttering a word.

18   The sign of the eleventh day, if you care to know,
will be so furious as to fill you with horror:
the graves you see closed will be opened;[6]
the bones will come forth from inside the enclosures.

19   No one will dare to look at the twelfth day,
for he will see great flames flying in the sky;
he will see the stars falling from their places
like leaves falling when they drop from the fig tree.[7]

20   With the others behind us, let us speak of the thirteenth day:
all humans will die, both young and old,
but a short time later they will be resurrected,
for righteous and condemned to come to the Judgment.

21   There will be terrible confusion on the fourteenth day:
the whole world will burn, the gold and silver,
the canopies and fabrics, the purples, silks and scarlets;
in the end not a rabbit will be left in his burrow.

22   On the final day, in the words of the prophet,
the proclaiming angel will sound his trumpet;[8]
each one of the dead in his coffin will hear it;
each with his sins will hasten to the Judgment.

23   All those never born and all who were engendered,
all those souls that were given life,
whether eaten by birds or scattered to the winds,
all will be gathered there together that day.

---

[5] Cf. Isa. 40:4.
[6] Cf. Matt. 27:52.
[7] See Rev. 6:13.
[8] See Rev. 11:15.

24   Those who never died, no matter what their age,
       whether children or middle-aged or the very old,
       all those thirty years of age,[9] the number of the Trinity,
       will come on that day before His Majesty.

25   The just will be placed on His right side,[10]
       the wicked and immoderate, on His left;
       the King in the middle, restored in appearance,
       near the Glorious One, perfect in charity.

26   There Judas the traitor will be brought forward,
       who through his ill fate betrayed his Lord;
       he will be given the honor he deserves;
       he could not possibly find himself in greater disgrace.

27   The Glorious King will turn to the righteous,
       His words to them will be temperate and delightful:
       "Come, you who are blessed by my precious Father,
       receive my kingdom, abundant and sweet.

28   Receive your reward for the service you did me,
       for when I was hungry you certainly fed me,
       you saw me thirsty and you gave me to drink,
       when I was naked you willingly clothed me.

29   When I came to your door for a place to stay,
       you were willing and glad to quickly offer me one;
       when I was in trouble you were ready to help:
       now I want to give you your reward for it all.

30   You shall be well rewarded for the service you did me:
       you shall reign with me *seculorum secula*;[11]
       you shall live in great glory and never see sorrow;
       you shall sing angelic praises before me forever."

31   He will turn to the left filled with anger and wrath;
       His news to them will be a harsh commandment:
       "Begone, you cursed servants of the devil,
       go with your master and your ruler.

32   Go and burn in the fire which is kindled
       for you and for Lucifer and all his troops;
       it has been decided you shall have no help,

---

[9] According to García, 1048, note 24c, all human beings, when they appear before the Judge, will evince the age of thirty, in honor of the Trinity. It shouldn't be forgotten that Christ died at the age of thirty-three.

[10] Quatrains 26–36 are based on Matt. 25:31–46.

[11] 'Forever and ever.'

for having served such a master you shall reap such reward.

33   When I was hungry and I was miserable,
     you refused to hear me or give me a morsel;
     you did not care if I suffered great thirst,
     and indeed you avoided giving me lodgings.

34   If you had given me anything at all,
     indeed I would have it stored for you now;
     but you were so cruel as to give me nothing;
     I have not forgotten how heartless you were.

35   When the person in need came to your door
     dressed in rags and begging in my name,
     you refused to give him even bread or wine;
     if you had cared for him, he would be your advocate today."

36   The angels in hell will be seized,
     with knotted ropes and burning chains;[12]
     they will lash them forward with deadly whips;
     may Jesus Christ protect us from such servants!

37   They will be taken to the fires, to the fires of hell,
     where they will never see light, only evil and affliction;
     each will be given his garment of sackcloth,
     each one of them weighing a hundred pounds.

38   They will be hungry and cold, shivering and hot,
     in turn, burning and freezing, and dreadfully thirsty;
     within their hearts there will be great affliction
     for refusing to believe the words of Holy Scripture.

39   They will be devoured by serpents and scorpions[13]
     who have sharp teeth and piercing stingers;
     they will be stung right to the heart;
     they will never be rescued at any time.

40   They will be given rotten suppers and worse lunches,
     great smoke in their eyes, great stench in their nostrils,
     sour wine on their lips, bitter gall on their palates,
     fire in their throats, colic in their loins.

41   Those who twist words will hang by their tongues,
     those who scorn and bear false witness;
     neither kings nor emperors will be pardoned:
     their servants will be like the masters that they were.

---

[12] See Jude 6.
[13] See Rev. 9:5, 19.

42   Men who are greedy for minted money,
who do not mind sinning to heap up riches,[14]
will have their mouths stuffed with their precious gold:
they will say that they never acquired such wealth.

43   There, crooked craftsmen and deceitful peasants
will give satisfaction for their dishonest labors;
there, cunning shepherds will make reparation,
for they are very clever in the art of concealment.

44   Some ordained priests who take offerings,
and live like seculars and keep filthy houses
will be shown no respect by the poisonous devils,
who will prick them sharply with goads for an offering.

45   Haughty men who steal from the unfortunate,
who take away their bread as well as their wine
will be bent over like hooks and go around begging;
the same will happen to wicked tax collectors.

46   Those unlucky enough to be envious,
those who grow pale over their neighbor's goods
will be kicked in hell by all who are there,
and treated like stepchildren by their stepmothers.

47   The torments of hell could hardly be told,
for many there are, and much greater than these;
may we be shielded from such blows by Jesus Christ
Who protected St. Peter on the angry waves.[15]

48   Let us change the subject and sing another tune;
let us linger no longer on an unpleasant tale;
let us return to the fine company of the righteous;
let us put into verse the good that we await.

49   The King of Kings and Righteous Judge,
Who ordains matters without any counselor,
at the head of His powerful procession
will enter into the glory of the true Father

50   The worthy company consecrated by Christ,
blessed by the Father and invited by the Son,
will enter heaven happy and content,
giving thanks to God and the Glorious Virgin.

51   There will be great rejoicing by the angels in heaven:
never was it greater on any single day,

---

[14] Cf. Ps. 39:7.
[15] See Matt. 14:29–30.

for they will see their company and pleasure increased;
God grant that we may enter into that fellowship!

52   Let us leave the sufferings of the ill-fated;
let us tell of the joys of those who are fortunate;
theirs will be greater and even doubled,
for their bodies will be united with their souls.

53   Their bodies and their souls will lie at rest;
their double joy is proclaimed by the Gospel;[16]
what is more, the condemned will endure double suffering:[17]
those words alone should stir us greatly.

54   We want to tell you what the first grace will be:
they will have eternal life, they will never die;
what is more, they will be so bright — I tell you no lie —
seven suns could not possibly shine so brightly.

55   Their eyesight will be very fine and sharp,
unhindered by any slope or mountain,
or hill or cloud or distance of miles:
they will see to the very ends of the earth.

56   They will receive the fourth grace for greater perfection:
they will be even swifter than the wind;
they will fly up and down completely at will;
it is written down, rest assured, I tell you no lie.[18]

57   They will be just as swift, and this is the truth,
as our minds within our very own selves
that flit tirelessly about as much as they want,
to any place or location that they choose.

58   The fifth joy they will have is worth more than all others:
they will be sheltered forever from anything evil;
a lord who rewards his servants this way
is one who is true, let no one think otherwise.

59   All will fervently praise the Lord;
all will have charity and love for each other;
they will not have to pray or clamor for peace,
or be on the lookout for any dark clouds.

60   May Jesus Christ lead us to that company,
where there is so much goodness and joy;

---

[16] See Rev. 18:6.
[17] See Jer. 16:18
[18] Cf. John 3:8.

may we be guided by our glorious and holy Mother Mary
who is the fountain of grace flowing every day.

61   When the King of Glory comes to judge,
as angry as a lion who is seeking food,[19]
who will await Him with bravery and daring?
for an angry lion is in no mood for joking.

62   The heavenly Virtues who, according to Scripture,
never did anything frivolous or foolish
will be filled that day with very great fear,[20]
for they will see the Judge immeasurably angered.

63   When the holy angels tremble with fear,
they who never sinned against their Lord,
what shall I, such a wretched sinner, do?[21]
Even now I am dreadfully frightened and fearful.

64   Although I may wish to hide from His sight,
it will be neither proper nor possible to do so;
I could not sustain an argument against Him;
I am ill prepared to appear before Him.

65   On that day there will be no petitioners;
all righteous and sinners alike will be quiet;
all will experience great fear and trembling,
but those on the left in much greater degree.

66   They will see with their eyes the fires of hell,
how the serpents keep their mouths wide open,
how they stick out their tongues and sharpen their teeth;
they will indeed perceive their evil intentions.

67   That will be the day, according to Scripture,
that will be very long and terribly bitter,[22]
wherefore we should all greatly fear it;
he who does otherwise will be sorely ill-fated.

68   The day will be long for those who are fortunate,
for they will never again be disturbed by night;[23]
it will be very bitter for the condemned
who will be forever dispossessed of goodness.

---

[19] Cf. Job 10:16; Ps. 17:12; Isa. 31:4; Hos. 13:8; Rev. 10:3.
[20] See Luke 21:26.
[21] Here too quatrains 63–65 recall the Sequence *Dies Irae*.
[22] See Amos 8:10; Joel 2:1–11.
[23] Rev. 22:5.

69   The Day of Judgment is greatly to be feared,
        more than anything else could possibly be;
        man will be forced to confront his evil deeds;
        he will be unable to conceal his wickedness.

70   Everything he did, whether big or small,
        excepting what was washed away by penance,
        everything will come before the public eye,
        to be recognized by all and hidden from no one.

71   There, the life stories of all people will be told;
        both good and bad alike will be severely reproached;
        as their houses will be open and without any doors,
        walls that were poorly bricked up will appear.

72   On Judgment Day there will be enormous grief,
        impossible for humans or angels to imagine;
        may Your divine grace help us, Jesus Christ,
        lest we fall at that time into the abyss!

73   If they look up above, they will witness God's anger;
        down below, the hellfire, kindled and burning,
        with a huge host of devils all around it;
        who will not be troubled by such a furious vision?

74   If they close their eyes so as not to see anything,
        the worm within will be gnawing their entrails;
        their wicked penance for their past lives
        that were base and filthy, fetid and corrupt.

75   May Jesus Christ protect us from such sights,
        all of us men and women who are Christians;
        let such divisions be the part of the devil
        who provides his friends with bitter rewards.

76   We who are Christians and believe in Christ,
        if we wish to escape from those visions,
        let us amend our lives, let us do penance:
        we will gain heaven and escape evil.

77   Let us say the *Pater Noster*[24] so that we may obtain this;
        let us praise the Glorious Lady, let us invoke her mercy;
        let us all sing *Ave Maria*[25] in her honor,
        so that we may reign with her and her Son.
        Amen.

---

[24] The prayer the "Our Father".
[25] 'Hail Mary.'

Bibliography

Primary Sources
(in addition to those given in Abbreviations)

Gonzalo de Berceo. *De los signos que apareserán ante del juiçio.* In *Obras completas,* intro. Rufino Briones. Logroño: Instituto de Estudios Riojanos, 1971.

Other Works and Sources of Reference

Andrés Castellanos, María S. de, ed. *La Vida de Santa María Egipciaca.* Madrid: Aguirre Torre, 1964.

Baró, José. *Glosario completo de los "Milagros de Nuestra Señora" de Gonzalo de Berceo.* Boulder: Society of Spanish and Spanish-American Studies, 1987.

Bartha, Jeannie K. "Four Lexical Notes on Berceo's *Milagros de Nuestra Señora.*" *Romance Philology* 37 (1983): 56–62.

————. *Vocabulario de los "Milagros de Nuestra Señora" de Gonzalo de Berceo.* Normal, IL: Applied Literature Press, 1980.

Blecua, J. M., ed. *El conde Lucanor.* Madrid: Castalia, 1969.

Cejador y Frauca, J. *Vocabulario medieval castellano.* Orig. 1929; repr. New York: Las Américas,1968.

Corominas, Joan, ed. *Libro de Buen Amor.* Madrid: Gredos, 1967.

————, and José A. Pascual. *Diccionario crítico etimológico castellano e hispánico.* 6 vols. Madrid: Gredos, 1980–1991.

Covarrubias Orozco, Sebastián de. *Tesoro de la lengua castellana o española.* Orig. 1611; repr. Madrid: Turner, 1977

Dutton, Brian. "A Chronology of the Works of Gonzalo de Berceo." In *Medieval Hispanic Studies Presented to Rita Hamilton,* ed. A. D. Deyermond, 67–76. London: Tamesis, 1975.

————. *A New Berceo Manuscript, Biblioteca Nacional Ms. 13149. Description, Study and Partial Edition.* Exeter Hispanic Texts 32. Exeter: University of Exeter Press, 1982.

————, ed. Gonzalo de Berceo, *Obras Completas.* 5 vols. London: Tamesis, 1967–1984.

————. "The Sources of Berceo's *Signos del juicio final.*" *Kentucky Romance Quarterly* 20 (1973): 247–55.

Goicoechea, Cesáreo. *Vocabulario riojano.* Madrid: Aguirre Torre, 1961.

Gulsoy, J. "The -i Words in the Poems of Gonzalo de Berceo." *Romance Philology* 23 (1969–1970): 172–87.

Heist, W. W. *The Fifteen Signs Before Doomsday.* East Lansing: Michigan State College Press, 1952.

Honnorat, S. J. *Dictionnaire Provençal-Français.* 3 vols. Orig. 1848; repr. Marseille: Laffitte Reprints, 1971.

Keller, John Esten. *Gonzalo de Berceo.* Twayne World Authors Series 187. New York: Twayne, 1972.

Koberstein, G., ed. *Gonzalo de Berceo, "Estoria de San Millán": Textkritische Edition.* Münster: Aschendorff, 1964.

Kulp-Hill, Kathleen, trans. *Songs of Holy Mary by Alfonso X, The Wise: A Translation of the* Cantigas de Santa María. MRTS 173. Tempe: Arizona Center for Medieval and Renaissance Studies, 2000.

Lanchetas, Rufino. *Gramática y vocabulario de las obras de Gonzalo de Berceo.* Madrid: Sucesores de Rivadeneyra, 1900.

Lappin, Anthony. *Berceo's Vida de Santa Oria: Text, Translation and Commentary.* Oxford: Legenda, 2000.

Latham, R. E. *Revised Medieval Latin Word-List.* London: Oxford University Press, 1965.

Lazar, Moshé, ed. *La Fazienda de Ultramar.* Salamanca: Cervantes, 1965.

Levy, Emil. *Petit Dictionnaire Provençal-Français.* Orig. 1909; 5th ed. Heidelberg: Carl Winter 1973

Machielsen, J. *Clavis Patristica Pseudepigraphorum Medii Aevi.* Vol. 2A. Turnhout: Brepols, 1994.

Marchand, James W. "Gonzalo de Berceo's *De los signos que aparesçerán antes del Juicio.*" *Hispanic Review* 45 (1977): 283–95.

Marden, C. Carroll, ed. *Libro de Apolonio.* Orig. 1922; repr. Millwood: Kraus Reprint Co., 1976.

Menéndez Pidal, Ramón,ed. *Cantar de Mío Cid. Texto, gramática y vocabulario.* 4th ed. Madrid: Espasa-Calpe, 1969.

Montgomery, Thomas, ed. *El Evangelio de San Mateo. Texto, gramática, vocabulario.* Madrid: Aguirre Torre, 1962.

Mount, T., and Annette G. Cash, trans. Gonzalo de Berceo, *Miracles of Our Lady.* Lexington: University Press of Kentucky, 1997.

Nebrija, Antonio de. *Vocabulario de Romance en Latín.* Orig. 1516; transcr.Gerald J. MacDonald. Philadelphia: Temple University Press, 1973.

Real Academia Española. *Diccionario de la lengua española.* 19th ed. Madrid: Espasa-Calpe, 1970.

Solalinde, A.G.,ed.*Milagros de Nuestra Señora.* 8th ed. Madrid: Espasa-Calpe, 1972.

Walsh, John K., ed. *El Libro de los Doze Sabios o Tractado de la Nobleza y Lealtad.* Madrid: Aguirre, 1975.

Willis, Raymond S., ed. *El libro de Alexandre.* Orig. 1934; repr. Millwood: Kraus Reprint Co., 1976.

———. *Libro de Buen Amor.* Princeton: Princeton University Press, 1972.

INTRODUCTION TO *THE HYMNS*

TRANSLATED BY JEANNIE K. BARTHA

Three *Hymns* are attributed to Berceo. Each is written in the *mester de clerecía*, and each is a song of praise to a member of the hierarchy of Heaven. In the first *Hymn*, the poet lifts up his voice to the Holy Spirit; in the second one, he addresses the Blessed Virgin Mary; the third *Hymn* is to Our Lord Jesus Christ. All three are composed of seven stanzas, the number seven having long been an integral part of Judaeo-Christian symbolism, and each *Hymn* is composed in Berceo's usual monorhymed quatrain.

The sources of Berceo's three *Hymns* are well-known hymns written in medieval Latin, widely circulated across Christendom. As was his custom, Berceo used known Latin sources, translating their content into Spanish, the vernacular language of his time, but enlarging upon the original as he translated and versified them.

The first *Hymn* can be given a title from the wording of its first line: *Veni Creator Spiritus* ('Come, Creator Spirit'), coming from the ancient Latin hymn with that opening line. The author of the original Latin was probably Rabanus Maurus (d. 856). Berceo in his Spanish version follows the thread of the Latin original, but does not translate as closely as he does in the other two *Hymns*. This may very well be due to the fact that several versions or renditions of this Latin hymn were in circulation in the thirteenth century and the Spanish poet followed a version different from the one that survives today. This explanation is made plausible by the fact that both of the other *Hymns* more closely follow the Latin sources.

The second *Hymn*, whose title, again from its first line, is *Ave Sancta Maria, Estrella de la Mar* ('Hail, Holy Mary, Star of the Sea'), comes from the Latin hymn *Ave Maris Stella* ('Hail, Star of the Sea') of unknown authorship. This hymn is known to have been sung as early as the ninth century, since a manuscript of St. Gall exists from that period. This is the most famous and most widely disseminated of the multitude of hymns written in honor of the Blessed Virgin Mary. The meter in Latin is trochaic dimeter catalectic, composed of three trochees in seven stanzas, the same number as the Bercean counterpart.

The third of Berceo's *Hymns*, his *Tu, Christe, Que Luz Eres* ('Christ, You Who are light') is the Spanish poet's rendition of the famous Latin hymn *Christe, qui Lux Es et Dies* ('Christ, Who are light and day'), also in seven stanzas.

These *Hymns* are seldom mentioned in histories of Spanish literature, yet they are three gloriously and deeply spiritual hymns which deserve a place in the repertory of Gonzalo de Berceo's creative contributions. They are poetically the equal of hymns in the vernaculars of many lands, and in quality they compare favorably to other hymns in medieval Spanish.

THE HYMNS

1.   Come, Creator Spirit, filled with sweetness,
visit our minds with Your holy light;
purge our breasts of wicked impurity,
fill them with Your customary grace.

2.   You are called Comforter, and rightly so,
sweet and worthy gift of the Lord our God,
vital fountain, living fire, charity and love,
unction that heals the sinful soul.

3.   From Your holy grace, from Your charity,
flow the seven gifts of great power;
You are called finger of the King of Glory;
You cause the barbarians to converse in Latin.

4.   Enkindle our minds with Your light:
in You may our souls obtain perfect love;
may our weak and sluggish bodies
be revived through Your perfect gift.

5.   May Your grace shield us from the deadly enemy;
grant we may live in peace, free from strife;
be our guide, may Your tent cover us,
that we may avoid doing anything evil.

6.   Give us the intelligence to understand the Father,
and together with the Father, to know the Son;
and as we obtain faith and wisdom from You,
how You three are one God and one power.

7.   Praised be the Father and His Son,
and You, Creator Spirit, who proceeds from both;
may the Son, Who was martyred on the cross for us,
send us the grace of the Holy Spirit. Amen.

II

1   Hail, Holy Mary, Star of the Sea,
ever matchless Mother of the King of Glory,
ever Virgin, for you would not sin,
gateway for sinners to enter into heaven.

2   To you the angel Gabriel said the word "Ave,"
a sweet and gentle word, sweeter than honey;
hold us firmly in peace, ever faithful Mother;
Eve, Abel's mother, became an "Ave."

3   Unbind the sinners who lie entangled,
give light to the blind who are sinful,
remove the evils that hold us fast,
and obtain for us the good things we lack.

4   Reveal yourself as a mother: be moved by pity,
offer our petitions to the King of Glory;
for God and charity, obtain for us the grace
from the Son Who assumed humanity within you.

5   Glorious Virgin Mother, single and unique,
filled with gentleness, more simple than a lamb,
obtain for us, Mother, the life that is true;
as holder of the key, open heaven to us.

6   Guide our lives that we may not corrupt them,
serve as our path that we may not stumble;
guide us, Lady, when we go from here,
that we may see God and rejoice with Him.

7   Praise to the Father, homage to the Son,
honor to the equally powerful Holy Spirit,
one God in three Persons: this is our faith,
one Kingdom, one Dominion, one King, one Being. Amen.

III

1   Christ, You Who are light that illumines the day,
You Who remove the darkness and make it go away,
I firmly believe that You are light, the light of my soul,
and that You generously bestow all light and goodness.

2   Lord and Holy Father, of You we beg mercy:
may we be protected by You through this night;
may we rest safe and secure from our enemies;
may we whom You redeemed have a good night.

3   Let us not be tempted by dreams from evil sources;
let us not be trampled on by the devil;
may our bodies not yield to the king of sin
who gives filthy, evil, and poisonous advice.

4   May our eyes obtain their natural sleep;
may our minds remain alert to justice;
may Your sacred right hand greatly shield
Your servants who love and adore Your face.

5   You, our Defender, cast Your glance upon us,
drive away the devil, a wicked impostor;
You, fine governor, rule Your servants
whom with great suffering You bought with Your blood.

6   Lord, remember us, deign to protect us,
lest our bodies should lose their souls;
Lord, Who would suffer the Passion for our souls,
do not abandon us or let us be lost.

7   You, the Almighty Father of the heavens,
with Your Son no less powerful than You,
and with the Holy Spirit, gracious with gifts,
grant us perfect death, our souls sweet repose.

Bibliography

Editions of Berceo's Works

Dutton, Brian, ed. *Los Himnos*. In Gonzalo de Berceo, *Obras Completas*, 3: 61–66. London: Támesis, 1975.

García, Michel, ed. *Himnos*. In Gonzalo de Berceo, *Obra completa*, with Isabel Uría, 1069–75. Madrid: Espasa-Calpe, 1992,

Gonzalo de Berceo. *Himnos*. In *Obras completas*, intro. Rufino Briones. 486–89. Logroño: Instituto de Estudios Riojanos, 1971.

Other Works and Sources of Reference

Bernárdez, Francisco Luis. "Gonzalo de Berceo como traductor de himnos litúrgicos." *Criterio* 26 (1953): 170–71.

Cejador y Frauca, J. *Vocabulario medieval castellano*. Orig. 1929; repr. New York: Las Américas, 1968.

Corominas, Joan, and José A. Pascual. *Diccionario crítico etimológico castellano e hispánico*. 6 vols. Madrid: Gredos, 1980–1991.

Dutton, Brian. "A Chronology of the Works of Gonzalo de Berceo." In *Medieval Hispanic Studies Presented to Rita Hamilton*, ed. A. D. Deyermond, 67–76. London: Tamesis, 1975.

Gulsoy, J. "The -i Words in the Poems of Gonzalo de Berceo." *Romance Philology* 23 (1969–1970): 172–87.

Honnorat, S. J. *Dictionnaire Provençal-Français*. 3 vols. Orig. 1848; repr. Marseille: Laffitte Reprints, 1971.

Keller, John Esten. *Gonzalo de Berceo*. Twayne World Authors Series 187. New York: Twayne, 1972.

Lanchetas, Rufino. *Gramática y vocabulario de las obras de Gonzalo de Berceo*. Madrid: Sucesores de Rivadeneyra, 1900.

Latham, R. E. *Revised Medieval Latin Word-List*. London: Oxford University Press, 1965.

Levy, Emil. *Petit Dictionnaire Provençal-Français*. Orig. 1909; 5th ed. Heidelberg: Carl Winter, 1973.

Marchand, James W. "The Hymns of Gonzalo de Berco and Their Latin
    Sources." *Allegorica* 3 (1978): 105–25.
Real Academia Española. *Diccionario de la lengua española.* 19th ed. Madrid: Es-
    pasa-Calpe, 1970.

INDEX

In the Index certain names, objects, positions and situations with common attributes are listed not as individual entries, but rather as components of the following categories: *animals, bishops, emperors, illnesses, kings, martyrs, monasteries, mountains named in the poems, musical instruments, persons named in the poems, places named in the poems, popes, prophets of Old Testament,* and *rivers named in the poems.* Following the Index is an Addendum listing the various titles and designations Berceo employs in describing Christ and Mary. Throughout the Index, footnote references are indicated by n (single) or nn (multiple).

A

Aaron, 397n37, 440
  See also Mary, mother of Jesus; symbols
Abel, 125, 226, 286, 462, 462n73, 500
Abderrahman, caliph, 366, 366n25, 370, 375
Abraham, 165, 425, 425n19, 446, 462, 462n73, 463
absolution, 88, 442, 471
  See also knights
Adam, 14, 105, 153, 155, 162, 339
Adam and Eve, 5, 15, 159, 159n42, 163n95, 168n121, 201, 250, 260, 263, 444
Aemilianus, St. *See* Millán, San/St.
Agatha, St. *See* martyrs
Agnes, St., 49
  See also martyrs
Almanzor, caliph, 322
alms and almsgiving, 31, 51n10, 177, 184, 236, 279, 392
  See also Dominic, St.; Lawrence, St.; Millán, San/St.

altar
  dedicated to Mary, 48, 63, 69, 71, 74, 92, 93, 118, 130
  dedicated to St. Dominic or San Millán, 288n187, 293, 299, 322, 363, 364, 365
  fixtures and linens of, 64, 64n5, 461, 461n72, 468, 468n89, 471n101
  of Old Testament temple, 203, 439
  offering of Old Testament and New Testament sacrifice at, 445–446
  significance of sides of, 291n193, 444–445, 465, 465nn82–83
  See also Millán, San/St.
Ambrose, St., 415
Amunna /Amuna (St. Oria's mother), 384, 385, 386, 391, 403, 404, 405, 406, 406n54, 411n63
  visions of, 406, 408–410, 410n60
anchorite/anchoress, 119, 263, 263n134
  See also Oria, St.